The 100 Most Important Sporting Events in American History

The 100 Most Important Sporting Events in American History

Lew Freedman

GREENWOOD™

An Imprint of ABC-CLIO, LLC

Santa Barbara, California • Denver, Colorado

Copyright © 2016 by ABC-CLIO, LLC

Library of Congress Cataloging-in-Publication Data

Freedman, Lew.
  The 100 most important sporting events in American history / Lew Freedman.
    pages cm
  ISBN 978-1-4408-3574-2 (hardback)—ISBN 978-1-4408-3575-9 (ebook)   1. Sports tournaments—United States.   2. Sports—United States.   3. Special events—United States. I. Title. II. Title: One hundred most important sporting events in American history.
  GV712.F74 2016
  796—dc23   2015022062

ISBN: 978-1-4408-3574-2
EISBN: 978-1-4408-3575-9

20 19 18 17 16   1 2 3 4 5

This book is also available on the World Wide Web as an eBook.
Visit www.abc-clio.com for details.

Greenwood
An Imprint of ABC-CLIO, LLC

ABC-CLIO, LLC
130 Cremona Drive, P.O. Box 1911
Santa Barbara, California 93116-1911

This book is printed on acid-free paper ∞
Manufactured in the United States of America

Contents

Introduction		ix
#1	Jackie Robinson	1
#2	The Miracle on Ice	6
#3	James Naismith and the Invention of Basketball	11
#4	Joe Louis	14
#5	Title IX	19
#6	Sports Come to Radio	22
#7	Sports Come to Television	26
#8	ESPN: Sports around the Clock	29
#9	Muhammad Ali Defies Uncle Sam	32
#10	Jesse Owens	37
#11	Cincinnati Red Stockings Go Pro	40
#12	The World Series	43
#13	Babe Ruth Transforms Baseball	46
#14	Red Grange Introduces Pro Football to the World	51
#15	The Great Jim Thorpe	54
#16	The NFL's Greatest Game	58
#17	Roberto Clemente	61
#18	Marvin Miller and Baseball Free Agency	66
#19	The NBA Integrates	69
#20	Texas Western Wins NCAA Basketball	72
#21	Hank Aaron Breaks Babe Ruth's Record	76
#22	Fritz Pollard, the NFL's First African American Coach	81

#23	The Black Sox Scandal	84
#24	Bill Russell, First African American NBA Coach	88
#25	Don Larsen's Perfect Game	92
#26	Joe Namath's Super Bowl Prediction	95
#27	Secretariat the Great	99
#28	Joe DiMaggio's 56-Game Hitting Streak	103
#29	Ted Williams Bats .406	107
#30	The Death of Dale Earnhardt	110
#31	Michael Jordan Plays While Sick	114
#32	Jack Nicklaus Reclaims Glory	117
#33	The Dream Team at the 1992 Olympics	120
#34	Richard Petty's 200th Win	124
#35	Lance Armstrong	128
#36	Kenny Sailors Invents the Jump Shot	131
#37	Pete Gogolak's Funny Kicking	135
#38	Introduction of the NBA Shot Clock	139
#39	Pete Rose, Charlie Hustle	142
#40	President Nixon's Ping-Pong Diplomacy	145
#41	Miami Dolphins Go 17–0	149
#42	Frank Robinson, First African American Manager	153
#43	Althea Gibson	157
#44	Women's Pro Basketball	160
#45	Johnny Vander Meer's Two No-Hitters	164
#46	The Houston Astrodome	168
#47	U.S. Soccer World Cup Champs	171
#48	Wilt Chamberlain Scores 100 Points in a Game	175
#49	Cy Young Wins 511 Games	179
#50	The Jack Dempsey–Gene Tunney Long Count	183
#51	Baseball's All-Star Game	187
#52	Bill Mazeroski's Amazing Home Run	191
#53	Michael Phelps	195

#54   Martina Navratilova Wins and Comes Out   198

#55   Magic Johnson Shows You Can Live with AIDS   203

#56   John Wooden's 10 NCAA Titles   207

#57   University of Connecticut Women's Basketball   211

#58   The Cal Ripken Streak   215

#59   Wayne Gretzky Changes Hockey   219

#60   Pat Summitt Wins Big and Inspires   223

#61   Jack Johnson Is Hated for Being Black and Good   227

#62   Fernandomania   231

#63   Frank Shorter Is Golden   235

#64   Wilma Rudolph   239

#65   Tiger Woods Tries to Be the Greatest   242

#66   Honus Wagner and Baseball Cards   246

#67   Pittsburgh's Immaculate Reception   250

#68   Babe Didrikson Zaharias   254

#69   Indiana State versus Michigan State   257

#70   A Basketball Sisterhood   261

#71   Marshall University's Plane Crash   265

#72   Oklahoma Football's 47-Game Winning Streak   269

#73   Tommie Smith's and John Carlos's Gloved Fists   273

#74   Jim Brown's Stunning Career and Departure   277

#75   Willie Mays's World Series Gem   281

#76   The Ice Bowl   284

#77   Rocky Marciano, Undefeated Champion   287

#78   A. J. Foyt   291

#79   Bobby Thomson Wins the Pennant   294

#80   Red Sox at Last   297

#81   Dan Jansen's Challenges   300

#82   The Fosbury Flop   303

#83   Win One for the Gipper   306

#84   Kerri Strug   309

#85   Loyola's 1963 Iron Men   313

#86   The Death of Len Bias   316

#87   Peyton the Great   319

#88   Bob Beamon's Leap   323

#89   Roger Maris Tops the Babe   326

#90   The National Hockey League Expands   329

#91   College Basketball's Game of the Century   333

#92   Baseball's Only Fatality   336

#93   The Earthquake World Series   339

#94   Libby Riddles Wins the Iditarod   343

#95   Baseball Teams Start City Hopping   346

#96   Monica Seles Is Stabbed   350

#97   Billie Jean King Steps Up for Women's Tennis   353

#98   Tommy John Surgery   356

#99   Fantasy Sports   360

#100   Soap Opera on Skates   363

Index   367

Introduction

Sport has never been bigger in America, has never played a bigger role in society than it does in the 21st century.

More than anyplace else in the world, in the United States sport dominates leisure time in more ways than most people can easily enumerate. They might run out of fingers to count on before they list the ways in which sports of all sorts have infiltrated daily life and conversation.

From simply playing games at the local recreation center to attending games in person, sport is a hobby in several ways. You can listen to games on the radio, or listen to 24-hour sports talk radio to hear the opinions of blustery hosts and their call-in telephone pals. You can sit in the living room in front of the television and not only watch the big game of the night, but keep right on watching through the night on 24-hour sports TV stations.

And if you don't happen to be at home, you can still tune in to play-by-play in ways unimaginable only a few years ago. At work you can cruise wherever your computer will take you for scores, opinions, news reports, feature stories, and chit-chat about your favorite hometown teams, your favorite sports, and ones you barely care about at all but feel compelled to keep up with.

Sports in the United States create frenzied, all-emotions-in fans who fit the true definition of fanatics. Sports fill the calendar to bursting, with seasons getting longer and longer. Baseball awakes in March, before the snow melts in the North, and doesn't close up shop for the year until nearly November, when trees shed their leaves. Basketball and hockey are on the agenda for at least six months. Football, which once was neatly compartmentalized in the autumn, opens training camp before the end of July and doesn't quit until February. NASCAR, the governing body of stock-car racing, which is not a team sport but has elbowed its way into the top echelon of popularity, barely pauses to take a breath or brake. The season begins in mid-February and does not conclude until the week before Thanksgiving.

You can Google sports history, just in case you forgot something you used to know, that you never knew before, or that you want to read about for the first time. You don't even need that desktop computer as large as a TV screen to do it, either.

You can find most of the same options on your smart phone. And going back to that TV for a moment, the computers have shrunk and the TV screens have grown larger in recent decades.

The middle-aged try to stay in shape playing their own games at a proficiency level lower than the professionals, even as they encourage their children to devote their energies to a sport of choice on local playgrounds and in local gyms, while playing for highly organized, sophisticated youth-league teams.

Hundreds of American athletes are nationally famous. Dozens are known throughout the world. Our leagues have gone global. Once all of our professional sports leagues were parochial in nature. There was even a thing in various sports called a "territorial draft," by which it was meant that a Boston team had first dibs on a player from New England, or that a Southern California team could put in a claim for an athlete from Los Angeles. Those notions seem quaint now.

In recent decades, especially over the last 20 years, baseball, basketball, and hockey, considered three of the four major professional team sports in the United States, have embraced internationalism. Where once the United States was isolationist in global politics, with large percentages of the populace committed to minding our own business, now not even the games we watch and play fit that description. The National Basketball Association, the National Hockey League, and Major League Baseball feature many, many players whose names the average American spectator can't even pronounce. Those fans don't think this is at all unusual and don't blink when Giorgio from Italy slides into the lineup next to George from Brooklyn.

Only football remains dominated by American-born players. That is because, outside of Canada, which features its own slightly different version of football, the rest of the world has not adopted the sport that Amos Alonzo Stagg helped develop more than a century ago. Still, the NFL is trying its best to go international, to woo countries that have no background in the sport whatsoever, by scheduling not just exhibition games, but regular-season, count-in-the-standings games in places like London and Mexico City.

For today's sports fans who are under 30 years old, this is all so-what stuff. This is what they grew up with and what they have always known.

But it wasn't always like this. These fans cannot recall a time when it was gossip-worthy bad form for a woman to sweat in sports competition. They may not be aware that when the federal government passed Title IX legislation guaranteeing high school girls and college women sporting opportunities, it was nearly as cosmically habit-changing for society as women's suffrage.

They do not recall the bad old days when African Americans were banned from participating in big-league baseball or pro football, when colleges throughout the South did not have a single African American player competing in football and basketball, or when schools all over the nation hesitated to suit up a starting basketball lineup that included more than at most two black players.

Much has changed over time. There has been revolution and evolution in sport, just as in society. Often, sport took tentative first steps, ahead of society's accepted norm, to right wrongs, to lead. For decades newspaper sports departments—in house, as well as on the street—were referred to as the toy department of the paper.

Many chose not to see, or were too blind to see, that the sports landscape was altering Americans' prejudices, was breaking down barriers, and was introducing common ground between peoples who were raised with uninformed suspicions, and worse, ugly hatreds.

Sports did not lift America out of the dark ages of race relations and discrimination against women and improve international relations just because fans got to know people of color, people whose first language was not English, and came to recognize that fairness to daughters was the same as fairness to sons. Sports have not solved all of America's problems, but they have helped broaden acceptance and improve society's thinking.

The twisting road of history is not mapped. History is written on the fly, but once the past is recorded, it cannot be changed, and it is easier to read backward than to project forward.

The true beginning of sport as we know it in the United States can be traced to 1869, when the Cincinnati Red Stockings became the first professional baseball team. The origins of the sport of baseball have been debated for about 150 years. For decades baseball embraced the notion that Civil War general Abner Doubleday invented the game on a grassy field in Cooperstown, New York, in 1839.

High officials of the sport were as eager to establish baseball's roots as any orphan searching for long-lost parents. Albert Spalding, a 19th-century baseball star and later the founder of the famed Spalding sporting goods concern, sought to pin down the elusive answer to baseball's beginnings, and a commission was formed in 1905 to study the matter.

This so-called blue-ribbon panel proved to be remarkably slow-moving in its research. Finally, in a report issued in 1907, the group credited Doubleday with creating the game. The commission relied solely on a letter written by a Cooperstown man named Abner Graves, who asserted that baseball was the brainchild of Doubleday.

For many years this explanation, buttressed by a yellowing baseball on display in the Hall of Fame in Cooperstown after it opened in 1939 and referred to as "the Doubleday ball," sufficed as an explanation for most. However, it should be noted that Henry Chadwick, one of the commission members, dissented from the final conclusion. Chadwick, who was selected for membership in the Hall of Fame much later, was a sports reporter who invented the box score and edited the first baseball guide sold commercially.

Chadwick's disappointment with the commission's ruling in favor of the Doubleday creation story was largely overlooked, because the majority opinion steamrolled him. Many years later, when more historians and researchers took an interest, the Doubleday tale was relegated to the category of myth. No one could even prove that Doubleday ever set foot in Cooperstown during his lifetime. Nor could anyone establish with certainty that he cared one whit about baseball.

Eventually historians showed that baseball most likely grew out of the English games of cricket and rounders and might well have been played in some form as long ago as the 1400s.

Among the earliest of baseball teams were the New York Knickerbockers, the Brooklyn Atlantics, and the Athletics of Philadelphia (though not the same ones that continue to play today in Oakland). Games were played with serious intent, but the players were not paid on a regular basis. There was no football, baseball, hockey, or anything else except likely boys in fields running sprints against one another for bragging rights. Most likely this is why in 1856 it occurred to a now long-defunct newspaper called the *New York Mercury* to bestow the compliment of "national pastime" upon baseball. This label stuck for more than a century for good reason and now lingers mostly for nostalgia.

The Cincinnati Red Stockings, forerunners of the Reds that represent the Queen City of Ohio today, emerged in 1869 as the first baseball team to provide salaries to players. At the time Harry Wright and George Wright were the most famous brother duo from the region, establishing the club, leading it, and starring for it. Those other Wright brothers, Wilbur and Orville, were from nearby Dayton, Ohio, before they migrated to Kitty Hawk, North Carolina, where they lifted off in the first airplane. Orville and Wilbur are better remembered, since their invention benefited humanity, whereas Harry and George's innovation only established a trend.

By successfully touring and taking on all comers, the Red Stockings showed that baseball could be profitable. Soon enough other full-time professional outfits sprang up, and in 1876 the National League—the same National League that makes up half of Major League Baseball in the 2000s—was formed.

Baseball was a sport, not a profession, and it took some time for fans to look favorably on the idea of ball players making money for playing a game.

Before baseball, thoroughbred horse racing, well established in other parts of the world, broke into the American consciousness with the introduction of three major races, which many years later would be linked together and labeled the Triple Crown. The Belmont Stakes in New York was first run in 1867. The Preakness Stakes was first contested in Baltimore in 1873. Finally, predating by a year the first organization of a major league was the first running of the Kentucky Derby in 1875.

In 1869 the first college football battle played out between Princeton and Rutgers Universities. Professional football still lay in the future. The Ivy League and the Big Ten were early bastions of the sport. Students and alumni were fascinated by the game and turned out in droves, requiring the construction of larger and larger stadiums beginning in the early years of the 20th century.

Late in the 19th century only those who ventured into the seedy world of fisticuffs joined baseball players in the professional realm. Boxers still fought bare knuckled, and in 1882 John L. Sullivan, the Boston Strong Boy, was proclaimed the first world heavyweight champion. By the time Sullivan retired in 1892, he had earned $1 million, an unfathomable sum at that time. He was the first athlete in any sport to do so. The bare-knuckle era ended when Sullivan's did, as did reliance on the old London Boxing Rules. They were replaced by the Marquess of Queensbury Rules, which called for the use of gloves on fists.

The first professional football player to earn any money for playing in a game was William "Pudge" Heffelfinger, who was deemed so valuable to the chances of the Allegheny Athletic Association in Pittsburgh in 1892 that the club paid him $500 for one game.

Clearly this was a much simpler time in the world of American sport. Sport was all about amusement, not big business. Sport, with few exceptions, especially upon the return of the Olympic Games to the modern era in Greece in 1896, was something engaged in for a nobler cause than filling a wallet. One represented his country, or his school, but by his early twenties moved on to the serious lifestyle of working at a career and raising a family.

When the Civil War ended in 1865, the Union freed the country's slaves. That did not guarantee automatic equality in all walks of life for African Americans. Hatred and discrimination did not evaporate overnight. Just about two decades after the battle of Appomattox, on May 1, 1884, Moses Fleetwood Walker, who had played on Oberlin College's baseball team the preceding few years, suited up with the Toledo Blue Stockings of the American Association, at that time a major league. This made him the first African American major leaguer, though he was ousted from the league because of pressure from influential white players at the end of the season.

Dr. James Naismith, a Canadian, invented basketball in 1891 at the Springfield, Massachusetts, YMCA. While teaching physical education he noticed that his pupils became bored with the curriculum, and he sought to interest them in something new. Famously, peach baskets were hung at two ends of a gymnasium, and the players became engrossed in the sport. The baskets were not hoops, but rather still retained their bottoms, so that play stopped every time someone scored while the ball was fished out.

Naismith scribbled out 13 rules of the sport, which were rudimentary, and in the ensuing century or so basketball mushroomed in popularity and escalated in speed, with players performing maneuvers unimaginable to the scholarly professor. In 2010 Naismith's handwritten "Magna Carta" of the sport sold at auction for $4 million, with the proceeds going to charity.

In some ways it is remarkable that the original rules were preserved, because little thought was applied to saving what much later came to be known as sports memorabilia.

Slowly but steadily, as the decades passed, the limited number of American sports expanded into a smorgasbord of choices.

The National Hockey League was founded in November 1917, though it is likely only the keenest of fans would be aware that the Canadian-born game was imported to the United States in such an organized fashion before the establishment of the National Football League.

Football was gaining in popularity in rugged factory towns throughout the East and Midwest, but mostly as a weekend diversion, better described in today's parlance as semipro. Communities embraced their hometown teams, and players were paid at most $50 a game, with many getting much less.

Founded as the American Professional Football Association in August 1920, a short while later the organization changed its name to the National Football League and began its inexorable rise in popularity, until it displaced baseball decades later as the most fanatically followed team sport in the country.

The baby among the professional sports leagues that play a major part in American life today is the National Basketball Association. The NBA was founded in New York City in June 1946 as the Basketball Association of America. In 1949 the circuit merged with the National Basketball League, and the new name was adopted.

All of these were fresh, landmark beginnings, the crawl-before-you-walk-before-you-run stages of the organizations that supply some of the best-known acronyms in the United States today. Except for college football, all were founded as business ventures. They were not propounding a sound mind and a sound body—the Greek ideal—so much as being created to make money for team owners and to entertain the public. They were amusements for people who had disposable income and could afford tickets offered for 50 cents or $1.

These sporting developments were basically confined to the nation's largest cities. Indeed, the period from the end of the Civil War through the 1880s was still the heyday of the Wild West in places like Dodge City, Kansas; Tombstone, Arizona; Colorado; Wyoming; and New Mexico. As the Cincinnati Red Stockings toured, buffalo roamed the prairie, and the railroad was in the process of connecting more of the East to the West. If there was no baseball team in a town, little attention was paid to the sport. Cowboys rode their horses and worked ranches, and the gunfighters of renown had their day.

In the early 1890s historian Frederick Jackson Turner proclaimed that the frontier had closed, ending an era in American history. Indeed, the Indian wars had concluded. Buffalo Bill Cody, who had pretty much seen it all and shaped much of it in his multiple roles, was no longer residing in the West, but was selling it around the world with extravagant Wild West shows.

In 1900 the average American laborer worked 60 hours a week. He didn't have either the time or the wherewithal to follow sports, whether horse racing, baseball, or boxing, essentially his only three choices if he wasn't a natural rooter for Hahvad or another Ivy League football team. He was supporting his family in a factory or up before dawn tilling the land to bring in a healthy crop.

The greatest shame of U.S. history is the institution of slavery. And despite being officially freed as the result of the North's victory in the Civil War, African Americans faced unending discrimination in most walks of life and in their daily routine.

Only retrospectively was the exclusion of Moses Fleetwood Walker from baseball deemed socially significant. It was an astonishing achievement when Jack Johnson became the first African American to win the heavyweight championship, in 1908 (a title he held until 1915). It was the grandest individual prize in sport at the time, and the racist elements ingrained in the sport were horrified by his triumph. A major reason was that inherent in the acquisition of the crown was the foundational belief that the heavyweight champion was the toughest man in the world.

Johnson was perpetually hounded through legal and extralegal means, verbally attacked, and dishonored by all manner of challenges throughout his reign. The discrimination and smear tactics were so overt that they rallied fair-minded whites to Johnson's side. But there were not enough of them, and they were neither outspoken nor powerful enough to help him.

The treatment of Johnson may be the first obvious instance of a big-time sporting figure becoming a symbol of a social cause in American sport. As a minority in a white majority country, Johnson wielded no clout beyond his powerful fists to make a statement that could be heard. History has for the most part sided with Johnson in terms of his being done wrong, but at that time social consciousness and sympathy for the underdog were hardly commonplace.

In social strata, athletes were on a par with actors. They were not looked at to effect change. It never would have occurred to an early football player to pen an op-ed piece for the *New York Times*, or to a baseball player to become an active member of a presidential candidate's campaign.

Little boys may have looked up to players, but to whatever degree athletes attained celebrity, it was one-dimensional, except for those lucky enough to elbow into vaudeville or the fledgling motion picture industry. It was difficult for players to build a name in their sport; that was up to the newspapers. In an era before electronic media, the public relied on sports reporters to inform them about what happened in the game, to provide the play-by-play. The reporters rarely left the press box, never entered the locker room, and only rarely, before games, on road trips, did they seek quotes from athletes describing how or why they did something. The most proficient athletes sometimes gained identity in the public mind by having their own columns (mostly ghostwritten by sportswriters). For the most part, those writings took the place of interviews and were forums open only to the biggest of stars.

Only on very special occasions, days when clocks paused, were Americans mesmerized by the common denominator of sport. The World Series, first contested in 1903, took center stage each October as the championship of the country's most popular team sport. Those springtime Saturdays when the fastest horses ran in Baltimore, Louisville, and New York were dates circled on the calendar. Once the Indianapolis 500 had been established in 1909, so was Memorial Day.

Baseball gained the trust of the populace first. From 1901 on, when the American League appeared on the Major League Baseball scene in competition with the National League, baseball ruled. There were 16 big-league teams, although they were not widely scattered geographically. All operated between Boston in the North, Washington, D.C., in the South, and St. Louis in the West.

In the less-populous country, those cities and their teams constructed fan bases intense in their rooting and deeply passionate about results. Baseball was the leader, far eclipsing football and hockey in glamour and newspaper column inches of coverage. Women's sports were nonexistent. Fans of winter sports did them, rather than watching them. Since the Winter Olympics were conducted far away, not even ardent supporters could get their news of gold medals earned in any timely way. Pro football's first task was to prove that it played a brand of the game superior to the colleges' version. Until that fact was established, and until the NFL stabilized the lineup of its teams, which did not occur until the 1930s, its credibility was soft.

Many a great game was contested, and many a satisfying championship was won, whether in baseball, football, and hockey; fleet animals running for glory and roses; or humans representing the United States in international competition. Yet from the first baby-stepping inception of sport, and for several decades, it would be difficult to impart special societal significance to any sport's results.

The games were played, the fans cheered, the results were recorded, and everybody went home. World War I was fought and won. World War II was fought and won. The United States flexed its might and convinced its citizens (especially during World War II) that it was on the side of right.

Next to such cataclysmic and world-shaping events, sport was nothing. No sport, no game, no championship could make the claim that it was changing the world, changing the way people lived, or transforming society. Only a handful of sporting developments predating World War II had a truly significant impact that affected people in more than one city.

So the real question is: How did we get from the Wright brothers of baseball and Pudge Heffelfinger of football to where we are now?

Make no mistake, where we are now is that sport on a daily basis means so much to so many that it monopolizes lives. Psychologists have studied fanatics and found that when their favorite team is winning or losing to a large degree, that affects their day, and winning or losing affects their long-term happiness. Americans are more emotionally invested in sport than ever before. In a society long called a melting pot, sport can be one of the biggest common denominators between strangers or between people so unlike in other ways they would otherwise have nothing to talk about.

To summarize the 100 most important sporting events in American history, it should first be noted that the list is not based on the most significant games per se, but gives more weight to sports developments that ultimately shaped individual habits or ways of thinking.

Games are defined by winners and losers, and since that is the yardstick that measures the worth of teams, this will never change. But it may be said that after World War II sport grew up, sometimes faster than the nation at large. Sport became a vehicle for change, not always willingly, sometimes quite grudgingly, but indisputably.

Good teams collect championships and frequently show off the milestones by installing banners in their arenas or flying pennants over their stadiums. To some extent, that is like counting your money in public.

In a long season of 162 baseball games, 16 football games, 82 basketball games, or 82 hockey games, results are transitory yet cumulative. Games can run together in memory. What truly counts, what truly matters, is when a game rises above its addition to the standings, when a development changes a sport for all time, or when the event becomes forever imbedded in memory.

This goes a long way toward explaining how this top-100 list was compiled. Events that occurred that affected the multitudes, not just a slice of a cheering faction, ranked highly. Political and societal change usually comes slowly. There is entrenched opposition to major change because there are many who prefer the status quo. Their reasons may be convoluted and wrong, particularly in the area of basic human fairness, where equality is at issue.

It takes time to change rules, laws, and attitudes, and rarely have sports leaders been enlightened enough to take steps within their empires that risk the wrath of a portion of spectators. The Berlin Wall came down because it was time. Likewise, Jackie Robinson broke the color barrier in Major League Baseball because others had put their necks on the line and lobbied for that change for years. When the U.S. Congress approved Title IX legislation guaranteeing equal opportunities for girls and women in high school and college sports, it was long past the time when females believed their only role in America was to be stay-at-home moms and housewives wearing prim costumes.

These are not the 100 biggest sporting events in American history. Those would be game results, and the list would have turned out very differently. In selecting the items on this list and their order, I emphasized their significance more than a final score. I placed importance on how much public reaction was affixed to the sporting development, as well as how much significance was attached to what occurred by society at large and the item's enduring place in history.

Rarely does sport change the world we live in, but at times it does have broad ramifications. They are not always planned or calculated. Sometimes they are a shock to everyone. Sometimes even events that come along on a schedule after being arranged do not produce the expected reactions.

The most highly rated sporting developments in American history have had great impact not only at the time they happened, but also decades later, when they are easily recalled by sports fans who were not even alive at the time. Moreover, those special moments are often just as readily recalled by the average person on the street who is not an avid sports fan. That is one true measurement of significance: a sporting event important not only in the sports world, but in the scheme of history.

I did not use a hard-and-fast points system of numbering to rank the most important sporting events. Hard-eyed evaluation of what transpired, coupled with its enduring nature, led me to a belief that selected turning points in sport were vastly influential, not only at the time they happened, but still today. Firsts can never be repeated, and a great deal of weight was placed on a pioneering development in a particular sport or one that affected all of sport.

One of the major reasons Americans are so conversant with, entranced by, and almost goo-goo eyed over sport is the ready accessibility of the games. For many years the only information available on sports was printed in newspapers, with a small group of magazines contributing. Sports began outreach to the millions living in far corners of the country through radio initially and then through television.

These media opened previously closed windows on the activities of individuals who up until then might as well have been fictional characters in novels, for all those living in smaller cities and towns knew about them.

Radio and television imparted both vivid description and information in much larger quantities than had previously been available. Their influence in creating sports fans and entertaining them is incalculable. Ironically, first with radio, and then with TV, owners of professional sports franchises initially resisted allowing their games, their property, to be given away over the airwaves. They were slow to understand that the broadcasts whetted people's appetite for more. Fans who listened to the game on the radio really wanted to be there, at the stadium, watching in person.

Teams could be described as operating in medieval times when it came to marketing, given how little marketing there was in the 1920s and 1930s. Clubs didn't sell T-shirts advertising their brand. They didn't sell baseball caps with insignias on the front. Kids did approach their athletic heroes for autographs, but not in droves. The last thing in the world they thought of doing with a signature obtained was selling it. Sports memorabilia didn't exist except for souvenirs of their careers saved by individual players. Some passionate fans may have saved early scorecards, or World Series programs, as well.

It should be noted, however, that baseball cards did exist. Despite many types of the little cardboard gems being packaged with cigarettes and tobacco products, the manufacturers still did seem to aim their wares at youths. There are always hoarders who save things that please them, and there are careless collectors who outgrow their hobbies and discard their "childish things." A surprising number of century-old cards remain in remarkably pristine condition

Sport as a whole remained fairly unsophisticated into the 1920s, as did the men who played in professional leagues. Early baseball players were far more likely to have come off the farm than through matriculation at a four-year college. Even football had not yet turned to the colleges as a farm system.

The Roaring Twenties, before the stock market collapse that bled into the Great Depression, represented a quantum leap in the manner in which sport was viewed. Larger-than-life athletes came along just as the country was shedding the post–World War I blues and looking to Charleston the night away, even if people couldn't legally stop for a drink after work.

Pretty much up until 1920, in baseball the game was the thing. After 1920, players became more sharply defined personalities, because of the way newspapers covered them. The men were no longer comparatively anonymous names in a box score, but had their exploits emblazoned in bigger headline type.

From the late 1910s on, but especially in the 1920s and 1930s, Americans came to know heavyweight champion Jack Dempsey, baseball slugger Babe Ruth, football star Red Grange, boxer Joe Louis, and track star Jesse Owens. These are all men who transcended sport, and while all are long deceased, they remain imprinted on the American consciousness in ways that few of the famous ever are.

What was still true after World War II, though, was the heinous lynching of blacks, the everyday discrimination against African Americans, and the deprivation of opportunity for athletic talents to reach the top. With such a larger percentage of Americans shut out of the American dream, the simple hiring of Jackie Robinson to play baseball for the Brooklyn Dodgers was such a huge departure from the historical norm that it shook the foundations of society.

In 1947 baseball was still by far the most popular team sport in the United States. The phrase "national pastime" was very much true. There was no second place among professional team sports, and second place in the hearts of sports fans was the most that football, basketball, and hockey could aspire to.

Simmering anger among American blacks who had gone off to war to defend the country's ideals against Nazis and other fascists was no longer buried beneath the surface. African American newspaper writers became louder and more vocal in their opinion columns, demanding that baseball offer jobs to the best African American players.

There was no more waiting for glacially moving baseball to act. The time was now. Only one baseball figure in authority had the fortitude to buck history and the disapproval of fellow executives. The statesman in the group was Branch Rickey, the general manager of the Dodgers.

Rickey understood there would be backlash. He knew that he, like Robinson, would be a minority of one in organizing the most visible of all possible challenges to the color barrier by signing an African American player to take the lead in beating down the sturdy walls that had been in place since 1884.

The single most important moment in American sporting history was the elevation of Jackie Robinson to the major leagues to play for Brooklyn in 1947. It was monumental in symbolic as well as literal significance because of baseball's long history of intolerance, the message sent to the world that from now on things would be different, and Robinson's magnificence on the diamond, proof positive that blacks were as good as whites in baseball.

As the most astute among observers comprehended, the success of Jackie Robinson portended a more just future. He opened the door of opportunity a crack, but his arrival in the big leagues heralded a flood of previously banned blacks and a revolution that altered not just baseball, but the lives of millions of African Americans. The symbolic meaning of Jackie Robinson was an infusion of hope where none had resided before.

Never before or since has the performance of one man on one team in one sport meant so much to so many. The world turns slowly, but it does keep on turning, and decades later, after Robinson's retirement, long after he was inducted into the Baseball Hall of Fame, and sadly, long after his death, which came too early, Major League Baseball recognized his contributions to that sport, all sports, and all Americans.

On April 15, 1997, the 50th anniversary of Robinson's debut with the Dodgers, baseball decreed that his No. 42 jersey number would be retired by all teams.

Those few players still active for certain clubs who wore 42 were grandfathered in, but when they left their team or retired, that was it for 42. This was a rare and grand tribute.

Robinson's barrier breaking represented the ultimate confluence of sport and social significance in the United States.

A ranking of such depth, of 100 events, will always occasion a variety of opinion, and indeed, it was not always easy to rate in order of the most important events in American sporting history. Always in my mind was the meaning of a sports development that transcended the playing field. There have been few times when American sports fans—and Americans from all corners of the nation—have been united by a sporting event. Each of the events listed here should have been big enough on its own merits to appear on the front page of newspapers nationally, or at the very least, on the front pages of newspapers where it took place.

As 1999 turned into 2000, numerous news agencies sought to rank the most important sporting event of the 20th century. Different criteria were used by one magazine, one newspaper, one television station, but almost uniformly the votes emerged in favor of the same event. The victory by a team of youthful, amateur players over the well-oiled Soviet hockey machine at the 1980 Winter Olympics at Lake Placid in New York was the game of a lifetime for most Americans.

One of the unlikeliest of big-game triumphs in all of sports history, the match pitted a huge underdog against what appeared to be an unbeatable giant, all played out against the backdrop of the Cold War and especially tense relations been the United States and USSR, the world's two major military superpowers. The Americans followed up by winning the gold medal, beating Finland.

Looking back over the convoluted and mythologized history of the Old West, I periodically applied a phrase about sorting fact from fiction: "When legend becomes fact, print the legend." Director John Ford, maker of many Hollywood Westerns, had one of his film characters say that.

In the case of the most emotional hockey game ever witnessed by Americans, the facts were so outrageous that they overshadowed legend.

By the nature of seeking out events that transcended sport and seeped into mainstream recognition, a large percentage of the sports events included in this listing took fans beyond the scoreboard. In almost all instances, they were the talk of the day, even before office buildings had water coolers. What happened yesterday or last night was on the tip of everyone's tongue, excitedly talked about with family, friends, neighbors, coworkers, and even strangers. Did you hear what happened at the stadium? Did you see what happened in New York?

The umbrella over sport is a very large one, and comparing a World Series game with an NCAA college basketball championship might be construed as an apples and oranges approach. No doubt the same may well be said of a singular athletic accomplishment and an act that forever changes the manner in which a sport is played or viewed.

Obviously almost any ranking that does not apply an empirical formula (though Lord knows what it would be for this kind of project) is subjective. The scales of justice are not calibrated, but I have attempted to balance them without prejudice.

There is a difference between special and historic. Winning the Super Bowl any year is special. Winning the Super Bowl for the New York Jets after the quarterback predicted an upset victory is historic.

Winning the Kentucky Derby, the Preakness, and the Belmont, the Triple Crown, is special. Secretariat winning the Triple Crown in unprecedented, dominant fashion is not only historic, but unforgettable.

We live in a transient society, often called a disposable society, with a short memory. Etching an achievement or development in granite is something that is always remembered. That is a pretty good yardstick for applying the term historic.

The listing mixes those events that affected society for all time in terms of off-the-field change with those that are highlighted in memory by on-the-field brilliance. Higher rankings were awarded to events that not only did Americans most strongly react to, but that changed the sports landscape for good or permanently changed perceptions of fans.

There have been many heavyweight champions, some worthy of the appellation great, from Muhammad Ali to Joe Frazier, from Jack Dempsey to Mike Tyson. But there was only one Joe Louis. At a time when boxing was one of the most avidly followed sports in the country and black fighters seeking titles in any weight class were routinely discriminated against, Louis not only set records for the longest reign and the most title defenses, but comported himself in such a gentlemanly manner that he changed many white fans' assessment of African Americans.

The same was true of Jesse Owens, whose dignified handling of a put-down from racist dictator Adolf Hitler in the 1936 Summer Olympics in Germany, winning gold medal after gold medal, is also very much legend.

When Title IX was approved by Congress, giving girls and women powerful official backing in their attempts to gain the same opportunities as boys and men in sport, the earthquake-like repercussions were felt for years despite some intransigence by athletic leaders. This legislation has had the most wide-ranging effect of any law passed by Congress regarding sport.

Most girls of the modern generation have not even heard of Title IX, and to them stories of their grandmothers being denied the chance to play on a volleyball or basketball team—which did not even exist for them—is incomprehensible, a relic of history as foreign to them as the assassination of President John F. Kennedy or just what did take place in Vietnam.

Given that in terms of history the ability of girls and women to compete in organized sports has been a brief window, not nearly as many women have contributed to the most important sporting events in American history as have men. In a sense, except for a small number of individuals and a smaller number of teams, women's sports history in this country virtually began with the passage of Title IX in the 1970s.

A fresh listing of a top 100 written 50 years from now no doubt would have a different cast. However, it remains important to recognize the achievements of special events highlighting women's athletic achievements.

Women started late, through no fault of their own. Tennis star Althea Gibson made her mark as an African American barrier breaker, the U.S. women's soccer team placed its stamp on the international scene, and the creation of the still-growing Women's National Basketball Association provided the biggest-ever forum on American soil for women's team sport. Other women who have shown what women of earlier generations might have been doing all along if they had been allowed to are tennis legends Martina Navratilova, Billie Jean King, and Monica Seles (though not only for their playing prowess); basketball coach Pat Summit; track star Wilma Rudolph; gymnast Kerri Strug; golfer and much more Babe Didrikson Zaharias; and Iditarod Trail Sled Dog Race champion Libby Riddles.

Sometimes memorable, indelible great moments were recorded in a single day, such as Bill Mazeroski winning the 1960 World Series with a home run, Richard Petty recording his 200th stock-car victory, Wilt Chamberlain scoring 100 points in an NBA game, Don Larsen pitching a perfect game in the World Series, Frank Shorter running to Olympic gold in the marathon in 1972, and Bobby Thomson smashing the shot heard around the world to give the New York Giants a pennant.

Firsts figure prominently on the list of the 100 most important sporting events in American history, from the first sports radio broadcasts to the first sports television broadcasts. Transcendent figures such as Babe Ruth, Roberto Clemente, Muhammad Ali, Jim Thorpe, Hank Aaron, and Joe Namath are all iconic names among the pantheon of America's greatest sports stars, and in all cases there was a moment to point to in their careers that was transformational.

One aspect of sport that provides quantifiable comparison across the years and generations is record keeping. Playing conditions may well have differed dramatically within the same sport between 1910 and 2010, yet still there is enough of a common denominator that we may recognize a special event, a special performance, or a special athlete. A regularly used sports cliché is that records are made to be broken.

When someone sets an all-time record, that should be duly noted and celebrated. It is never safe to claim that the record will last a long time, and an example from the autumn of 2014 makes this point most graphically. On November 15, a running back named Melvin Gordon rushed for 408 yards in one game for the University of Wisconsin, setting a mark for the most yards gained on the ground in the large-school NCAA category. Gordon received his share of "attaboys." Yet just one week later, on November 22, a running back named Samaje Perine rushed for 427 yards in one game for the University of Oklahoma. Bye-bye record. Even by the standards of the cliché, that was remarkably swift eclipsing of a major record.

Included in this listing are certain records that are almost guaranteed never to be broken—the forever group. When the marks were recorded, they were recognized as significant. With the passage of time, they appear unassailable. In several cases, rule changes, evolution of styles of play, and different approaches in the way coaches use their players seem certain to help preserve those numbers for all time.

If a sports betting parlor in Las Vegas—another phenomenon that did not exist when Babe Ruth ruled the earth, or at least American League pitching—placed odds on certain of these records being broken, they might go up on the big board at 100–1. In truth, for some of these accomplishments, those would be short odds.

No baseball pitcher is ever going to top Cy Young's 511 victories. No baseball hitter is likely to achieve a .400 batting average again. No baseball pitcher is ever going to toss three no-hitters in a row. The odds do stack up against another NFL quarterback topping the yardage and touchdown passes accumulated by Peyton Manning in 2013, though one must stop short of using the word impossible for that one. One hopes that there will never be a more significant or worse sports incident than the 1919 Black Sox scandal.

Many events examined on this list are firsts. They cannot be repeated, and seconds never measure up to firsts. It is like the fall of Humpty Dumpty from that great wall. Poor Humpty could never be put back together again. In sport no one can go back in time and become the first at something. In these cases, the first African American major league player, the first African American professional team sport coach, the first all-black college basketball championship lineup, the setting in motion of pro football's quantum jump in popularity, are not records to be broken, but breakthroughs forever to be admired. They will never be surpassed.

Alas, in some cases the deaths of notable athletes figured into the way they are remembered or the special event they are linked to. Dale Earnhardt Sr. died in his race car. Roberto Clemente died on a mission of charitable mercy. Ray Chapman perished on a baseball diamond.

Professional and college sports teams fly around the country on chartered jets, hurriedly shifting locations for the next game. It is remarkable that over the last 60 years or so, when airplane flights replaced train travel as the most common method of transportation, no major league baseball, football, basketball, or hockey team has been involved in a fatal plane crash. With hundreds more teams flying the skies, college teams have not been so fortunate. Perhaps the greatest tragedy in college sport was the fatal plane crash that wiped out the Marshall University football team in November 1970. The death toll was 75. Although the horrible incident is memorialized and always remembered on the West Virginia campus, the school did rebuild its football team in an inspirational manner, leading to a movie about the event.

Most objective observers of the American sporting scene would say that professional sports, to whatever degree they were involved, were shamefully slow in welcoming African Americans to play and equally derelict in providing in opportunities for women. That is why, when it finally happened, it was so noteworthy that Major League Baseball opened its doors to blacks, and the ripple effect throughout society led to other sports doing the same.

So many significant racial and sexual sporting barriers have been hacked through and trampled in the dust that anyone spoiling for an equal-rights fight might find nothing left to accomplish. The big wars have been won, and only skirmishes, individual challenges, seem to remain, with a possible exception or two on a grander scale.

Someday, in some sport, some spectacular athlete will come along and add a name to the list of socially prominent sports stars we revere. Perhaps that will be the first woman to make her mark playing Major League Baseball. I'm not sure where to rank something that has not yet occurred, but if we live long enough there is every reason to believe that day will come.

Yes, that person will be remembered as a pioneer. And yes, that news will play out on the front pages of newspapers, on radio and television, as well as on computers and cell phones. When the woman in question throws her first pitch, or smacks her first hit, the whole country will know it and applaud.

The 100 Most Important Sporting Events in American History

#1 Jackie Robinson

Jackie Robinson was always feisty, especially when standing up for his rights. That attitude became a problem for him in the military when superior officers engaged in racist behavior and he refused to take it. In one case Robinson literally refused to move to the back of a bus, becoming so enraged at the driver that charges were eventually lodged against him, and he was court-martialed.

Robinson brought the same fierce pride to baseball, and he needed every ounce of courage and determination as the pioneer African American who opened a door that was a steel barrier with a heavy lock on it, to provide opportunity to others.

He was born January 31, 1919 in Cairo, Georgia, into a family of sharecroppers, and his mother Mallie, a single parent, moved the family to California in hopes of finding a better life after his father, Jerry, abandoned the clan. The youngest of five children, Robinson was introduced to sports by his older brothers, especially Mack, who in 1936 won a silver medal in the Summer Olympics.

After high school Robinson enrolled in nearby Pasadena Junior College, then after two years became a student at the University of California at Los Angeles. It was there that Robinson showed he could compete against the best. He lettered in four sports: football, basketball, baseball, and track. An all-around talent, Robinson won a National College Athletic Association title in the long jump. In November 2014 UCLA paid homage to Robinson by retiring the number 42, which he wore while playing for the Brooklyn Dodgers; the Bruins applied that honor to all of the school's sports teams.

The year 1941 was a big one in young Robinson's life. He met freshman Rachel Isum, who eventually became his wife; he left school early and ventured to Honolulu to play football for the Hawaii Braves; and he competed as a running back for the Los Angeles Bulldogs, part of a West Coast pro league. At that point it seemed likely that if Robinson was going to become known for his participation in any professional sport, it would be football.

When the Japanese bombed Pearl Harbor in December of that year, Robinson was swept up in the conflict. He also found himself in the midst of that bus-riding conflict, but was ultimately acquitted of charges of insubordination and granted an honorable discharge.

Robinson, a sturdily built five foot eleven and 195 pounds, dabbled once again in football with the Bulldogs, but then accepted a job as athletic director at what was then Sam Houston College in Austin, Texas. Not long afterward he was approached to play baseball for the esteemed Kansas City Monarchs and came under the guidance of manager Buck O'Neil, who later became the first African American coach in the majors.

Baseball star Jackie Robinson was the most transformative figure in sports history. At a time when African Americans were agitating for more opportunities in society and when baseball was by far the most significant team sport, Robinson made history when he broke into organized ball with the Montreal Royals in 1946 and then the Brooklyn Dodgers in 1947. (AP Photo/John J. Lent)

By 1945, as African American troops returned home from fighting overseas, they were in no mood to accept being treated as second-class citizens. Simultaneously, sportswriters at the nation's premier African American newspapers agitated for blacks to be welcomed into the national pastime. For decades the Negro Leagues had offered so-called separate-but-equal baseball playing, and much as in the public schools, conditions imposed on players were far from equal. All-time great African American baseball players such as Satchel Paige, Josh Gibson, Cool Papa Bell, Buck Leonard, Smokey Joe Williams, Bullet Joe Rogan, Oscar Charleston, John Henry Lloyd, and Judy Johnson were barred from the top echelon of the sport in the United States.

Commissioner Kenesaw Mountain Landis and the baseball teams' owners denied there was any policy against signing African American players. They provided weak excuses about how it just so happened that none were on major league rosters. A specific appeal was made to the Pittsburgh Pirates to offer tryouts to stars in their backyard playing for the Homestead Grays and the Pittsburgh Crawfords, but they never happened. Jackie Robinson did participate in a sham tryout with the Boston Red Sox and was rejected. The Red Sox also had the opportunity to obtain Willie Mays and passed on that.

Plotting carefully and quietly while all of this was taking place, Brooklyn Dodgers general manager Branch Rickey, known for his innovations in a long executive career in the sport, had dispatched a scout to find the perfect African American player to break the color barrier. Rickey pored over the biographies of numerous prospects. He wanted someone of great skill and fortitude, but who could hold his temper in check when the verbal and physical assaults from racists began on the field. Rickey wanted someone who was married and would not be a playboy. He wanted someone not too old and set in his ball-playing ways. Robinson was not close to being the Negro Leagues' star with the most glittering resume, though he was an all-star shortstop for the Monarchs in 1945.

Mindful of the politics of the time and the likelihood that team owners would oppose him, Rickey floated the rumor that he was trying to start a new pro league for black players. When Robinson was invited to Rickey's New York office, he thought that was what Rickey wanted to talk about. Rickey had built the "Gashouse Gang" St. Louis Cardinals into world champions and introduced the minor league farm system. Now, through a combination of wanting to do the right thing about racism in baseball and advancing his own interests by hiring the best players available, he sought to change the world.

Robinson was his anointed choice as the avenging angel against injustice. Rickey's only worry was whether the fiery Robinson could hold in check his basic nature to retaliate when inevitable discrimination flared up. In what became a famous comment, Rickey said he wanted someone who had the courage NOT to fight back, for two years. On November 1, 1945, Robinson signed with Brooklyn. At this juncture Rickey was aided in his efforts by Commissioner A. B. "Happy" Chandler, a former U.S. senator. Landis had died in 1944. The anti-Robinson faction felt it could count on Chandler because he was from Kentucky. Instead, Chandler backed Rickey and Robinson.

Robinson spent the 1946 season with the AAA minor league Montreal Royals, in a cosmopolitan, international city, suffering limited pushback. The real ordeal of his career began in Florida during spring training in 1947, when locals fought to keep his housing separate from the rest of the team. Some Dodgers resented his presence, but when rumors of a possible boycott reached Rickey, he informed the players that he would trade anyone who wanted to leave. National League president Ford Frick stepped in and threatened to suspend any player who boycotted a game because of Robinson. It may have been Frick's finest hour in the job.

Rickey had banked on Dodgers players supporting Robinson as a teammate and ignoring his race, but that development was slower to materialize than he expected. Eventually—and Rickey did dispose of some players—their backing came through.

Aside from whatever level of altruism Rickey maintained, he publicly said that he had brought in Robinson because he would help Brooklyn win more games and put more people in the seats at Ebbets Field. This proved to be true. Beginning April 15, 1947, the day he made his big-league debut, and moving forward, Robinson was a huge gate attraction. African American fans who had never considered attending a big-league game turned out for his appearances, not just in Brooklyn, but all around the National League.

Regrettably, players on other teams sprinkled their heckling of the Dodgers' new player with racist invective, and once its severity led to a public dressing down of Philadelphia player-manager Ben Chapman. The virulent, steady verbal attack by Chapman was unsettling. Another time Robinson was spiked and bled through his uniform.

"I have to admit that this day, of all the unpleasant days in my life, brought me nearer to cracking up than I ever had been," Robinson said.[1]

Fans also shouted racial slurs at Robinson from the stands in other ballparks. The stress was constant and cumulative. Robinson knew he had to succeed on the field or naysayers would claim that black ballplayers were not good enough for the majors, and who knew when an African American would get another chance?

Robinson channeled his anger into his performance. He played with inner fire, stealing bases and taking the extra base, challenging pitchers who threw high and inside on him, and hitting his way to acclaim. He became an overnight celebrity in the black community, touted and feted and honored everywhere until he reached the point of exhaustion. It took all of Robinson's energy to excel as Jackie Robinson the ballplayer. He was not enthusiastic about embracing Jackie Robinson the symbol, yet he did so because he understood how important that was.

Despite Rickey's constant support, the companionship of Robinson's wife Rachel, and some backing from teammates, Robinson's very public workdays subjected him to enormous pressure. It was a miracle he didn't snap, but he persevered.

At age 28 Robinson was an old rookie, though he needed every one of those years of maturity to cope with his status. That year he won the first rookie of the year award. During a 10-year career, as he became more accepted and other African Americans followed him into the majors, from Larry Doby with the Cleveland Indians to Roy Campanella and Don Newcombe with his own Dodgers, Robinson became a star at second base, first base, whatever position he played.

When he retired after the 1956 season, Robinson had compiled a .311 batting average, won a most valuable player award, and helped lead Brooklyn to six pennants and one World Series crown. He was inducted into the Baseball Hall of Fame in 1962. Despite his hair going white prematurely, his body breaking down from the effects of diabetes, and his gradual descent into near-blindness before his death at age 53 in 1972, Robinson never stopped campaigning for racial justice.

The level of notoriety Robinson reached across the United States made him a household name during his baseball career. To African Americans he was a hero. To right-thinking other Americans he represented progress in racial relations. To haters he was an archenemy.

Jackie Robinson's legacy has never faded. Rachel continued to lobby for the same causes Jackie believed in. Now their children have taken up the cudgel. Long after his death, Robinson was awarded the Presidential Medal of Freedom and the

Congressional Gold Medal. There is a Jackie Robinson Little League in Chicago. Every Major League Baseball team has retired jersey number 42, although one day each season every player on every team trots onto the field for a game wearing that number. *We are all 42*. In 2013 a Jackie Robinson biographical movie entitled *42* was released, bringing home to younger generations the struggles Robinson faced to integrate baseball.

Robinson credited the assistance and example of Joe Louis, his own role model, for showing him the way. A year after Robinson integrated baseball, President Harry Truman integrated the armed forces. In 1955, a year before Robinson retired from the Dodgers, Rosa Parks refused to give up her seat on a bus in Montgomery, Alabama, and the civil rights movement was growing. The Reverend Dr. Martin Luther King Jr. called Robinson "a legend and a symbol in his own time" who "challenged the dark skies of intolerance and frustration."[2]

In 1999, shortly before the dawn of the 21st century, *Time* magazine named Robinson one of the 100 most influential people of the 20th century. Indeed, Robinson's influence on American society was mighty, and only a small part of it was due to his being a very good baseball player.

NOTES

1. Jackie Robinson, as told to Alfred Duckett, *I Never Had It Made* (Hopewell, NJ: The Ecco Press, 1995), 59.
2. Rachel Robinson, "A Pioneer in Civil Rights," *Boston Globe*, March 2, 2005.

FURTHER READING

Eig, Jonathan. *Opening Day: The Story of Jackie Robinson's First Season*. New York: Simon & Schuster, 2008.

Falkner, David. *Great Time Coming: The Life of Jackie Robinson from Baseball to Birmingham*. New York: Touchstone, 1995.

Kahn, Roger. *Rickey & Robinson: The True, Untold Story of the Integration of Baseball*. New York: Rodale, 2014.

Rampersad, Arnold. *Jackie Robinson: A Biography*. New York: Ballantine Books, 1997.

Salisbury, Mitchell, Hersch Rothmel, Marion Pagios, Philippa Naugle, Devin Martin, Avery Mansfield, and Sean Knox. "The African American Athlete (Commodity, Image, & Narrative)." Paper presented at Academic Excellence Conference, Keene State College, New Hampshire, 2015.

#2 The Miracle on Ice

On the eve of the 1980 Winter Olympics in Lake Placid, the tiny community in upstate New York that had also hosted the games in 1932, the U.S. national hockey team played an exhibition game at Madison Square Garden against the powerful Soviet Union.

In the February 9 game, the Russians clobbered the Americans 10–3. Few were surprised. Despite this being the culmination of a 61-game pre-Olympic practice tour that had begun in September 1979, the Americans were regarded as callow boys, college kids with limited experience. The USSR was *the* international powerhouse of the time, winner of Olympic gold in 1956, 1964, 1968, 1972, and 1976. The Soviet Union was also the two-time defending world champion and winner of three other hockey golds, at the world championships in the 1970s.

In that era before professionals skated into the games, Americans playing in the National Hockey League were not eligible to compete. A few years later Mikhail Gorbachev would begin to remake the Soviet Union into a more open society, and Russians would cross the ocean to play pro hockey as teammates with Americans and Europeans.

However, in 1980 the USSR was very much considered the evil empire, the Cold War nemesis. Members of its sports teams were treated as professionals, living and breathing their sports, but officially they were not pros. So the very best players from the USSR continued to be eligible for the Olympics and world championships.

Few fans of the sport gave the Americans any chance to win gold, and pessimists could not see them even winning a medal.

Complicating matters were geopolitics. The Soviets had invaded Afghanistan, and U.S. president Jimmy Carter demanded that they withdraw. In 1980 the Soviets weren't budging, although later that ill-advised adventure became known as Russia's Vietnam, a reference to the U.S. involvement in Southeast Asia that resulted in bitter domestic division and military failure.

Tension had ebbed and flowed between the two nuclear superpowers since the end of World War II. Although mutual suspicion never seemed to evaporate, this period was a low point. This was Communism versus Capitalism on the ice.

If anyone in Lake Placid harbored optimism about the long-term chances of the U.S. team, it was the U.S. team members. They had lived together, trained together, played together, and endured the sometimes harsh rhetoric and even more demanding practices of coach Herb Brooks, on a leave of absence from the University of Minnesota. Aloof and unyielding, Brooks was the dictator of the team. He had selected his men carefully, sometimes ignoring statistics and banking on the heart and spirit he saw within a prospect.

Even Brooks recognized that he had been as much warden as coach. But he thought that's what it would take to whip the guys into the best shape of their lives to play the best hockey of their lives.

"I would never ask my family, my loved ones, to do what I asked them to do," Brooks said.[1]

While the best Soviet players enjoyed international reputations, especially fabulous goaltender Vladimir Tretiak, the Americans were epitomized by captain Mike Eruzione. From Winthrop, Massachusetts, and out of Boston University, Eruzione was one of the oldest players at age 25, and he had skated through two minor league seasons on an amateur contract. He was not the fastest of skaters, nor did he possess the hardest of shots. On a team of underdogs, Eruzione was used to that status.

"None of the colleges thought I could play Division I hockey," Eruzione said of barely being recruited for the top level of NCAA play, never mind becoming an Olympian.[2]

In some ways Eruzione was the quintessential Olympian. He was a homebody, telephoning his family to the tune of $90 a month in an era before cell phones and when he had no income. He did the little things right on the ice to bug opponents. He believed—even before the squad played an Olympic game—that being captain of the U.S. hockey team would be the highlight of his skating life, even if he got his previously denied chance to play in the NHL.

The six-month road trip to strange arenas led the players to their new home at Lake Placid Olympic Fieldhouse and culminated with Americans on the ice against Sweden on February 12. The United States and Sweden tied 2–2, but it took Brooks pulling goalie Jimmy Craig out of the net to achieve the tie on a last-ditch goal with 27 seconds left. The tie was actually a good sign, because Sweden was a power on the international stage.

Nobody got too worked up because it was the opener, but the United States began opening eyes when it torched Czechoslovakia 7–3 in its next game. The Czechs were supposed to be in line for a silver medal. By the time the United States bested Norway 5–1 after a sluggish start, fans were sitting up and taking notice.

After trailing 1–0, Eruzione tied the game 1–1, and then Mark Johnson, Mark Pavelich, Mark Wells, and Ken Morrow scored.

The United States kept winning its way through the preliminary round and at 4–0–1 advanced to the medal round to face the Russians. In 1980, television had not yet taken complete control of the Olympic schedule for the convenience of prime-time audiences. A request to move the game to 8:00 p.m. for a prime-time

U.S. audience was denied by the Soviets. So the showdown versus the USSR took place at 5:00 in the afternoon, to be shown later to U.S. fans on tape delay. There may never have been a hockey game played on U.S. soil that created as much anticipation.

Early in the tournament Eruzione had said, "For a team to beat us here it will have to overcome the emotion of the crowd." It was a toss-up whether the field-house would provide home-court advantage or home-country pressure.[3]

The U.S. squad was the youngest and most inexperienced among the 12 Olympic teams. The Russians were the most talented and experienced. The Olympic Fieldhouse held 8,500 fans, and a semifinals ticket was tougher to obtain than a discount seat on an airline at Thanksgiving.

Some 35 years after the event, Americans are used to chanting, "U-S-A! U-S-A!" when the mood strikes them as they watch their brethren compete in international contests. But in 1980 it was a relatively fresh phenomenon, and the reverberating shouts of the fans told a very emotional story in very few letters. The patriotism in the building was extreme. More than just a hockey game, for fans this confrontation seemed to symbolize a nonshooting battle proving the superiority of one country's lifestyle over another's. There was a tremendous amount of "Beat the Commies" sentiment in the air. The inside of the arena offered a frenzied atmosphere of patriotism, with fans waving small American flags and singing "God Bless America."

One of the Soviet greats, forward Vladimir Krutov, gave his country a 1–0 lead in the first period, instilling a minor sense of dread in fans who recalled the 10–3 drubbing of a few weeks earlier. Buzz Schneider tied the game for the United States, and Sergei Markarov, another famous Russian player, put his team ahead 2–1. A key moment occurred near the end of the first period when Tretiak, the usually brilliant netminder, made a sloppy play, failing to smother a 100-foot shot from Dave Christian.

More dramatically, Johnson, whose father coached the University of Wisconsin team and became the head of USA Hockey, out-hustled the defenders for a last-gasp shot that tied things at 2–2.

Russian coach Viktor Tikhonov made a stunning move between periods, yanking Tretiak and replacing him with backup Vladimir Myshkin. Players on both teams were flabbergasted. Later in life Tikhonov conceded it was the worst move he ever made in coaching.

By the end of two periods it was apparent that the swifter-skating Soviets could penetrate the U.S. defense, but the last line of that defense, Craig, was almost always there to stop them. Still, after 40 minutes of play the Soviet Union led 3–2, and there was a disquieting buzz in the house. At the time there had been no appreciable drop-off with Myshkin in net, but as the minutes ticked off in the third, the

United States played with more urgency. When Craig made a save (and he made a lot of them, finishing with 36), he shoved the puck ahead to his teammates to start the offense further up ice.

When Krutov went off for high-sticking, the Americans capitalized on the power play, the fleet Johnson netting his second goal. The tension was palpable in the arena, with the score 3–3. Back and forth the sides skated at high-octane speed, the Russians pressing, swarming Craig, the United States clearing the puck and taking runs at Myshkin.

Ten minutes exactly remained on the clock as the puck rolled into the face-off circle to Myshkin's right. Eruzione skated hard for it, his stick drawn back as he thought "shot" before he touched the puck. He fired, and the puck soared past Myshkin. The roar of fans in the fieldhouse practically registered on the Richter scale. Rarely has the intonation of "USA!" rubbed so many tonsils raw.

It was 4–3 United States, and now the Americans had to protect the lead.

The players focused and skated; the fans sat and worried. Agonizingly, the clock ticked down, second by second, minute by minute as the most startling and magnificent upset in American sports history inched toward reality. As the last seconds disappeared on the clock, broadcaster Al Michaels uttered a call for the ages: "Do you believe in miracles?"

Fans stood and sang "The Star-Spangled Banner." Players hugged one another and whooped. Somehow they had done it, polished off the big, bad Russians, and deep down a portion of their psyche would not process that information. The players walked around as if in a daze, as if they hadn't slept in a month.

"I'm so drained I don't know what I'm going on," said U.S. forward John Harrington.[4]

For all the pomp and hype, for all the satisfaction gained by

Called "The Miracle on Ice," the victory by the United States Olympic hockey team over the Soviet Union in 1980 resonated around the world and was capped by the capture of the gold medal over Finland. The triumph over the Soviet Union is considered one of the greatest upsets in sports history and was considered the most significant sporting event of the 20th century. (AP Photo)

edging the Soviets, the job wasn't done. All the victory did was advance the Americans to the gold medal game. A loss would have been the most anticlimactic finish of all time. But the United States came through once more, defeating Finland 4–2 and capturing the gold.

"We'll probably wake up tomorrow and still won't believe it," Johnson said.[5]

President Carter, who immediately extended an invitation to the White House, might have thought the same. He told Brooks in a celebratory phone call that nobody at the White House could get any work done until their triumph was recorded.

Outside the fieldhouse, people danced in the street, shouted "USA!" over and over, and toasted the team and the country with something strong.

The glow of that victory has never faded. Once the games ended, the players went their separate ways, some back to their colleges, some on to the pros. Dave Christian joined his father Bill and uncle Roger, who had been members of the other U.S. Olympic champion hockey team in 1960, as a gold medal winner. Defenseman Ken Morrow went directly into the New York Islanders' lineup and was a member of the same season's Stanley Cup champions. He played a part in all four Islanders 1980s Cup championships. Mark Johnson had a lengthy pro career and has had a lengthy coaching stint leading the University of Wisconsin's women's hockey team.

Mike Eruzione retired from hockey, and the captain of America's favorite team became a much-in-demand public speaker and a fund-raiser for his alma mater, Boston University. Eruzione was right. Nothing he could do in hockey would eclipse his Olympic role. When he said that, though, Eruzione never imagined he would score the winning goal over the Russians, the goal that Americans remember best of all those they have ever seen.

NOTES

1. Lewis Freedman, "U.S. Hockey Team Opens against Sweden Today," *Philadelphia Inquirer*, February 12, 1980.

2. Lewis Freedman, "A Lot of People Thought He Couldn't but Mike Eruzione Thought He Could," *Philadelphia Inquirer*, February 11, 1980.

3. Lewis Freedman, "Home Court Isn't So Cozy, Athletes Find," *Philadelphia Inquirer*, February 16, 1980.

4. Lewis Freedman, "A U.S. Miracle in Lake Placid," *Philadelphia Inquirer*, February 23, 1980.

5. Lewis Freedman, "U-S-A, U-S-A, U-S-A, U-S-A, U-S-A, U-S-A," *Philadelphia Inquirer*, February 25, 1980.

FURTHER READING

Chevreux, Laurent, Wim Plaizier, Christian Schuh, Wayne Brown, and Alenka Triplat. "The Miracle on Ice." In *Corporate Plasticity*, 39–42. New York: Apress Media, 2014.

Coffey, Wayne, and Jim Craig. *The Boys of Winter: The Untold Story of a Coach, A Dream, and the 1980 U.S. Olympic Hockey Team*. New York: Crown, 2005.

Powers, John, and Arthur C. Kaminsky. *One Goal: A Chronicle of the 1980 U.S. Olympic Hockey Team*. New York: Harper & Row, 1984.

Wendel, Tim. *Going for the Gold: How the U.S. Olympic Hockey Team Won at Lake Placid*. New York: Dover, 2009.

#3 James Naismith and the Invention of Basketball

The date of birth of basketball can be pinpointed. Unlike baseball, which lived under a surreal and unbelievable cloud as an origin story; unlike hockey, which was an imported game from Canada; and unlike football, which grew out of rugby and other knockoffs, basketball is the purest of sports.

From its extremely humble beginnings as a teaching tool to cure students of boredom during winter, basketball has become the most global of games with American roots and the most international of games, after soccer.

For those who are unaware that there are more than 200 countries in the world, it should be noted that the National Basketball Association knows because its games are televised in more than 200 countries.

It would be a wonder if Dr. James Naismith could have imagined that. Certainly he did not envision the geometric growth and expansion of his game when he sat down at a desk one day in Springfield, Massachusetts, and drew up 13 simple rules for a new sport. It was named basketball because the implements of the game were a round ball (actually a soccer ball) and a basket, initially an 18-inch-square wooden one that had held peaches.

Naismith was born in 1861 in Canada. Basketball was born in 1891 at the International YMCA Training School in Western Massachusetts. Often overlooked is that Naismith was under orders from his superior at the "Y," Dr. Luther Gullick, to come up with a new game that would help keep track athletes in shape and that wasn't too rough. Gullick may well have had football in the back of his mind when issuing that portion of his instructions.[1]

Dr. James Naismith's goal was to invent an indoor game that would hold the interest of his students at the Springfield, Massachusetts, YMCA training school. That's how the sport of basketball was created in 1891. He lived long enough to see basketball become part of the Summer Olympics. (AP Photo)

The first basketball game was played in Springfield on December 21, 1891.

Originally designed to be played nine-on-nine, basketball was later refined to the five-on-five game seen today. Compared to the sport that the entire world plays in the 2000s, it might be said that Naismith's basics were a rough draft. To illustrate how far the sport has come, the original rules did not include a provision for dribbling. Because the basket retained its bottom, the pace of play was turtle-like, and it was decades before anyone implemented a jump shot to score with or a 24-second clock to speed up play. Dunking the ball was not part of a player's repertoire in the 1890s.

Despite those handicaps, basketball caught on. The first college game was contested in 1896 between the University of Iowa and the University of Chicago. By then, still tinkering, Naismith had replaced peach baskets with the iron hoops more familiar to present-day players.

Naismith's quickly dashed-off rules were modified many times in the coming years. He coached basketball at Kansas University, and when he visited Indiana, the state that wishes it was home to the invention of basketball because of its fervent embrace of the game, he admitted basketball had been virtually raised to an art form there.

In 1936 Naismith, who would pass away two years later at age 77, was fortunate to witness the introduction of his game to the Summer Olympics in Berlin. Naismith was always proud of his creation, but he died long before basketball really took hold in the nation's consciousness and overseas.

Naismith's name is still associated with the game in several ways. The sport's hall of fame, which is located in Springfield because he invented it there, is called The Naismith Memorial Basketball Hall of Fame. Each year an outstanding male college player is presented with the Naismith Award, emblematic of the finest player in the county.

The first National Invitational Tournament crowning a college basketball champion took place at Madison Square in 1938, with six teams competing and Temple University winning. The now-more-famous and prestigious NCAA tournament held its inaugural event in 1939 with eight teams in Evanston, Illinois, on the campus of Northwestern University. Oregon was the first champ.

While it was not until after World War II that basketball organized itself well enough to create leagues that morphed into the NBA, as early as the 1920s some prominent teams were formed and barnstormed throughout the country. One of the most renowned was the Original Celtics, so named because they were the survivors of a pre-1920 squad called the New York Celtics. Another club was the New York Renaissance, or Rens, an all-black team that was formed in the 1920s. A first American Basketball League was spearheaded by George Preston Marshall, better known later as the owner of the Washington Redskins. The league existed from 1926 to 1931.

Players became bigger and stronger and more agile, but it was not until the 1940s, when guard Kenny Sailors was competing for the University of Wyoming, that anyone regularly left his feet to take a shot. The one-hand and two-hand set shot ruled the sport, alongside short push shots and layups.

After World War II two leagues competed for players and attention, the Basketball Association of America and the National Basketball League; they merged into the NBA in 1949.

The more people who played—an estimated 300 million do so today—and the better coaching they received, the more sophisticated basketball became. Eventually teams discovered the value of the fast break, pushing the ball up-court more swiftly in order to disrupt defenses and prevent them from getting set. Higher scores resulted.

However, there was no prohibition against teams in college or professional basketball holding onto the ball indefinitely and slowing the pace of the game to a crawl. Syracuse Nationals owner Danny Biasone was wise enough to realize that fans wanted to see scoring, and he introduced the 24-second shot clock in 1954. A particularly egregious example of boredom masquerading as excitement occurred when the Fort Wayne Pistons topped the Minneapolis Lakers, 19–18, on November 22, 1950.

College basketball resisted for a time. North Carolina, one of the best programs in the land, took advantage of the rules and frequently went into stall games under legendary coach Dean Smith. The Tar Heels called it their four-corner offense. In 1985 the NCAA signed off on a 45-second clock, and in 1993 the possession limit without a shot was reduced to 35 seconds. Women's college basketball is played with a 30-second shot clock. The supervisors of college and pro play want the players to take shots and score points, and whatever strategies a coach devises must work within the framework of the time limits assigned.

Postwar Europe had more important things on its agenda than basketball, but as the decades passed and the United States dominated Olympic and world championship play, some nations began fielding more proficient teams that on the odd day could best the Americans. The NBA was in the forefront of major sports in international marketing, and the caliber of play improved steadily overseas.

It is difficult to guess what would astonish Naismith the most about the simple game he invented: that by the 2014 season there were about 100 foreign-born players on NBA rosters, or that his handwritten, original rules sold for $4 million at auction a few years ago.

Each year more and more young foreign players are selected before hopeful American collegians in the league's annual player draft. Long after James Naismith saw his first Olympic basketball game, the world has embraced his invention more fully than ever.

NOTE

1. Rob Rains and Hellen Carpenter, *James Naismith: The Man Who Invented Basketball* (Philadelphia: Temple University Press, 2009).

FURTHER READING

Grundy, Pamela, Murry Nelson, and Mark Dyreson. "The Emergence of Basketball as an American National Pastime: From a Popular Participant Sport to a Spectacle of Nationhood." *The International Journal of the History of Sport* 31, nos. 1–2 (2014): 134–155.
Naismith, James, and William J. Baker. *Basketball: Its Origin and Development*. Lincoln, NE: Bison Books, 1996.

#4 Joe Louis

On June 22, 1937, Joe Louis won the heavyweight championship of the world by knocking out James J. Braddock in the eighth round of a scheduled 15-round bout. At that time the heavyweight crown was the most prized individual title in sport.

Although the heavyweight title remains a highly coveted reward, the respect and fame accorded to the man who possessed the belt in the 1930s was far greater than it is now. During that period in American history the three major sports that fans followed and cared about the most were baseball, boxing, and thoroughbred racing.

Not only was the heavyweight champ the king of his sport, at that time limited to eight weight classes and minus the multiple governing bodies that have fractionalized the glory, as the biggest of all champs, he was viewed symbolically as the toughest man in the world.

It was no surprise that Louis, who was born in 1914 into a poor family in unincorporated Chalmers County, Alabama, but mostly grew up in Detroit, shredded Braddock's defenses. "The Brown Bomber," as Louis was called in that politically incorrect era because of the color of his skin, was heavily favored to win.

But not everyone was happy about it. While African Americans rejoiced by literally dancing in the streets of Harlem and in other black neighborhoods of big cities around the country, there was a vocal and scheming core of fans and promoters appalled that "a Negro" had captured the most important title in their sport.

It was the first time since the demise of the extremely unpopular Jack Johnson, 22 years earlier, that an African American had ascended to the top of the division. The road to the number 1 contender ranking had been a rocky one. His manager and trainer plotted and planned and creatively built Louis's image for years before he got a shot at the title. Essentially, they worked to position him in the public mind as the anti-Johnson, who had flaunted his fondness for white women, had boasted about his boxing conquests at every opportunity, and bragged about his greatness to newsmen. To some degree Johnson was a Muhammad Ali a half century too early.

By contrast, Louis was soft spoken, gentlemanly outside of the ring, never publicly celebrated his victories, and though he packed thunder in his fists, he was always careful to avoid controversy. This was by the design of his handlers, but the role came naturally to the more discreet Louis.

Louis stood six foot two and in his prime generally fought at around 200 pounds. With chest bared he appeared massively muscular, and the power in his hands helped him become one of the best-known men in the country—and most definitely the best-known and most admired black man at a time when blacks were routinely treated with disrespect and faced lynch mobs in the South.

Working his way up the hard way, Louis was 32–1 after thumping Braddock. But by then he was a known quantity around the United States. While politically indifferent, Louis gained in worldliness and savvy as he matured and was exposed to more and more places and situations.

Naïve at the time, Louis had already proved his mettle under pressure and as a somewhat surprising ambassador for all Americans in his 20th pro victory when he deconstructed Primo Carnera at Yankee Stadium in 1935. A mountain of a man at six foot seven and 260 pounds, Carnera was from Italy and nicknamed "The Ambling Alp." He was suspiciously guided to a share of the heavyweight title by corrupt handlers, who fixed many of his fights.

Rated among the very best boxers of all time, Joe Louis held the heavyweight championship for a record 22 defenses and controlled the crown for 12 years. Louis was credited with improving race relations and also was greatly admired for his role as a morale builder for U.S. troops during World War II. (Library of Congress)

Although by the time Louis fought Carnera, the latter had been exposed as a fraudulent talent, the atmosphere surrounding the bout was exceptionally tense. Italy had invaded Ethiopia, and many Americans viewed Carnera as a representative of the warlike regime. More than ever, the American black community hoped for a Louis trouncing of his foe as a symbol of payback to the Italians. Louis obliged his fans with a sixth-round technical knockout.

En route to the heavyweights title, Louis lost just once, stopped by German Max Schmeling in 1936. Louis and others were caught off guard by the way dictator Adolf Hitler embraced Schmeling as the living embodiment of the superiority of the white race. Only gradually was the United States becoming aware of the atrocities being perpetuated by Hitler as he set his sights on conquering Europe.

Four fights after disposing of Braddock, Louis gave Schmeling a shot at the title. No bout that Louis contested ever meant more to him. By 1938 the world's political climate had shifted, and Schmeling, who considered New York his second home, was confused and demoralized when he was attacked as a Nazi on this visit.

The second Louis-Schmeling bout was staged on June 22, 1938, at Yankee Stadium. It in no way resembled the first one. Louis fought with an undeniable fierceness, plowing through Schmeling's defenses with ease and pummeling him to the canvas. The championship distance was 15 rounds, but Louis put Schmeling away in one and sent him to the hospital.

For Louis the victory was redemption. For Americans it was a cannon shot across the bow of Hitler's discriminatory policies. The irony of an African American being the toast of the nation was not focused on by many, but to a degree this was the origin of Louis being looked upon as a great patriot, an image enhanced by his actions during World War II.

Unlike most boxing champions, who survive at the top either briefly or for a handful of years at most, Louis embarked on a record 25-defense reign between 1937 and 1948, repelling all comers. When he joined the army during World War II, Louis could have been commissioned an officer. Instead he went into the service as a private. He did not fight, but promoted. He was a roving morale soldier. It is estimated that Louis boosted the spirits of a million servicemen around the globe. Less publicized was how he used his clout to report racial injustice to army authorities. At this time he first met soon-to-be-famous baseball player Jackie Robinson and helped him with such a case. Robinson later said that he could not have become the baseball barrier breaker he was hailed for being without Louis laying the groundwork.

Almost daily Louis gained in stature for his willingness to forego big money at the height of his career. Twice he put his title on the line, with all proceeds going to an armed service. Speaking at a navy relief dinner, Louis eschewed advice on his talk and spoke from the heart. In part, he said, "We can't lose because we're on God's side."[1] Initially some felt Louis got it backward, meaning to say God was on the U.S. side, but the more people thought about it, the more Louis's sentiment was praised, and he was credited by many for "naming the war." Depicting Louis wearing a battlefield helmet and wielding a bayonet-tipped rifle, the army displayed him and his words on a recruiting poster.

Louis engaged in several epic bouts that boxing historians consider significant, but it was the totality of his life that made him an American hero. He relinquished the heavyweight crown voluntarily in 1948, made an ill-advised comeback, and retired with a 66–3 record (plus one no decision).

However, Louis had squandered much of the money he earned and ended up owing back taxes, for which the Internal Revenue Service hounded him for years. He could never get ahead. Americans, remembering his contributions to the country when he was needed, lobbied for the tax to be forgiven, and eventually it was.

In retirement Louis remained in the public eye as a greeter at Caesars Palace in Las Vegas, a job he enjoyed, and was a popular figure at ringside when the gambling town hosted major fights.

After dealing with failing health for a number of years, Louis passed away in 1981 at age 66. In death his memory has been honored in many ways. A huge sculpture of Louis's fist is on display in downtown Detroit. The Joe Louis Arena is where the Detroit Red Wings play hockey. A statue of Louis was erected in Alabama, not something he would have imagined when his family fled north for racially rooted economic reasons. In 1982 Louis was voted the Congressional Gold Medal, the legislative body's highest civilian honor. He was also pictured on a postage stamp in 1993, the first boxer to be so singled out.

When Louis died, although he was not technically eligible, then president Ronald Reagan waived the rules and permitted the former champ to be buried at Arlington National Cemetery.

The subject of uncounted thousands of words penned by journalists, possibly the most notable sentence written about Louis—at a time when race was a huge issue for many and African Americans were subjected to often-brutal discrimination—was authored by a New York sportswriter: "Joe Louis is a credit to his race—the human race."[2]

NOTES

1. Bill Libby, *Joe Louis: The Brown Bomber* (New York: Lothrop, Lee & Shepard Books, 1980), 165–166.
2. Jimmy Cannon, *New York Post*, cited in Libby, *Joe Louis*.

FURTHER READING

Bak, Richard. *Joe Louis: The Great Black Hope*. Dallas, TX: Taylor Publishing, 1995.
Freedman, Lew. *Joe Louis: The Life of a Heavyweight*. Jefferson, NC: McFarland, 2013.
Margolick, David. *Beyond Glory: Joe Louis vs. Max Schmeling and a World on the Brink*. New York: Vintage Books, 2006.
Mead, Chris. *Joe Louis: Black Champion in White America*. New York: Dover Publications, 2010.
Roberts, Randy. *Joe Louis: Hard Times Man*. New Haven, CT: Yale University Press, 2010.

#5 Title IX

Before Title IX, basketball for girls was a peculiarly adjusted version of the sport, played six to a side, with only three of the players allowed to cross half court. That's if a high school had a team for girls at all.

College sports for women consisted of a small number of teams with no serious travel paid for, inferior equipment, and inconvenient practice times because the men had first claim on the gym.

When the U.S. Congress passed Title IX legislation into law in 1972, although it was rare for citizens to remember such an arcane label for a bill, it triggered a revolution that transformed the landscape of sport across the country, initiating effects that still ripple today.

Although many people think of Title IX as a piece of sports legislation, it was not specifically focused on sports participation. In part the ruling read, "No person in the United States shall, on the basis of sex, be excluded from participation in, be denied the benefits of, or be subjected to discrimination under any education program or activity receiving federal financial assistance."

The House sponsor was Rep. Edith Green of Oregon. The Senate sponsor was Birch Bayh of Indiana. President Richard Nixon, perhaps thinking to curry favor with the women's vote in the upcoming 1972 presidential election, signed the measure into law.

The key word in that legislative sentence was the word "education." Title IX was construed to mean any program whatsoever accepting federal funds. That included universities and public school systems.

Yet Title IX's most visible effects were on the playing fields. It was interpreted to mean equal opportunity for girls and women's participation in sports. It took some massaging and subsequent court actions to spell out some definitions, but now, 40 years after Title IX's passage, there is little mystery about its impact.

Four decades ago, a school or college might have had a 50–50 male–female student body, but by no means were expenditures on sports for males and for females distributed equally. A university might have a dozen men's teams and two women's teams. The men's teams might have four coaches and the women's teams one head coach and an unpaid or underpaid assistant. Men's teams might travel in a chartered plane. Women's teams might well travel by bus. Men's teams might have spanking new locker rooms. Women's teams might change in the ladies' room.

In some cases abruptly, in other cases gradually and steadily, Title IX's application revamped athletic programs. A college with a football team might give out 50 scholarships. That meant a woman's program must provide 50 scholarships.

There is no women's sport played that has as large a squad, so in some places a by-product of the new law was that men's sports became casualties. Schools with limited funds dropped non-revenue-producing men's teams in favor of starting up women's teams.

There was much outcry among fans of the departed teams, but no one caught women opposing such moves. They were reaping new benefits and loving every opportunity that had previously been denied.

It is important to note that Title IX heralded a sea change in American society, but it was also an outgrowth of the women's movement, which spotlighted lack of equality in the workplace, where women were shut out of certain jobs altogether and received less than equal pay for equal work in other places. These women grew up in an era in which it was considered not ladylike to sweat in public. One old saw had it that women didn't sweat, they perspired. It was also considered inappropriate for them to wear slacks in public instead of dresses, and except at the beach it was forbidden in many forums for them to show bare legs by wearing shorts.

As women broke out of being pigeonholed as stay-at-home wives and mothers with no responsibilities beyond cleaning house and cooking meals, they were also able to raise competitive daughters, who if born earlier would not have been able to play high school sports or had the chance to play in many, if any, college sports.

For today's teenaged females, the idea that their mothers, and certainly their grandmothers, were virtually banned from competitive sports seems incomprehensible. Was America really like that then? they might ask. Yes, it was.

What was it like in the dark ages of women's sports? Tara VanDerveer, an iconic women's basketball coach at Stanford, has said that when she was in college in 1974, she and other players at Indiana used to sit around wondering what their lives would be like if they could receive scholarships, play on TV, and travel by airplane instead of in a cozy little van.

"At the time it was all total, total fantasy," she said.[1]

Soon all of their fantasies came true.

A *Sports Illustrated* 2012 report, relying on information provided by the Women's Sports Foundation, indicated that by 1972 nearly 300,000 girls were competing in some kind of high school sport, but by 2011 that number had surpassed 3.1 million.

By the time Congress actually got the message that change was needed, girls (and their parents) and women were challenging long-held assumptions, rules, and ways of doing things. Girls won the right to compete in Little League baseball roughly at the same time that Title IX was approved. The national-caliber Yale women's rowing team held protests because they were given equipment that was inferior to that of the men's team.

During the dark ages of sport during the 20th century, women were second-class citizens, often not allowed to compete at all. Even when there were teams they were often given old uniforms and inferior transportation to games until Title IX was passed by the U.S. Congress. The 1972 law empowered women and opened myriad doors of opportunity. (Paul Morigi/Invision for espnW/AP Images)

Title IX did not spring into reality perfectly formed, and there have been a number of amendments to the basic premise over the years. But Title IX is basically undefeated in court; no challenge that would have diluted it or exempted men's teams from its application due to funding issues has ever succeeded.

Disgruntled senators and even the NCAA, the governing body of collegiate sport, did not go down without a fight, but in the end they were defeated. In 1971, even before the approval of Title IX, women sought to make inroads in college sport by working around the NCAA, not with it. The Association for Intercollegiate Athletics for Women (AIAW) was founded in 1971.

Operating on a shoestring—yet operating—the AIAW produced some legendary basketball teams, such as Immaculata of Pennsylvania, before the NCAA was forced to beef up women's sports.

"I will always remember that time, how positive it was for women's athletics," said Cathy Rush, who coached the Mighty Macs of Immaculata to three AIAW championships.[2]

Life has changed so dramatically for young women with sports aspirations that they take for granted the opportunities to play for sports teams that previous generations never had. Billie Jean King, the legendary tennis player and campaigner for equal rights for women in sport, has said that it is important that subsequent generations understand the fights that preceded them.

"I think the more you know about history, the more you know about yourself," King said.[3]

NOTES

1. Kelli Anderson, "The Power of Play," *Sports Illustrated*, May 7, 2012.
2. George Dohrman, "Chance to Be a Champion," *Sports Illustrated*, May 7, 2012.
3. Catherine Pearson, "Billie Jean King to Young Women on Title IX: 'Now It's Your Turn,'" *Huffington Post*, June 23, 2012.

FURTHER READING

Brake, Deborah. *Getting in the Game: Title IX and the Women's Sports Revolution*. New York: NYU Press, 2012.

Byrne, Julie. *O God of Players: The Story of the Immaculata Mighty Macs*. New York: Columbia University Press, 2003.

Rose, Deondra. "Regulating Opportunity: Title IX and the Birth of Gender-Conscious Higher Education Policy." *Journal of Policy History* 27, no. 1 (2015): 157–183.

#6 Sports Come to Radio

In the early days of professional and college sports fans had to be there, in the stadium, to know what was going on and to find out the result on the same day.

Soon newspapers began sending reporters to games to write stories for the next day's paper so fans could read about what happened when they couldn't make it to the scene of the game.

Then along came radio, and now fans could listen to games in the comfort of their living rooms. The cost of doing so was free, making it not a half bad deal.

The invention and evolution of radio was a roughly 80-year process that originated with the discovery of electromagnetic waves and involved harnessing them so that voices could be projected over a long distance with the right equipment.

The first Major League Baseball game was broadcast on radio in Pittsburgh in 1921. Radio was the first form of electronic media that allowed sports fans not inside the arena to follow a game live, often from their own homes. (AP Photo)

The biggest developmental breakthroughs were made by Guglielmo Marconi and Reginald Fessenden around 1900. Wireless telephony became radio by 1910.

By 1920, boxing fans were privileged to listen to the first-ever sporting event on the radio. On September 6 of that year heavyweight champion Jack Dempsey defended his title against Billy Miske in Benton Harbor, Michigan, and radio station WWJ out of Detroit, which is still going strong, broadcast the bout. Founded barely two weeks before the fight, WWJ claims that it was the first radio station in the world to broadcast regularly scheduled programming.

On November 25, 1920, the first play-by-play broadcast of college football aired, featuring the University of Texas against Mechanical College of Texas, now better known as Texas A&M. The station was WTAW.

Better remembered than those two events—perhaps because radio and baseball were wildly popular easy listening companions—was the first broadcast of a major league game on August 5, 1921, by KDKA in Pittsburgh. The game featured the Pirates versus the Philadelphia Phillies, and Harold Arlin was the man on the microphone. Arlin, who was more engineer than broadcaster, handled mike duties for just five years in the 1920s before switching back to his preferred job.

Later in 1921, on October 5, WJZ for the first time broadcast a World Series. This one featured the New York Yankees against the New York Giants.

Broadcasting baseball changed the habits of fans. The first choice always was to be on hand for the game, but there were not always enough tickets to go around, and not everybody could make it to every game they wanted to attend. Prior to radio, during the earliest days of the World Series, when the need to know was imperative, fans collected in centralized public areas to have updates relayed to them. Telegraph wires sent play-by-play to a newspaper office or the like. And fans stood around waiting to hear of hits clubbed and runs scored far away.

Radio was a much better substitute. People could actually hear commentary from the stadium, hear the crowd buzzing in the background, and do so at home where they could visit the refrigerator for a snack between innings, keep an eye on the kids, or even walk away for a couple of innings and then return.

The visual aspect was still up to listeners' imagination, but they definitely heard a lot more, and the pleasure of an announcer's company and his insightful knowledge being passed on enhanced the ball game experience. It was almost like being there.

Baseball team owners were slow to recognize that radio could be a plus for their teams. Most viewed radio broadcasters not as journalists, but as agents of companies trying to steal something. The owners spent their money trying to build up their teams, but these radio guys wanted to give the product away for free to listeners.

Well into the 1930s, team owners were skittish about having their games broadcast. They believed fans would stay home and listen instead of coming to the ballpark and spending money. At that time several cities had teams both in the American League and National League, and the owners of the Chicago Cubs and Chicago White Sox, Philadelphia Phillies and Philadelphia A's, Boston Red Sox and Boston Braves, and New York Giants and New York Yankees agreed not to broadcast their away games when the other team was playing at home.[1]

At the time the equivalent of later television's tape delay was the reconstructed studio broadcast. An announcer plucked the play-by-play off the teletype, and working in a cubicle-sized space instead of a ballpark, re-created the action, complete with sound effects, one play at a time. Several owners banded together and pledged to not even allow that minimalist broadcasting to take place.

Several years passed before owners viewed radio as anything other than a threat, not a vehicle to use to promote their businesses. Arguments were constantly made that broadcasting games would make more fans want to attend games in person, but the club owners did not see it that way.

In 1933, future Hall of Fame baseball executive Larry MacPhail took over the reins of the Cincinnati Reds. Owner Powell Clancy owned radio stations, and MacPhail sold him on the idea of broadcasting his team's games on his station. MacPhail also brought the idea of baseball games on the radio to the Brooklyn Dodgers when he changed jobs. MacPhail's main announcer was Red Barber, the twangy-talking southerner who became one of the great play-by-play men.

Radio brought the games to the people, marking a change in strategy of building the fan base from youths up.

A reluctance to alter old habits and fear of a drain on their financial investments led many owners to wait years before they comprehended the force for good that radio could be. Nowadays it would be inconceivable for a professional American sports team to play out its season without a radio contract. That just doesn't happen.

Sports announcers, who were never seen, were made into celebrities and household names beginning in the 1940s and 1950s. Barber, Mel Allen with the New York Yankees, Curt Gowdy with the Boston Red Sox, and others became major personalities in their home cities and graduated to national broadcast work, while also handling football and other sports in the baseball off-season.

Much later, after play-by-play was entrenched in the daily experience, sports talk radio burst onto the scene, with studio hosts opening the air waves to passionate fans who called in and expressed their opinions.

Some sports talk radio programs date to the 1940s, but they were not common. The explosion of sports talk radio occurred in the 1980s, and one pioneer was WFAN in New York, which on July 1, 1987, became the first 24-hour sports talk radio station. Programmers realized that fans enjoyed hearing themselves talk about sports as much as listening to the games.

NOTE

1. Alex French and Howie Kahn, "The Sound and the Fury," *Grantland*, July 11, 2012.

FURTHER READING

Barber, Red, and Robert Creamer. *Rhubarb in the Catbird Seat*. Lincoln, NE: Bison Books, 1997.

Borelli, Stephen. *How About That! The Life of Mel Allen*. New York: Sports Publishing LLC, 2005.

Gantz, Walter, and Nicky Lewis. "Sports on Traditional and Newer Digital Media: Is There Really a Fight for Fans?" *Television & New Media* 15, no. 8 (2014): 760–768.

Greenberg, Mike, and Mike Golic. *Mike and Mike's Rules for Sports and Life*. New York: ESPN Books, 2010.
Halberstam, David. *Sports on New York Radio*. New York: McGraw-Hill, 1999.

#7 Sports Come to Television

The technology that made mass-produced television sets possible was slow to evolve, from a blurry picture first seen in the 1920s to the improved quality that made the TV set a post–World War II phenomenon that changed the habits of American families.

TV sets with adequate pictures were available in very small numbers in the late 1940s, but high-quality black-and-white sets became overwhelmingly popular in the 1950s, a decade of recovery from the war and a seeming age of innocence.

Feeding into the fact that more workers had additional leisure time, TV viewing captured households with all kinds of fresh programming that had never been seen before. Sports on the tube became part of the entertainment landscape, although its roots dated back to 1939.

The first televised sporting event was a college baseball game played between Ivy League rivals Columbia and Princeton on May 17, 1939. The announcer was the famous Bill Stern, but the game was not nearly as memorable as his career.

The site was Baker Field on the Columbia campus in New York, and the game was part of a doubleheader. Only the second game was televised on NBC. Stern was speaking to a cozy little audience. Although there has never been a time in the history of TV ratings when a Columbia-Princeton baseball game would have dominated the airwaves, it was estimated that there were only 400 TV sets in the vicinity capable of viewing the contest, assuming they were all turned on.

During his long career Stern broadcast football on the radio for years and was a well-known network sports personality when it was first possible to become one. This college broadcast was notable only because it was a first.

A few months later Major League Baseball appeared on television for the first time. The August 26, 1939, game between the Cincinnati Reds and the Brooklyn Dodgers was called by Red Barber. Once again, in the same manner that baseball owners had resisted the advance of radio, they were skeptical that televised games would do them any good. For a time they stuck with the notion that there was no reason to give away their product for free. Eventually, of course, every club developed its own local television deal to promote the team, and the teams enthusiastically embraced the idea of being shown on national television.

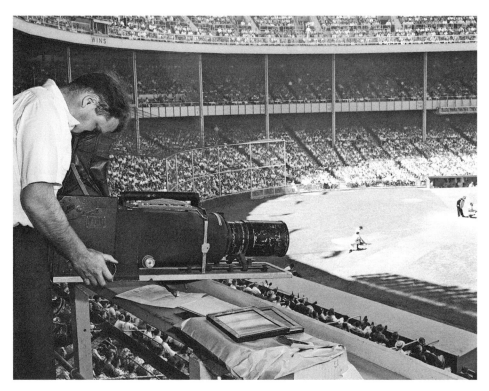

Television followed radio as the electronic medium that allowed fans away from the stadium to tune into live games. The first Major League Baseball game was telecast on August 26, 1939. Television watching and sports watching boomed in the 1950s. (AP Photo/Ed Ford)

Initially there was a *Game of the Week*, and that was the only time besides the all-star game and World Series that baseball was shown nationally. Now a fan of just about any team can find a way to watch just about every game when he feels like it.

Also in 1939, on October 22, the first professional football game was aired, pitting the Philadelphia Eagles against the Brooklyn Dodgers, the short-lived football franchise (they were done by 1944) that borrowed the name of the baseball team.

Sport by sport, television introduced viewers to live-from-the-scene pictures. The first hockey game was shown on TV on February 25, 1940, when the National Hockey League rivals Montreal Canadiens and New York Rangers faced off. Just three days later the first basketball game was televised, a college matchup between Fordham and the University of Pittsburgh.

The first time the World Series was shown on the air was the 1947 showdown between the New York Yankees and the Brooklyn Dodgers. The broadcast booth housed Bob Edge, Bob Stanton, and Bill Slate, none of whom is a household name today.

Something only the most accomplished of *Jeopardy* contestants would guess is the event that carried TV from black and white to color coverage. The first color broadcast was of the Davis Cup (tennis) between the United States and Australia on August 26, 1955.

Typically, American homes were single-set owners, and shows that were fun for the whole family, children's programming, and sporting events competed for attention in the 1950s. As time passed the medium grew and grew, to the point that nothing dominates TV programming like sports coverage.

Once again, TV proved adept at whetting fans' appetites. After watching their heroes on the small screen, viewers were more likely to want to attend a live game and see them up close in the flesh. Television's influence and power extended the reach and impact of sports. There were millions of American sports fans, but only a fraction of them, in the thousands, could afford tickets to the biggest games or obtain them.

The remainder became a captive audience in front of the World Series, the NFL championship game, the NBA Finals, the NCAA tournament, the Indianapolis 500, Wimbledon, and the Winter and Summer Olympics, and television networks found it lucrative to sell advertising to woo those stay-at-homers. The sports leagues that had once looked askance at inviting TV cameras into their homes learned that they could squeeze tremendous rights payments out of the networks to help finance their businesses. They discovered that TV was a very useful and friendly partner.

Sportscasters became as recognizable and popular as movie performers, and such personalities as Howard Cosell, Al Michaels, Bob Costas, Keith Jackson, Dick Enberg, Vince Scully, Chris Schenkel, John Madden (whom some forgot was even a football coach), Pat Summerall (who many never knew played pro football), and Harry Caray received high salaries and fame.

Forget that audience of perhaps 400 watching Columbia-Princeton. The audience and appetite for sports on TV was gargantuan. Millions watched World Series games and NCAA college basketball games. No other event could compete with professional football for interest to the extent that the Super Bowl championship game, now played on the first Sunday in February, has almost taken on the trappings of a national holiday. Fans plan Super Bowl parties the way they plan Thanksgiving dinner and Christmas parties. They lay in provisions, clearing grocery store shelves of snacks and liquor stores of beer.

Of the top 10 most-watched television programs in American history, 8 are Super Bowls. Number 1 is the 2011 Super Bowl between the Green Bay Packers and the Pittsburgh Steelers, with 111 million viewers. In non-sports programming, only the series finale of *M*A*S*H* in 1983, in third place, and the *Cheers* finale in 1993 cracked the top 10.

The consistently high and record-breaking TV ratings support the assertion that pro football is the most popular sport in the United States.

Once shown only on Sunday afternoons, pro football is now routinely televised on Sunday nights, Monday nights, and Thursday nights as well, and on a couple of Saturdays after the college football season ends.

"If there is a saturation point, we haven't seen it yet," NFL vice president Brian Rolapp said in 2014.[1]

NOTE

1. Ken Belson, "On Pro Football: The N.F.L.'s Juggernaut May Risk Market Saturation," *New York Times*, August 30, 2014.

FURTHER READING

Galily, Yair. "When the Medium Becomes 'Well Done': Sport, Television, and Technology in the Twenty-First Century." *Television & New Media* 15, no. 8 (2014): 717–724. doi: 1527476414532141.

O'Neill, Terry. *The Game Behind the Game: High Pressure, High Stakes in Television Sports*. New York: St. Martin's Press, 1990.

Ribowsky, Mark. *Howard Cosell: The Man, the Myth and the Transformation of American Sports*. New York: W. W. Norton.

#8 ESPN: Sports around the Clock

Since ESPN—the Entertainment and Sports Programming Network, based in Bristol, Connecticut—has been around for more than 35 years, many millions of Americans do not recall what TV sports watching was all about before ESPN came into existence in 1978 and made its debut on September 7, 1979.

ESPN was the first cable TV network devoted to just one subject. Too many to count have followed, but ESPN was there first and developed the model.

The announcement of the creation of a 24-hour, around-the-clock sports network was met with a certain amount of bemusement, even by the most ardent of sports fans. What was going to be shown at 3:00 a.m.? When ESPN began it didn't have much programming and had to be inventive to fill the hours it was on the air.

Fanatics could watch sports at any hour of the day, and that was intriguing. But they were at best only tangentially interested in Australian Rules football, shows on fishing in the Bahamas, women's gymnastics, or minor league anything. They wanted more big-time stuff, and in the beginning ESPN didn't have either the resources or the credentials to procure it.

The beginnings were simple. The network was conceived and started by Bill Rasmussen, Scott Rasmussen, and Ed Eagan, a trio of entrepreneurs who probably could not have imagined the major footprint ESPN would leave on the sports world. Eventually, it crashed the private party of the three-cornered network power brokers and the hold they had on showing big-time sports.

Once thought of as a quaint little idea, ESPN has grown into a player any time rights fees are put up for grabs, and just about the only thing of interest to the sporting public that ESPN hasn't fought to acquire is the Olympics. That will probably happen one of these days.

Along the way ESPN began calling itself "The Worldwide Leader in Sports," and no one has been able to refute that claim. Leading up to the 2013 football season, Fox Sports decided to take the challenge and go head to head against ESPN with its own 24-hour sports network, called Fox 1. The programming included a *SportsCenter*-like news show.

The major difference for Fox was that the network was not a start-up as ESPN had been in the late 1970s, but rather was well established on the air and available in 90 million American homes immediately, compared to ESPN's 99 million total through its several networks. Also, Fox already owned the rights to a fair amount of sports programming and was able to shift some major league play-off games to Fox 1 in October 2014.

Fox was not underplaying its task of taking on Goliath, however.

"ESPN, quite frankly, is a machine," said the network's programmer, Billy Wagner, acknowledging the difficulty of the challenge.[1]

Originally, ESPN management was clever in going after any potentially fascinating programming that either seemed undercovered or came cheaply. ESPN played a huge role in promoting boxing in the 1980s with regular cards, and the NCAA should be forever grateful for the manner in which ESPN seized upon the postseason men's basketball tournament as it mushroomed into a mega-property. All along the way ESPN showed that there was an audience for college basketball on just about any day of the week at almost any time of the evening, even if the teams performing had no geographic relevance to the viewer.

One of the early innovations that helped establish ESPN was the introduction of the nightly sports highlight show, patterned after network news programs. The show was called *SportsCenter*—and it still is. The network used the dual-anchor concept, introducing the half-hour show with Lee Leonard and George Grande.

Leonard opened the inaugural *SportsCenter* with these words: "If you love sports. . . . If you really love sports, you'll think you've died and gone to sports heaven."[2] It wasn't the Gettysburg Address, but those words spoken in 1979 seem to be as applicable now as they were then.

A staple of *SportsCenter* has been witty repartee between the hosts and clever commentary about the highlights while still informing. The show reached the apex of influential hosting when Dan Patrick and Keith Olbermann teamed up. They were as entertaining and as erudite as any pairing on television.

Chris Berman joined ESPN within a month after it was founded. Bob Ley was there at the beginning, too. They are the only two ESPN on-air regulars who have been with the network virtually from its first show.

When times were tough, Anheuser-Busch, maker of Budweiser, the beer most closely identified with sports and a company that knows who its drinkers are, spent $1.4 million on ESPN advertising.

A breakthrough for ESPN, which was still struggling financially, came in 1982 when the network inked a deal to televise the NBA. This was ESPN's first venture into professional sports. A second significant moment occurred when ESPN obtained rights to show some NFL games, which led to ESPN's *Sunday Night Football*. The football league and the TV network helped one another keep growing.

Founded in 1978 as a fledgling 24-hour cable TV sports network, ESPN transformed the landscape for the coverage of the sports world. It has grown into a behemoth that reaches 90 million homes and includes several programming channels. (AP Photo/Bob Child)

ESPN was renowned for plucking the best talent from other media outlets and for promoting its homegrown people as well. The goal was to feature a well-known specialist in each professional sport and on college sports.

In 1992 ESPN introduced its own radio network, and in 1998 it began producing *ESPN The Magazine*, a biweekly publication that has been one of the first truly serious challengers to *Sports Illustrated*'s market niche. A true conglomerate these days, there are now several ESPN splinter networks: ESPN2; ESPNU, featuring college games in less-publicized sports; and ESPN Classic, which shows great games of the past. And there is also the ESPN Web site and the usual array of social networking communication outlets.

An aid to ESPN's credibility over the years was the revelation in interviews, jokes, and off-the-cuff comments that many athletes watch the highlight shows, crave the opportunity to be on the highlight shows, and regularly converse with selected ESPN broadcasters as if they are buddies as much as interviewer and interviewee.

ESPN is now ubiquitous. Once begging to be allowed in the door, ESPN now has so much clout that it tells leagues when to play games.

NOTES

1. Michael Hiestand, "Fox Sports Launches Direct Challenge to ESPN Dominance," *USA Today Sports*, March 6, 2013.
2. James Andrew Miller and Tom Shales, *Those Guys Have All the Fun* (Boston: Little, Brown, 2011), 3.

FURTHER READING

Evey, Stuart. *Creating an Empire: ESPN—The No Holds Barred Story of Power, Ego, Money and Vision That Transformed a Culture*. Chicago: Triumph Books, 2004.
Freeman, Michael. *ESPN: The Uncensored History*. Dallas, TX: Taylor Trade Publishing, 2001.
Smith, Anthony F., and Keith Hollihan. *ESPN the Company: The Story and Lessons behind the Most Fanatical Brand in Sports*. Hoboken, NJ: John Wiley & Sons, 2009.

#9 Muhammad Ali Defies Uncle Sam

Considered one of the best boxers of all time and assuredly the sport's biggest personality of all time, Muhammad Ali, born Cassius Clay in Louisville, Kentucky, helped change perceptions of American blacks during the tumultuous period of the civil rights movement. During the height of his fame in the 1960s and 1970s, Ali was believed to be the best-known person in the world.

Winning an Olympic gold medal in 1960 and capturing the heavyweight championship of the world for the first of three times in early 1964 gave Ali a forum to speak out on issues of the day, and he did so. However, he was so clever and creative that even when he took controversial stands, Ali could entertain and make people laugh at the same time.

"Float like a butterfly, sting like a bee," became Ali's mantra.[1]

Most athletes up until then had been of the aw-shucks variety, avoiding politics and refraining from issuing verbal opinion essays that might get them in trouble with the paying customers. Ali didn't care. He had the courage to take unpopular stands and not back down. If newspaper reporters asked him what he thought, he told them what he thought.

That included informing the world about how good he was. This defied the accepted practice of speaking of one's own athletic prowess modestly. Not only did Ali proclaim himself "The Greatest," he repeatedly told everyone how beautiful he was, too. He was a handsome man, but mostly it was about shock value, making people listen and pay attention.

He could be outrageous, spontaneously making up poetry about his next opponent and what round he would be defeated in, but with a great sense of self-awareness, his teasing would be accompanied by a wink. His face was a pliable mask. Sometimes he frowned, apparently in deadly earnest. Sometimes he smiled his million-watt smile. Other times he let all of the pretense drop and became plain old Muhammad Ali for a moment. Maybe, since it is difficult for those words to fit with the name Muhammad Ali.

Ali was six foot three, and although his weight varied by the fight, he was often around 215 pounds. He possessed supremely quick hands and feet. The hands allowed him to flick deadly jabs, and the feet carried him around the ring on his toes, making him very hard for an opposing fighter to catch up to.

There were multiple stages to Ali's career. In the beginning he was Cassius Clay, and he moved his mouth as fast as those hands. He was working his way up the ranks through the other contenders, and he was a brash, funny man. Young people especially loved his act. Some older boxing fans wanted to see him get knocked out, because they didn't like his attitude.

Clay won the heavyweight title from Sonny Liston in early 1964 and then revealed he was changing his name to Muhammad Ali. While Americans have always had quite a capacity for reinvention, and actors and actresses in particular had often changed their names, they did so for marketing purposes. Americans didn't know quite how to respond to someone changing his name for religious

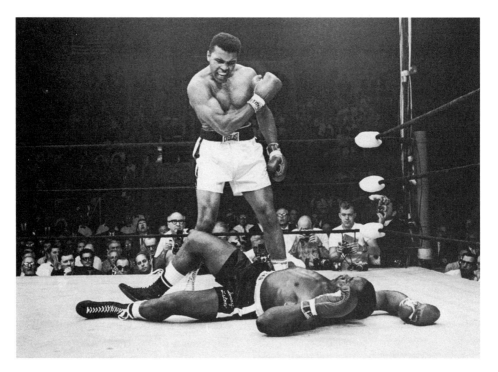

Heavyweight champion Muhammad Ali, one of the most colorful and accomplished fighters of all time, put his mouth where his political beliefs were when he refused to be inducted into the U.S. Army because of his religious beliefs. Ali lost 3½ years of his prime years before winning a Supreme Court appeal reinstating his power to box. (AP Photo/John Rooney)

reasons. They also didn't quite know what to make of his religion. To mainstream America, the Black Muslims had been portrayed as white haters, if people had heard of them at all.

Ali may have talked 100 miles per hour in interviews and in prefight camp, predicting his victories almost to the round, but inside the ring he put on an even better show with his superior skills. He blew through all of the top contenders, raising his record to 29–0 by 1967.

Already a lightning rod, Ali became an even more polarizing individual, splitting the nation politically in its perception of him as either liberal or conservative.

Drafted into the army during the Vietnam War, Ali refused induction as a conscientious objector, stating that his religion prevented him from going to war.

"I ain't got no quarrel with them Viet Cong," Ali said.[2]

It had often been said of individual citizens—no matter who they were—that they couldn't fight the government. Ali showed that if the cause was just, you could, and you could win. Short of money, with no boxing income, Ali toured college campuses as a speaker against U.S. involvement in Vietnam. One thing Ali could do besides box was talk.

As Ali battled his induction in the courts, he was stripped of his right to box in every state and of his passport. It took the intervention of the U.S. Supreme Court, after he had been sidelined from the sport for 3½ years, for Ali to resume his career.

The lost years in Ali's prime between ages 25 and 29 could never be recovered, and while his fights were confined to courtrooms another great heavyweight emerged on the scene and seized the title. When Ali's exile ended, Joe Frazier was the champ.

A clash between the current champ and the former champ was inevitable, but no one foresaw the ferocity and evenness of perhaps the most intense rivalry in all of sport. Frazier was not as glib as Ali, though away from the ring he was generally a nice man, a hero in South Carolina, where he grew up, and in Philadelphia, where he then resided. He possessed a vicious left hook, and his body punches could level a man.

Ali had to work off his ring rust before meeting Frazier, but he had a fresh constituency in his corner: young people, college students, who admired him for sticking to his principles and refusing induction. At the time many college students of much lesser renown were fleeing to Canada to avoid the draft. Ali's political stance had also made him many enemies, and those boxing fans who saw him as a traitor backed Frazier.

Frazier and Ali met at Madison Square Garden on March 8, 1971, in an event billed as "The Fight of the Century" before it even happened. Then the bout lived up to the hype. This was not Ali's finest hour verbally. On many occasions he sought to get into opponents' heads and psyche them out. He did this with Frazier, but went too far with his insults, calling him ugly, accusing him of being a tool of the white establishment and of being an Uncle Tom. It was not a pretty picture, and Frazier never truly forgave Ali for that behavior. That barrage enraged him, and he paid Ali back with his fists.

Frazier won a unanimous 15-round decision to keep the crown, Ali's first loss. Over the following years, Frazier lost the crown to George Foreman and then faced Ali a second time in New York City, in 1974. This confrontation was won by Ali in a unanimous 12-round decision and set up Ali's next shot at the title against Foreman in "The Rumble in the Jungle" in Zaire in October 1974.

This bout demonstrated Ali's international appeal. He had already fought in England, Canada, West Germany, Switzerland, Japan, Ireland, and Indonesia, but never before in Africa in a predominantly black country. While Foreman was also black, it was obvious from the fans' treatment of Ali when he ran in public and went through his workouts that he was the popular one.

At the time Foreman was another Liston, surly to many, unlike the friendly, cuddly demeanor he adopted later when he made a comeback, and with fists of dynamite. It did not seem possible that the 32-year-old Ali could stand up to the big man's blows. Yet on this occasion Ali truly did fool the world, adopting an unusual and risky strategy called "the rope-a-dope" that had Foreman punching himself out in the heat as Ali took his punches while reclining against the ropes.

The trick worked, and Ali regained the crown. Four fights later, in the Philippines, Ali outlasted Frazier in their third battle, winning by technical knock-out in the 14th of 15 scheduled rounds, when Frazier's friend and trainer Eddie Futch refused to let his man take any more punishment and threw in the towel. Once the "Thrilla in Manila" was over, both protagonists went to the hospital for recovery. They had each fought his heart out.

Of the brutal bout, Ali said, "That was the closest I've come to dying."[3]

Eventually, after losing and regaining the heavyweight crown a third time, Ali retired with a record of 56–5. He was 39, and even he agreed that he had stayed too long. That became evident later in life when Ali was afflicted with Parkinson's disease, which gradually eroded his motor system and ironically robbed him of speech.

Before he retreated almost altogether from the public eye, however, Ali was a secret, and then wildly popular, choice to light the Olympic torch before the Summer Games in 1996 in Atlanta.

In 2005 George W. Bush awarded Ali the Presidential Medal of Freedom. The world that had sometimes treated Ali harshly some 40 years before had become a vastly different place.

NOTES

1. Vi-An Nguyen, "21 of Muhammad Ali's Best Quotes: 'Don't Count the Days; Make the Days Count'," February 22, 2014, communitytable.parade.com.

2. Official Muhammad Ali Web site, http://www.ali.com (accessed April 2, 2015).

3. David Jones, "Poisoned by Hatred He Couldn't Let Go, the Champ Who Lost the World's Longest Grudge Match," *Daily Mail*, November 9, 2011, http://www.dailymail .co.uk/news/article-2059249/Joe-Frazier-dead-Boxing-champ-poisoned-Muhammad-Ali -hatred-let-go.html (accessed May 2, 2015).

FURTHER READING

Ali, Muhammad, and Richard Durham. *The Greatest: My Own Story*. New York: Random House, 1975.

Hauser, Thomas. *Muhammad Ali: His Life and Times*. New York: Simon & Schuster, 1992.

Mailer, Norman. *The Fight*. New York: Random House, 2013.

Remnick, David. *King of the World: Muhammad Ali and the Rise of an American Hero*. New York: Vintage Books, 1998.

#10 Jesse Owens

The scene at the Summer Olympics in 1936 in Berlin often includes descriptions of Nazi dictator Adolf Hitler turning away from American Jesse Owens and leaving so he didn't have to shake hands with a black man during a medal ceremony.

Certainly that would have been keeping with Hitler's odious racial politics. Hitler had been congratulating winners, but no one was 100 percent sure if he did it to snub Owens because he was African American and his skin color did not jibe with Hitler's views of white supremacy, or he just stopped hanging out at the Games.

Nonetheless, it was Owens, through his magnificent and dominating performance, who snubbed Hitler, with grace, dignity, and athleticism, merely by proving him wrong.

James Cleveland Owens was born in 1913 in Oakville, Alabama, and he was nine years old when his large family abandoned its stifling existence in a rural portion of the state where African Americans were openly discriminated against and could not easily fight their way out of poverty. The family moved to Cleveland, Ohio, seeking better opportunities.

Owens attended Ohio State University, where he was a star on the track team. On one day at the Big Ten Conference championships in Michigan in 1935, during a 45-minute span Owens broke three world records and tied a fourth one. The lithe and powerful five-foot-ten, 165-pound Owens long-jumped 26 feet, 8¼ inches (a world mark that stood for 25 years), ran the 220-yard dash in 20.3 seconds, completed the 220-yard low hurdles in 22.6 seconds, and tied the 100-yard dash mark in 9.4 seconds.

There has never been a single-day track and field feat like it, and it is quite possible no athlete in any sport has had a better day. That Big Ten accomplishment foreshadowed Owens's brilliant Olympic showing in Germany a year later, when he captured four gold medals.

Yet as important as he was to the Buckeye track team, when the squad traveled Owens was forced to lodge in black-only hotels and eat at black-only restaurants,

By reasonable measurement Jesse Owens was the most famous, revered, and greatest track and field star in American history. The Ohio State graduate, who set four world records in one day at the Big Ten Championships, catapulted to worldwide fame in 1936 by winning four Olympic gold medals in Germany as dictator Adolf Hitler sneered at blacks as an inferior race. (Library of Congress)

and because he received no scholarship, Owens worked part-time when he was attending school.

In Berlin Owens, who was 23 at the Olympics, won the 100-meter dash in 10.3, the 200-meter dash in 20.7, and the long jump, and anchored the U.S. winning 400-meter relay in 39.8 seconds.

It was such an extraordinary performance that Owens returned to the United States a hero, one of the first African Americans to become a household name through his athletic achievements. Owens's early life in Alabama and his family's move north during the Great Migration paralleled the early life of heavyweight champion Joe Louis.

Louis won the heavyweight crown in 1937, and the two men, who knew of each other, finally met a bit later and became life-long friends. Unlike Louis, however, Owens excelled in an amateur sport, one that was strictly governed at the time to prevent any tint of professionalism. While Louis eventually made millions of dollars, Owens struggled financially at various times after becoming a national figure.

The myth of the heavyweight championship was that the belt's owner was the toughest man in the world. The label placed on the winner of the Olympic 100-meter dash has always been "world's fastest human."

While American blacks were heartfelt in their joy and celebration of Owens's efforts, unlike in later years, when such a renowned Olympic champion would have reaped a windfall of endorsements and appearance fees at future track meets, that avenue was not open to him. When Owens returned to the United States following the Games, after he had made some appearances in Sweden, the U.S. Olympic Committee took away his amateur eligibility, in essence ruining any remaining competitive track years Owens had. For most, holding his time in Sweden against Owens in this way seemed to be the act of an ungrateful nation.

Owens has been acclaimed for his brilliance in Berlin and hailed as someone who in the best way he knew how stood up to Hitler's ugly policies at a time when the dictator was trying to pretend to the world that he was merely an economic reformer who bore no ill will against other countries or races.

Albert Speer, one of Hitler's henchmen, who was entrusted to design many of the structures of the Third Reich, later wrote that Hitler was very much annoyed by Owens's repeat successes. Still later it was reported that Owens actually possessed a photograph of Hitler shaking his hand and congratulating him, although such a picture has not had widespread dissemination.

At one point Owens noted that President Franklin D. Roosevelt never invited him to the White House to congratulate him on his achievements and never even sent a telegram. Owens said FDR really snubbed him, not Hitler. Owens was not a complainer, but he was candid with interviewers later and pointed out that he may have been touted as a hero in the United States, but as a black man he still had to ride in the back of the bus, and "I couldn't live where I wanted."[1]

Owens enjoyed a long, happy marriage, but never quite attained the heights in the professional world that he had reached in track and field. He was 66 when he died of lung cancer, and Louis was crushed when he heard of his friend's death, which predated his by only two years.

If anything, Owens has been better appreciated in death than he was in life. However, he was able to receive one singular honor in person, the Presidential Medal of Freedom, from President Gerald Ford in 1976. In 1990, Owens was posthumously awarded the Congressional Gold Medal.

At other times Owens has been recognized by the naming of parks after him; by his alma mater Ohio State, which each spring promotes a track meet called the "Jesse Owens Track Classic"; and by appearing on a list of the greatest African Americans. Twice his likeness has appeared on postage stamps, in 1990 and 1998.

Life was at its best for Owens when he was allowed to run free.

"I let my feet spend as little time on the ground as possible," Owens said. "From the air, fast down, and from the ground, fast up."[2]

In 2013 one of Owens's gold medals was auctioned off. The man who had difficulty making a living to support his family because he couldn't bank acclaim and respect would have been astonished to learn that it sold for more than $1.4 million.

NOTES

1. Larry Schwartz, "Owens Pierced a Myth," ESPN.com, February 6, 2013.
2. Alex Altman, "Usain Bolt: The World's Fastest Human," *Time Magazine*, August 18, 2009.

FURTHER READING

Edmonson, Jacqueline. *Jesse Owens, A Biography*. Santa Barbara, CA: Greenwood Press, 2007.

McRae, Donald. *Heroes without a Country: America's Betrayal of Joe Louis and Jesse Owens*. New York: Ecco, 2002.

Owens, Jesse, with Paul Neimark. *Jesse: The Man Who Outran Hitler*. Robbinsdale, MN: Fawcett, 1985.

Schaap, Jeremy. *Triumph: The Untold Story of Jesse Owens and Hitler's Olympics*. Wilmington, MA: Mariner Books, 2008.

#11 Cincinnati Red Stockings Go Pro

While the origins of baseball remain somewhat murky, there is no mystery about which team became the first professional outfit in the sport. The Cincinnati Red Stockings of 1869 signed up 10 players as their roster and paid them all salaries.

Not only were the Red Stockings the first professional baseball team, but all future teams in the four major American team sports—baseball, hockey, football, and basketball—could look at the Red Stockings as the forerunner of their own fledgling pro efforts.

The man who did the most to shape the Cincinnati team was Harry Wright, who actually had been a cricket player before migrating to baseball. Wright was born in England, and his father was a professional cricket player. That other sport brought Wright to Cincinnati in 1865 when he was hired by the Union Cricket Club and met George Ellard.

He helped organize and manage, and played for, the Red Stockings. The squad was founded in 1866, but became a professional team three years later when the players embarked on an ambitious barnstorming tour, taking on all comers.

Most distinctively, the Red Stockings were identified by their long, red stockings, a look that was unique at the time. Wright was the driving force behind the team doings, though businessman Ellard, who knew Wright from cricket dealings, was a key organizer. By 1869 the Red Stockings were joined by George Wright, Harry's younger brother. George played shortstop and was the Red Stockings' best player. Harry played center field.[1]

Cincinnati became a member of the National Association of Base Ball Players (NABBP) and during that 1869 season went 57–0 in games against other member teams. The Red Stockings also played games against nonmember teams and finished with a 65–0 record. The 10 players whom Wright and Ellard rounded up were on salary for eight months, starting March 15. This marked the first time that baseball was a full-time job for an entire team.

Cincinnati was legally able to boast a professional lineup because for the first time the NABBP permitted payments to

Forerunners of the Cincinnati Reds of the National League, the Red Stockings became baseball's first professional team in 1869 under the direction of player-manager Harry Wright. Their success and popularity helped lead to the founding of the National League in 1876. (Library of Congress)

players instead of limiting competition to amateurs. This arrangement did not last very long, because by the end of the 1870 season both the Red Stockings in Cincinnati, as well as the NABBP, were defunct. But the floodgates had been opened, at least for squads who wanted to be classified as professionals. Other teams did woo star individual players with cash payments, but they did not surround those team leaders with other paid professionals.

That situation was about to change, though, with the move to full-time professionalism under way. The Red Stockings and the NABBP represented a stepping-stone to Major League Baseball, which traces its roots to the still-operating National League, founded in 1876.

As an outfielder, Harry Wright was the first player to back up infielders during plays and to make outfield positioning changes in mid-game. Multitasking, Wright also served as manager and general manager and made sure the club got to the next appointment on its schedule on time.

As a hitter, Wright batted .276, but that only included appearances between 1871, when he was already 36, and 1877. By then the Red Stockings had moved to Boston. They were the Reds before the Cincinnati Reds and the Reds before the Red Sox. Wright formed the Boston club with some of the same players in 1871 after the Cincinnati club folded. Eventually, in 1953, Wright was voted into the Baseball Hall of Fame, though the recognition came for his off-field activities.

The 1869 Red Stockings roster consisted of Harry Wright and George Wright, pitcher Asa Brainard, catcher Doug Allison, first baseman Charlie Gould, second baseman Charlie Sweasy, third baseman Fred Waterman, Andy Leonard in left field, Carl McVey in right field, and one bench player to fill in, Dick Hurley.

Of the non-Wright brothers the best-remembered player is Brainard. The right-hander was the stalwart of the mound for the Red Stockings, throwing almost three-quarters of all innings Cincinnati played that debut year. Brainard pitched for the Brooklyn Excelsiors for the first half of the 1860s, including the entire Civil War period, and played for other teams in the early 1870s, after his Cincinnati adventures. Brainard was only 47 when he died of pneumonia shortly before the National League was founded.

George Wright resembled his brother, right down to their bushy sideburns, but big brother also had a bushy beard, and George did not. George Wright was also selected for the Baseball Hall of Fame. The reasons Wright was chosen were his fielding prowess and for being a career .301 hitter, not for the kind of extracurricular organizational work Harry did.

Under the Wright brothers' influence the Boston Red Stockings won four championships in six years as part of the National Association.

When the new National League was formed, George became the first batter in the history of that circuit when play opened on April 22, 1876. George, who was 12 years younger than Harry, continued to play through 1882, but he also managed the Providence Grays in 1879. George Wright had two athletic sons, but they excelled in tennis, not baseball.

Harry retired as a player in 1877, but continued to manage through 1893.

Although the NABBP has been forgotten by all but the most thorough of researchers, the Cincinnati Red Stockings do live on in memory, if only of some fans, as the answer to the trivia question asking what the first professional baseball team was.

However, the historical lineage between the Red Stockings and the NL's Cincinnati Reds—even if it is mostly words, not fact—is strong in Cincinnati. The Queen City is very proud of its roots as the home of the first professional team, and although it is unofficial, the opening day of the new baseball season each spring is treated much like a holiday. Children skip school, adults play hooky from work, and the city throws a parade to celebrate the return of baseball action. It is on that day that reminders of the Cincinnati Red Stockings, and their history in the community, are most actively publicized.

NOTE

1. "National Baseball Hall of Fame," http://www.baseballhall.org.

FURTHER READING

Devine, Christopher. *Harry Wright: The Father of Professional Baseball*. Jefferson, NC: McFarland, 2003.
Guschov, Stephen D. *The Red Stockings of Cincinnati: Base Ball's First All-Professional Team and Its Historic 1869 and 1870 Season*. Jefferson, NC: McFarland, 1998.
Leventhal, Josh. *A History of Baseball in 100 Objects*. New York: Black Dog & Leventhal, 2015.
Okrent, Daniel. *The Ultimate Baseball Book*, *Expanded and Updated Edition*. Wilmington, MA: Mariner Books, 2000.

#12 The World Series

The American sports fan of a certain age will remember the wars between the National Football League and American Football League and the competition for survival between the National Basketball Association and the American Basketball Association, all of which ended in mergers.

But long before present-day fans were born, the same kind of intense feelings permeated the frosty relationship between the National League and the challenging American League in baseball. Since the two leagues have lived under the umbrella of harmony for more than a century, not much thought is devoted to the beginnings of their oh-so-tight connection.

The reality is that the NL was the established league, dating back to 1876, when the American League came along in 1901. They were competitors for players and fans, at first not of any mind to be pals. The National League had already outlasted other assaults on its supremacy and believed it would do so again.

But the American League was stronger than the other upstarts, and rather than fight any longer, by 1903 the leagues were working toward forging a tentative peace that would preclude player raiding. Before the season even ended, since the respective teams had such large leads in the standings, the owners of the Pittsburgh Pirates in the NL and the Boston Red Sox in the AL held talks proposing a postseason championship series to determine the best team in the game.

The Red Sox, managed by Jimmy Collins and owned by Henry Killilea, finished 91–47. The Pirates, managed by Fred Clarke and owned by Barney Dreyfuss, finished 91–49. They were led by Honus Wagner, "The Flying Dutchman" at shortstop, who batted .355 and is considered one of the greatest players of all time.

Played between October 1 and October 13, the first World Series was a best-of-nine series. The Red Sox, riding the pitching of the magnificent Cy Young, who went 28–9 during the regular season, and Bill Dineen, topped the Pirates five games to three. Pittsburgh was shorthanded on pitching, but ace Deacon Phillippe stood in. Phillippe pitched five complete games, winning three of them, but couldn't hold off the Sox.

The first World Series game was slated for 3:00 p.m. on October 1, 1903, and was played at Boston's Huntington Grounds. As the visiting team, Pittsburgh batted

The first World Series was played in 1903 between the Boston Red Sox and the Pittsburgh Pirates and was won by Boston. The existence of the championship series represented a thaw in tense relations between the more-established National League and upstart American League, founded in 1901. (AP Photo)

first, and Boston was in the field first. Young, for whom after his death the award for the leagues' best pitchers was named, threw the first pitch in Series history.

There was no World Series in 1904 because of squabbling. New York Giants manager John McGrew refused to participate in a competition against the American League champion Red Sox, who finished 1½ games ahead of the New York Highlanders. In the future, not even world wars interrupted the playing of the World Series. The only other year since 1903 that no Series was held was 1994, when a bitter labor strike cut short the season and wiped out the play-offs as well.

As the two leagues did learn to coexist, the World Series became an annual event starting in 1905. As fans flocked to baseball, making it the preeminent team sport in the country, the World Series became the most closely followed and popular sporting event on the calendar. Each October the nation came to a virtual standstill as two teams battled for a world title.

Before the days of radio, fans sought information from any source they could find. When radio began broadcasting the Series, nearly every household, it seemed, was tuned into the game. When TV advanced coverage, the same proved true. During World Series games, other forms of leisure activities virtually ceased.

Fans were mesmerized by one-day championships such as the Kentucky Derby, Indianapolis 500, or a major prize fight, but when it came to overall interest, nothing compared to the World Series. For decades all of the games were played in the afternoon, and workers tried their best to listen to the proceedings while on the job. It was hard to hold the attention of schoolchildren once the first pitch of a game had been thrown, especially if the hometown team was involved.

Throughout the 1950s and into the 1960s, the national pastime ruled the sports world. With the ascension of football and its surge to primacy, and the splintering of TV audiences as cable spread its tentacles and rolled in a tidal wave over the three network channels, there was no longer such a thing as a captive audience. In 1978 it was estimated that 44 million people watched the World Series in the United States, a record. In 1980 approximately 55 million people watched the sixth game of the Series between the Philadelphia Phillies and the Kansas City Royals.

What the World Series showed was that even the casual fan would drop what he was doing to follow or watch a major championship. The World Series was the first sporting competition to be classified as an event, because it represented the culmination of a long season crowning a champion in the most popular sport in the land.

The season ended abruptly in August 1994, although when the regular season schedule was halted, there was hope play would resume and that a Series could still be contested. Baseball purists were appalled by the absence of the World Series that year. Also hurt were players and managers, especially those affiliated with teams that were leading their leagues at the time.

The New York Yankees were ahead in the American League. The Montreal Expos were ahead in the National League. While the Yankees seemed to make an appearance in the World Series almost every year, this looked like the best team the Expos ever had. The manager was Felipe Alou, the old San Francisco Giants out-fielder, and he felt his club was on a special ride that year, as it turned out, one never to be repeated.

"It took away an opportunity," said Alou, speaking eight years later. "That took away my only opportunity to be in the play-offs. It's frustrating. It's emptiness."[1]

Even though the World Series has lost some of its clout because of fractional-ized attention in a glutted sports world and among nonsports fans, it remains one of the most prominent annual events on the sports calendar, and anyone with even a passing interest in the sport usually knows what team won the championship and what team was the loser.

NOTE

1. Jack Curry, "Baseball: Lost Games, Lost Dreams," *New York Times*, August 26, 2002.

FURTHER READING

Abrams, Roger I. *The First World Series and the Baseball Fanatics of 1903*. Boston: Northeastern University Press, 2003.
Dabilis, Andy, and Nick Tsiotos. *The 1903 World Series: The Boston Americans, the Pittsburgh Pirates and the First Championship of the United States*. Jefferson, NC: McFarland, 2004.
Ryan, Bob. *When Boston Won the World Series: A Chronicle of Boston's Remarkable Victory in the First World Series*. Philadelphia: Running Press, 2003.

#13 Babe Ruth Transforms Baseball

Nearly 60 years after his death, there is no mystery who is being talked about when someone mentions the nickname "The Babe."

Although he did not invent the home run, George Herman "Babe" Ruth might as well have. He perfected it, turned it into baseball's premier weapon, and virtually single-handedly changed baseball from a low-scoring game played with careful attention to advancing base by base to one that emphasized power.

Babe Ruth was the nuclear weapon that transformed baseball, and during the Roaring Twenties he created more excitement than any other person in the United States, in or out of sports. After the Black Sox scandal of 1919 tarnished baseball's image and destroyed public confidence in the sport because of the Chicago White Sox fixing the World Series, Ruth proved to be a savior.

Not only did Ruth inject more pizzazz into the sport than it had ever offered before, he also uplifted the New York Yankees to greatness; became a hero to little boys, whom he charmed; and through his gargantuan appetites and personality entertained fans and sportswriters off the field as well.

Even though Ruth died of lung cancer in 1948, he lives on clearly in memory today, and baseball fan or not, most Americans know his name.

Ruth was born in Baltimore in 1895, where he had a troubled youth. He was on the wild side, and when his parents decided he couldn't be controlled and was "incorrigible," they deposited him at an orphanage. Distraught at first, Ruth adapted, and this is where he learned how to play baseball. He became so good at the game that in his late teens, when the priests who supervised the orphanage felt he was ready to go out into the world, he was brought to the attention of the minor league Baltimore team.

A left-handed thrower as well as a left-handed batter, Ruth, it is sometimes forgotten by the casual fan, was also a superb pitcher, and when he made his major league debut for the Boston Red Sox in 1914, that was his primary role. When discussion turns to who was the greatest player in baseball history, those who vote for Ruth can toss in the evidence that as his secondary skill he was a star pitcher. He was good enough to compile a 94–46 pitching record (67 percent wins) and earn an American League earned run average title with a 1.75 mark in 1916, when he won 23 games. He won 24, his career high, the next year. At one point Ruth owned the record for the most consecutive scoreless innings thrown in the World Series.

At six foot two and 215 pounds, before he gained more weight in his belly as a result of his out-of-control eating and drinking habits, Ruth was exceptionally strong. He hit so well during his time in the lineup as a pitcher that the Red Sox began spotting him in the outfield on days between starts.

In 1920, in need of cash, Red Sox owner Harry Frazee, prompted by New York's Ed Barrow, who had shifted from being Frazee's employee, made one of the most ill-advised deals of all time and shipped Ruth to the Yankees. In New York Ruth really thrived, accepting the change to a full-time outfield slot and foregoing pitching.

Timed to coincide with the introduction of the more lively baseball, which replaced the older, dead ball, Ruth in New York created a sensation because he could bash the ball all over the lot and out of it, too, far more regularly than anyone else who had ever played the game. He was an explosion waiting to happen each time he stepped into the batter's box.

People like Ty Cobb were proponents of the "scientific" method of playing baseball, advancing on the bases one at a time, throwing in stolen bases and bunts and relying on the hit-and-run for a single run at a time. Ruth was the antidote to this approach, a one-man rally who with one swing cleared the bases with two-run homers, three-run homers, and grand slams, putting up multiple runs with a single swing. Another of his nicknames was "The Sultan of Swat."

Baseball had never seen anything like Ruth. In 1918, when Ruth was a part-time position player and the dead ball still ruled, he won his first American League home-run title. Ruth clouted 11 homers, tying with Tillie Walker of the Philadelphia Athletics. Ruth began changing the universe in 1919 when he smashed 29 homers for the Red Sox to win another home-run title. Overlooked because it is an insignificant number compared to Ruth's subsequent achievements, that total represented the all-time single-season home-run mark.

In 1920, while Cy Williams of the Phillies was leading the National League with 15 homers, Ruth was bashing 54 for the Yankees. That same season he became the first player to hit 30, 40, and 50 home runs in one year. Ruth was the talk of baseball, and his exploits so thrilled New York owner Jacob Ruppert that he dove into construction of a much bigger and more palatial ballpark. The demand of ticket buyers to watch Ruth send baseballs into orbit led to the new Yankee Stadium, which opened in 1923, being described as "The House That Ruth Built."

It has become a sportswriting cliché to describe an athlete as a one-man wrecking crew, but even if the phrase was not invented for Ruth, it most certainly could have been. In 1921, the season after Ruth's 54 homers set a new standard, he hit 59, breaking his previous record.

He wasn't finished, either. In 1927, as the cornerstone of the "Murderers Row" Yankees, Ruth set a new record once more, smashing 60 home runs. That single-season record stood until 1961, when Roger Maris, another Yankee, broke it with 61 home runs.

"Sixty! Count 'em, 60," Ruth shouted in the Yankee dugout. "Let's see some other son of a bitch match that."[1]

Ruth did have a strong sense of self-worth. He knew he was responsible for putting fannies in the seats at Yankee Stadium and routinely sought raises. Sometimes there was hard bargaining, but Ruth was the highest paid player in the game by far and maintained that level. In 1930 he played for $80,000. When someone pointed out that he was making more money than President Herbert Hoover, Ruth replied, "Why not? I had a better year than he did."[2] Given that the nation was in the midst of the Great Depression, Ruth's comeback was indisputable.

Although the lively ball did introduce a new scoring trend in baseball, and other sluggers emerged to join Ruth as practitioners of the long ball, no one could match him. He was the trendsetter, the human symbol of the home run. Much to players like Cobb's disgust, as great as they were at other facets of the game, it was Ruth who wowed the public. He seemed to always rise to the occasion and to always be in the news due to his gregarious personality and the Yankees' domination of the sport.

On October 1, 1932, during a tense moment in the World Series against the Chicago Cubs, the myth of Ruth collided with the reality of Ruth, and what happened has never quite been sorted out. The setting was game 3 of the Series in the fifth inning as Wrigley Field fans razzed Ruth

Babe Ruth was baseball's greatest slugger of all time, the man who made the home run into a lethal weapon. Ruth's true breakthrough came with the New York Yankees when he smashed a record 54 homers, making him the first player to hit 30, 40, and 50 homers in a single season. (AP Photo/National Baseball Library, Cooperstown, NY)

and Cubs players harangued him. A bit irritated by the verbal abuse, Ruth still stepped calmly into the batter's box against Chicago pitcher Charlie Root.

Only the fuzziest of video is available to interpret, but the story goes that Ruth accepted two strikes from Root, holding up a finger each time, counting them, and then pointing his hand or bat at the distant center-field wall. Ruth promptly deposited the next pitch into another area code for a home run, a clout forever after referred to as "Ruth's called shot."

Ruth circled the bases laughing hard, but not a huge amount of attention was lavished on the play in the next day's coverage. The story took hold from there, though, and expanded in detail and the telling thereafter. Ruth never thoroughly explained the gesture, nor did he ever deny it. He knew a good story when he heard it.

"I didn't exactly point to any spot," Ruth said later. "All I wanted to do was give that thing a ride out of the park anywhere."[3]

When Ruth retired at age 40, after 22 big-league seasons, in 1935, he was already a legend. He had collected 714 homers, a mark that most believed would last forever. It took nearly 40 years for someone to catch up. During his amazing career Ruth also scored 2,174 runs, gathered 2,214 runs batted in, batted .342, and had a lifetime .474 on-base percentage, at least partially because he walked 2,062 times. He led the league in homers 12 times.

Just as important for baseball, Ruth led the league in autographs given, making youngsters feel happy and spreading goodwill about the game.

While baseball was not an international game at the time, Ruth did participate in a tour that brought the sport to Japan before World War II, and he was besieged by admirers there as well.

After retiring as a player, Ruth desperately wanted to manage the Yankees, but the call never came. He remained a goodwill ambassador for baseball and a beloved figure for the rest of his life. If anything, his stature has grown since his death at age 53.

NOTES

1. Robert Creamer, *Babe: The Legend Comes to Life* (New York: Pocket Books, 1976), 308.
2. Ibid., 352.
3. Ibid., 367.

FURTHER READING

Fitts, Robert K. *Banzai Babe Ruth: Baseball, Espionage and Assassination during the 1934 Tour of Japan.* Lincoln: University of Nebraska Press, 2013.

Montville, Leigh. *The Big Bam: The Life and Times of Babe Ruth.* New York: Broadway Books, 2006.

Sherman, Ed. *Babe Ruth's Called Shot: The Myth and Mystery of Baseball's Greatest Home Run.* Guilford, CT: Lyons Press, 2014.

Stevens, Julia Ruth, and Bill Gilbert. *Babe Ruth: Remembering the Bambino in Stories, Photos & Memorabilia.* New York: Stewart, Tabori and Chang, 2008.

Weintraub, Robert. *The House That Ruth Built: A New Stadium, the First Yankees Championship, and the Redemption of 1923.* New York: Back Bay Books, 2013.

#14 Red Grange Introduces Pro Football to the World

A transcendent figure in football, Red Grange parlayed his remarkable skills and public image in college football into a role uplifting the image of professional football across the country.

At a time when pro football was struggling for an identity and a foothold in the American sports consciousness, the arrival of Grange on the pro scene with the Chicago Bears and a frenzied, intensely followed, and successful whirlwind national tour raised the status of the pro game.

Grange's given name was Harold, but before he finished his schooling at the University of Illinois the world called him "Red." It also called him a number of other nicknames propagated by sportswriters, the most famous being bestowed on the fleet running back by Chicago sportswriter Warren Brown. Brown took one look at Grange's sprinting ability with the football and referred to him as "The Galloping Ghost."

Others referred to Grange as the "Wheaton Iceman." After his birth in Forksville, Pennsylvania, in 1903, Grange's family moved to Wheaton, Illinois, a Chicago suburb. At that time, before refrigeration was widespread, Grange worked delivering ice blocks to homes for the purpose of keeping their food fresh. The six foot, 180-pound back said he built his powerful muscles by toting the ice.

Grange was a stupendous high school athlete, earning 16 varsity letters in four sports while scoring 75 touchdowns for Wheaton's football team. At Illinois he rewrote the Big Ten school's record book and gained national fame through one spectacular game performance.

On October 18, 1924, Illinois faced an exalted Michigan team. Not only did Grange run the opening kickoff back 95 yards for a touchdown, he never did stop scoring touchdowns that day. He scored four touchdowns in the game's first 12 minutes, adding runs of 67, 56, and 44 yards to the kickoff return. Grange scored a fifth TD later, and Illinois romped. The performance prompted legendary sportswriter Grantland Rice to write a poem about Grange.

Those who watched Grange run were enthralled by his skill, but his number 77 uniform also made him easy to pick out on the field. Grange was a three-time all-American for the Illini, and his jersey was retired.

Watching from a not-so-great a distance of 150 miles from Champaign, Chicago Bears founder, owner, and coach George Halas was intrigued by Grange's ability and wanted to land him for his NFL team after Grange graduated. However, events took an unpredictable turn once Grange completed his eligibility.

One day at a movie theater, Grange was approached by a stranger. The man's name was C. C. Pyle, and he had a proposition for Grange. Pyle, a promotional whiz who was sometimes disparaged by critics, who said his initials stood for "Cash and Carry," told Grange that if he threw in with him he could make him rich. He guaranteed Grange at least $100,000 and maybe more if he signed on for a tour on which he would be the headliner.

At that time, although he had begun to examine his future, Grange had not thought much about playing the professional game. He was astonished when Pyle told him he could make that much money.

In that age of amateur sports many influential people, including Grange's coach Bob Zuppke, frowned on his going pro and thought he should try a more sedate career. But Pyle sold the idea to Halas, and the barnstorming tour was set.

Pro football was still an unstable enterprise. Between the founding of the NFL in 1920 and the early 1930s, teams came and went with startling rapidity, folding in midseason, failing to make payroll, and disappearing from the standings. Grange was the most popular of college players, known all over the nation.

With Grange in the lineup and the Bears his supporting cast, the group crammed a tremendous amount of football into a short period and played for some very large audiences. The tour pace was demanding, almost ridiculous, and at times Grange was so bruised and battered from the matchups against local teams that he had to sit out the occasional game.

The Pyle-arranged tour consumed 66 days and consisted of 19 games over the late fall and into the early winter of 1925 and 1926. The game against the New York Giants at the Polo Grounds attracted 70,000 people and alleviated the debt acquired by Giants owner Tim Mara, perhaps rescuing that franchise from oblivion.

Grange and the Bears created excitement wherever they traveled. He was like the star of a Broadway play on the road. Newspapers invested hundreds of column inches on the player and team, and hundreds of thousands watched the games in the flesh. Pyle's instincts were on the money, and to Halas's satisfaction, this tour proved conclusively that there could be an appetite for pro football. Historians agree that the Grange-fronted tour helped legitimize the NFL in the eyes of sports fans in a manner that regular season games on their own had yet to do.

Pyle did make Grange, who otherwise would still have been taking classes in Champaign, Illinois, a rich man. Over time, in an era when sports memorabilia were virtually nonexistent, there were such items available as a Red Grange doll. Pyle also obtained endorsements for Grange. However, the playing arrangement was not a one-and-done deal. Grange was under a long-term contract to Pyle. Once the tour ended, Grange was a free agent in search of a team. The college draft lay in the future. Having proved his worth as a drawing card, Grange came at a high price. Halas, who had the inside track, didn't want to pay it. The always-thinking

Red Grange, the nation's most prominent college football player, after scoring six touchdowns in one game against Michigan, in 1925 made the sudden leap from the University of Illinois to the Chicago Bears for a barnstorming tour that helped put professional football on the map. (Library of Congress)

Pyle subsequently started an entirely new league just to showcase Grange. The first American Football League included a team named the New York Yankees, which it was hoped people would confuse fondly with the baseball Yankees.

Grange played the 1926 season in New York, but when the league floundered he did sign with the Bears and played the rest of his pro career with Chicago. A severe knee injury robbed Grange of the mobility he had displayed in college, but he was still good enough as a player to team in the backfield with hulking fullback Bronco Nagurski and served Bears championship teams as a defensive back, as well.

Whether it was for the star quality of his personality, his unusual skills on the field, or a combination of many things, Grange was greatly admired, and those who watched him play football remembered it.

Damon Runyon, one of the most talented writers of that generation, once described Grange this way: "He is three or four men rolled into one. He is Jack Dempsey, Babe Ruth, Al Jolson, Paavo Nurmi and Man O' War."[1]

Later in life Grange became a Bears broadcaster, and he was a charter member of the Pro Football Hall of Fame in Canton, Ohio, when it opened in 1963. Grange's shiftiness made him an excellent player, but his biggest contribution to football may well have been the star quality that enabled him to front that memorable tour.

NOTE

1. Gerald Eskenazi, "Football Hero of 1920's, Dead at 87," *New York Times*, January 29, 1991.

FURTHER READING

Carroll, John M. *Red Grange and the Rise of Modern Football*. Urbana: University of Illinois Press, 1999.
Grange, Red, and Ira Morton. *The Red Grange Story: An Autobiography*. Urbana: University of Illinois Press, 1993.
Poole, Gary Andrew. *The Galloping Ghost: Red Grange, an American Football Legend*. Boston: Houghton Mifflin Harcourt, 2014.

#15 The Great Jim Thorpe

By any measure, Jim Thorpe is the greatest Native American athlete of all time. When Thorpe won the Olympic gold medal in the decathlon in 1912 in Stockholm, he met King Gustav V of Sweden. The king shook Thorpe's hand in congratulations at the closing ceremonies and said, "Sir, you are the greatest athlete in the world." Thorpe responded, "Thanks, king."[1]

The person who wins the Olympic decathlon at the Summer Olympics every four years is acclaimed the greatest athlete in the world by dint of the triumph. The decathlon is a 10-event competition that includes running and field events, testing speed, endurance, power, and strength. Thorpe also won the gold medal in the pentathlon, a five-event competition that has since been discontinued.

Pentathlon competition was a one-day affair. Decathlon events were spread over two days.

King Gustav, the host for the fifth Olympics, could not have known how accurate his statement was. Thorpe's athletic prowess far superseded his enduring victory in the decathlon.

In later years he starred as a professional football player and also played Major League Baseball, which was probably his third best sport. He even barnstormed as

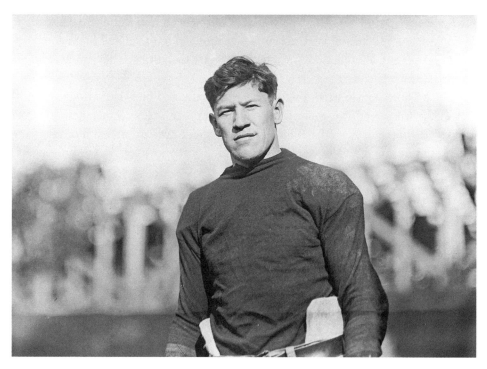

Track and field, football, and baseball, Jim Thorpe excelled at them all, earning the title of "World's Greatest Athlete." He won the gold medal in the Olympic decathlon, starred in pro football, played for the New York Giants in the National League, and was the first commissioner of the National Football League. (Library of Congress)

a member of an all-Indian basketball team. If a sport was available, Thorpe tried it and excelled at it. At six foot one and 200 pounds, Thorpe could do it all.

When votes were tabulated in 1950, Thorpe was selected as the best U.S. athlete of the first half of the 20th century. In another vote taken at the end of the 20th century, Thorpe won again.

Thorpe, a Sac and Fox Indian, was born in Oklahoma in 1888 and died in California in 1953. Much like those other most famous minority athletes of the pre-1950 era, Joe Louis and Jesse Owens, Thorpe starred at his specializations but did not always receive his due, and he did not always have an easy time of it away from the playing fields. The injustice he suffered that was most famously reported was being stripped of those Olympic medals because of charges of professionalism. He had played some semipro baseball for $2 a game before the Games. The medals were later reinstated.

Young Thorpe attended Native American schools, though he kept running away from them. Eventually he enrolled at the Haskell Institute in Kansas, a boarding school. In 1904, when he was 16, Thorpe became a student at the Carlisle Indian School in Pennsylvania, and it was there he blossomed and first gained notice as an athlete, although not for a few years. By then both of his parents and his brother Charlie had died.

Once Thorpe got started, though, no one could stop him. He introduced himself to the track team by clearing the high-jump bar at five foot nine—in street clothes. He dabbled in lacrosse and even won an intercollegiate ballroom dancing championship, more evidence that if physical effort was involved, Thorpe would be a contender.

One day, according to Thorpe, he was strolling past the high-jump pit and stopped to watch the athletes practice.

"After a while they had set the bar at five feet, nine inches and none of them could jump over it," Thorpe said. "They were just about ready to call it a day when I asked if I might try it. I had a pair of overalls on, a hickory shirt, and a pair of gymnasium shoes I had picked up in the gym that belonged to someone else. I looked like anything but a high jumper."[2]

Thorpe made his jump and improved from there.

Interestingly, Thorpe had to beg to be allowed to try football, because he had no experience with the game and the team was already good. Coach Pop Warner, one of the most famous early coaches in America, thought a couple of belts from sturdy defenders would disabuse Thorpe of his desire. Instead, once handed the ball, Thorpe skirted past the defense, outrunning the whole team. And then he did it again.

After that Thorpe was a critical member of the team. Carlisle upset Harvard in 1911 when the Crimson was ranked number 1 in the country. In 1912 Carlisle won a national championship as Thorpe scored 25 touchdowns. The United States had waged wars against various Indians and broken tribal treaties with many within living memory of millions of Americans, so Carlisle students were not always embraced wherever they traveled. But the school did play very good football.

"Carlisle had no traditions," Warner said, "but what the Indians did have was a real race pride and a fierce determination to show the palefaces what they could do when the odds were even."[3]

Once Thorpe's amateur eligibility was revoked, he was the object of major league teams' recruiting wars. Thorpe signed with the New York Giants, and following the 1913 season the Giants and Chicago White Sox embarked on a groundbreaking world tour. Thorpe's name was known in some of the other countries because of his Olympic championships, and he got to meet more royalty.

Anyone who can collect a check for playing major league baseball has a certain amount of talent and has accomplished something that thousands of shut out young men would yearn to be able to do. It's just that baseball wasn't really Thorpe's best sport. His career average was .252. Thorpe could do almost anything athletic well enough to fit in at the top level of the sport. One myth about Thorpe that makes him sound more like a freak of nature than a serious athlete was a story claiming that on the 10-day boat ride to Sweden for the Olympics, Thorpe didn't even bother to train. Olympic teammates refuted that story and talked of working out with Thorpe.

Later that same year Thorpe signed to play professional football, which was in its infancy in terms of sophistication. By 1915 he was a member of the Canton Bulldogs. The Ohio club was one of the most stable around, and with Thorpe the key to the offense, Canton won some pre-NFL championships. After that league was founded, Canton was accepted into the new structure and competed into the mid-1920s.

Although he really wasn't expected to sit at a desk and sign paperwork, when the NFL was founded in Canton—for one year operating as the American Professional Football Association—Thorpe was appointed the first commissioner. The money men behind the franchises appreciated Thorpe's reputation and history in the sport and wanted him as a front man for credibility. The founding of the NFL in Canton in August 1920 was a major reason that the NFL later backed the placement of the Pro Football Hall of Fame there.

Thorpe continued to play pro football well into the 1920s, with his final on-field action in 1928 being for the Chicago Cardinals, a forerunner of today's Arizona Cardinals. Thorpe also coached several teams between 1915 and 1926.

Once age began catching up to Thorpe and he was no longer able to compete in sports at a professional level, he and his family struggled with finances. At times Thorpe was forced to cope with discrimination against Native Americans, but he didn't help himself as much as he might have. A major issue for Thorpe was alcoholism, and that contributed to his demise at age 64. He was impoverished at the time of his death.

Shortly after Thorpe died, his widow Patricia became angry at Oklahoma authorities because they would not erect a statue of the deceased athlete. In a peculiar arrangement, the Pennsylvania community of Mauch Chunk agreed to change its name to Jim Thorpe and build a monument there honoring the athlete. The town leaders' motivation was tourism.

This was fine with Thorpe's wife, because she wanted him to be remembered and honored. Patricia gained control of Thorpe's remains, and he was buried in Pennsylvania. It is unknown if Thorpe ever passed through the community of about 4,800 people in life, but it is located only 100 miles from Carlisle.

NOTES

1. Robert W. Wheeler, *Jim Thorpe: World's Greatest Athlete* (Norman: University of Oklahoma Press, 1975), 110.

2. Ibid., 50.

3. Ibid., 36.

FURTHER READING

Anderson, Lars. *Carlisle vs. Army: Jim Thorpe, Dwight Eisenhower, Pop Warner and the Forgotten Story of Football's Greatest Battle.* New York: Random House, 2008.

Bruchac, Joseph. *Jim Thorpe: Original All-American.* New York: Speak, 2008.

Buford, Kate. *Native American Son: The Life and Sporting Legend of Jim Thorpe.* New York: Knopf, 2010.

Cook, William A. *Jim Thorpe: A Biography.* Jefferson, NC: McFarland, 2011.

King, C. Richard, ed. *Native Americans and Sport in North America: Other People's Games.* New York: Routledge, 2014.

#16 The NFL's Greatest Game

The 1958 National Football League championship game between the New York Giants and the Baltimore Colts loomed as a suspenseful way to end the season. It was that and more—much more. The game turned into an epic, and its impact became a catalyst for pro football to become the number 1 sport in America.

The first championship to run into overtime in pro football history, the game introduced the words "sudden death" into public sporting lexicon, and the suspense, coupled with the influence of the game on television programming, helped it earn the label "The Greatest Game Ever Played."

New York won the Eastern Division title and Baltimore won the Western Division title, during an era of play that predated lead-up play-off games to the championship match as well as the Super Bowl. The game was scheduled for December 28, 1958, at Yankee Stadium.

Both teams entered the contest with 9–3 records. The Giants had been more of a powerhouse lately and won the 1956 NFL crown. The Colts had been patiently built by coach Weeb Ewbank, who had inherited a bottom-of-the-league franchise.

Each club was also loaded with stars on both sides of the ball. They had very capable offenses and stingy defenses, and a number of players on both teams would later be enshrined in the Pro Football Hall of Fame.

The first quarter was fairly nondescript, with the Giants taking a 3–0 lead. The Colts owned the second quarter, scoring two touchdowns and taking a 14–3 lead into halftime. Although Baltimore quarterback Johnny Unitas, nicknamed "The Golden Arm," was already quite popular with Colts fans, this game gave him a national platform to show the nation how special he was. The same was true of his favorite receiver, Raymond Berry. Berry was regarded as a slow-poke end, albeit one with grand hands and great moves. Running back Lenny Moore was a Hall of Famer, as was offensive lineman Jim Parker.

Defensively the Colts featured such devastating hitters at Gino Marchetti at defensive end and Art Donovan at defensive tackle.

New York was quarterbacked by Charlie Conerly, who was protected by Roosevelt Brown and aided in making big yardage by Frank Gifford, Kyle Rote, and Alex Webster. The Giants' proud defense was led by linebacker Sam Huff, defensive end Andy Robustelli, and defensive back Emlen Tunnell. It was during this period that the now-common spectator cry of "Dee-fense! Dee-fense!" was initiated by Giants fans.

New York fought back with a touchdown in the third quarter against Baltimore's one field goal. Late in the game the Colts' defensive leader, Marchetti, snapped a bone in his leg and was helped off the field. Rather than accept medical treatment, he gritted his teeth and remained on the sidelines, refusing to leave until the championship was decided. The Giants took the lead in the fourth quarter and had the Colts pinned at their own 14-yard line as the clock was running out. It was then that Unitas took over.

Unitas went on to a storied career, but his career was almost stillborn before he obtained employment with the Colts. He had played college ball at Louisville, and NFL teams showed minimal interest in his future. The Pittsburgh Steelers drafted him in the ninth round, but barely glanced at him in training camp before cutting him. Famously, Unitas was playing semipro ball for $6 a game when he got a second chance with the Colts.

With his trademark crew cut and black shoes, in modern parlance Unitas might be called a geek. When he took the football field, though, Unitas was a general, a creator, a clutch player of imperturbable demeanor.

In more recent decades of NFL play, statistics have been kept to determine how often a quarterback leads a winning comeback scoring drive. Such series have gained the appellation "two-minute drill." This is when quarterbacks try to rally their teams by throwing and hurrying them down the field to record a survival score. That is exactly what Unitas did during the waning minutes against the Giants, routinely firing balls to Berry as the Colts ate up yardage. Seven seconds remained on the clock when Baltimore's Steve Myhra kicked the tying field goal from the 17-yard line. Tie game at 17 as time ran out.

There had never been a tie in an NFL championship game, and the rules determining what happened next after 60 minutes of play had only been recently introduced by Commissioner Bert Bell. They had never been used, however, and when the gun sounded ending regulation time, the players did not know what to do. Many thought the game was over and that they would be declared co-champions.

Not so. Referee Ron Gibbs knew what to do. He gathered the co-captains of both clubs at midfield for a second coin toss of the game. He informed them that the first

The 1958 National Football League's championship game has been called the best game in history. The Baltimore Colts' defeat of the New York Giants was certainly the most influential. It was the first time sudden-death overtime was played, and the large viewing audience demonstrated the nation's appetite for more pro football on TV. (AP Photo)

team to score in any manner would be the winner. That's where the "sudden death" phrase came in. Teams did not get a chance to retaliate if the other team scored.

New York won the coin toss and naturally took the ball. But after a fumbled kickoff gave them possession on their own 20-yard line, the Giants couldn't move the ball and punted. The Colts received the ball on their own 20.

The story goes that because the game had run long, more and more viewers tuned in late and were enthralled by the drama. Ratings indicated 45 million people watched, an enormous number for the time, but one that likely would have been much larger if the New York City area had not been blacked out.

As if the Giants had not had their fill of Unitas after the tying drive, he now did it all over again. It took Baltimore 13 plays to score the winning touchdown. The score occurred on a one-yard burst by Alan Ameche and is the subject of a famous photograph. Ameche has his head down, his shoulder pointed forward as he expects rugged resistance at the goal line, but the hole opens, and he seems to be all alone on the field as he plunges into the end zone.

At the end Unitas made the call to go for the TD instead of another chip-shot field goal.

"He was confident and we were very confident in him," said Colts end Jim Mutscheller.[1]

The final score was Baltimore 23, New York 17. The Colts did not try for an extra point.

This game, which earned the description of greatest ever, is definitely the most important NFL game of all time. It introduced a golden age of pro football, when fans demanded more and more games be shown on television; it helped provide motivation for the creation of the upstart American Football League, which was able to survive its challenge to the NFL because of its own TV contract; and it proved to NFL owners that they had a property that was on an upswing in the public eye.

They did not quite recognize that fans would have an insatiable appetite for their game—fed by television—but they would learn that soon enough.

NOTE

1. Jeff Miller, "Shaky Myhra Made the Kick That Mattered Most," ESPN.com, December 8, 2008.

FURTHER READING

Bowden, Mark. *Best Game Ever: Giants vs. Colts, 1958, and the Birth of the Modern NFL.* New York: Atlantic Monthly Press, 2009.
Callahan, Tom. *Johnny U: The Life and Times of Johnny Unitas.* New York: Crown, 2010.
Gifford, Frank, and Peter Richmond. *The Glory Game: How the 1958 NFL Championship Changed Football Forever.* New York: HarperCollins, 2008.

#17 Roberto Clemente

Before he died in a plane crash trying to help earthquake-stricken residents of Nicaragua, Roberto Clemente was a role model for all Latin American baseball players. After the accident took his life at a young age, while he was still active for the Pittsburgh Pirates, he graduated to veritable sainthood.

Clemente, born in Carolina, Puerto Rico, in 1934, was one of the pioneer base-ball players of Hispanic heritage who made breakthroughs to stardom in the 1950s and paved the way for the influx of hundreds of additional Latin American players, who have became a routine part of Major League Baseball today.

When Clemente broke in with the Pirates in 1955, and through the early part of his 18-season career, which ended in 1972, the United States had not yet adapted to Spanish-speaking residents, and the percentage of Latinos in the country was much smaller than it is today.

Rather than Americans embracing cultural differences, it was felt to be incum-bent on those who spoke Spanish as a first language to fit in with mainstream America and to adapt to an American way of doing things. Some sportswriters routinely referred to Clemente as "Bob" rather than Roberto. In fact, on some of Clemente's first baseball cards he was also called Bob.

A proud man, Clemente had no intention of foregoing his own way of life in favor of assimilation. His adaptation consisted of bashing the baseball over the fence, running the bases, fielding and throwing with abandon, and growing into one of the biggest stars in the sport. He despised being quoted in accented English when he was trying hard to accommodate sportswriters in their language.

"I think it was ignorance on the part of the people then," said former Pirate broadcaster Nellie King. "The culture at that time in this country was difficult. You had to be white and you had to speak English."[1]

Clemente was dark skinned, and Pittsburgh and the United States were hardly free of racism in 1955. An inability to speak without an accent contributed to Clemente's early frustration with the Pirates and their hometown.

It took time for Pittsburgh fans to understand Clemente, and it took Clemente some time to adapt to some aspects of daily U.S. life without compromising himself. Bridging the language gap was the universal language of baseball. In English or Spanish, or any other language, Clemente was a superb player.

Before he was through, the man who owned right field at Forbes Field and then Three Rivers Stadium was named an all-star in 12 seasons, won 12 Gold Gloves, won a Most Valuable Player Award, collected 3,000 hits, and compiled a .317 bat-ting average. He won four National League batting titles.

Pie Traynor, one of the Pirate greats from the past, was always impressed by Clemente.

"He's a four-letter man," said Traynor, a Hall of Fame third baseman. "He can hit, run, field and throw."[2]

Not only did Clemente win over the fans in Pittsburgh, he also gained admirers throughout the game because of his all-around skills and for carrying himself with great dignity. Although Clemente was not the first Hispanic star to become a hit in the majors, he was one of the first, and his was one of the biggest and most enduring names. He became an idol not only to fellow Puerto Ricans, but also to players from such countries as the Dominican Republic, Mexico, and Nicaragua, and any other Spanish-speaking lands that sent forth young players trying to make it in the big time. The Roberto Clemente Fan Club grew by the season.

Clemente was not a huge man. He stood five foot eleven, and his listed playing weight was 175 pounds. But he looked bigger in the field. He had long arms and a rifle arm that cut down runners silly enough to try to extend a double into a triple. His number 21 Pirates jersey became well-known throughout the league.

The Pirates had not won a World Series since 1925, and the community was hungry for a championship. Clemente was a regular and star for the 1960 and 1971 clubs that delivered world championships to the old steel town. Following the 1960 campaign, Clemente and a fellow Puerto Rican, Orlando Cepeda, flew home and were greeted by a crowd of 18,000 people. The championship had elevated Clemente's status even more in Puerto Rico. The next year, 1961, Clemente won his first batting title with a .351 average.

As Clemente aged from the 20-year-old rookie he had been in 1955, he matured on and off the field, and in a sense the city matured with him. As Clemente continued to excel for the Pirates—he never played for any other big-league team—Pirates fans became fonder of him.

Clemente won the National League Most Valuable Player Award in 1966 when he blasted 29 home runs, drove in 119 runs, scored 105 runs, rapped out 202 hits, and batted .317. The next season, Pirates manager Harry Walker said of Clemente, "he is just the best player in baseball, that's all."[3]

The 1971 season was another special one for the Pirates. Clemente batted .341, and Pittsburgh won the second World Series of his career. The Pirates won 97 games and bested the Baltimore Orioles in a seven-game championship series. During one game in the regular season, partially due to injuries to their usual starters, the Pirates became the first team in history to field an all-black starting lineup. Manager Danny Murtaugh said he didn't even notice when writing out the lineup card. Clemente, Willie Stargell, Rennie Stennett, Gene Clines, Manny Sanguillen, Dave Cash, Al Oliver, and Jackie Hernandez were the position players. It also happened to be pitcher Dock Ellis's turn in the rotation.

Injuries diminished Clemente's contributions in 1972, limiting him to 102 games. He still batted .312, and he drew within a single hit of the career milestone of 3,000. On September 30 Clemente nearly sat out, willing to rest on 2,999 hits during the off-season and pick up with the 1973 season. But he changed his mind and suited up.

Clemente came to bat twice, clouted a double off New York Mets hurler Jon Matlack, and left the game. He reached 3,000 exactly.

Some months later Managua, the capital of Nicaragua, was devastated by a 6.2 earthquake that killed 6,000 people, injured 20,000, and left 250,000 homeless.

Roberto Clemente stroked his career 3,000th hit for the Pittsburgh Pirates in the last at-bat of his career. Already an icon and an idol among Latin American players, the Puerto Rican native further enhanced his legend by perishing at 38 on a mercy flight that was carrying supplies to earthquake ravaged Nicaragua. (AP Photo)

Moved by the plight of the people suffering after the December 23, 1972 temblor, Clemente organized shipments of food and medical supplies from San Juan to aid the suffering region. Clemente was 38, an aging baseball player, but his stature had grown significantly, and he could use his fame to help others.

He had supervised other flights, but caught wind of some of the supplies being diverted into greedy hands rather than going to those most in need, so he decided he would accompany the latest load. Clemente was aboard when the heavily laden jet took off and almost immediately crashed into the ocean. His mission to help others had turned tragic. Clemente went down with the plane, and his body was never found. It was December 31, 1972, New Year's Eve.

The shock of Clemente's disappearance and death spread throughout the baseball world and the Latin American world and was greeted with disbelief and grief.

It was an event of tremendous sadness as the world celebrated the arrival of a New Year with optimism.

Clemente was married, and he and his wife Vera had three sons. In the decades since his premature death they have grown up and helped perpetuate his legacy. Clemente is in no way forgotten. The Baseball Hall of Fame waved its five-year-after-retirement waiting period to allow Clemente to be voted in the next summer. A statue of him as a baseball player stands outside PNC Park, the current home of the Pirates. There is another statue of Clemente in Puerto Rico.

In 1984 a U.S. postage stamp of Clemente was issued. The honors have poured in as remembrances of Clemente the player and Clemente the man. Pittsburgh renamed a bridge for him. There is also a Clemente Park in Pittsburgh. His jersey number was retired by the team.

In 1971 Major League Baseball initiated a commissioner's award to recognize public service and charitable acts made by players on each team. In 1973 the name was changed to the Roberto Clemente Award, and the annual winner of the prestigious award is announced each year during the World Series. Willie Mays of the Giants won the first award. In 2014, for the first time ever, there were two recipients, Paul Konerko of the Chicago White Sox and Jimmy Rollins of the Philadelphia Phillies.

The only number retired by all teams throughout baseball is Jackie Robinson's number 42. There has been some discussion, spearheaded by Latin Americans, about Clemente's number 21 also being retired. There is some symmetry to the proposal. While admired by all, Robinson's courage made him a hero to African Americans, and Clemente's humanity made him a hero to Latin Americans.

NOTES

1. Bruce Markusen, *Roberto Clemente: The Great One* (Champaign, IL: Sports Publishing, 1998), 48.
2. Ibid., 81.
3. Ibid., 157.

FURTHER READING

Clemente Family. *Clemente: The True Legacy of an Undying Hero*. New York: Celebra, 2013.

Maraniss, David. *Clemente: The Passion and Grace of Baseball's Last Hero*. New York: Simon & Schuster, 2007.

Nathan, Daniel A. "Sports History and Roberto Clemente: A Morality Tale and a Way Forward." *Journal of American History* 101, no. 1 (2014): 184–187.

O'Brien, Jim, and Roberto Clemente Jr. *Remember Roberto: Clemente Recalled by Teammates, Family, Friends, and Fans*. Pittsburgh, PA: James O'Brien Publishing, 1994.

#18 Marvin Miller and Baseball Free Agency

Even before the end of the 19th century, baseball players seemed to be involved in a low-grade war with owners over low pay, lack of benefits, and being bound in perpetuity to a team by the reserve clause once a contract was signed.

Whenever a rival league sought to compete with the National League, whether it was the American Association, the American League in 1901, and later (challenging both of them) the Federal League, for a brief period of time players gained the upper hand and saw widespread salary increases.

As soon as the competing leagues failed, the players' leverage disappeared, and salaries dropped again. Players claimed that if they signed a contract for one year, when the year was up they were free agents, eligible to sign to play for anyone they wished. Owners countered that the contracts had built-in options, and they could not become free agents.

The core of these issues never varied. For decades the contentious situation continued. It took court decisions, coupled with the formation of a union and the hiring of a brilliant labor negotiator named Marvin Miller, for the players to win their arguments. The result, in terms of player rights and movement between teams, redrew the landscape of Major League Baseball and enriched players in ways they never could have imagined.

By 1965 the Major League Baseball Players Association, tired of being shunted aside by the more powerful owners, had embarked on a nationwide search to hire someone who could break free of the old patterns. The quest led them to Marvin Miller, a New Yorker born in 1917 who had worked for the United Steel Workers. Neither the players nor Miller realized upon his hiring in 1968 that the new executive director was about to become one of the most influential men in baseball history.

"Marvin Miller, along with Babe Ruth, and Jackie Robinson, is one of the two or three most important men in baseball history," said respected broadcaster Red Barber.[1]

Unifying the players' clout as he surveyed the scene, Miller first negotiated an increase in the minimum salary from $7,000 to $10,000. (Now it is more than $500,000.) He also helped formalize procedures for player complaints to be heard. Soon afterward Miller worked to establish a three-person independent panel to judge disputes rather than leaving the decisions to the commissioner.

A landmark owner-player dispute unfolded in 1969 when St. Louis Cardinals outfielder Curt Flood claimed that his longtime employer had no right to trade him

Although he never faced a fastball or swung a bat, Marvin Miller was one of the most influential figures in the history of Major League Baseball. The executive director of the Major League Players Association negotiated the policies that greatly increased salaries and free agency policies that provided fresh opportunities for players. (AP Photo)

to the Philadelphia Phillies because he didn't want to go there. The Flood case went to the U.S. Supreme Court, and although it was decided against him, Flood was determined to pursue the case, despite being warned by Miller that he would never get another job in baseball. What Miller told Flood—something that reso-nated—was that his efforts would aid future generations of players.

While the Flood case dragged on, Miller rode point on other player issues. Owners were stunned when players stayed away from ballparks on strike for a 13-day period in early 1972 while Miller bargained for a $500,000 increase to the pension fund. Miller was not above convincing players to strike to make a point. They needed to be taken seriously by the owners, he felt, and there was no better way to show the bosses how serious they were. Usually the discouraged owners, worried that the labor strife would kill the golden goose, capitulated. The owners knew only too well that they had had a good thing going, siphoning off profits and keeping their labor costs low for decades.

In 1974, with Miller guiding him, future Hall of Fame pitcher Jim "Catfish" Hunter broke from his Oakland A's contract to become a free agent, because

Oakland owner Charlie Finley had missed the deadline for a contractual annuity payment. Hunter received big money to play for the New York Yankees.

Also in 1974, Andy Messersmith, then pitching for the Los Angeles Dodgers, and Dave McNally, a hurler for the Baltimore Orioles, challenged the reserve clause. They played out the season for their teams without signing new contracts and said they had fulfilled their obligations under the option clause. The courts agreed, and for the first time players had won limited access to free agency.

Believing that too many players entering free agency at once would defeat the purpose of the decision and result in lower salaries being paid, Miller negotiated a deal with the owners to restrict free agency to players with more than six years of big-league service. That way, he told the players, they would be a scarcer and more valuable commodity, and the bidding for their services would jump. The scenario played out as Miller had predicted.

Periodically owners felt they had to fight back. Twice during the 16 years that Miller spent as executive director, owners locked the players out. Miller was the hired leader of the players union until 1982, and when he stepped away from office the minimum salary had skyrocketed to $326,000.

Miller's reading of the marketplace was correct. Players may have been nervous at first about cutting ties to a team they had spent years with, but they discovered that if they were good enough, other owners wanted them badly enough to pay millions of dollars for them to swap uniforms. Baseball, unlike football and basketball, has no salary cap. While fans of today are shocked to read about the size of long-term contracts, which might commit more than $300 million to one player, ironically it is the owners themselves who set the market standard.

An economist at the basic level, Miller would never criticize a situation for having gone too far. All the owners had to do was stop digging deep to pay out the multiyear, multi-million-dollar deals. They just didn't have the self-discipline to do so.

"I think he's the most important baseball figure of the last 50 years," said former commissioner Fay Vincent upon learning of Miller's death in November 2012. "He changed not just the sport, but the business of sport permanently."[2]

Miller was 95 when he passed away. There were Veterans Committee votes taken when he had come close to being elected to the Baseball Hall of Fame for his impact on the sport, and it is generally believed he will be elected at some point.

NOTES

1. Allen Barra, "Runnin' Scared: Once Again One of Baseball's Greatest Is Kept from Cooperstown," *Village Voice*, November 27, 2007.

2. Ronald Blum and Ben Walker, "Marvin Miller Obituary," *Associated Press*, November 27, 2012.

FURTHER READING

Burk, Robert F. *Marvin Miller: Baseball Revolutionary*. Urbana: University of Illinois Press, 2015.

Miller, Marvin. *A Whole Different Ball Game: The Inside Story of the Baseball Revolution*. Chicago: Ivan R. Dee, 2004.

Snyder, Brad. *A Well-Paid Slave: Curt Flood's Fight for Free Agency in Professional Sports*. New York: Viking, 2007.

#19 The NBA Integrates

There was no Jackie Robinson figure involved when the National Basketball Association integrated its rosters in 1950.

Only three years after Robinson broke Major League Baseball's color barrier, the circumstances were quite different. There was no lone pioneer standing alone on a ledge. And compared to baseball, the national pastime and number 1 team sport in the nation, at that time pro basketball was viewed more as a fringe sport.

There was also no well-thought-out, highly orchestrated plan à la Branch Rickey to ease one player into the spotlight. For the most part, integration of the NBA took place as much by happenstance and coincidental timing as by intention. That is why public recognition of the barrier breakers has always been minimal and seems more to be viewed as the answer to a trivia question than anything else.

The 1950–1951 NBA season began with three African American players, who each played a slightly different role in the integration of the league. Nat "Sweetwater" Clifton was a member of the New York Knicks. Chuck Cooper was a member of the Boston Celtics. And Earl Lloyd was a member of the Washington Capitals.

Cooper, who competed in college for Duquesne, was the first African American drafted in the history of the league. Clifton was the first to sign a contract. And Lloyd was the first to actually appear in a game, because his team opened the schedule a day before the others.

Although the room was a small one, with a limited number of people present, the story of the drafting of the six-foot-five Cooper leaked out and was talked about in low tones. Boston owner Walter Brown, who presided over the club that was later the first to start five blacks, announced the Celtics' selection of Cooper. There was silence in the room until one other owner quietly informed Brown that Cooper was black—as if he didn't know. Brown thundered that he didn't care if he was "striped, plaid, or polka dot," Cooper was the Celtics' choice.[1]

Cooper had been a second-team all-American in college. After graduation he signed to play for the Harlem Globetrotters, but switched to the Celtics when given the opportunity. Cooper was never an NBA star, but played in the league from 1950 through 1956 and recorded a career scoring average of 6.7 points a game.

Understanding the difference in their situations, Cooper did not put himself in the same class as Jackie Robinson as any kind of heroic figure.

"I wasn't alone," he said. "I didn't have to take the race-baiting and the heat all on my own shoulders like Jackie Robinson. Besides, any black coming after Jackie, in any sport, had it easy compared to the turmoil he lived through."[2]

At various times, though not from his teammates, who were supportive, Cooper had racist verbal abuse heaped on him. He roomed with Bob Cousy, not only the leader of the Celtics, but someone who was emerging as one of the biggest stars in the league. Cousy, who is white, considered such treatment of Cooper to be shameful, and he became an early member of the NAACP. Once, when the Celtics were on an exhibition tour in the South, Cooper was prohibited from staying in the same hotel as his teammates. He left town early by train, and Cousy went with him.

Clifton, who possessed a powerful, six-foot-eight, 220-pound physique, was originally from Chicago, but attended Xavier University of New Orleans. Clifton was older than the others. He spent three years in the army during World War II fighting in Europe, before resuming his athletic career.

Before signing with the Knicks at 27, he played basketball for the all-black New York Rens and spent some time with the Harlem Globetrotters. Although his nickname of "Sweetwater" stemmed from a boyhood love of drinking soda, it was catchy enough to follow him throughout his career.

Clifton's debut in the NBA occurred four days after Lloyd's. In his career, Clifton averaged 10 points and 9 rebounds a game and made the 1957 all-star team. Regarded as a fine all-around athlete, Clifton was a major figure in the sport of 16-inch softball, a specialty of the Chicago area, and he is a member of the Chicago 16-Inch Softball Hall of Fame.

Known for his generous charitable work, Clifton was inducted into the Naismith Basketball Hall of Fame in 2014.

Lloyd, who was from Virginia, played college ball at historically black West Virginia State, an NAIA school, where the sturdy, six-foot-five, 225-pound forward, nicknamed the "Big Cat," was a great scorer. One season, West Virginia State went unbeaten. After Brown stunned the other owners with his draft choice, Washington stepped up and selected Lloyd in the ninth round of the 1950 draft.

On October 31, 1950, Lloyd made his debut against the Rochester Royals, and so did African Americans in the NBA. The next day Cooper made his debut with the Celtics.

With much less fanfare than Major League Baseball, the National Basketball Association integrated its rosters with more than one player for the 1950–51 season. The Boston Celtics first drafted Chuck Cooper, the Washington Nationals chose Earl Lloyd (pictured), and the New York Knicks signed Nate "Sweetwater" Clifton. Clifton was the first African American to sign a contract and Lloyd was the first to get into a game. (AP Photo)

Never a pro star, Lloyd did enjoy a solid 10-year career in the NBA, averaging 8.4 points and 6.4 rebounds a game, and he played for the 1955 Syracuse Nationals' championship squad. That was also Lloyd's best individual season, during which he averaged more than 10 points a game. In the early 1970s Lloyd also coached the Detroit Pistons. In recognition of his role in integrating the NBA, Lloyd was inducted into the Hall of Fame in 2003.

Although Lloyd, Clifton, and Cooper are highlighted as the African American pioneers of the NBA, three other African Americans played lesser roles in opening up the league to blacks.

Harold Hunter joined the Washington Capitals in 1950, but was cut from the team before the regular season started. He did go on to make a major impact in basketball, coaching at Tennessee State University, with the U.S. National Team, and with the U.S. Olympic team.

Harold DeZonie joined the Tri-Cities Hawks for five games late in 1950, but it was said that he quit the game because of the racial discrimination he encountered.

Long before the other five sought employment in the NBA, an African American named Harry "Bucky" Lew attempted to play professional basketball with a team in Lowell, Massachusetts, signing in 1902. When several members of his team fouled out of a game, his coach initially preferred to play four-on-five rather than insert him into the lineup. Angry fans disapproved.

"The fans got real mad," Lew said, "and they almost started a riot, screaming to let me play. That did it."[3]

Much later, the NBA became known as the most progressive of major sports leagues in the United States, with more opportunities for black players on rosters proportionately than in any other sport, becoming the first modern pro league to hire an African American coach, and opening up front office leadership posts for African Americans.

NOTES

1. Chuck Cooper Foundation, http://chuckcooperfoundation.org.
2. "Chuck Cooper, N.B.A. Player," *New York Times*, February 7, 1984.
3. David Howell, "Six Who Paved the Way," *NBA.com*, April 23, 2013.

FURTHER READING

Lloyd, Earl. *Moonfixer: The Basketball Journey of Earl Lloyd*. New York: Syracuse University Press, 2010.
Thomas, Ron. *They Cleared the Lane: The NBA's Black Pioneers*. Lincoln: University of Nebraska Press, 2004.

#20 Texas Western Wins NCAA Basketball

All-white versus all-black. That shouldn't have been the issue in the 1966 NCAA men's basketball championship game, but it was. Texas Western of El Paso, Texas, which fans knew little about, met Kentucky, a program of basketball royalty even then, at Cole Field House, in College Park, Maryland, on March 19, 1966.

Texas Western's team marked the first time that all five starters for a college basketball team were African Americans. As it so happened, Kentucky, king of the Southeastern Conference, started five white players.

The Miners, Texas Western's nickname, became one of the most famous squads in college basketball history as a result of their 72–65 victory over the Wildcats and their Hall of Fame coach, Adolph Rupp, who had never recruited a black athlete.

"What a piece of history," said one-time prominent college coach Nolan Richardson, who in his younger days played at Texas Western. "If basketball ever took a turn, that was it."[1]

Texas Western's triumph was regarded as a milestone for African American college basketball players and an event that helped move the all-white SEC to begin offering scholarships to black players.

Texas Western, the name of which was later changed to the University of Texas at El Paso, finished 28–1 that season. The Miners' triumph came at the height of the civil rights movement, when breakthroughs in different walks of life in American society were occurring with regularity.

The Miners were led by coach Don Haskins. Haskins, who was nicknamed "The Bear," coached Texas Western from 1961 to 1999, and always insisted that he was not trying to make a statement with the 1965–1966 squad, but was merely playing the best players on the roster. He never sought acclaim for being a barrier breaker, nor did he accept it readily when it came his way anyway.

Although the Miners had a few local players on the roster, the main men who started and scored the majority of the points were from cities far away. Point guard Bobby Joe Hill was from Detroit. Center Nevil Shed, forward Willie Cager, and guard Willie Worsley were all from New York City. Forward Harry Flournoy and guard Orsten Artis were from Gary, Indiana. The biggest talent in the club was powerful David Lattin, a six-foot-six sophomore from Houston.

The makeup of a team like Texas Western, with players brought in from distant places, and featuring an all African American starting lineup, would be commonplace in the 2000s. In the mid-1960s, it was extraordinary. Texas was not exactly a bastion of liberalism, so the black players were always on guard for slights and prejudiced remarks and outright issues of discrimination.

They became a tightly knit unit on the floor, but also off of it, banding together for a common cause. That became a cause célèbre as the Miners marched through the NCAA play-offs in March 1966. Compared to the impact and attention the 68-team tournament garners today, the NCAA play-off games of 1966 were a county fair.

Only 22 teams were invited to participate. Texas Western was placed in the Midwest Regional along with Cincinnati, Kansas, Oklahoma City, and Southern Methodist. The road to the Final Four was a demanding one for the Miners, whose regional quarterfinal was essentially a play-in game.

Nonetheless the Miners dispatched Oklahoma City, 89–74. Texas Western was known for its precise offense and stifling defense, and although the squad might have been a latecomer in terms of national respect and attention, the players did not flinch in the face of tough showdowns.

Cincinnati had been one of the top teams in the country for the entire decade and the Miners battled to top the Bearcats, 78–76, in the regional semifinals. In the regional final, Texas Western edged Kansas, 81–80.

One of the reasons coaches did not want to recruit several black players at once—if they recruited them at all, which depended on where they were located in the country—was the false reputation African American players had for being undisciplined, playground-style competitors. The irony was that the Miners only ran when they got steals on defense. Otherwise they wore teams down with their half-court offense.

"We played the most intelligent, the most boring, the most disciplined game of them all," said Miner guard Willie Worsley of the Final Four teams.[2]

That sent the Miners to the Final Four in Maryland. In the national semifinal, Texas Western outlasted Utah, 85–78. The Utes were led by star forward Jerry Chambers, a tremendous scorer who actually won the Final Four MVP award, and who averaged more than eight points a game in a six-year professional career.

Kentucky came into the tournament with a number 1 ranking and just one loss in 28 games. During Rupp's long tenure, the Wildcats were the bullies of the SEC, the dominant team almost every year. This particular bunch did not have much height and was labeled "Rupp's Runts."

Just because they were undersized, however, did not mean the Kentucky team lacked talent. Featured were sharpshooting guard Louie Dampier, who enjoyed a long career with the American Basketball Association, and six-foot-four Pat Riley, a scrappy player, who later became a widely admired NBA coach and front-office executive.

Tommy Kron, Larry Conley, and Thad Jaracz were also key contributors. Dampier, Riley, and Jaracz received all-American recognition, and all five starters earned first-, second-, or third-team conference honors.

Most believed that the iconic Rupp and his talented crew, who had defeated Dayton, Michigan, and Duke to reach the championship contest, would be able to harness Texas Western's running game and capture the crown. Rupp, known as "The Baron of the Bluegrass," retired with 876 victories (then the most in college basketball history) and four national championships. Texas Western prevented him from adding a fifth.

Completely ignored in the preseason ratings, the Miners had made their case for consideration throughout the regular season, moving up to number 3 nationally by the time tournament play began.

And by the championship game, no one was taking them lightly. The game was close throughout, with Texas Western leading 34–31 at the half, as the 14,253 fans in attendance buzzed over the prospect of an upset. While the game was tight, Texas Western never relinquished the lead in the last 30 minutes of play. Kentucky, led by Dampier and Riley, who each knocked down 19 points, scrambled to keep up.

The Miners' scoring was split among seven players, with Hill the high man with 20 points. The one player Kentucky could never successfully defend against, though, was Lattin, who scored 16 points and ripped down 9 rebounds. Artis added 15 points. Hill, Artis, and Worsley each played all 40 minutes of the game.

As time passed and the significance of the Texas Western group seemed to gain in importance in many minds, the team and Haskins received numerous honors. A

Texas Western's victory over Kentucky in 1966 is the most famous triumph in NCAA men's basketball championship-game history. The Miners' all-black lineup was a first, and they defeated an all-white Wildcats team that in some quarters represented the perpetuation of segregation in college sport. (AP Photo)

book called *Glory Road* told the story of the Miners' championship run and was followed by a 2006 movie of the same name.

Haskins compiled a 719–353 record during his long coaching career in El Paso and was enshrined in the Naismith Memorial Basketball Hall of Fame in 1997. He was also enshrined in the College Basketball Hall of Fame in 2006. He died at age 78 in 2008.

The Miners as a team were inducted into the Naismith Hall in 2007.

It seems difficult to believe that Haskins did not think more about the nature of his all-black starting lineup than he said he did, but assistant coach Moe Iba said that was Haskins.

"The fact that he was doing something historic by playing five blacks, that probably never crossed Don's mind," Iba said. "Hell, he'd have played five kids from Mars if they were his five best players."[3]

NOTES

1. Frank Fitzpatrick, "Texas Western's 1966 Title Left Lasting Legacy," ESPN.com, November 19, 2003.
2. Ibid.
3. Ibid.

FURTHER READING

Fitzpatrick, Frank. *And the Walls Came Tumbling Down: Kentucky, Texas Western, and the Game That Changed American Sports*. New York: Simon & Schuster, 1991.
Haskins, Don, and Dan Wetzel. *Glory Road: My Story of the 1966 NCAA Basketball Championship and How One Team Triumphed against the Odds and Changed America Forever*. New York: Hachette Books, 2005.

#21 Hank Aaron Breaks Babe Ruth's Record

Hank Aaron was never flamboyant. Not for more than five minutes in his long baseball career. But he played so well for so long that he walked away from the sport as one of the greatest players of all time and the owner of a passel of records.

No record Aaron set was more impressive or more revered than when, in 1974, he topped Babe Ruth's career home-run total of 714. Although the former Braves superstar's mark has since been eclipsed by Barry Bonds, the moment of Aaron's ascension is seared into the memories of millions of fans.

It represented a triumph of consistency at a high level and perseverance in the face of obstacles, and once again, in an America that had not quite caught up to the equal rights doctrine that was a founding principle of the country, it also represented conquering the ugliest sort of racism.

By nature a quiet man, Aaron was born in 1934 in Mobile, Alabama, and made his major league debut with the Milwaukee Braves in 1954. He came to prominence in the 1950s, when the Braves were one of the finest teams in baseball, winning one World Series and playing in another. He was surrounded by great talent like Hall of Famers Warren Spahn and Eddie Mathews.

Aaron was also part of the first great collection of African American talent that entered the majors in the years after Jackie Robinson made it possible for blacks to play for any team. He was one of the first great African American stars of the next generation to reap the benefits of Robinson's breakthrough.

This did not mean his early baseball experience was free of racism; it was not. Somewhat lost as an 18-year-old in Wisconsin, as a 19-year-old Aaron was the focus of much racial invective while playing for Jacksonville, Florida, in the Sally League. That was, he was glad to note, the last Aaron saw of the minors.

"Playing in the Sally League was quite a bad experience for me," Aaron once said. "Some of the names I was called, I had never heard them in my life—Jigaboo, burr-head."[1]

Aaron was six foot tall and weighed 180 pounds in his prime. His was not a meaty build, and his surprising power stemmed from his wrists. He may not have resembled a behemoth, but the player nicknamed "Hammerin' Hank" could belt homers with the best of them.

Year after year, Aaron entertained fans in the Midwest and the knowledgeable ones who turned out to see him when the Braves traveled. In an era far more removed from the mass media hype of the present, those who lived in American League cities rarely got a chance to see him play. He was a regular in the all-star game, and the Braves did compete in those two World Series. Otherwise, baseball fans had to be alert to pick up Aaron's games on the *Game of the Week* when the Braves took their turn.

Aaron batted from the right and for the majority of his career was a right fielder, picking up three Gold Gloves roaming that area. He was remarkably durable, hardly ever incurring injuries that caused him to sit out for very long. Slowly, steadily, his lifetime statistics began to pile up. Other greats were cut down by injury. Others watched their skills fade as they aged. Aaron kept on rolling.

A 25-time all-star (including in years when there were two all-star games), Aaron won the 1957 Most Valuable Player Award, and four times by 1967 he led the National League in home runs. He won two batting titles, four RBI titles, and led the NL in runs scored three times.

By the 1973 season it was apparent that if steady Aaron continued at his usual pace, he was going to catch up to Ruth's record of 714 home runs, which had stood since 1935. As Aaron's homers mounted up, he began receiving thousands of letters from baseball fans and members of the public. (At the end of 1973 the U.S. Postal Service presented a plaque to Aaron for receiving more mail—930,000 pieces—than anyone else in the country who was not a politician.)

But not all of those letters were from well-wishers. Mixed in with the letters of praise and adulation was distressing hate mail. Some of the letters were death threats.

Aaron and members of his immediate family began receiving protection from the FBI, and he began staying in hotels separate from his teammates, registering under assumed names. The situation was pathetic and outrageous. Aaron was hunting down one of the most revered of records in all of sports, and he could not enjoy it. The irrationality of some of the letters pointed up two things: how beloved Babe Ruth was and how deeply the United States was still mired in the muck of racism.

Aaron hit 40 home runs in 1973 at age 39, a remarkable feat in itself. He blasted number 713 on September 29, one day before the end of the regular season, but alas, could not tie Ruth in the final game of the season.

Being positioned on that precipice for the entire off-season proved extremely stressful to Aaron, as he had to wait six months to try to hit that magical homer. During the off-season the barrage of mail continued.

There was controversy at the start of the next season. The Braves, who had moved to Atlanta several years earlier, opened on the road and wanted Aaron to break Ruth's record at home, where the team's fans could most enjoy it and where the Braves could reap the benefits of large attendance figures. The plan was for Aaron to sit out the first three games of the season in Cincinnati, but Commissioner Bowie Kuhn ordered the Braves to play him in at least two of the three games.

Sure enough, on his first swing of the 1974 season, Aaron belted a home run off Reds pitcher Jack Billingham to tie Ruth.

"Thank-you very much," Aaron said to cheers when the game was stopped for a few minutes, "and I'm just glad it's almost over with."[2]

The Braves were satisfied when Aaron did not break the record on the road, and the home-run watch resumed in Atlanta on April 8. The Braves were right about one thing: the local fans were fascinated and wanted to be on hand for history. For the game against the Los Angeles Dodgers, a team record 53,775 fans turned out. The game was also on national television.

Every Aaron at-bat now was an event. Aaron walked in the second inning, the suspense building. He then stepped into the batter's box in the fourth inning against

Demonstrating all-around superb play year after year in his long career, Hank Aaron broke Babe Ruth's career home-run record with a mighty swing on April 8, 1974, in Atlanta. This was the 715th blast of Aaron's career. He retired with a record 755 homers, a mark later broken by Barry Bonds. (AP Photo)

LA southpaw Al Downing. Aaron swung and connected, and the ball sailed toward left-center at Fulton County Stadium, clearing the wall and landing in the Braves' bullpen, where it was snared by Atlanta reliever Tom House.

As Aaron circled the bases, two teenaged fans darted onto the field to congratulate him, though at first they merely scared him. House dashed through the outfield to home plate to deliver the ball to Aaron, as the game paused and festivities ensued. Broadcasters had had a long time to think about what they might say when the record was busted. Vince Scully, handling broadcast duties for NBC, was his usual eloquent self in a memorable commentary.

Once Scully announced that the ball was "gone," he went silent for several minutes and let the sounds of the scene permeate the broadcast, from bursting fireworks to the prolonged cheering. Then he spoke up.

"What a marvelous moment for baseball," Scully said. "What a marvelous moment for Atlanta and the state of Georgia; what a marvelous moment for the country and the world. A black man is getting a standing ovation in the Deep South for breaking a record of an all-time baseball idol. And it is a great moment for all of us, and particularly for Henry Aaron."[3]

After spending his entire career with the Braves, for the final two seasons of his playing days, Aaron returned to Milwaukee as a designated hitter for the expansion Brewers, then in the American League. He retired after the 1976 season at age 42, with 23 seasons under his belt. Besides the home-run record, Aaron collected 2,274 runs batted in, also a record, one that is still standing. His lifetime average was .305, and he smacked 3,771 hits, third on the all-time list.

Aaron was inducted into the Baseball Hall of Fame in 1982. In 1999 baseball created the Hank Aaron Award, given to the best offensive player in each league each year. Statues of Aaron were erected outside the ballparks in both Milwaukee and Atlanta, and he received the Presidential Medal of Freedom in 2002 from President George W. Bush.

NOTES

1. Tom Stanton, *Hank Aaron and the Home Run That Changed America* (New York: William Morrow, 2004), 22.

2. Ibid., 206.

3. Vince Scully, NBC broadcast, Atlanta Braves-Los Angeles Dodgers, April 8, 1974, www.youtube.com/watch?v=GvfYg_kNtTk.

FURTHER READING

Aaron, Hank, and Dick Schaap. *Home Run: My Life in Pictures*. Tampa, FL: Total Sports, 1999.

Aaron, Hank, and Lonnie Wheeler. *I Had a Hammer: The Hank Aaron Story*. New York: Harper Perennial, 2007.

Bryant, Howard. *The Last Hero: A Life of Henry Aaron*. New York: Anchor, 2011.

Vascellaro, Charlie. *Hank Aaron: A Biography*. Santa Barbara, CA: Greenwood Press, 2005.

#22 Fritz Pollard, the NFL's First African American Coach

In the late 1970s and early 1980s there was an outcry for the National Football League to hire its first African American head coach. It was long overdue, the argument went, and there were qualified candidates.

The only thing wrong with the discussion was that there had already been an African American head coach in the league. It had occurred so long before and had passed through the night sky so quickly that the more modern-day debate overlooked the tenure of Fritz Pollard.

Born Frederick Douglass Pollard, he grew up in the Rogers Park area of Chicago at a time when it was virtually an all-German neighborhood. That's how he acquired the nickname Fritz.

The NFL was founded as the American Professional Football Association in 1920 and changed its name in 1921. The Chicago Cardinals were there at the beginning and are now the Arizona Cardinals. The Chicago Bears were there at the beginning as the Decatur Staleys. And the Green Bay Packers joined up in 1921.

Aside from those teams, the franchises originally welcomed as members in the fledgling league are all defunct, including the Akron Pros. Like many of the first NFL clubs, the Akron team was founded as a semipro club. The Akron team started play in 1908 as the Akron Indians. The name was changed to the Pros in 1920 when the team went pro, although in 1923 it reverted back to the Indians, then folded in 1927.

In 1921 Pollard was co-coach of the Pros, making him the first African American coach not only of an NFL team, but of any in the four major team sports leagues in the United States. He also coached the Hammond Pros for a handful of games a few years later. His coaching tenures were brief, and for a time his achievement was forgotten or overlooked.

Pollard was born in 1894 in Chicago and enjoyed a long life, living to be 92. In pictures of him as a young man he resembles a jazz musician more than a hardy football player, but he was highly regarded for his talent. At five foot nine and 165 pounds, Pollard was no giant, but it was not uncommon for running backs to be that size at the time.

As a youth Pollard attended Lane Tech, and when he first dressed out as an end for the high school team, he weighed 89 pounds. Pollard attended Brown University, where he was an all-American. In 1916 Brown and Pollard competed in the first Rose Bowl. As the only black on the squad, Pollard was subjected

Although for years his pioneering contribution was overlooked, Fritz Pollard was the first African American in the National Football League. Pollard was the player-coach of the Akron Pros in 1920. (AP Photo)

to discrimination on the train going west and at the hotel in California. It was hardly the only time in his life he had to overcome prejudice.

After college, in 1920, Pollard and Bobby Marshall became the first two African Americans to play in the new NFL. With Akron, Pollard got to play against the legendary Jim Thorpe. Of course he knew who Jim Thorpe was, and he surmised that Thorpe knew who he was.

The men engaged in a short exchange, Pollard said. "He said, 'Hello, little black boy.' I said, 'Hello, big black boy.'" Pollard said Thorpe was taken aback.[1]

That year, the NFL's inaugural season, Pollard played in the backfield for Akron, and the Pros won the first NFL title with an 8–0–3 record. One of Pollard's teammates was Paul Robeson. Robeson, later famous as a singer, actor, and a civil rights activist, had been an all-American player at Rutgers. Pollard sought Robeson for the Pros, and while Robeson studied for his law degree at Columbia University he played in the NFL. Robeson, who was six foot three and 220 pounds, played one year with the Pros and another season with the Milwaukee Badgers before moving on to his other endeavors.

Pollard was not only one of the first two African Americans in the league. When he took a turn as signal-caller in addition to his running back play, Pollard also became the first African American to play quarterback in the NFL.

In 1921 Pollard was a player-coach when Akron finished 8–3–1.

"I wanted the honor of being the first black coach," Pollard said decades later when interviewed by NFL Films in a video adapted for use by the Pro Football Hall of Fame.[2]

Pollard also acknowledged that he was fairly small for the NFL even then and "no one had any sympathy for me."[3]

He was also subject to some hard-nosed play, in which prejudiced whites were not content merely to tackle him, but also tried to injure him. Pollard mostly tried to ignore them, and when he popped up from the ground he did so with alacrity, trying to show that he was not hurt.

"I looked at them and grinned," Pollard said.[4]

In 1925 Pollard coached the Hammond Pros, an Indiana-based team located near Chicago.

At one time or another between 1920 and 1926, Pollard and five other African Americans suited up for Hammond. During this period there were only nine African American players in the NFL. That was as far as things went for the time being. Pollard and the other blacks were no longer welcome after 1926, and until 1946 no other black players competed in the NFL. It is believed that Washington Redskins owner George Preston Marshall, an influential leader who was an avowed racist, helped block inclusion of African Americans in the league during that period. Opportunities for black players began opening up again after World War II, at roughly the same time that Jackie Robinson made his impact on Major League Baseball.

After his NFL career ended, Pollard stayed in football, organizing all-black barnstorming teams. He coached some of them, too. The most prominent among them was the Chicago Black Hawks. The club played all-white squads in the Chicago area and then in winter adjourned to the West Coast to meet teams there in milder weather. The Black Hawks folded in 1932 during the Great Depression.

After his football career ended, Pollard engaged in a number of successful business pursuits, starting a coal company, working as an agent for black stage talent, and engaging in several other ventures.

After a gap of about 60 years, the NFL's first black coach of the modern football era was hired by the then Los Angeles Raiders in 1989, when former lineman Art Shell was brought on board. Not much was written about Fritz Pollard at the time—he had died three years earlier—and it took some time for the misconception about Shell being the first black coach to be corrected.

In 1954 Pollard was inducted into the College Football Hall of Fame, and in 2005 he was inducted into the Pro Football Hall of Fame. The hall's description of Pollard calls him "a pro football pioneer in more ways than one."[5]

Pollard, a handsome man who maintained his hair and looks in old age, was 80 when he sat down with NFL Films to reminisce. He was still spry enough to throw around a football in his driveway.

"I think I am a very fortunate man," Pollard said of his overall good health, a statement that could be applied to his entire life.[6]

NOTES

1. *1974 Interview with Fritz Pollard*, www.nfl.com/videos/nfl-videos.
2. Ibid.
3. Ibid.
4. Ibid.
5. Pro Football Hall of Fame, www.profootballhof.com (accessed May 3, 2015).
6. *1974 Interview with Fritz Pollard.*

FURTHER READING

Caroll, John M. *Fritz Pollard: Pioneer in Racial Advancement*. Urbana: University of Illinois Press, 1998.

Duru, N. Jeremi. "The Fritz Pollard Alliance, the Rooney Rule, and the Quest to Level the Playing Field in the National Football League." *Virginia Sports and Entertainment Law Journal* 7 (2007): 179.

Rhoden, William C. *Third and a Mile: From Fritz Pollard to Michael Vick—An Oral History of the Trials, Tears and Triumphs of the Black Quarterback*. New York: ESPN Books, 2007.

#23 The Black Sox Scandal

The greatest shame of baseball—besides its refusal to offer full opportunity to African American players for more than 60 years—was the Chicago White Sox players' fixing the 1919 World Series at the behest of gamblers.

These nefarious efforts shook the credibility of the nation's most popular sport and could have ruined the game. Some details of the plot to sell out the World Series, who actually tried to win, and who actually tried to lose, remain in dispute. But the broad overview is known, and the repercussions of the bold scheme were marked.

In 1919 the Chicago White Sox were the best team in the American League and won the pennant. They were heavily favored to win the World Series over the National League champion Cincinnati Reds. The Reds were a good club, but not viewed as having enough firepower and all-around talent to defeat the White Sox.

At that time gambling was commonplace in baseball, and it has long been suggested that Arnold Rothstein, a kingpin of the Chicago underworld, dreamed up the plan to throw the Series Cincinnati's way and clean up while betting on the underdogs. However, others in the gambling world were involved, and although the effort became more and more complicated, it did not unravel.

In the end the White Sox lost the best-of-nine Series to Cincinnati, 5–3. Rumors circulated during the games that they were not all on the up-and-up, and Hugh Fullerton, a prominent sportswriter of the era, kept track of plays he thought were suspicious. The World Series ended, there was considerable conjecture, but no proof came out, and time passed without any concrete action being taken. The Reds celebrated their championship. The White Sox slinked into the off-season.

Owner Charles Comiskey and manager Kid Gleason were among those who were uneasy about what they witnessed, but they made no declarations. The good of the game was at stake, so they swallowed any concerns they might have uttered. Months after the World Series ended, Fullerton wrote a provocative newspaper series telling the public that the results may have been fixed and that the White Sox may have lost on purpose.

The 1920 season began and was played, but eventually a grand jury was impaneled, and as pressure mounted, several White Sox regulars, including stars, were called to testify. At one point it was revealed that confessions had been signed by ace pitcher Ed Cicotte and exalted hitter "Shoeless" Joe Jackson. Eight players were indicted, and the case went to trial, whereupon it was learned that any confessions penned by Jackson and Cicotte had disappeared.

Meanwhile, in the aftermath of the World Series and while suspicions were being hurled around like snowballs, top baseball officials met and decided they needed to take a firmer grip on the game and run off the gambling element. They approached a federal judge named Kenesaw Mountain Landis to become the sport's first commissioner. Landis demanded many changes, but baseball was so anxious to hire a law enforcer that they acceded to every one. Landis ended up with a contract for life and the dictatorial authority to make unilateral decisions that he felt were in the best interests of the sport.

When the White Sox players went on trial in Chicago, they were treated more like celebrities than like accused lawbreakers. They were acquitted and celebrated in relief, ready to resume their careers in the 1921 season. The iron-fisted, white-maned Landis had another fate in store for them.

He had watched the proceedings closely, scrutinizing every word of testimony, and come to some conclusions. Although there was some doubt about whether all of the players charged received bribes of up to $10,000, and there was also some doubt about whether some of the players went along with the fix and did not try their best, he did not care. All of them were aware of the proposed scheme, had either witnessed or participated in discussions about throwing games, and had done nothing to prevent the fix from playing out.

Landis took the hanging-judge approach and banned all eight players from baseball for life. Nearly a century later, long after all of the White Sox players involved have died, their names are still tainted with ignominy and remain on

Considered the most disgraceful scandal in sports history, the Black Sox Scandal of 1919 nearly destroyed Major League Baseball. Accused of fixing the World Series, the Chicago White Sox saw eight players banned for life after they lost to the Cincinnati Reds, including legendary hitter Shoeless Joe Jackson. An offshoot of the scandal was the hiring by the owners of baseball's first commissioner, Kenesaw Mountain Landis. (AP Photo)

baseball's banned list. The eight players are Cicotte, Jackson, Buck Weaver, Oscar "Happy" Felsch, Claude "Lefty" Williams, Fred McMullin, Charles "Swede" Risberg, and Arnold "Chick" Gandihl.

When the players exited the Chicago Criminal Court building, supposedly a little boy looked up at Shoeless Joe and said, "Say it ain't so, Joe," to which Jackson supposedly replied, "Yes kid, I'm afraid it is." While that encounter has taken root in lore, most doubt it really happened.[1]

As an immediate side effect, not specifically germane to the punishment, Landis's ruling gutted the White Sox's lineup and reduced the club from one of the best in the American League to one of the worst. The White Sox did not win another pennant for 40 years, long after the death of Comiskey, although other members of his family had remained involved with the team for most of that period.

Cicotte might have been a borderline Hall of Famer. He recorded one of the best career earned-run averages, won 29 games in a season, and is credited with being the inventor of the knuckleball. But Cicotte was the linchpin of the scheme. Pitching the first game of the Series, he purposely hit a batter as the signal that the fix was on, and he did collect $10,000. Risberg and Gandihl were regarded as the ringleaders.

Jackson, one of the sport's rare .400 hitters (.408 in 1911), said he never wanted to be part of any deal, tried to return money left in his hotel room, and tried to report the plot to Comiskey, but was rebuffed. He said he then tried his hardest in the games. In later years, some, notably slugger Ted Williams, took up the cause of getting Jackson, a lifetime .356 hitter, reinstated so he could be considered for the Hall of Fame, but the commissioner's office never took any action.

Likewise, Weaver, the third baseman, listened in on the plot in its planning stages, but said his only crime was not ratting out his teammates. He played his best, he said, and Weaver devoted far more effort over the following 35 years to clearing his name. His appeals to baseball went on long after Landis died while still in office in 1944, but were unsuccessful.

Other than the eight accused, the rest of the White Sox were known as the "Clean Sox." One was Hall of Fame catcher Ray Schalk who years later said that if pitcher Red Faber had been able to participate, the White Sox would have "beaten the Reds despite the gamblers."[2] Faber, another Hall of Famer, missed the Series altogether because of injury.

The ramifications of the players' sleazy decision to fix the outcome of the World Series damaged the game's image and might have had longer-lasting effects if not for the introduction of the lively ball in 1920, which enabled Babe Ruth to lift the game from the rubble. It literally was a whole new ballgame in the 1920s, when Ruth energized crowds with his awesome slugging.

Cicotte lived a quiet life out of the limelight after his disgrace, residing on a farm in northern Michigan. He once broke his silence in an interview with prominent Detroit sportswriter Joe Falls, saying he had lived a clean life ever since the scandal and that if taking the bribe was the worst thing he ever did, he could live with that.

Landis was baseball's first commissioner, and while the structure of the game's administration has changed in other ways, there has always been a commissioner's name at the top of the letterhead on the sport's stationery. Landis was given a mandate to clean up the sport, to do whatever it took to eradicate gambling elements from the game, and the ripple effects of his zero tolerance stand, forbidding players, coaches, managers, and other insiders from gambling on baseball, are still felt today. Inappropriate gambling remains one of baseball's cardinal sins.

NOTES

1. Art Spander, "Shoeless Joe Jackson Carries a Label He Doesn't Deserve," *The Sporting News*, June 4, 1984.
2. "Ray Schalk, Obituary," *The Sporting News*, June 6, 1970.

FURTHER READING

Asinof, Eliot. *Eight Men Out: The Black Sox and the 1919 World Series*. New York: Holt Paperbacks, 2000.
Carney, Gene. *Burying the Black Sox: How Baseball's Cover-Up of the 1919 World Series Fix Almost Succeeded*. Washington, DC: Potomac Books, 2006.
Lamb, William F. *Black Sox in the Courtroom: The Grand Jury, Criminal Trial, and Civil Litigation*. Jefferson, NC: McFarland, 2013.
Nathan, Daniel A. *Saying It's So: A Cultural History of the Black Sox Scandal*. Urbana: University of Illinois Press, 2005.

#24 Bill Russell, First African American NBA Coach

Bill Russell has been acclaimed as the greatest winner in team sport. The six-foot-nine center for the Boston Celtics was the leader of and a member of 11 NBA championship teams in 13 seasons during the greatest pro basketball dynasty ever assembled.

In addition, before Russell set foot on an NBA court, he had won an Olympic gold medal and twice led the University of San Francisco to NCAA championships. Where Russell went, titles were sure to follow.

Russell played for the Celtics between 1956 and 1969, and he revolutionized pro basketball with his shot-blocking ability. Unlike any player who had come before him, and few who have come after, Russell had the leaping talent and skill to block an opponent's shot and catch it in the air rather than simply swat it into the crowd. That ability enabled him to start innumerable fast breaks for the Celtics.

"On offense, it's possible to take a break, to stand around a bit, let other players take over," Russell said. "On defense, if you take a break, a good offensive team will burn you."[1]

Surrounded by Hall of Fame talent at every position and guided by the brilliant coaching of Red Auerbach, Russell was the right player at the right time for the

Boston Celtics center Bill Russell (left) with previous coach Red Auerbach, is considered the greatest winner in team sports. The 6-foot-9 star led Boston to 11 NBA titles in 13 years ending in 1969. Adding to his fame and accomplishments, Russell became the first African American head coach in major American team sports for the final three seasons of his career. (AP Photo)

right team. Auerbach coached the Celtics to nine titles in 10 years, but in 1966 decided that he wanted to step away from the bench and concentrate on front-office personnel moves.

Knowing that Russell, a man of great pride and a finicky personality, would not take to coaching by just anyone, Auerbach approached his star and asked him if he would be interested in succeeding him. Russell accepted the challenge, which was doubled by the fact that he had no plans to retire.

"I wasn't offered the job because I was a Negro," Russell said at the time. "I was offered the job because Red figured I could do it."[2]

The hiring of Russell as coach of the world champions made him the first African American head coach in any prominent American team sport since Fritz Pollard's brief leadership role in the NFL in the early 1920s. The switch was effected with a minimum of fanfare at the same time that controversy was brewing in baseball, where lobbying had been increasing for some time to give an African American a chance.

Starting with the 1966–1967 season, Russell worked as a player-coach, relying on some of his savvy teammates to send in tips on moves to him while he was on the court.

Auerbach's move was barrier breaking, but it made plenty of sense to the Celtics and Boston fans. Although Boston was seen as somewhat of a racist northern town, and Russell had complained about racism in the community when he arrived as a player, if you were a Celtics fan you had had considerable time to get used to both Russell and numerous other African American players on the scene.

Between the late 1950s and mid-1960s, when Russell ascended to the coaching job, the Celtics had been in the forefront of using black players. Auerbach never counted, but the Celtics were the first NBA team to ever employ five African American starters. The occasion was December 26, 1964, when Hall of Fame forward Tommy Heinsohn was injured. Overlapping with Russell were such African American Hall of Famers as guards Sam Jones and K. C. Jones and forward Tom Sanders. Plus there were top guns like Willie Naulls, who filled in for Heinsohn on that day. Young John Thompson, long before he became a famous college coach at Georgetown, served as Russell's backup for a while. Veterans like Sihugo Green and Woody Sauldsberry also did some Celtics time.

The Russell coaching tenure was a success, although the Celtics dynasty was at risk as a whole as he—the foundation of it all—aged and several other stars were coming to the ends of their careers. Auerbach was a personnel magician, bringing in players who had been discarded by teams for which they excelled, squeezing out a couple of useful years from them as they filled out their resumes with championship runs.

Players like Naulls, Bailey Howell, and Clyde Lovellette had been stars elsewhere, but played smaller, yet still critical, roles with Boston at the tail end of their careers.

The first season under Russell, the Celtics finished 60–21, ordinarily a good enough record to top the Eastern Division. However, that season, with Russell's rival Wilt Chamberlain at center, the Philadelphia 76ers reached the franchise's apex to that point of its existence and not only beat out the Celtics during the regular season, but eliminated them from the play-offs. This was only the second time in Russell's NBA career that Boston did not win the crown.

Philadelphia was so good that year that it was widely believed that this marked the end of the Boston dynasty and perhaps the beginning of a new one by a team located 300 miles away. The 1967–1968 season results seemed to support that notion. Boston finished 54–28 that season, again a very good showing, but not good enough to top the 76ers.

But in an epic seven-game series, the Celtics upended the 76ers to advance to another Finals, where they defeated the Los Angeles Lakers in a six-game set.

One by one the aging Celtic greats were retiring, and Auerbach was hard pressed to resupply through the college draft, because they were always last in the pecking order. Around the league, a point had been reached at which some teams did not want to trade with the Celtics, because they found themselves repeatedly burned by the results.

During the 1968–1969 season, which would prove to be Russell's last as coach, although he didn't announce it, the Celtics looked their age. Their regular-season mark was 48–34, quite respectable, but it left them just fourth in the East. It was a long road through the play-offs, with the disadvantage of not having home-court seventh games if Boston was to win an 11th title.

"The Celtic 'system' was designed to permit intelligent, winning players to endlessly use their own curiosity and creativity to accomplish results," Russell said.[3]

They did so. Bob Cousy and Bill Sharman were long gone. K. C. Jones had retired, and so had Heinsohn. The remaining stalwarts, besides Russell, were Sam Jones, Sanders, and John Havlicek, and the Celtics had a spate of new young guards, including Larry Siegfried and Don Chaney, Mal Graham, and Emmette Bryant.

The Lakers, so often thwarted by the Celtics, were spoiling for revenge, and had the seventh game at home in L.A. this time when the knotted series headed for the finale. In a careless gesture of optimism, team officials had not only sent clusters of balloons to the ceiling of The Forum, they had passed out brochures outlining how the postgame celebration would unfold. These were the Lakers of Wilt Chamberlain, Jerry West, and Elgin Baylor, an extraordinary collection of talent. But once the Celtics read the instruction brochures, their motivation burned on the extra fuel.

Boston prevailed once again, banking the team's 11th championship. Russell announced he was finished as coach and retired with two championships won on his watch. Russell was the first of many African American head coaches in the NBA, a league that has proven itself more open-minded over a longer period than the other three major U.S. team sports leagues. Among Russell's black successors who won NBA titles coaching was his old friend K. C. Jones, who twice won crowns with Boston in the 1980s.

NOTES

1. "Bill Russell: 12 Quotes about Basketball," *Christian Science Monitor*, November 2, 2013, www.csmonitor.com/Bill-Russell-12-quotes.

2. D. L. Chandler, "NBA Legend Bill Russell Became First Black Coach in Pro Sports 46 Years Ago Today," *NewsOne*, April 18, 2012, www.newsone.com/2003287/bill-russell-first-black-coach-in-pro-sports/.

3. "Bill Russell: 12 Quotes about Basketball."

FURTHER READING

Freedman, Lew. *Dynasty: The Rise of the Boston Celtics*. Guilford, CT: Lyons Press, 2008.

Nelson, Maury. *Bill Russell: A Biography*. Santa Barbara, CA: Greenwood Press, 2005.

Russell, Bill, and David Falkner. *Russell Rules: 11 Lessons on Leadership from the 20th Century's Greatest Winner*. New York: New American Library, 2001.

Russell, Bill, and Alan Steinberg. *Red and Me: My Coach and My Lifelong Friend*. New York: HarperCollins, 2010.

Russell, William F. *Second Wind: The Memoirs of an Opinionated Man*. New York: Random House, 1979.

#25 Don Larsen's Perfect Game

In all of the Major League Baseball played over nearly 140 years, there has only been one game like Don Larsen's 1956 gem for the New York Yankees. On October 8, 1956, the right-hander, born in Michigan City, Indiana, in 1929, pitched the first and only perfect game in World Series history.

The World Series began in 1903, and it is the showcase competition of baseball, crowning the season. The Series results in the naming of a champion for the season. Every play is magnified in importance, and with the eyes of the whole baseball world on the participants, every play and move is more highly pressurized than games contested during the regular season.

During the 1950s the Yankees were the dominant team in baseball, far superior to all other contenders. Under manager Casey Stengel, New York won 10 pennants in 12 years, between 1948 and 1960. This was one of the greatest runs in the history of the game, and the 1956 Series fell in the middle of this powerhouse team's streak. The Yankees were supremely talented at all positions, and that included having depth among starting pitchers.

Larsen, who spent 14 years in the majors with several teams, was not one of the best pitchers in the league. His lifetime record was 81–91, and he suffered through some awful seasons, including a 3–21 mark with the Baltimore Orioles in 1954, one of the worst single-season marks of all time.

Never before and never since: New York Yankee right-hander Don Larsen threw the only perfect game in World Series history on October 8, 1956, to beat the Brooklyn Dodgers, 2–0. There has only been one other no-hitter in big-league post-season play. (AP Photo)

However, the 1956 season was Larsen's best. He finished 11–5 in the regular season with a 3.26 earned run average and earned Stengel's trust as a spot starter and long reliever. Larsen stood six foot four, weighed about 215 pounds, wore a crew cut, and was known as a player who enjoyed the night life. In fact, it has often been stated—true or not—that the night before fate reached out and tapped Larsen on the shoulder, he had been out late partying. By then Larsen had earned the nickname "Gooneybird" for his off-field antics. In a famous quote—Stengel had many of them—about Larsen's exploits, Stengel commented on a one-car auto accident involving Larsen: "He was either out pretty late or out pretty early."[1]

None of the background mattered on this day, though. The Yankees' opponent was the Brooklyn Dodgers, a team New York had outlasted a few times in recent Series. The first game was played on October 3 at Ebbets Field, and Brooklyn won,

6–3. The second game, also at Ebbets Field, also went to the Dodgers, 13–8. Larsen was hit hard in that one.

The Yankees won the next two games in Yankee Stadium, 5–3 and 6–2. Larsen got the nod to start game 5, also at Yankee Stadium before 64,519 fans. Sal Maglie started for the Dodgers, and he was pretty stingy. The Yankees scored a single run in the fourth inning and another single run in the sixth for a 2–0 lead. Altogether New York only touched the Dodgers for five hits, one of them a Mickey Mantle home run.

So the game was close and suspenseful throughout. Larsen had to be as good as he was in order to win it. A baseball perfect game consists of nine innings of perfects wherein the opposition does not score a run, get a hit, or put anyone on base. That means there are 27 men up at the plate and 27 men sent back to the dugout making outs. At that time Larsen's effort was just the sixth perfect game in the then 80 years of major league history, including the regular season and World Series.

Aside from the unexpected drama of Larsen's performance, the Yankees needed to win the game to take the World Series lead. The Series was knotted 2–2, and whichever team was going to win, this was most likely to be the turning point. A 3–2 lead with two games to go would put the winner in a commanding position.

Larsen was so dominating that day that he threw just 97 pitches in the complete game. His control was so sharp that only once, while Dodger shortstop PeeWee Reese was batting, did he go to three balls on a hitter, so Larsen did not even come close to walking anyone.

By the eighth inning, there was not a person in the ballpark who did not realize what was going on. Larsen handled the three Dodger batters effortlessly, leaving only the ninth inning ahead. By that point Larsen had struck out six Brooklyn hitters.

As the top of the ninth dawned for the visiting Dodgers, there were no doubt many sitting in Yankee Stadium biting their nails or holding their breath. Showing that his effectiveness wasn't waning, Larsen got ahead two strikes and no balls to Brooklyn outfielder Carl Furillo, who flew out to right field. One down.

Next up was dangerous Brooklyn catcher Roy Campanella, who that season won his third National League Most Valuable Player Award. If Larsen felt he had to be extra careful with Campanella, it didn't really show. Once again he got ahead two strikes and no balls before Campanella grounded out second to first.

History came down to a last chance for Brooklyn. It was pitcher Maglie's turn at bat, and there was no way he was coming to the plate. Manager Walt Alston inserted Dale Mitchell to pinch hit.

Mitchell, a lifetime .312 hitter, was coming to the end of his career and was a late-season pickup for Brooklyn, only appearing in 19 regular-season games. In fact, except for one more pinch-hitting assignment, in game 7, this was the last at-bat of Mitchell's career. Once again Larsen worked the batter to 0–2, but this time he sneaked the last pitch past Mitchell, striking him out, looking to end the game and crown the perfect-game achievement.

The swiftly worked game took just two hours and six minutes to complete, and the moment the ball nestled into New York catcher Yogi Berra's glove, he sprinted to the mound and leapt into Larsen's arms. The celebratory picture is the most remembered image from the day.

"When it was over, I was so happy I felt like crying," Larsen said.[2]

Brooklyn regrouped and won game 6, but the Yankees steamrolled the Dodgers in game 7 to win the Series. Larsen was named Most Valuable Player.

The World Series perfect game remains the signature moment of his career for Larsen, who is in his eighties, and stands as one of the greatest games in baseball history.

NOTES

1. *Baseball Almanac*, http:www.baseballalmanac.com/quotes (accessed May 3, 2015).
2. Ibid.

FURTHER READING

Barra, Allen. *Yogi Berra: Eternal Yankee*. New York: W. W. Norton, 2010.
Berra, Yogi, and Tom Horton. *Yogi: It Ain't Over*. New York: McGraw-Hill, 1989.
Larsen, Don, and Mark Shaw. *The Perfect Yankee: The Incredible Story of the Greatest Miracle in Baseball History*. New York: Sports Publishing, 2012.
Paper, Lew. *Perfect: Don Larsen's Miraculous World Series Game and the Men Who Made It Happen*. New York: New American Library, 2010.

#26 Joe Namath's Super Bowl Prediction

Joe Namath grew up in the coal country of Western Pennsylvania and played college football at Alabama, but he didn't seem to be truly at home in football until he joined the New York Jets.

Namath's personality was a perfect fit for the Big Apple. He was flamboyant and colorful, ate up the New York night life, and definitely earned his nickname, "Broadway Joe."

Namath was born to be a star, and New York made him one. Of course he contributed, with his talent on the field and brashness off it. Right from the start, when Namath was drafted as the number 1 pick in the American Football League draft in 1965, he became the symbol of more than just a good football player.

A half century ago, Namath signing a contract for $400,000 made him front-page news. For someone who was about to start living large, the dollar signs attached to his name enhanced his status. The implication of Namath's signing by the AFL, the upstart league formed in 1960 that was doing battle for credibility with the established National Football League, carried import. It demonstrated that the younger league was working toward equal footing and might have the resources to do so.

Namath, who stood six foot two and possessed an easy charm, was regarded as a suave playboy. He wore fur coats and bantered with the sports media. He came through on the field as well, gaining all-star status.

But decades later Namath is best remembered for his outspoken confidence before Super Bowl III, when the Jets, champions of the AFL, were taking on the Baltimore Colts, champions of the NFL. The arrangement of a championship contest between the two leagues was the forerunner of a complete merger.

Public opinion favored the older NFL as the stronger league, and the way the first two Super Bowls turned out, most of the evidence did tilt in favor of the NFL. The Green Bay Packers breezed past the Kansas City Chiefs and the Oakland Raiders in those games.

Yet Namath was undaunted, even in the face of what appeared to be a dominating Colts club. The Colts, coached by future Hall of Famer Don Shula, finished 13–1 in the regular season, with a backup quarterback to boot. The legendary Johnny Unitas was injured in the preseason, and Earl Morrall stepped in as his replacement. Morrall turned in his finest season and won the league's Most Valuable Player Award. The Colts steamrolled the opposition with such stars as tight end John Mackey, defensive back Bob Boyd, defensive lineman Bubba Smith, and linebacker Mike Curtis.

The Jets went 11–3, and besides Namath featured such stalwarts as receivers Don Maynard and George Sauer, running back Matt Snell, and defensive back Johnny Sample.

Namath and the Jets refused to believe that they were the inferior product, and Namath defied protocol by "guaranteeing" that New York would beat Baltimore in the January 12, 1969, Super Bowl in Miami.

It was critical for the Jets to make a good showing to enhance the stature of the AFL, and not many football people predicted that they could do it. The hullabaloo surrounding the game weighed heavily in favor of the Colts being "the greatest team of all time" and the Jets being patsies who would be easily overrun.

Brash, out-spoken, and the highest paid player in football when he signed with the New York Jets for $400,000, former Alabama quarterback Joe Namath brought creditability to the American Football League and forever established himself in football lore when he accurately predicted his team would upset the Baltimore Colts in Super Bowl III. (AP Photo)

The betting odds set by the well-known Jimmy the Greek made the Colts a 17-point favorite. The *New York Daily News* listed Baltimore as a 16-point favorite. Baltimore added two playoff wins to its regular-season total and appeared fearsome on defense, with four shutouts. The Colts crushed the Cleveland Browns, 34–0, in the NFL championship game. Baltimore's numbers made a good case for its supporters.

Namath, whose season-long stats were not as good across the board as Morrall's, followed the news and became irritated that almost no one was giving his team a chance to win the big game. He was offended when that chatter spilled over to friends of his. He began telling people he knew to bet on the Jets, because point spread or not, New York was going to win.

By the time the Jets headed south to Miami, Namath was setting the stage. His statements to New York sportswriters were becoming bolder and bolder. He watched film, and in his mind the AFL was deep in quarterbacks who were better than

Morrall. For *New York Times* columnist Dave Anderson he listed Daryle Lamonica of Oakland, John Hadl of San Diego, Bob Griese of Miami, and himself as those who could outplay the Colts' leader. Then he threw in his own backup, Babe Parilli.

Namath wasn't playing around. He truly believed what he was saying. This kind of rating was not done by prominent players. The only athlete of Namath's stature who really let loose with thoughts in such a manner was Muhammad Ali. The others kept mum about what they really thought about foes. It was the old approach of not giving the other guys bulletin board material to rile them up. Namath didn't care. He was providing bulletin board material that he knew would aggravate the Colts.

In Fort Lauderdale, where the Jets made their final preparations, Namath ran into Lou Michaels, who was from the same area of Pennsylvania but was a defensive lineman for the Colts. They got into an argument in a bar. Namath told Michaels the Jets were going to kick the heck out of Baltimore. Michaels thought Namath was ill-mannered and was acting inappropriately for a pro athlete. Michaels almost blew a gasket when Namath called Unitas "an old man" who "was over the hill."[1]

Finally, at a banquet before the Super Bowl where he was being awarded his league's MVP award, Namath responded to a heckler with the most vivid declaration of his life. "The Jets will win Sunday," he said. "I guarantee it."[2]

The furor that followed was slow to build, both in newspapers and in conversation. It gained greater currency later. About 90 percent of the people on the scene picked Baltimore to win. Namath gained fame for being a true believer who said what he was going to do and then went out and did it.

Although this was unprecedented, the New York papers, usually quick to pick up on any minor development, did not go to town on this "guarantee" until it became reality. To the sportswriters on the scene, it was the same sort of stuff Namath had been talking about all week. It was emblazoned across the newspapers in Miami, though, and New York coach Weeb Ewbank was less than pleased.

"I could have shot him for saying it," Ewbank said.[3]

When game day arrived, Namath was proven correct and the rest of the world was proven wrong. The Jets, by then 18-point underdogs, pulled off one of the great upsets in pro football history, besting the Colts 16–7.

After a scoreless first quarter, alarming enough for Baltimore, the Jets never trailed. Fullback Snell scored a touchdown on a four-yard run, and New York added two field goals by Jim Turner in the second quarter, for a 13–0 halftime lead. The Jets intercepted Morrall three times in the first half.

Turner added a third field goal for a 16–0 lead, before the Colts scored a touchdown in the fourth period. Baltimore became so desperate to make something happen on offense that Shula sent Unitas into the game after he had not played throughout the regular season.

Namath completed 17 of 26 passes for 206 yards and was the game's MVP.

Sample was one Jet who couldn't believe that Namath had made good on his guarantee.

"The thing was, we all thought we'd win the game," Sample said. "We had studied film on the Colts and we were really confident. But a guarantee?"[4]

Namath, now in his seventies, has never stopped hearing about his boldness.

"I can't tell you how many times I have had people tell me they used our win as a motivating force," Namath once said. "We sent a message to all the underdogs out there."[5]

NOTES

1. Mark Kriegel, *Namath* (New York: Viking, 2004), 261.

2. Ibid., 268.

3. Pro Football Hall of Fame, "He Guaranteed It: Joe Namath Made the Super Bowl Truly Super," http://www.profootballhof.com/history/release.aspx?RELEASE_ID=822 (accessed May 3, 2015).

4. Ibid.

5. Ibid.

FURTHER READING

Boyle, Robert. "Show-biz Sonny and His Quest for Stars." *Sports Illustrated*, July 19, 1965.

Gruver, Ed. *From Baltimore to Broadway: Joe, the Jets, and the Super Bowl Guarantee*. Chicago: Triumph Books, 2009.

Namath, Joe, and Dick Schaap. *I Can't Wait Until Tomorrow . . . 'Cause I Get Better Looking Every Day*. New York: Random House, 1969.

Telander, Rick. *Joe Namath and the Other Guys*. California: Holt, Rinehart and Winston, 1976.

#27 Secretariat the Great

They called the gallant thoroughbred "Big Red," and for many Secretariat is the greatest race horse of all time. His 1973 campaign, sweeping the Kentucky Derby, the Preakness Stakes, and the Belmont Stakes, lives on in memory because it was so extraordinary.

For one American spring Secretariat was the most famous sports figure in the land. At the time the three-year-old, ridden by Ron Turcotte and trained by Lucien

Triple Crown winner Secretariat is regarded by many as the greatest thoroughbred horse of all time. The 3-year-old's victories in the Kentucky Derby, Preakness, and Belmont Stakes were all captured in record times that still stand more than 40 years later. (AP Photo/Bob Daugherty)

Laurin, dominated the news, exciting the populace the way few racehorses across the decades have had the power to do.

Secretariat won the Triple Crown, the first horse to do so in 25 years, but it was the manner in which he surpassed all comers that added so marvelously to the sport's lore.

This is an age when in all manner of competition, athletes, human or otherwise, tend to get bigger, faster, and stronger; training methods have matured; and equipment has improved. Yet for 40 years Secretariat's racing speed has reigned supreme in the most hotly contested events that engage the racing public.

The best of the best of their generations have come to the starting gates at all three of the premier events for more than four decades, yet none of the best horses that have won those coveted titles has run faster than Secretariat.

A large chestnut colt, Secretariat's bloodlines were sound, something of extraordinary import in horse racing, which carefully traces its history back for hundreds of years. Secretariat's sire was Bold Ruler, out of Somethingroyal at The Meadow in Virginia.

Secretariat grew to stand more than 16 hands tall and to weigh nearly 1,200 pounds. The horse was owned by a woman named Penny (Tweedy) Chenery, and Meadow Farm's colors were blue and white.

The horse was foaled in 1970, and as a two-year-old Secretariat's promise was revealed, winning five races in a row after a slow start. That made him the winter book favorite for the 1973 Kentucky Derby at Churchill Downs in Louisville, the 1¼-quarter-mile classic that is the premier American horse race.

Those closest to Secretariat knew he was a special horse, but until the horse won a Triple Crown event that hadn't been proven.

On the first Saturday in May Secretariat went off as a 3–2 favorite, but broke last from the starting gate. If his slow start sucked the breath from fans, the long-striding thoroughbred of great heart demonstrated there was nothing to worry about. He picked off the faster starters one by one and cruised under the wire in 1 minute, 59⅖ seconds.

The buzz began immediately. This was the fastest time ever recorded for the distance at the Downs in a race that dated its start to 1875. Called the Run for the Roses, the Derby has also been termed "the most exciting two minutes in sports," and it definitely was when Secretariat ran. The record pace the horse set in 1973 still stands. The margin of victory was 2½ lengths over Sham, the early leader.

Two weeks later Secretariat's handlers took him to the Preakness Stakes in Baltimore, the second leg of the Triple Crown. Once again Secretariat perpetuated his bad habit of coming out of the gate last. But in a freight train of a move, he accelerated past virtually the entire field at once and again relegated Sham to second place by 2½ lengths.

On the day of the race there was a malfunction with the electronic timing mechanism and hand-held watches recorded a wide disparity from the time shown on the big board. Times ranged from 1:53⅖ to 1:55. Although it was conceded that Secretariat had run pretty darned fast for the 1³⁄₁₆ of a mile at Pimlico Race Course, the controversy prevented the thoroughbred's time from being recognized as an official record.

However, in 2012 the Maryland Racing Commission conducted a special hearing using sophisticated timing and videotapes and concluded that Secretariat had actually covered the distance in 1:53. That is the fastest time ever for the distance and now is officially acknowledged as the Preakness's best.

Despite the impressive manner in which Secretariat seemed to find another gear to pass the competition, Sham's relatively close finishes did not discourage his seconds, and they put him up against Secretariat in the Belmont Stakes three weeks later. The Belmont, with its long 1½-mile course, has often been the graveyard of hopes for Triple Crown contenders that travel to New York for a coronation after capturing the first two legs in Kentucky and Maryland.

Several other three-year-olds had been scared off by Secretariat's strength and speed, and the Belmont went off with five horses, Secretariat being the 1–10 betting favorite. That meant if Secretariat won, the payoff would be just $2.20 on a $2 bet.

Secretariat did win, with perhaps the most dominating big-race victory in the history of the sport. Sham broke quickly, setting an almost insane pace, but Secretariat ate up the ground, passed Sham as if he were standing still (which by then he almost was), and roared away. Secretariat's margin of victory was 31 lengths. Secretariat and the horses trailing him could not be seen on the same TV screen at the same time.

Race caller Chic Anderson was astonished even as he called the race. "Secretariat is blazing along!" he said. "He is moving like a tremendous machine. Secretariat by 12! Secretariat by 14! An unbelievable performance!"[1]

The winning time was 2:24, not only a record for the Belmont Stakes, but a record for the distance, which also still stands. It was an astounding showing. Once again Secretariat had electrified racing fans and even Americans who cared little for the sport but became enthralled by his running. Chenery had many years to reflect on Secretariat's greatness and the joy he brought her and on the 40th anniversary of his Belmont run, when she was in her nineties, she provided an answer to why she thought the horse was so spectacular.

"What made him so special was that physically, he had no flaws," Chenery said. "His conformation was about perfect. He got more out of his stride and was very well balanced. He didn't get tired; he responded to it."[2]

Secretariat was retired from the track with $1.3 million earnings.

"It was a hot day," said jockey Ron Turcotte, 40 years after Secretariat's brilliant Belmont. "But it was beautiful. He was the best ride you ever wanted to have. He is the greatest horse that ever lived. Whenever he was right, no horse could beat him."[3]

There have been many great horses in the Triple Crown events, but there are few humans who would argue with Turcotte's assessment.

Secretariat, as was to be expected, was outlived by his human connections. He died in 1989, and when trainer Laurin was given the news, he was inconsolable.

"This is a terrible day for me," Laurin said. "I trained the greatest horse that ever lived, the greatest of them all. And now he's gone."[4]

NOTES

1. *Secretariat Belmont Stakes 1973 & Extended Post Race Coverage*, https://www.youtube.com/watch?v=cS4f6wiQJh4 (uploaded August 19, 2007).

2. Melissa Hopert, "The Rail: Reliving Secretariat's Magical Ride 40 Years Later," *New York Times*, June 8, 2013.

3. Ibid.

4. Neil Milbert, "Trainer Mourns Secretariat's End," *Chicago Tribune,* October 5, 1989.

FURTHER READING

Nack, William. *Secretariat*. New York: Hyperion, 2010.

Scanlan, Lawrence. *The Big Red Horse: The Story of Secretariat and the Loyal Groom Who Loved Him*. New York: HarperCollins, 2010.

Scanlan, Lawrence. *The Horse God Built: The Untold Story of Secretariat, the World's Greatest Racehors*e. New York: Thomas Dunne Books, 2007.

Woolfe, Raymond G., Jr., and Ron Turcotte. *Secretariat*. New York: The Derrydale Press, 2010.

#28 Joe DiMaggio's 56-Game Hitting Streak

New York Yankee center fielder Joe DiMaggio authored just about the greatest two months in baseball history during the season of 1941. From May 15 until July 16, Joltin' Joe banged out at least one hit in every game that his team played.

After being stopped from hitting safely in a game against the Cleveland Indians, DiMaggio walked off the diamond with a 56-game hitting streak. It is one of the most admired records in baseball, and no one before or since has come within 11 games of it. Second place on the all-time hitting streak belongs to Wee Willie Keeler with 45. Right behind him is Pete Rose with 44.

DiMaggio, who died in 1999 at age 84, grew up in the San Francisco area and was the most famous of three brothers, who were sons of a fisherman but ended up playing major league ball. Older brother Vince paved the way, and younger brother Dom starred for the Boston Red Sox. Only Joe became a Hall of Famer, for his accomplishments between 1936 and 1951, and was one of the most dazzling players to wear Yankee pinstripes.

The graceful DiMaggio batted .325 lifetime, hit 361 home runs, won two batting titles, was a 13-time all-star selection and a nine-time World Series champion, and won three American League Most Valuable Player awards. He excelled in all facets of the sport and was an icon of the game, but his 56-game hitting streak is

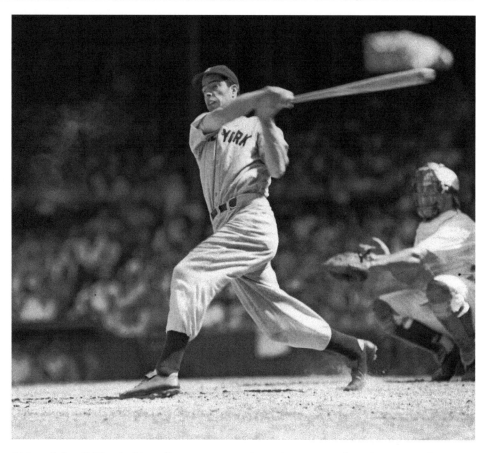

Although Joe DiMaggio himself once put together a longer streak in the minors, his Major League 56-game hitting streak for the New York Yankees in 1941 is considered to be one of the sport's unbreakable marks. (AP photo)

the achievement that most readily comes to mind when baseball fans of later generations recall his career.

In 1933 DiMaggio hit in 61 straight games for the San Francisco Seals in the Pacific Coast League.[1] It is likely that no one except West Coast fans would have remembered if he had not challenged the mark and set the all-time major league record less than a decade later. The previous PCL consecutive-game hitting streak was 49 games. DiMaggio recalled later that when his march to a new record gained traction, much attention was paid.

"When my streak passed its 30th game, attendance increased at every park I played," DiMaggio said.[2]

DiMaggio's memorable hitting streak began on May 15, fairly early in the season, with a one-for-four day against the Chicago White Sox. It extended for most of those two months before DiMaggio was shut down on a series of hard shots to Cleveland's Ken Keltner, who speared them at third base to retire him.

Some days DiMaggio was hotter than others, but during the streak he never went to bed hitless, overall batting .408. He bashed 15 home runs and knocked in 55 runs, nearly one per game, during the streak.

DiMaggio's success began with gradual awareness in the local New York papers that he was accumulating a limited hitting streak. As he continued to bat safely day after day, more sportswriters took notice and brought more notoriety to his ongoing achievement.

At the time the record hitting streak was considered to be Keeler's, although for years it was accounted for as a 44-game hitting streak, and not until long after DiMaggio surpassed it did research show that it should have been a 45-game streak. Aside from Keeler, whose accomplishment was recorded in 1897, the modern record was considered to be the 41-game streak notched by the St. Louis Browns' George Sisler.

In 1922, the year when Sisler, like DiMaggio and Keeler a Hall of Famer, put together his streak, he batted .420. DiMaggio tied and passed Sisler on the same day during a doubleheader against the Washington Senators on June 29, 1941.

DiMaggio met with reporters between games of the doubleheader after catching Sisler and expressed his pleasure at doing so.

"I'm tickled," he said. "Who wouldn't be? It's a great thing. I've realized an ambition."[3]

In the second game a DiMaggio single propelled him past Sisler, and he relaxed by his locker and entertained the sportswriters yet again on the same day.

"I'm glad the strain is over," he said.[4]

DiMaggio tied Keeler (the 44) on July 1. Less well-remembered is that after the Indians broke DiMaggio's streak, he hit in 16 more straight games, giving him hits in 72 out of 73 games.

As the number of games in which DiMaggio slashed a base hit kept climbing, he became national news in cities that didn't even have Major League Baseball teams. Baseball was king in America in the early 1940s, and DiMaggio was revered, not only in New York, but among fans everywhere. He kept chugging along, and assuredly by the time DiMaggio surpassed Sisler and Keeler, tickets were virtually impossible to purchase for his games. Fans lined up around the block in hopes of picking off a secondhand ducat.

In 1961 when Roger Maris was chasing Babe Ruth's single-season record of 60 home runs, he almost caved in to the pressure of public attention and the barbs of newspapermen who either did not want to see the record broken at all or preferred that Mickey Mantle do it.

DiMaggio was under similar, if perhaps not quite as intense, media scrutiny, and there was enough attention to shake the nerve of a shy man. In retirement DiMaggio became nearly reclusive at times, but during his playing days he met his obligations to sportswriters without becoming contentious.

Dom DiMaggio, playing with the Red Sox, said he noticed no discernible difference in Joe's behavior as he kept on ripping out those base hits, unlike Maris, who felt so much pressure that his hair began to fall out in clumps. The two brothers socialized and ate dinner together during the streak on the days when the Yankees and Red Sox played.

"I didn't notice any change in Joe during the streak," Dom DiMaggio said. "I was glad to see him holding up so well."[5]

Joe hit in his 50th straight game on July 11 against the St. Louis Browns. He reached 51 straight the next day, again versus the Browns. DiMaggio hit in both ends of a doubleheader against the Chicago White Sox on July 13, and games 54 and 55 in the streak also came at the expense of the White Sox.

Ironically, the pitcher who surrendered two hits to DiMaggio on July 15, game number 55 in the streak, was the same Eddie Smith who had allowed the first hit in the streak on May 15.

The next day, DiMaggio hit in his 56th game in a row. He collected two hits that day against the Indians, one off Al Milnar and the other off Joe Krakauskas.

It was not known at the time when DiMaggio failed to obtain a hit in his 57th straight game that the Heinz 57 condiment manufacturing company was prepared to close a $10,000 deal with the center fielder if he hit in 57 straight games. He came that close.

"I can't say that I am glad it's over," DiMaggio said after the Indians stopped him. "Of course, I wanted to go on as long as I could."[6]

What DiMaggio didn't realize at the time was that the streak would go on and on in people's minds and even outlive him. Nearly 75 years after DiMaggio hit in 56 straight games, practically no one believes it is a record that will ever be broken.

NOTES

1. Dennis Gafney, "DiMaggio's 61-Game Hitting Streak, Pacific Coast League," *PBS. org*, http://www.pbs.org/wgbh/amex/dimaggio/peopleevents/pande07.html (accessed January 3, 2015).

2. Tom Clavin, *The DiMaggios* (New York: HarperCollins, 2013), 46.

3. Lew Freedman, *DiMaggio's Yankees* (Jefferson, NC: McFarland, 2011), 171.

4. Ibid., 172.

5. Clavin, *The DiMaggios*, 134.

6. Ibid., 135.

FURTHER READING

Cramer, Richard Ben. *Joe DiMaggio: The Hero's Life*. New York: Simon & Schuster, 2001.
Jones, David. *Joe DiMaggio: A Biography*. Santa Barbara, CA: Greenwood Press, 2004.
Kennedy, Kostya. *56: Joe DiMaggio and the Last Magic Number in Sports*. New York: Sports Illustrated, 2011.

#29 Ted Williams Bats .406

When Boston Red Sox slugger Ted Williams hit .406 in 1941, it was recognized as an extraordinary achievement. What no one realized at the time, however, was that no Major League Baseball player would reach the .400 barrier again.

As Williams's achievement approaches its 75-year anniversary, there have been few serious challenges to that hallowed average in all of those years.

Any time a player batted .400, it was deemed a special accomplishment. But as the first four decades of the 20th century passed, it became a rarer and rarer feat. A decade and a half into the 21st century, the modernization of baseball makes it less likely than ever that any batter will reach the territory where Williams left off.

Teams employ more relief pitchers who throw faster, and hitters must constantly adjust to the fresh arms they face in later innings. That style of play has taken a toll on batting averages.

Williams, the San Diego–raised left fielder for Boston, is regarded as one of the greatest hitters of all time. He retired in 1960 with a .344 lifetime average and 521 home runs. His .482 on-base percentage is the best of all time. Williams, who died in 2002 at 83, is one of the sport's mythic figures. He spoke in a voice that echoed John Wayne's, and he achieved his impressive lifetime statistics despite missing years of his prime while serving his country during World War II and the Korean War.

Prior to 1941, the last player to hit .400 in a season was the New York Giants' first baseman, Bill Terry, who batted .401 in 1930. The last American League batter to do so was the Detroit Tigers' Harry Heilmann, who hit .403 in 1923. Hugh Duffy, playing for the Boston Beaneaters in 1894, recorded the highest average of all time when he batted .440.

"I can say this about Teddy," said Duffy, who monitored Williams's progress closely that season and knew him well. "I have never seen a hitter better than Williams in all my life, and that goes for [Ty] Cobb, [Babe] Ruth, [Rogers] Hornsby, and all the rest."[1]

Ted Williams surpassed the .400 milestone in the most dramatic fashion possible in 1941 by collecting six hits in eight at-bats in a double-header. When Williams batted .406 more than 70 years ago, no one realized he would be the last man to hit .400. (AP Photo/Ted Sande)

Williams was on fire in the batter's box for most of the season. He put together jaw-dropping stretches. He batted .436 in May and .536 between May 17 and June 1. During a 23-game hitting streak, Williams hit .487.

Anyone who is going to hit .400 over the long baseball season can't afford a slump of more than a minute or two. Williams stayed near the benchmark all season, and while it had been just 11 years, since a player had hit so well for so long, the excitement began to build nationwide. Fans beyond his Boston base wanted Williams to hit .400. Some may not have seen it in their lifetimes. No one had seen it done for a while.

Right before the last series of the regular season (and Boston would have no postseason), Williams found himself in a pickle. He had a 1-for-7 day. In a doubleheader against the Washington Senators September 24, Ted went 0-for-3 and 1-for-4. That dropped him to just one point over .400 going into the wrap-up three-game series at Philadelphia. In the September 27 contest Williams went 1-for-4 again, and he woke up gazing at the number .400 next to his name in the statistics on the last day of the season.

Legendary stories and accomplishments surround Williams's career, but none was more telling than his approach to recording his .400 season when the final weekend of play began. In mid-September Williams was sitting on a .413 batting average. But he went into a mini-slump over the season's final two weeks and entered a September 28 doubleheader against the Philadelphia Athletics with an average of .39955. By baseball standards it would have been rounded off to .400, and Williams would have had his official .400 season. But to Williams that seemed an inappropriate way to conclude the year. Sitting down was the coward's way out, and he refused to do that.

Boston was led on the field by player-manager Joe Cronin, a close friend of Williams as well as his boss. Knowing the mathematical situation, Cronin asked Williams if he would like to sit out the games and preserve his .400 mark. Williams declined the offer. He said he would play both games, swing away, and let the situation play itself out according to fate. Williams took the risk of dropping well under .400.

The night before the A's games, Williams could not sleep. He walked the dark streets of Philadelphia accompanied by trainer Johnny Orlando. He kept saying that he was going to do it. He was going to hit .400.

The next day Williams proved his mettle all over again by blasting out six hits in eight at-bats to finish at .406. Lost to most fans except for historians was the fact that sacrifice flies were then scored as outs that were counted against a hitter's average. It was only later that the time at-bat for that play was removed from calculations. If the current sacrifice fly rule had been in effect, Williams would have batted .416 that season.

Somewhat remarkably, Williams did not let much of the joy he felt shine through in the clubhouse after the game. He did quietly tell Orlando, though, "I'm a good hitter."[2]

The left-handed swinging Williams, who played through the 1960 season, was only 22 years old in 1941. He not only won the American League batting title, he also led the league in runs scored with 134, home runs with 37, and walks with 147, and had an on-base percentage of .553 and a slugging percentage of .735.

Williams came in second in the Most Valuable Player voting behind Joe DiMaggio, who made his own history that year by hitting in 56 consecutive games, but Williams led his New York Yankees to the pennant and World Series championships.

In 1994 Tony Gwynn of the San Diego Padres batted .394 in a labor-dispute-shortened season (games stopped on August 12) to lead the National League in hitting. That is the closest any other player has come to batting .400 since Williams's 1941 season.

In 1980 George Brett of the Kansas City Royals hit .390, the closest anyone in the American League has come to .400 since Williams's milestone year. Also, Williams himself (at age 38) and Rod Carew of the Minnesota Twins each batted .388, Williams in 1957 and Carew in 1977.

Williams once said: "Baseball is the only field of endeavor where a man can succeed 3 times out of 10 and be considered a good performer."[3]

Or, in Williams's case, 4 times out of 10.

Ted Williams never hid the fact that he loved to hit and that he wanted to excel as a hitter more than as an all-around player.

"A man has to have goals for a day, for a lifetime," he once said. "And that was mine, to have people say, 'There goes Ted Williams, the greatest hitter who ever lived.'"[4]

He pretty much accomplished that goal.

NOTES

1. Ben Bradlee Jr., *The Kid: The Immortal Life of Ted Williams* (New York: Little, Brown, 2013), 179.
2. Ibid., 194.
3. Ross Atkin, "9 Quotes from Ted Williams on His Birthday," *Christian Science Monitor*, September 18, 2012.
4. Ibid.

FURTHER READING

Montville, Leigh. *Ted Williams: The Biography of an American Hero*. New York: Broadway Books, 2004.
Williams, Ted, and John Underwood. *My Turn at Bat: The Story of My Life*. New York: Fireside, 1988.

#30 The Death of Dale Earnhardt

The remarkable stock-car racing career of Dale Earnhardt ended in shocked silence, appropriately enough on a racetrack, when his car slammed into a retaining wall at the Daytona International Speedway in Florida.

Few events in the history of NASCAR, the governing body of stock-car racing, shook up the sports world the way the untimely death of Earnhardt in 2001 affected the sport and the American landscape.

In those days stock-car racing was still battling to obtain front-of-the-sports-section coverage. Earnhardt's death catapulted the sport (in the wrong way) onto the front pages of newspapers.

The nationwide outpouring of sympathy and sadness caught some big-city news hounds unawares, and they only gradually, and belatedly, grasped the significance of the driver nicknamed "The Intimidator." Due to his wearing all-black outfits, people also had taken to calling Earnhardt "The Man in Black."

Earnhardt was born in 1951 in North Carolina. At the time of his death he had won seven stock-car season-long championships, tying the once-thought-to-be unassailable record held by Richard Petty. During his driving career Earnhardt posted 76 victories and 428 top-10 finishes.

In many ways Earnhardt had become the face of the sport. His success gave him stature as the most famous driver, but his personal style combined bluntness in his speaking away from the track with aggressive, hard driving on it. Earnhardt was seen as a manly man whose overpowering personality and take-no-prisoners driving style made him an icon.

Earnhardt drove as if he expected to win every race, and once he said that very thing: that he aimed to win every race he entered. He uttered many comments about how badly he wanted to win and how he had disdain for second place or lower. "You win some, you lose some, you wreck some," turned out to be the story of Earnhardt's life.

Earnhardt had a legion of fans who burst into full-throated roars whenever his number 3 car was glimpsed, and to them he could do no wrong, even if others sometimes found him abrasive. Earnhardt seemed to be a man of some contradictions. Absolutely devoted and determined to success on the track, he had a limited formal education, yet the business savvy to build a racing empire that earned him millions of dollars.

The son of an early racer, Ralph Earnhardt, and the father of Dale Earnhardt Jr., repeatedly voted the most popular driver on the circuit, Dale Sr. bridged the rough-edged era of the early days of NASCAR and the more modern and sophisticated era. He projected an aura of indestructibility and assurance that made it all the more stunning when he met his demise on a racetrack at age 49.

Ralph Earnhardt was a short-track driver whose time in NASCAR coincided with its fledgling beginnings, and the Earnhardts were not rich. Dale always knew what he wanted to do, and typical of the way he led his life, he went after NASCAR success at full throttle. While Dale made his NASCAR debut in 1975 with a 22nd-place finish at the Charlotte Motor Speedway, he did not easily slide into the top class of drivers. He won one race in 1979. Widely regarded as a driver with great potential, as soon as he settled into a prominent role with a team, Earnhardt plucked his first Winston Cup championship in 1980.

He built upon that start and over the coming years became the biggest star in the game, winning race after race all over the country, and year after year either salting away another title or contending for the biggest prize in the sport. In a comparison to the outsized personality of baseball star Reggie Jackson, it was apparent that Earnhardt was the straw that stirred the drink in stock-car racing. He was the most visible driver on the circuit, the best driver, and the most forceful.

Earnhardt also won season-long points titles in 1986, 1987, 1990, 1991, 1993, and 1994. Although it was not considered likely that Earnhardt would top Petty's record 200 victories, no one bet against Earnhardt setting a new standard for championships.

By 2001 Earnhardt was the king of the asphalt, and on February 18, 2001, in the season-opening Daytona 500, not only was Earnhardt a participant, but he had other cars in the prestigious race. Son Dale Jr. was driving one, and new teammate Michael Waltrip, whose career Earnhardt was rescuing with this opportunity, was in another.

During the closing laps of the race Earnhardt realized his guys were in a tremendous position to go one-two in a race that he did not feel he could win. He adopted the role of protector, trying to block other cars from closing in on Waltrip and Dale Jr.

Waltrip cruised across the finish line for the biggest win of his career. Dale Jr. was right behind for a 1–2 finish. They had begun celebrating at the finish line, expecting Dale Sr. to join them on the track at any moment. But on the final lap there was a mishap as the next three cars hurtled for the finish. Earnhardt's car and the car driven by Sterling Martin touched, and Earnhardt's car spun in front of Kenny Schrader's car before hitting the wall front-end first.

It did not appear that Earnhardt had hit the wall at high speed or in devastating fashion. It was the kind of accident common in stock-car racing, not terribly violent, and of the type drivers walked away from with minimal bruising or perhaps a broken bone. But Earnhardt did not climb out of the vehicle. Emergency workers dashed to the scene and were dismayed by what they found.

Earnhardt had suffered a basilar skull fracture, a rare injury, and died from it. Word of his death spread slowly after medical experts sought frantically to revive him. When the news was announced, few could believe it. Earnhardt was too big, too tough, to die like that. The crash itself did not look that serious. It was inexplicable and horrifying news.

The accident was investigated and shown to be somewhat of a fluke. However, it was determined that if Earnhardt had been wearing an available protective device just then making its way into the sport, he might not have been seriously injured. This piece of equipment is called a HANS Safety Device, and it protects the head and neck. Soon after Earnhardt's death, NASCAR made the equipment mandatory for drivers, and in the nearly 15 years since Earnhardt died in his car the sport has virtually eliminated fatalities.

No one in NASCAR was more stunned or more deeply affected when Earnhardt died racing than Dale Jr., in the same profession and on the same track on the same day. Dale Jr. always loved Daytona, one of the sport's main showcases, and it was as if the very atmosphere had been poisoned when his father perished in the Daytona 500.

"I lost the greatest man I ever knew, my dad," he said.[1]

The death of legend Dale Earnhart in a crash on the track during the 2001 Daytona 500 was one of the most stunning developments in NASCAR history. The shocking demise of the sport's top driver led to the adoption of safety devices that have saved uncountable lives since. (AP Photo/Chris O'Meara)

In the aftermath of Dale Earnhardt's death came a tremendous outpouring of appreciation and affection for the man who more than any other then racing had helped build the sport. Fans wanted to let Dale Jr. and other NASCAR people know they were going to miss Dale Sr. Some fans were angry, vented at Sterling Martin, and threatened him. They blamed him for killing Dale Sr.

Dale Jr. called them "psycho fans"[2] and went out of his way to talk with Martin as reassurance, and he issued public statements calling for people to stop threatening Martin.

NOTES

1. Dale Earnhardt Jr. and Jade Gurss, *Driver #8* (New York: Warner Books, 2002), 348.
2. Ibid., 351.

FURTHER READING

Gillispie, Tom. *Angel in Black: Remembering Dale Earnhardt Sr.* Nashville, TN: Cumberland House, 2008.

Montville, Leigh. *At the Altar of Speed: The Fast Life and Tragic Death of Dale Earnhardt.* New York: Broadway Books, 2002.

Souter, Gerry. *The Earnhardts.* Santa Barbara, CA: Greenwood, 2009.

#31 Michael Jordan Plays While Sick

A large body of opinion favors the notion that Michael Jordan is the best basketball player who ever lived. He made a good case for that assertion during his years with the Chicago Bulls, when the franchise won six NBA crowns.

A five-time Most Valuable Player and 14-time all-star, Jordan was a transcendent player who averaged 30.1 points per game in his 15-season career with the Bulls and Washington Wizards after leading North Carolina to an NCAA title.

With Jordan in the lineup the Bulls reached the NBA finals six times, and six times the six-foot-six guard was named MVP of the final round of the play-offs. No occasion was more dramatic than the 1997 finals against the Utah Jazz.

Jordan was the king of the highlight reels, a deadly shooter in the clutch, and a nine-time member of the NBA's all-defensive team. He won every honor a player can win, and he also won off the court, acquiring the largest number of corporate sponsors and leading the way for athletes in the endorsement field.

Jordan developed his legend through his consistent excellence on the court and by leading his teams to championships. However, his defining moment (in a career chock-full of highlights) was probably his performance against the Jazz when the Bulls won their fifth championship.

Born in New York, Jordan moved to North Carolina early in his childhood. He was 33 by the time of the 1997 finals. His reputation was well-established as a player who could and would do just about anything on the court to help his team win. The Bulls did plenty of winning during the 1996–1997 regular season under coach Phil Jackson, finishing 69–13.

Besides Jordan, right-hand man Scottie Pippen, another future Hall of Famer; Toni Kukoc; Steve Kerr; Ron Harper; Bill Wennington; Luc Longley; and the colorful rebounding maven Dennis Rodman were prominent Bulls.

That season Jordan averaged 29.6 points a game, winning his ninth and next-to-last scoring title. The Bulls ripped through the early rounds of the play-offs to capture the Eastern Division title. They blitzed Washington, 3–0 in the first round. They easily handled Atlanta, 4–1. In the eastern finals, Chicago topped Miami, 4–1.

While the supporting cast was more than capable, Jordan was regarded as the go-to man at crunch time in close games and the player who could elevate his game at will. No other team had a player who was in Jordan's league.

Still, the Jazz were exceptionally talented. Utah finished 64–18 that season and also featured two future Hall of Fame players, forward Karl Malone and guard John Stockton. They were coached by Jerry Sloan, who also ended up in the Naismith Memorial Hall of Fame in Springfield, Massachusetts.

Malone was the perfect power forward and averaged more than 27 points a game that season. Stockton was just about the purest passer in NBA history and owns the all-time assists record. The muscular, six-foot-nine Malone was the league's MVP in 1997, his first of two such honors. It was not

Six-time NBA champion Michael Jordan is considered the greatest basketball player ever in many quarters. But the Chicago Bulls star perhaps reached the apex of his accomplishments when he came out of a sick bed to destroy the title hopes of the Utah Jazz in June of 1997. (AP Photo/Jack Smith)

easy for any star to claim that prize when Jordan was playing, but Malone edged him out that season. For Jordan, who used any potential slight to fuel his motivation, having Malone named MVP and then facing him in the finals made the last play-off round personal.

The Jazz dominated their half of the bracket almost as thoroughly as Chicago did its side. Utah came out of the West after polishing off the Los Angeles Clippers, 3–0; the Los Angeles Lakers, 4–1; and the Houston Rockets, 4–2. The Jazz players were hungry for a championship, but not more so than the two stars who were in their thirties and anxious to capture a ring. Malone and Stockman did not care one whit what Jordan and the Bulls had accomplished. To that duo they were just an obstacle standing between them and their long-sought NBA title.

By the time the series ended the Jazz would be sick of Jordan, not the other way around. The first game went to the Bulls 84–82, and sure enough, Jordan hit a shot at the buzzer to give his team the victory. The Bulls went ahead 2–0 by capturing the second game, 97–85. Both games were played at the United Center in Chicago.

Things changed when the series shifted to Salt Lake City. If fans thought the Bulls' early statement wins decided things, they were surprised. Utah roared back with two straight triumphs, 104–93 and 78–73, at the Delta Center. The best-four-out-of-seven championship round was deadlocked at 2–2.

The fifth game in the series was pivotal. The winner would go up 3–2 and be a single victory away from clinching. However, the Bulls had a major problem. Jordan woke up ill. He was running a high fever, had the sweats, and was so weak he could barely stand up for long, much less run up and down the court to play championship-level basketball.

Jordan's sweats began in the middle of the night leading up to the June 11 contest. He said that when he awoke perspiring from his fever, he got scared. His body felt so leaden he could hardly move. He said he felt paralyzed. When Jordan stood up he felt dizzy and actually believed for a short while that he might have been drugged. He felt like throwing up and had no energy.

Jordan spent most of the day in bed. He was dehydrated and lost weight. He did not rise for the day in his hotel room until 3:00 p.m. It seemed doubtful that he would be able to suit up in his iconic number 23 jersey that night. He appeared at the Delta Center around 4:30 p.m., and Pippen said he had never seen his teammate looking worse. Pippen did not even think that Jordan had the strength to pull on his uniform, never mind play.

In a sense, Jordan went right back to bed when he reached the arena. He found a dark room and tried to relax. Those who saw him thought he looked pale and out of sorts and that he seemed to lack the necessary energy to play against the NBA's best. Coach Phil Jackson thought he would be without his main man, but Jordan surprised him. He appeared in the locker room and told Jackson, "I can play."[1]

Jordan actually looked as if he needed a note from his mother, or his doctor, to be allowed on the court. But much was at stake, and Jackson took his cue from Jordan. If Jordan was game to give it a go, the coach would provide him with a forum.

What followed was one of the most astounding performances of Jordan's career. During the first quarter he could hardly run up and down the court. But at some point some inner fortitude clicked in and took over. Although at more than one stage of the game Jordan appeared on the verge of keeling over, he managed to play 44 of the game's 48 minutes. Once Pippen helped him off the court, Jordan's arms wrapped around Pippen in order to stay on his feet.

Yet in this game that the Bulls had to have, Chicago felled the Jazz, 90–88. Jordan scored 38 points on a night when he had no business playing at all. Two days later, back in Chicago, the Bulls won 90–86 to earn another NBA title.

It was Michael Jordan's gutsy showing in game 5, when he refused to allow his sick body to let him down, that everyone talked about. It was one of the crowning achievements of Jordan's basketball career and lives on in NBA lore.

NOTE

1. Rick Weinberg, "Jordan Battles Flu, Makes Jazz Sick," ESPN.com, http://sports .espn.go.com/espn/espn25/story?page=moments/79.

FURTHER READING

Halberstam, David. *Playing for Keeps: Michael Jordan and the World He Made*. New York: Broadway Books, 2000.
Jordan, Michael, and Mark Vancil. *For the Love of the Game: My Story*. Washington, DC: Crown Books, 1998.
Lazenby, Roland. *Michael Jordan: The Life*. New York: Little, Brown, 2014.

#32 Jack Nicklaus Reclaims Glory

Some believe that Jack Nicklaus is the greatest golfer of all time. He won a record 18 major championships and along with Arnold Palmer engaged in the most stirring one-on-one duels in the history of the sport.

"The Golden Bear" was born in 1940 and first gained attention at Ohio State University in his home state. He turned pro in 1961. Nicklaus won his first title on the Professional Golf Association tour when he simultaneously won his first major at the U.S. Open in 1962.

Before turning professional, Nicklaus twice won the U.S. Amateur, in 1959 and 1961. At one time that was among the most prestigious crowns in the world. Now the acknowledged majors of professional golf are the Masters, the U.S. Open, the PGA Tournament, and the British Open. By the time he was 26, Nicklaus had captured this grand slam of titles for the first time. Before Nicklaus emerged as the record holder, the legendary Bobby Jones had won the most majors, 13.

Nicklaus was selected as the PGA Player of the Year five times, and four times he topped the leaders on the money list. In all, Nicklaus won 73 pro titles, making him third on the all-time list.

When it came to his golfing style, Nicklaus, who took up the sport when he was 10, was renowned for his long, straight driving and ability to hit greens. Those characteristics enabled him to get close to the pin and were of great assistance, since he was not widely regarded as a great putter. Nicklaus was a more cautious player. Despite his keen driving ability, he did not just let it rip with all his might. He showed some conservatism in his game.

Nicklaus always let it be known that winning majors was a primary goal, and he set his sights on the four biggest tournaments year after year. He won the Masters in Augusta, Georgia six times, the U.S. Open four times, the British Open three times, and the PGA five times.

Most of Nicklaus's major victories were recorded in the 1960s and 1970s. He did pick off three more in the 1980s. However, he pretty much stopped winning the biggest tournaments in 1980. Yet he continued to play as he aged, still contending for other tournament titles. He was in no hurry to give up his passion.

Nicklaus' 18th and final major came at the Masters in 1986, six years after he had won his last major and at a time he when he had been hearing whispers that he should retire. 'His championship at Augusta that spring was the icing on his career. It was also the most unexpected triumph of his career, one that neither he nor his opponents on the 18 holes of Augusta saw coming. To some degree, besting the field at the Masters that year was the grandest win of Nicklaus's long career and is one of the most dramatic and exciting victories in the history of the sport.

Leading up to the Masters of April 1986, Nicklaus could pick up a newspaper and growl as he read unflattering stories suggesting he was over the hill and should quit big-time golf. Much as it is poor judgment to prick a real sleeping bear, the Golden Bear responded with anger to what he took as an insult.

Viewed by many as the greatest golfer of all time because of his 18 major championships, Jack Nicklaus put the icing on his career with his stunning triumph at Augusta National to win the Masters in 1986. At 46 years of age his best years were felt to be behind him, but he fooled everyone. (AP Photo/Phil Sandlin)

While no one would begrudge Nicklaus his place on a professional golf course, it was a virtually unanimous opinion that his championship era had passed. Instead, in the face of both criticism and doubts, at 46 years of age Nicklaus went out and won one more major, one more Masters. He made the galleries fall in love with him all over again and party like it was 1970. He electrified the watchers.

Nicklaus wasn't really even in the hunt for the title until the back nine of the final round. Then he turned back the clock to display his mastery on the course one last time, under the brightest of lights while listening to the loudest of his supporters.

As the tournament approached its conclusion, Nicklaus blistered the back nine at Augusta in 30. He shot a 65 for the last round for a seven-under-par score. Indeed, he gained that total under par in just 10 holes. On the 17th hole Nicklaus hit to within 18 feet of the hole and then dropped a putt. The shot culminated a stretch in which he shot eagle, birdie, birdie before an 18th-hole par.

This was a man nearing the age of players on the Senior Tour, yet who never flinched as the pressure increased and the cheers followed his every step, growing louder as he walked.

Nicklaus shot 74–71–69–65 over the 72 holes for a nine-under-par 279, getting better each day during the tournament and sneaking up on the field with his great final run. After Nicklaus nailed a birdie on the 16th hole on the final day, broadcaster Jim Nantz proclaimed, "And there's no doubt about it, the Bear has come out of hibernation."[1]

Tom Kite and Greg Norman tied for second place, one stroke behind Nicklaus.

"Obviously, I'm just tickled pink," Nicklaus said. "Some people said I was done, washed up, through."[2]

For a guy who was as defensive as anyone in reacting to those kinds of comments, Nicklaus was also candid about where his game stood in relation to his heyday.

"I'm not as good as I was 10 or 15 years ago," Nicklaus said. "I don't play as much competitive golf as I used to, but there are still some weeks when I'm as good as I ever was."[3]

When it was over and Nicklaus had held off the charges of many younger players, he slipped on the Masters green jacket for a sixth time and collected a purse of more than $144,000. It was a remarkable achievement. The 1986 Masters was the last of Nicklaus's majors, a capstone to a brilliant career (which did not end there), and made him the oldest golfer to win the venerable tournament. That remains true to this day.

After his final round, championship secured, there were tears in Nicklaus's eyes as he announced that his victory and his week were "unforgettable."[4]

If he could have, Nicklaus would have played tournament golf forever. He stayed active with at least a limited schedule for as long as he could. The last event of Nicklaus's playing career was the 2005 British Open. He was 65.

NOTES

1. David Newbery, "1986—The Bear versus the Shark," *InsideGolf.com*, http://insidegolf.rvrapid.com/default.aspx?iid=115966&startpage=page0000028#folio=28.

2. Ron Balicki, "40 Reads: '86 Masters Rates as Jack's Finest Hour," *Golfweek.com*, https://golfweek.com/news/2015/mar/11/masters-1986-jack-nicklaus-augusta-national-pga-40/?print.

3. Dan Jenkins, "The Greatest Masters," *Golf Digest*, June 1986.

4. Rick Weinberg, "20: Nicklaus Birdies 17, Wins Masters at 46," ESPN.com, http://sports.espn.go.com/espn/espn25/story?page=moments/20.

FURTHER READING

Nicklaus, Jack. *Jack Nicklaus: Memories and Mementoes from Golf's Golden Bear*. New York: Stewart, Tabori and Chang, 2007.

Nicklaus, Jack, and Ken Bowden. *Jack Nicklaus: My Story*. New York: Simon & Schuster, 2007.

Shaw, Mark. *Jack Nicklaus: Golf's Greatest Champion*. New York: Sports Publishing, 2013.

#33 The Dream Team at the 1992 Olympics

For decades basketball was considered an American game, and consistent with that prevailing view, the U.S. men's national basketball team dominated play in the Summer Olympics from the time the sport was introduced in 1936 until 1972.

The Olympics was the last bastion of amateurism, and the players selected to represent the United States in international competition were college players or Amateur Athletic Union stars. Professionals were not permitted to play.

For the United States, the 1972 Games in Munich differed from preceding every-four-year competitions in that its basketball team lost to the Soviet Union. That event has long been considered by American sports fans to be the greatest single robbery of a result they have ever seen. Over and over again the Soviet players were given fresh chances to score in the final seconds, until they did so. To this day, the Americans have refused to accept the second-place silver medals.

Basketball was invented in 1891 at a Springfield, Massachusetts, YMCA by a professor seeking to create fresh diversion for students in the winter. That man was James Naismith, who was born in Canada. He drew up simple rules that served as the foundation of the sport and lived long enough to see his game included on the Olympic calendar.

In the 20-year period between 1972 and 1992, much changed in both the Olympic movement and the basketball universe. The world became more enamored of basketball, and it grew in popularity in country after country. It took time for the caliber of play to catch up, but eventually the United States, which was still sending amateurs to represent it at the Games, lost its aura of invincibility and began losing in world championships and the Olympics.

At the same time the players representing the other nations—even the best ones—understood that Americans were not sending their best team. The hundreds of Americans playing in the National Basketball Association, the world's most elite league, were ineligible because they were professionals.

Gradually, sport by sport, the International Olympic Committee accepted professionalism in athletics, and players and competitors in a wide variety of sports became eligible to play for their country in the Games.

Although some less-informed American basketball fans believed that NBA players were allowed to compete in the Olympics because the United States was tired of losing, in reality movers and shakers within the international basketball community were the ones who sought the admission of pros. They believed that if they never played against the best, they would never become the best.

Their view prevailed, and in 1992 for the first time the Games were opened to all, and NBA pros were invited to become members of the U.S. national team.

In prior decades many famous American basketball players best known for their NBA stardom had played in the Olympics and won Olympic gold medals. But they did so before turning pro. Among those stars and future Hall of Famers were Clyde Lovellette, K. C. Jones, Bill Russell, Jerry West, Oscar Robertson, Walt Bellamy, Michael Jordan, Chris Mullin, and Patrick Ewing.

The inclusion of the NBA's best was set for the 1992 Games in Barcelona, Spain, and it transformed Olympic basketball. The United States assembled the most formidable basketball team of all time. All but one player was an NBA standout. As a nod to the college game, which previously had supplied most of the players, one college player was included on the roster.

Well-known and wildly popular worldwide, the American players stayed in a five-star hotel instead of the Olympic village. They were under constant security surveillance. Whenever some of the players ventured out, they were mobbed for autographs and treated like rock stars.

"It was like Elvis and the Beatles put together," said coach Chuck Daly of the Detroit Pistons.[1]

There was no question about which team would win the gold medal. That year the men's basketball competition was not about a battle for first place as much as it was about showing the world what the best players could do when teamed together and let loose.

Christian Laettner from Duke was the lone college player selected. The rest of the all-star bunch featured Michael Jordan, Larry Bird, Magic Johnson, Charles Barkley, Karl Malone, John Stockton, David Robinson, Clyde Drexler, Patrick Ewing, Scottie Pippen, and Chris Mullin.

The games within the Games were no contest. Daly's biggest task was to divide up playing time. Bird was suffering from a bad back, the injury that would lead to his retirement soon after the Olympics. But while the players had supreme confidence and knew they could pretty much flex their muscles at will any time an opponent (if ever so briefly) made a run, they enjoyed being on the worldwide stage to showcase their abilities.

"It was like, the guys lost in '88, and so then they sent in the Navy Seals," Ewing said. "We were the Navy Seals. We were the elite forces, the elite of the elite forces. We came in, and we kicked butt and took names and got everybody back home safely."[2]

The U.S. team opened against Angola, an African representative, and won 116–48. Illustrating how famous the American players were, players on the other team sought their autographs and asked them to pose for pictures.

Conceived as a way to spread the gospel of basketball more thoroughly around the world, the United States Olympic team of 1992 that romped to the gold medal included such luminaries as Larry Bird, Michael Jordan, Magic Johnson, Charles Barkley, and others. That group was called "The Dream Team." (AP Photo/John Gaps III)

Besides the humongous margin of victory, the game is often remembered for a hard elbow Barkley delivered to a much smaller Angolan player. In some ways this was Barkley's Olympics. He led the team in scoring with 24 points, mingled with the masses on the streets of Barcelona enjoying the night life, and cracked up sportswriters who listened to his postgame monologues.

While some members of the U.S. press corps took Barkley to task for this not only intentional, but unnecessary, elbow, Angola's coach Victorino Cuhna said it was no big deal.

"Oh, we don't get upset because Charles Barkley does the same thing in NBA games," Cuhna said.[3]

He was right about that.

In the following games the Americans defeated Croatia, 103–70; Germany, 111–68; Brazil, 127–83; Spain, 122–81; Puerto Rico, 115–77; Lithuania, 127–76; and Croatia again, 117–85, in the gold medal game.

There was no doubt which was the best team.

"It wasn't a gloating thing, it wasn't bragging, it was just, 'This is what we came to do,'" Malone said. "We didn't come there to try and make world peace. We came there to win the gold medal and bring it back home and say to the other countries, 'Now you've had our best.'"[4]

The Americans made a huge impact on and off the court, and although the most far-sighted among international basketball officials understood a Rubicon had been crossed, the everyday U.S. fan and player viewed the series of wipeouts as a flexing of national muscle. To them it was a restoration of U.S. basketball to the throne to which it was royally entitled.

Yet nearly a quarter of a century later, with perspective added to the mix, it is obvious that the intended purpose of the international administrators was fulfilled. Worldwide the caliber of basketball is far superior to what it was in 1992. More and more international players of this generation have reaped the benefits of their home-country basketball associations' efforts to grow the sport.

Among the foreign players in the NBA are Manu Ginobili and Luis Scola from Argentina, Andrew Bogut from Australia, Tiago Splitter from Brazil, Bojan Bogdanovic from Croatia, Bismack Biyombo from the Congo, Rudy Gobert from France, Dirk Nowitzki from West Germany, and Giannis Antetokounmpo from Greece.

There are more foreign-born players in the NBA playing professionally every year. These twenty-somethings grew up with more resources at their disposal and with more efficient and learned coaches than their predecessors had. This is all a by-product of the decision to invite professionals into the Olympics and what the greatest single team ever assembled accomplished in 1992.

NOTES

1. Larry Siddons, "Chuck Daly, Basketball Coach of 'Dream Team,' 'Bad Boys' Dies," *Bloomberg.com*, http://www.bloomberg.com/apps/news?pid=newsarchive&sid=aBJ2fmA Pcxz8.

2. Lang Whitaker, "The Dream Will Never Die: An Oral History of the Dream Team," *GQ*, July 2012.

3. Harvey Araton, "Barkley's Elbow Fouls a U.S. Rout," *New York Times*, July 27, 1992.

4. Whitaker, "The Dream Will Never Die."

FURTHER READING

Daly, Chuck, and Alex Sachare. *America's Dream Team: The 1992 USA Basketball Team.* Nashville, TN: Turner Publishing, 1992.

McCallum, Jack. *Dream Team: How Michael, Magic, Larry, Charles, and the Greatest Team of All Time Conquered the World and Changed the Game of Basketball Forever.* New York: Ballantine Books, 2013.

#34 Richard Petty's 200th Win

They called him "The King," and Richard Petty earned it. The man who dominated the early days of stock-car racing won the NASCAR championship seven times, and in a mark that likely will never be approached, never mind broken, won 200 races in his career.

It was a different era when Petty raced, and one characteristic of that period, from the late 1950s into the early 1970s, was the number of races the NASCAR circuit offered before it was somewhat streamlined. In 1967 alone, Petty won 27 races, more than most NASCAR drivers win during their entire careers.

Although he was hungry to put his foot on the pedal at a younger age, Petty's father Lee made him wait until his 21st birthday to visit the starting line in a NASCAR race. The day Richard had been waiting for finally arrived in 1958. He had been itching to drive for years, but couldn't afford to try it without his daddy's help. So he waited, impatiently, for his chance.

Born in North Carolina in 1937, Petty was the son of a former NASCAR champ, Lee Petty. Richard's son Kyle was also a successful racer. The Petty name is royalty around the racetrack.

Petty grew up around racing, but his uncles grew tobacco.

"To say that I was a product of my environment would be the understatement of the century," Petty said of his upbringing around racing. "I grew up in a world of fast cars and the constant talk of racing."[1]

Once Petty began racing those stock cars he adapted quickly, became tough to beat, and eventually demonstrated a breathtaking dominance. He won his first race on July 18, 1959, in Columbia, South Carolina. It was a 100-miler, and he was driving an Oldsmobile. For most of the rest of his driving career Petty drove Plymouths, though he did commit to Fords for a while in 1969 and in the closing stages of his career drove other cars.

One of the things that eventually developed in NASCAR racing was more sophisticated tracks that were better cared for than some of the old, chewed-up tracks in the early days of the circuit. Petty saw them all. Every town across the South seemed to have a track where NASCAR paused for a race.

"It took talent to drive them all because the tracks were so different," Petty said.[2]

He was the man who could do it, though, and Petty racked up wins all across the region at all types of distances. Before NASCAR went mainstream in the sports world and tracks were built near the nation's biggest cities, it used to be said that stock-car racing was the national sport of the South. Petty captured some of his earliest victories in Charlotte, North Carolina; Martinsville, Virginia; Hillsboro, Virginia; North Wilkesboro, North Carolina; Huntsville, Alabama; and Spartanburg, South Carolina. Petty had the daring and skill to drive the small tracks with their tight turns, but also to make a splash in NASCAR's biggest money, attention-getting races.

During his racing days Petty won the Daytona 500 seven times as part of his affinity for speed on every size of track where NASCAR ran. He also won at Darlington and Atlanta; Rockingham, North Carolina; and Bristol, Tennessee.

What distinguished Petty from many of his competitors, besides winning so often, was the example he set in hanging out with fans and signing autographs. Petty was at all times approachable and not only became beloved to stock-car fans, but elevated the profile of the sport and showed other drivers how to behave with crowds.

When Petty was voted the Most Popular Driver by fans, he responded with the same famous humility he showed people at all times.

"That meant a lot to me because I had always tried to treat everyone right," Petty said, "and not to let success go to my head."[3]

In addition to winning 200 times, Petty recorded 712 top-10 finishes and earned the pole for the start of races 123 times. He made the number 43 iconic in stock-car racing. He also won $7.7 million in prize money as a driver.

When it comes to the all-time NASCAR list of winners, Petty is so far ahead he is considered over the horizon. David Pearson, a contemporary of Petty's, stands second on the list, with 105 victories. Third is Jeff Gordon, who has had 92 wins

With a grand sense of timing and place, legendary driver Richard Petty won his 200th NASCAR race on July 4, 1984, at the Daytona International Speedway. That was the final triumph of Petty's career, and the 200 victories is viewed as an untouchable record. (AP Photo/Elliot Schecter)

but has announced his retirement following the 2015 season. By coincidence, Gordon's first NASCAR race, on November 15, 1992, was Petty's final race.

Dale Earnhardt Sr. tied Petty for the most seasonal championships won, seven, and had the potential to win more, but was killed at Daytona in 2001.

In the fall of 1991 Petty decided it was time for him to retire from driving race cars. He announced that the 1992 season would be his last. He had spent 34 years' seasons competing, but had not won a race in recent years. Petty had earned a spot in the winner's circle for the final time in his career eight years earlier.

On July 4, 1984, at the Pepsi 400 at Daytona, Petty took the checkered flag to capture his 200th race.

"Before I won my 100th race . . . people said it was an impossible feat," Petty said, "just because nobody had ever done it. Well, on July Fourth at Daytona—naturally everything big has happened there—probably the major event of my racing life took place. I won my 200th race. The papers and magazines say it's a record that will never be broken."[4]

NASCAR.com produced a list of the sport's records that are least likely to be broken, and Petty's 200 wins was voted number 1. No one else has come close to

200 wins yet, and even if someone does someday catch up to the King, it will be years and years from now.

Petty did not escape from his potentially dangerous sport unscathed. He raced in an era when the fatality rate for drivers was much higher than it is now. Twice he suffered a broken neck, and had numerous concussions, as well as injuries to other body parts, in his 1,184 NASCAR starts.

"Seeing where they started and where they are now, they've kept up with it as good as they could," Petty said in 2015 of NASCAR's efforts to make safety improvements. "Nothing will ever be 100 percent safe."[5]

It is not as if Petty faded into the woodwork when he stepped out of a car for the last time, either. He promptly began running his own team with other drivers. He was the car owner for Petty Enterprises. He met with some success in that role, although not nearly as much as he had behind the wheel. Eventually the team was sold.

Petty was given the Presidential Medal of Freedom in 1992, and in 2010 he was inducted into the NASCAR Hall of Fame as part of its first class.

Petty is still a visible figure in the stock-car world, making public appearances and attending races. As the most famous driver of all time, Petty still has a multitude of endorsement contracts. He may be in his late seventies now, but Petty retains an unmistakable look in public.

If you see Richard Petty, the King, at a racetrack, he will invariably be wearing his trademark sunglasses and cowboy hat. He will also likely be smiling broadly and signing autographs for his legion of fans. Petty is still a man of the people.

NOTES

1. Richard Petty and William Neeley, *King Richard I: The Autobiography of America's Greatest Auto Racer* (New York: Paperjacks Ltd., 1987), 39.
2. Ibid., 147.
3. Ibid., 185.
4. Ibid., 246.
5. Mike Hembree, "What Does Richard Petty Think about NASCAR's Safety Effort?" *USA Today*, March 20, 2015.

FURTHER READING

Beekman, Scott M. *NASCAR Nation: A History of Stock Car Racing in the United States.* Santa Barbara, CA: Praeger, 2010.

Bongard, Tim, and Bill Coulter. *Richard Petty: The Cars of the King.* New York: Sports Publishing, 1997.

Petty, Richard. *Richard Petty: King of the Road.* New York: Macmillan, 1997.

#35 Lance Armstrong

Lance Armstrong, the king of the bicycle, was an inspiration to millions of Americans for beating cancer and winning the Tour de France seven times, and then was disgraced when it was shown and he admitted that he had cheated all along, using performance-enhancing drugs.

Armstrong was born in 1971 in Plano, Texas. He emerged as the greatest U.S. bicycle rider for his triumphs in the world's most popular and demanding bicycle race, a showcase event in France each summer. Armstrong won the race in 1999, 2000, 2001, 2002, 2003, 2004, and 2005. One can search for a list of Tour de France winners and see Armstrong's name there as the champion in those years, but now his name has a line drawn through it. The point is to remember that he won on the course, but because he broke the rules, his titles were stripped from him.

At age 25 Armstrong was diagnosed with advanced testicular cancer, which had spread to his brain, lungs, and abdomen. His future appeared bleak, and doctors believed that he would not be able to beat the disease. Instead, Armstrong rallied, recovered, and came back to his sport better than ever.

The cancer diagnosis was shocking, and the harsh assessment of what the chemotherapy treatment would do to him was almost unbelievable to Armstrong. He related his memory of being informed of that in his best-selling book, *It's Not about the Bike*: "I'm going to kill you," the doctor told him. "Every day I'm going to kill you and then I'm going to bring you back to life. We're going to hit you with chemo and then hit you again, and hit you again. You're not going to be able to walk."[1]

Armstrong also endured brain surgery, and he was not confident he would live through the process.

"How do you confront your own death?" he said. "Sometimes I think the blood-brain barrier is more than just physical, it's emotional, too."[2]

Before his illness, Armstrong had been a budding star on the world cycling scene. He had won a one-day world cycling championship in 1993. He also had won two stages in the Tour, the prestigious event conducted over different courses each year, that routinely covers about 2,500 miles.

From 1998 on, Armstrong showed remarkable strength, speed, and staying power, becoming the most dominant racer in the world. Year after year he fought off all comers to win the Tour de France. He became the most visible recovered cancer patient in the United States and embraced the role of being an inspiration to millions battling the disease or who had loved ones fighting it.

For a bicycle racer, the Tour de France is the pinnacle of the sport. Armstrong was hungry to prove his abilities at this elite level. Few dispute that it is one of the most physically challenging of sporting events because of its length, terrain, and high-quality competition.

"I think it may be the most gallant athletic endeavor in the world," Armstrong has said.[3]

Armstrong was a brilliant competitor in the individual time trials. He routinely gained separation from the other best riders in those tests, hammering the pedals and winning by many seconds or sometimes even a minute or more.

He was surrounded by an excellent team, attacked well in the mountains, and eventually broke the peleton, or pack. Armstrong vividly embraced the final short distance in Paris on the day he won his first Tour.

Lance Armstrong has been both the greatest hero in American bicycling history for winning the Tour de France seven times and the biggest villain for confessing he cheated by taking performance-enhancing drugs. (AP Photo/Michel Spingler)

"I felt a swell of emotion as we rode onto the Champs-Elysees for the first time," he said. "The entire avenue was shut down for us and it was a stunning sight. The number of American flags swirling in the crowd stunned me."[4]

In 1997 Armstrong founded the Lance Armstrong Foundation to support victims of cancer. The organization sold millions of yellow rubber plastic wrist Livestrong bracelets and raised $325 million. His achievements on the bike, coupled with Armstrong's active Livestrong support and willingness to devote energy to the fight against cancer, made him one of the most admired athletes in the United States.

Before Armstrong, bicycle riding was popular as an activity for all ages, but bicycle racing was of limited interest to sports fans. Armstrong transformed American interest in the sport and especially raised the profile of and attention paid to the Tour in his home country. He was a household name, viewed as the best bicycle racer ever produced by the United States.

However, at the same time that Armstrong was becoming a hero to many in the United States, he was looked at with suspicion in Europe. To many cycling fans and reporters, his story was just too good to be true. Allegations that Armstrong used drugs to aid his performance popped up regularly and persisted for years.

Time after time Armstrong shouted down accusers, aggressively set lawyers on them, and sued them in court. Time after time he repeated that he had never failed a drug test administered at a race. This went on for years. Armstrong was the face of the sport, and he was in the forefront of defending international cycling from anyone who attempted to undermine its credibility by labeling him and others chronic drug users.

Some prominent cyclists did fail drug tests, and they were suspended for a year at a time. Armstrong skated through all challenges. Reporters dug in harder, seeking smoking-gun evidence that Armstrong had violated the rules. In the absence of hard proof, though, they could not make an unassailable case in the media. He referred to critics as being part of a witch hunt and denounced sportswriters as practitioners of tabloid journalism.

Armstrong appeared to be a pillar of the sport. He was the best rider and the biggest winner, brought glory to his American teams, was a spokesman in the fight against the deadliest disease, and had single-handedly lifted his sport up to beyond also-ran status on American sports pages.

It took a long time, but ultimately, to the horror of defenders, supporters, and believers, Armstrong's empire collapsed. After many years of decrying his detractors as liars, Armstrong was proven to be the liar and admitted to his long-running scam.

The beginning of the end for Armstrong came when another American Tour competitor, Floyd Landis, confessed to using performance-enhancing drugs and accused Armstrong of doing the same. A federal investigation followed, but Armstrong seemingly escaped with little permanent damage to his reputation, until the U.S. Anti-Doping Agency leveled serious charges in 2012.

Armstrong was accused of doping and trafficking in drugs. Former teammates stood against him and revealed their knowledge of the inner workings of the U.S. cycling teams Armstrong had led.

In January 2013 Armstrong appeared in a televised interview with Oprah Winfrey, for the first time reversing his long-standing denial of taking illegal drugs to improve his bicycle riding. Nearly eight years had passed since Armstrong's last Tour de France championship.

During the televised interview Armstrong said he had had to "win at all costs" and that he believed he could not have won the Tour de France without the help of performance-enhancing drugs. Armstrong listed the names of numerous drugs he had used during his tenure at the top of the world of bicycling. He said he had not felt that he was cheating, and had even looked up the definition in the dictionary.

He said because everyone was taking drugs, he looked at his own reliance on the artificial as "a level playing field."

"I view this situation as one big lie that I repeated a lot of times."[5]

This further sparked a downward spiral of Armstrong's reputation, led to his being stripped of all his Tour de France championships, and prompted former sponsors and endorsers to sue Armstrong to recover money spent on him. The Lance Armstrong Foundation is now called Livestrong. It lives on to help people, but Armstrong severed his connection with it. Some 80 million Livestrong bracelets have been sold.

There has probably never been another story like this one in American sports history, a roller-coaster of incredible highs and lows.

NOTES

1. Lance Armstrong and Sally Jenkins, *It's Not about the Bike* (New York: Berkley Books, 2001), 99.
2. Ibid., 112.
3. Ibid., 215.
4. Ibid., 256.
5. Liz Clarke, "Lance Armstrong Confession Gets Specific in Oprah Winfrey Interview," *Washington Post,* January 17, 2013.

FURTHER READING

Albergotti, Reed, and Vanessa O'Connell. *Wheelmen: Lance Armstrong, the Tour de France and the Greatest Sports Conspiracy Ever*. New York: Gotham, 2014.
Armstrong, Lance, and Sally Jenkins. *Every Second Counts*. New York: Broadway Books, 2013.
Hamilton, Tyler, and Dan Coyle. *The Secret Race: Inside the Hidden World of the Tour de France*. New York: Bantam Books, 2013.
Walsh, David. *Seven Deadly Sins: My Pursuit of Lance Armstrong*. New York: Atria Books, 2013.

#36 Kenny Sailors Invents the Jump Shot

From the time Dr. James Naismith invented the game of basketball until the mid-1940s, basketball was essentially a game played beneath the rim. Players shot flat-footed. They didn't "sky" as the term came to be called when latter-day athletes

Growing up in rural Wyoming, Kenny Sailors developed an unusual shot that turned into a revolutionary change for the game of basketball. Sailors, captain of the 1943 University of Wyoming NCAA titlists and a veteran of the early days of the NBA, introduced the jump shot at the highest levels of the game. (AP Photo)

developed phenomenal leaping games.

The one man, more than any other, who introduced a dramatic innovation that showed jumping could be more profitable than staying grounded, was a guard for the University of Wyoming named Kenny Sailors, the captain of the Cowboys team that won the NCAA title in 1943.

Sailors, born in 1921 and now in his nineties, is a member of the College Basketball Hall of Fame in Kansas City, Missouri, where his exploits as a three-time all-American and his creativeness are extolled.

When Sailors was of junior high school age in the 1930s, he was living on a farm in Hillsdale, Wyoming, with his mother and his older brother. Bud was five years older and more than five inches taller. When the boys engaged in one-on-one basketball play in the back yard, big brother took no mercy on little brother, regularly blocking his shot.

One day Kenny decided he had had enough of that. As usual, Bud was moving in to swat Kenny's shot to the cow pasture. But Kenny fooled him, jumping in the air and only then releasing his shot at the hoop. The jump shot was born.

The way Sailors remembers this seminal moment in basketball's evolution, he was 13 years old and stood around five-foot-six. Bud, who topped out at six-foot-five, was on his way to his full height, if not already there.

"It was just a weapon that came naturally," Kenny Sailors said of his eureka moment. "He was big, but he was fast enough to stop my drive."[1]

The younger Sailors couldn't quite get around Bud, so he elevated over him when Bud least expected it.

As the years passed Sailors perfected his form and accuracy. He employed the jumper to great effectiveness in high school and at Wyoming, where he was the leader of the best team in school history. On the way to the national title, the Cowboys played some games in Madison Square Garden, and Sailors became a sensation for his aerial tricks. He was featured on the cover of *Life* magazine and demonstrated that the jump shot could be a devastating weapon.

The Cowboys defeated Georgetown in the NCAA championship game, and Sailors was chosen the most outstanding player of the tournament. He is the oldest living outstanding player in the three-quarters of a century of the play-off's existence.

The result was not a blowout, but in an era with no shot clock and lower scoring games, the 12-point margin in a 46–34 finale was enough. Still, it was only late in the contest that the Cowboys realized they were going to be national champions.

"They were a good ball club," Sailors said. "It seemed as if we beat them pretty handily, but they weren't a bad team. We played control ball and occasionally threw in a fast break."[2]

Sailors was an accomplished ball handler as well as a sharp shooter from outside. His quickness allowed him to drive past defenders to the hoop, and one of his opponents who tried to cover him praised Sailors.

"He's the fastest man I ever tried to guard," said Georgetown back-court man Billy Hassett.[3]

After serving in the military during World War II and finishing his schooling at Wyoming, Sailors joined the fledgling NBA and played for five seasons. It was here, for the first time, that Sailors ran into prejudice against his shot. As many pioneers do, Sailors met resistance when he brought his shot along with him. His first pro coach told him it was reckless to leave one's feet to shoot.

Sailors earned one all-star mention during his limited NBA career and had one season in which he averaged 17.3 points a game. By the end of the 1950s basketball had been transformed. Stars at the beginning of the decade shot one-handed or two-handed set shots, feet firmly planted on the ground. The next generation of scorers all employed the jump shot, and the game has never looked back, even as it has become more athletic, with fancier drives to the hoops for layups or through the use of dunk shots.

The jump shot became such an ingrained aspect of the game that rarely did anyone stop to think about a time when it was not a routine part of the sport. Future players grew up using the jump shot from the time they first visited playgrounds, throughout high school, during their college days, and on into the pros. No one could remember a time when the jump shot was not the most effective offensive weapon. It was as natural as dribbling.

In 1965 Hall of Fame coach Joe Lapchick gave Sailors credit for introducing the jump shot as the world knows it.

"Sailors started the one-handed jumper, which is probably the shot of the present and the future," Lapchick said.[4]

To a large degree Sailors's history was forgotten by the average fan, something he always attributed to the fact that he went off to Alaska in 1965 and spent the next 35 years living there, away from mainstream college basketball. He was also a somewhat quiet man who was never a self-promoter.

Later in life, though, as historians investigated different eras of hoops, Sailors's story moved to the forefront, and he was frequently sought out by newspaper sportswriters and television sportscasters. His contribution to the game became more publicized and venerated.

In 2012, when Sailors was inducted into the college hall, he went in with several more recent stars, including Earl "The Pearl" Monroe, one of basketball's most awesome scorers.

Monroe, who sat next to Sailors on a dais during a press conference, was asked what he thought basketball would be like if Sailors had not invented the jump shot. Monroe paused for a moment and then said, "I guess we'd all be dunking. I can't imagine the game being played without the jump shot."[5]

In mid-January 2015 an ESPN crew happened to be in Laramie to televise a University of Wyoming basketball game. The color commentator was Hall of Fame coach Bob Knight, and he asked to meet Sailors. The session was arranged at Sailors's home by the school's sports information director.

Later that night during the game, Knight issued what amounted to a personal tribute to Sailors as the camera panned the rafters to focus in on Sailors's number 4 honored jersey, the university's only basketball shirt hanging above.

Knight told the viewers that Sailors deserved to be in the Naismith Memorial Hall of Fame, that his induction was way overdue, and that it was "criminal" that he had not already been enshrined in Springfield, Massachusetts.[6]

The day happened to be Sailors's 94th birthday.

After hearing the Knight testimonial, famed basketball announcer Dick Vitale chimed in on twitter: "Kenny Sailors, ex-Wyoming star, invented the jump shot. Should be in HOF as contributor says: Bob Knight & I agree."[7]

Although not as spry as he once was, Sailors lives just a mile from the University of Wyoming's basketball arena and still tries to attend as many games played by his alma mater as he can.

A member of the school's athletic hall of fame and an athlete who has been recognized as a treasure by the school, to his amazement Sailors saw a 22-foot statue of himself as a player being erected outside the arena as part of a fresh construction project.

Remembering his back-on-the-farm beginnings of long ago, that is something Kenny Sailors never thought he would see.

NOTES

1. Lew Freedman, *JUMP SHOT: Kenny Sailors, Basketball Innovator and Alaskan Outfitter* (Portland, OR: Westwinds Press, 2014), 9.
2. Ibid., 64.
3. Ibid., 65.
4. Ibid., 73.
5. Ibid., 194.
6. Bob Knight, ESPN basketball telecast, January 14, 2015.
7. Dick Vitale, https://twitter.com/dickiev, January 14, 2015.

FURTHER READING

Botkin, Brad. "Birth of the Jump Shot," *CBSsports.com*, http://www.cbssports.com/collegebasketball/feature/25067625/jump-shot.
Sailors, Kenny, and Lew Freedman. *Hunting the Wild Country*. Anchorage, AK: Glacier Press, 1994.

#37 Pete Gogolak's Funny Kicking

From the early days of football into the 1960s, before most current football fans were born, kickers who booted extra points and field goals and also kicked off to start the game, or after touchdowns, approached the oblong ball with a totally different method than is seen today.

Those kickers, from Lou Groza to Lou Michaels, from Gino Capalletti to Sam Baker, possessed a similar run-up. They approached the football from the same direction: straight on. A couple of steps and boom! Their first contact with the ball came from their toes. Groza, indeed, was nicknamed "The Toe."

Then along came Pete Gogolak. Gogolak was the first practitioner of the sideways approach to the football. He and others who followed charge the ball from the right or the left, not from right in front of it. This was called the soccer style of kicking the football. The point of contact with the ball is the side of the foot, a much bigger area of the appendage striking the ball. It was an import from Europe and was initially met with skepticism.

Some ridicule was attached to this peculiar method of booting the ball. Part of it was resistance to change. Part of it was because the straight-ahead method was the only one that anyone had ever used.

Born Peter Kornel Gogolak in Budapest, Hungary, in 1942, the kicker grew up playing soccer. By the time he was attending Cornell University, however, Gogolak

A man ahead of his time, Pete Gogolak from Hungary became the first player in NFL history to kick field goals with the soccer style that became the commonly accepted way for pros to score points with their foot when he broke into the game in 1965. (AP Photo)

had become a football player who kicked his own way. Gogolak was six-foot-one and weighed 190 pounds, so he pretty much looked like an athlete, even though a half century ago kickers were often disparaged for being specialists not involved in contact.

The birth of the soccer-style kick in American-style football dates to 1961, when Gogolak booted a 41-yard field goal for Cornell. When he finished college Gogolak was drafted by the Buffalo Bills, then members of the American Football League. The AFL, in competition with the established NFL, was considered more inclined to take chances and try innovative ideas.

As a 22-year-old rookie for Buffalo in 1964, Gogolak received tremendous attention for his newfangled style, in part because he was very successful with it. He attempted 46 extra points and made 45 of them. He attempted 29 field goals and hit 19 of them. By scoring 102 points, Gogolak made people think about his innovation.

The next season Gogolak proved that his performance was no fluke. He scored 115 points on 28 field goals and 31 extra points.

Although his showing should have solidified his standing with the Bills, Gogolak was not exceptionally well paid. The pervasive thinking was that unless a player also contributed in a position on the field, he was taking up important roster space. Buffalo paid Gogolak just $10,000 in his first season. Even after he broke the century mark in points, the team's offer for the next year was just $13,500. Under the rules of his contract Gogolak could take a pay cut (he played for $9,900 in 1965) and play out his option.

He did so and found the market receptive. Gogolak took more money to join the New York Giants, for whom he played the remainder of his 11-year career. Only twice during his ensuing years with the Giants did Gogolak approach his single-season points high with Buffalo. One season he scored 107 points, and another he scored 97 points. In 1970 kicked 25 field goals.

A few years after Gogolak made his pro football debut, his younger brother Charlie, who played for Princeton, joined him in the NFL. One thing that Pete's success did was put his brother in the spotlight.

Charlie, who was two years younger, became the first kicker ever to be a number 1 draft pick, when the Washington Redskins selected him in 1966. Naturally Charlie, who was also born in Hungary, employed the same soccer-style way of kicking a football. He played professionally for six years with the Redskins and with the Boston Patriots as they were changing their name to the New England Patriots. Unlike the larger Pete, Charlie was kicker-sized. He stood just five-foot-ten and weighed 165 pounds.

On November 27, 1966, Pete's Giants and Charlie's Redskins met in a regular-season game at D.C. Stadium in Washington. In one of the most unusual high-scoring games in NFL history, the Redskins topped New York, 72–41. Charlie kicked nine extra points, and Pete kicked five extra points. The total of 14 extra points combined is equal to the NFL all-time record. In another game Pete Gogolak kicked eight extra points.

By the time Pete Gogolak retired he was the Giants' all-time leading scorer, and his Bills-Giants total was 863.

Gogolak was most famous for introducing the new way to kick a football, but he also played a role in effecting the merger between the AFL and the NFL. The AFL was founded in 1960, and its creation not only provided more jobs for players, it helped drive up salaries. Teams in both leagues bid for the best players.

As the AFL refused to die and its owners invested lavishly in trying to secure the best available players coming out of college each year in the draft, both sides fought the war on another front: stealing established players. Pete Gogolak had won all-AFL honors in 1965, but he jumped leagues. This was an aspect of the feud between the leagues that owners hated the most.

Gogolak was an Ivy League graduate, so although he wanted to continue playing pro football, he was smart enough to realize he had a certain amount of leverage when the Bills came in with their limited-raise offer.

"It was like a slap in the face, frankly," Gogolak said years later. "We won the AFL championship. I proved myself. I asked for $20,000 and they wouldn't talk to me."[1] Gogolak liked Buffalo and wanted to stay there, but he took the pay cut for his second season to play out his option and see if another team might be attracted to him.

Gogolak became a free agent on May 1, 1966. Just before that, he said, "they didn't talk to me for two years and then they offered me $20,000. I said, 'No, thank you.'"[2]

Actually, when the free agent deadline arrived, a worried Gogolak had no offers.

"I was surprised that none of the other AFL teams had called me," he said. "A lot of teams needed a kicker."[3]

Soon afterward, however, the Giants contacted him with an impressive offer. Gogolak got a raise to $35,000 a year and signed a four-year deal. "I not only started the soccer-style kick, but maybe I started the merger."[4]

While not all present-day kickers are aware of who was the first to try extra points and field goals with a soccer approach, there are no NFL kickers anymore who employ any other style. Pete Gogolak showed the world the way, and his method became so ingrained that the kicker of today probably believes it was always done that way.

NOTES

1. Matt Warren, "Pete Gogolak Discusses His Role in the AFL-NFL Merger," *Buffalo Rumblings*, SB Nation, May 17, 2011.
2. Ibid.
3. Ibid.
4. Ibid.

FURTHER READING

Freedman, Lew. *New York Giants: The Complete Illustrated History*. Minneapolis, MN: MVP Books, 2012.

Gogolak, Pete. *Nothing to Kick About: The Autobiography of a Modern Immigrant*. New York: Dodd Mead, 1973.

Gogolak, Pete, and Ray Siegener. *Kicking the Football Soccer Style: With Tips on Playing Soccer*. New York: Holiday House, 1972.

#38 Introduction of the NBA Shot Clock

When basketball was invented in 1891, it was a static game. It would be barely recognizable to the modern fan. One could say the fundamentals got the game going, but the bells and whistles were added later.

During the early days of basketball, and right up to and beyond the establishment of the National Basketball Association, there were no rules prohibiting how long a team could remain in possession of the ball without taking a shot.

The modern fan would be totally turned off by that form of the game. Teams tended to stall when playing a superior foe. The coaches figured if they shortened the length of the game by running off clock time, they had a better chance to keep the score low and closer, and they just might pull off an upset.

One problem was that on occasion some teams took that strategy to the extreme. The NBA is a latecomer to the national sports scene compared to baseball, football, and hockey. Professional basketball leagues did not form until after World War II. Then more than one appeared, in hopes of taking advantage of the new national prosperity and increased leisure time. It was quickly learned that one league was enough, and after a few years of dueling leagues, the NBA emerged.

After some teams folded, some teams merged, and only the most fortunate of teams survived, the league still struggled to gain traction in the sports entertainment market. It was not doing anyone much good if fans paid to enter an arena, then ended up booing the play because they were being bored to death by teams that held the ball and took a shot only once every several minutes. There was plenty of time to visit the restroom or the concession stand, but the main show could sometimes drive even the most ardent fan nuts.

One of the most egregious of sins was for a team leading in the game to go into a stall so that there was no chance of the opponent making a comeback and catching up. That drained all of the suspense out of the sport.

The Minneapolis Lakers were the NBA's first dynasty. In the early days of the league the Lakers won championships almost every year. The Lakers featured a six-foot-ten center named George Mikan, a former all-American from DePaul. Mikan was basketball's first great big man. He was so good that nobody could cover him, and he dominated other teams with shorter personnel.

Surveying the landscape, some teams believed the only way they had a chance to beat the Lakers with Mikan in the middle was to stall. On November 22, 1950, the Fort Wayne Pistons and the Lakers played what must be characterized as one of the worst games in NBA history. Fort Wayne topped the Lakers, 19–18. The score in the fourth quarter—12 minutes per quarter—was 3–1. Basketball fans were lucky the teams didn't kill the sport right there. Not long after that the Pistons played the Lakers again, and since the slow-down game had worked once, pulled it out again. The game went into six overtimes, but the teams did not play to win as much as they played not to lose. During each overtime period the teams shot only once.

"That was the way the game was played—get a lead and put the ball in the icebox," said Boston Celtics Hall of Fame guard Bob Cousy. "Before the new rule, the last quarter could be deadly."[1]

How could they make the public fall in love with professional basketball? The answer was to provide more action.

While those Fort Wayne games were an extreme example of milking the rules to the max to possibly create a win, low-scoring games with stagnant play occurred all too often. The hero riding to the rescue of the NBA, and perhaps all basketball, since all other levels of play beyond high school eventually adopted a shot clock, was Syracuse Nationals owner Danny Biasone.

"The adoption of the clock was the most important event in the NBA," said Maurice Podoloff, who was the league's first president.[2]

Biasone invented the NBA shot clock, setting the timer at 24 seconds per possession, during which time a shot had to be taken or else the ball would be forfeited. Since there was no precedent, Biasone devised his own formula in choosing 24 seconds. Using the eye test—games he enjoyed watching—coupled with statistics from the box scores of those games, he came up with a plan.

He saw that in those games he liked, each team took about 60 shots, for a total of around 120 shots per game. In other words, there was action, instead of holding the ball. The NBA game consisted of 48 minutes, and he broke the minutes into seconds and then divided 120 into the total. The result was 24 seconds as an average per shot.

Biasone implemented the plan on his own in a Nationals scrimmage and found the results pleasing. He lobbied the league to adopt the 24-second shot clock, and it came into use for the 1954–1955 season. While it is strange to contemplate now, since the 24-second clock is a staple of the NBA, players adapting from no time limit to this time limit actually began to rush their plays. They had to get used to the changeover.

When the American Basketball League came into existence for a few years in the early 1960s, the ABL used a 30-second shot clock—a little tinkering there to be different.

When women's college basketball began to take hold in 1969, the Association for Intercollegiate Athletics for Women, which predated the NCAA in sanctioning women's ball, introduced a 30-second clock. That time limit for taking a shot is still in use.

The modern NBA really got its start during the 1954 season with the introduction of the 24-second shot clock. The new rule sped up the game and increased scoring, making the pro game more fan friendly. (AP Photo/Michael Okoniewski)

The Women's National Basketball Association uses a 24-second clock, the same as the male pros.

NCAA men's basketball was slow to change. Although he was not the inventor of the four corners stall, the late University of North Carolina coach Dean Smith was the most visible proponent of it in the 1960s and beyond. Smith often pulled out the strategy of widely spreading the floor and refusing to shoot when his team had a small lead, forcing the opponent into desperate measures. Eventually, for the 1985–1986 season, NCAA men's basketball ceased being a holdout and introduced a 45-second clock.

This was indeed a compromise, allowing plenty of time to shoot. For the 1993–1994 season the NCAA went a step further and cut the shot clock to 35 seconds. That is where it sits today, though there is discussion about reducing the time of possession to 30 seconds.

There is no doubt that a shot clock speeds up play. After all these decades, despite the minor differences in the amount of time on the clock at varying levels, all players have grown up with the shot clock in their background. It should be noted, however, that there is no shot clock in American high school basketball. Those teenaged teams can take as long as they wish to shoot.

It is hard to imagine what would have become of professional basketball, with its built-in cap on excitement, if teams had continued to dribble to their hearts' content and continued to produce games with scores like that of the infamous 19–18 contest.

NOTES

1. "History of the Shot Clock," *NBA.com*, October 22, 2001, http://www.nba.com /analysis/00422949.html.
2. Ibid.

FURTHER READING

Hubbard, Jan, ed. *The Official NBA Basketball Encyclopedia*. New York: Doubleday, 2000.
Longan, Patrick E. "The Shot Clock Comes to Trial: Time Limits for Federal Civil Trials." *Arizona Law Review* 35 (1993): 663.
Pluto, Terry. *Tall Tales: The Glory Years of the NBA, in the Words of the Men Who Played, Coached, and Built Pro Basketball*. New York: Simon & Schuster, 1992.

#39 Pete Rose, Charlie Hustle

The thing that fans and other players couldn't get over about Pete Rose when he broke into Major League Baseball was that he never stopped moving. Even when he walked, he ran. If a pitcher threw him four balls, he ran to first base. That's what earned him the nickname Charlie Hustle.

Rose was destined for greatness on the baseball diamond, but he also became an American tragedy.

As a big-league player, mostly for the Cincinnati Reds, with a major stop in Philadelphia for the Phillies and a cameo for the Montreal Expos, Rose spent 1963 to 1986 in the majors. He was one of the most admired players in the game because of his work ethic, his winning attitude, and his achievements, which were outsized by any standard, but seemed more so because it appeared Rose accomplished so much through sheer effort, not pure talent.

Rose stood five-foot-eleven and weighed 190 pounds, but in some ways he was considered a small man in the game. He was not speedy, but always got where he was going in plenty of time. He was not a flashy fielder, but he was chosen an all-star 17 times, representing a record five different positions. Rose did not demonstrate much power, but he always hit in the clutch, always hit in any situation. Fittingly, he was a switch-hitter who could adapt to any situation.

During his long career Rose won three National League batting titles and finished with a .303 lifetime average. He was a key cog in the Big Red Machine's dominant teams of the 1970s and played for three World Series champs, one of them the 1980 Phillies. While Ernie Banks, the late Chicago Cubs star, was known for his phrase, "Let's play two" as a symbol of always being ready for the next game, Rose was just as willing to play a doubleheader every day of the season. He seemed durable enough to do it, too, since he led the league in games played five times.

Baseball's career hits leader and the inspirational leader of the Cincinnati Reds and then the world champion Philadelphia Phillies, Pete Rose was banned from the game for gambling in 1989. Despite his achievements, that suspension has kept Rose from Hall of Fame consideration. (AP Photo)

Rose's trophy case was full. Besides the three championship rings, he was rookie of the year and won a Most Valuable Player award.

It may not be as well known as some of Rose's accomplishments, but his ability to stay healthy and play for a long time culminated in his becoming the major league leader in games played, 3,562. He has the most at-bats, 14,053. He also has the record for the most singles, and he made the most outs. Without being a power hitter, he smacked 160 home runs and drove in 1,314 runs. Without being especially fleet afoot, he stole 198 bases.

What Rose is best known for, however, is collecting the most hits in baseball history, 4,256. That earned him the nickname "The Hit King," which he likes to apply to himself as well.

Rose moved into third place on the all-time list on August 10, 1981, bypassing Stan Musial. Rose slashed a single off St. Louis Cardinal reliever Mark Littell to reach 3,631 hits and trail only Ty Cobb and Hank Aaron. This took place at Philadelphia's Veterans Stadium, and the team sent 3,631 balloons skyward when

Rose stroked the hit. Firecrackers were set off, too. Stan "The Man" Musial was in the house to congratulate Rose, pledging to stay for as long as it took during a three-game Phillies-Cardinals series.

"I had goose bumps for six or seven innings," Rose said. "I'll probably have pneumonia tomorrow." The phone rang during Rose's press conference, and he joked, "Tell the President to wait a minute." It was President Reagan, who for some reason took four tries to get through to Rose to congratulate him.[1]

After Rose digested his latest accomplishment, he was inevitably asked if he believed he could catch Ty Cobb's record.

"I am 40 years old now, and Cobb's record is still 560 hits away," Rose said, not sounding terribly confident. "At my age it's pretty difficult to think of matching that one. But given a few more good seasons, who knows? If I get close enough, I certainly would make a try for it."[2]

There was drama in Rose's pursuit of Ty Cobb. Cobb played for 24 seasons between 1906 and 1928 and retired with a .366 batting average, the highest average in history. The Detroit Tigers center fielder won 12 batting titles and three times batted over .400. Many consider Cobb the greatest ballplayer of all time. He also stole 897 bases and six times led the American League in steals.

Although historical revisionists credit Cobb with 4,189 hits, for decades his most famous record was considered to be 4,191. When it became apparent that Rose was the first player since the days of Cobb who had a chance to exceed 4,000 hits and possibly to surpass Cobb, that was the number he was chasing. Rose earned that Hit King title by cracking Cobb's record and retiring with 4,256 hits, 3,215 of them singles. Major League Baseball has stuck to the 4,191 figure, although researchers demonstrated that two Cobb hits were counted twice. Rose shot far enough past the old mark, anyway. The day Rose celebrated breaking the record was September 11, 1985, with a single, off of San Diego Padres pitcher Eric Show. If the smaller Cobb total is counted, Rose actually broke the record on September 8, off of Reggie Patterson of the Chicago Cubs. However, no one noticed at the time.

Another notable Rose batting achievement was his 44-game hitting streak of 1978. Rose hit safely from June 14 to August 1. He was in pursuit of Joe DiMaggio's major league record 56-game hitting streak, and he got closer than anyone else had since DiMaggio set the mark in 1941. The pre-1900 record belongs to Wee Willie Keeler, also credited with a 44-consecutive-game hitting streak. Like Cobb's total, though, researchers have since tampered with the number, crediting Keeler with batting safely in 45 straight games.

When Rose retired in 1986 he was on top of the world, a surefire first-ballot Hall of Famer once his five-year waiting period ended. By 1989 he was managing the Reds, but he was being investigated for betting on baseball games. That is the cardinal sin of the sport, a stupendous no-no infraction dating back to the Black Sox

Scandal of 1919, when the Chicago White Sox fixed the World Series and commissioner Kenesaw Mountain Landis subsequently banned eight players for life.

Baseball's investigation of Rose led to his being barred from the game for life, and he has officially been out of the sport for more than a quarter of a century. That has kept Rose's name from even being entered on the ballot for Hall of Fame consideration. In early 2015 Rose appealed for reinstatement, but no decision was immediately forthcoming from commissioner Rob Manfred.

After being on the outs for so long, Rose, who originally denied his guilt and continued to do so for some time, but eventually confessed, felt he had served his punishment. Others agreed, but still others want to see Rose frozen out of the sport and prohibited from being a candidate for the Hall of Fame.

While no one denies that Rose is deserving of membership in the Hall of Fame for his achievements on the field, there are many who believe he should not be allowed into the hall in Cooperstown, New York, because of his off-field actions.

Rose, who was 74 when he submitted the petition to Manfred, has said many times he believes he had done enough penance and deserves to have his suspension lifted.

NOTES

1. Lew Freedman, "Rose Drives to Hit Mark," *Orlando Sentinel*, August 11, 1981.
2. Michael Strauss, "Rose Breaks Musial's Career Hit Record," *New York Times*, August 11, 1981.

FURTHER READING

Kostya, Kennedy. *Pete Rose: An American Dilemma*. New York: Sports Illustrated Books, 2014.
Rose, Pete, and Rick Hill. *My Prison without Bars*. New York: Rodale Press, 2000.
Rose, Pete, and Roger Kahn. *Pete Rose: My Story*. New York: Macmillan, 1989.

#40 President Nixon's Ping-Pong Diplomacy

The phrase "Ping-Pong diplomacy" is applied to one event and one event only in the public mind, and it garnered the most attention the sport of Ping-Pong has ever received. The current younger generation of Americans cannot remember a time when the United States was not at least on speaking terms with China.

But for decades China was viewed as a sleeping giant of an enemy, the world's most populous country being run by a Communist government, which was turned inward and was suspicious of what lay beyond its borders.

China also fought on the side of North Korea during the Korean War of the early 1950s. The American political Right viewed China under Chairman Mao and subsequent Chinese hardliners as public enemy number 2 behind the Soviet Union. Taiwan was the U.S. ally in the region, and to differentiate "our" friend in Taiwan from the big, bad China, the huge land mass of Asia was called "Red China."

"It's hard for us to really understand just how little direct contact Americans and Chinese had with each other," said Clayton Dube on the occasion of the 40th anniversary of the trip in 2011. Dube was associate director of the University of Southern California's U.S.-China Institute. "It was a place much talked about and it was a place where the imagination ran wild."[1]

Right-wing politicians in the United States were opposed to conciliation in any form with the Communist leadership. President Richard Nixon, who was a candidate of the Right, had long established his anti-Communist credentials. It was easier for Nixon, with his ingrained policies, to make an overture to China than it would have been for Jimmy Carter or any other Democrat.

Nixon and his prominent secretary of state, Henry Kissinger, cared not a whit about Ping-Pong as an activity, but ingeniously employed the game to U.S. advantage. For most Americans, Ping-Pong was a basement recreational activity, way, way down the list of sports. It was viewed as a hobby game. When friends or neighbors came over, the house paddles were picked up and the little plastic white balls were slammed around for a time. The accurate name for the sport is table tennis, and its governing body in this country is USA Table Tennis. The average citizen sticks with Ping-Pong.

The Chinese took Ping-Pong more seriously and produced some of the world's top players. Indeed, on occasion a pair of Chinese players could be found giving half-time exhibitions at NBA games, where their incredible skills required use of virtually the entire court and their tricky spin serves and wicked returns made audiences gasp in admiration.

The U.S. Table Tennis team was participating in the world championships in Japan in 1971 when it received an unexpected invitation to visit China. Travel to China in those days for Americans was extremely limited and rare, with special permission required. The invitation from the People's Republic of China was accepted. The trip, with journalists in attendance (another surprising aspect of availability for reporters who had been requesting the opportunity to write from that nation for years, but were always being turned down), took place on April 10, 1971.

That was the first time an official American delegation of any type had visited the Chinese capital (then called Peking and now called Beijing) and been

Conservative President Richard Nixon was credited with creatively using the comparatively unheralded sport of Ping-Pong to open diplomatic relations with China in the 1970s despite China being the world's largest Communist nation. (AP Photo)

welcomed into China since 1949, after Mao's Communist Army drove Chiang Kai Shek from the mainland to Taiwan. One other group, of 11 Americans, had visited China for a week earlier in 1971, based on statements that their beliefs were consistent with the Black Panther Party, which expressed its support for Mao's politics.

It was never 100 percent clear why the invitation was extended to the Ping-Pong players, but partially through circumstances and partially through individual efforts to ignore politics, some top American players and some top Chinese players had practiced and played together and gotten to know one another.

Once the American Glenn Cowan was playing with a Chinese world champion and missed the departure of his team bus from a practice facility, and he was able to hitch a ride with the Chinese team back to his living quarters. The mere sight of the American and Chinese players mingling created an international sensation.

Tim Boggan, the official historian of USA Table Tennis, was one of the Americans who made the trip into China. At the time he was president of the

International Table Tennis Federation. Years later he laughed because "Ping-Pong" was being written about in newspapers all over the United States in a positive way despite reporters almost universally ignoring the use of "table tennis" as the sport's proper name.

"I never thought I would be happy to see the words Ping-Pong," Boggan wrote. "Those words are hated" because of the "Ping-Pong table in the basement" image. However, Boggan did call the development "the story that rocked the world."[2]

Whether the world at large believed the slogan or not, China had begun its gradual reintegration into international sport by stating, "Friendship first, competition second." This was at the least one way to live up to that slogan. Ping-Pong was a Chinese sport in which many of the most talented athletes in the country shone. In other words, it was a Chinese strength. Forty-some years ago, China would not have invited a basketball team to visit from the United States.

Mao, China's supreme leader, initially squashed the idea of inviting the American team to visit China, then changed his mind. Nine players and a small support group made the trip, and while they were in the country they played nonserious matches against Chinese players, but also saw sights like the Great Wall.

That small step through athletics led to Nixon's much more significant visit to China in February 1972 and the beginning of the normalization of relations between the two superpowers. Appropriately, Nixon attended a Ping-Pong match on his trip.

After the American table tennis players visited China, Nixon secretly opened talks with China and then sent Kissinger to Peking as a go-between to make the arrangements for his own breakthrough, breathtaking presidential visit. The Ping-Pong venture is so well remembered because it was a rare use of sport to facilitate improved relations between countries, and because nothing quite like it has followed.

"Never before in history has a sport been used so effectively as a tool of international diplomacy," said Chinese Premier Chou En-lai. Nixon called the interaction "the week that changed the world."[3]

Also in 1972, two months after Nixon visited China and posed for pictures shaking hands with Mao, between April 12 and 30 a Chinese Ping-Pong delegation came to the United States. Zhuang Zedong, who had been involved in the initial events with Cowan, was a leader of the group.

The Richard Nixon Foundation commemorated the 40th anniversary of the 1971 events. Part of the program consisted of Ping-Pong matches.

"It is the Ping-Pong that got the two countries together," said Qiu Shaofang, who was China's counsel to the United States in Los Angeles during that commemoration.[4]

NOTES

1. Matt Stevens, "When the Little Ball Moved the Big Ball Four Decades Ago," *Los Angeles Times*, July 8, 2011.
2. Tim Boggan, "Ping-Pong Oddity," in *History of U.S. Table Tennis*, Vol. V, Pt. 1 (USA Table Tennis, 1999), http://www.usatt.net/articles/ppoddity01.shtml.
3. David A. DeVoss, "Ping-Pong Diplomacy," *Smithsonian Magazine*, April 2002.
4. Stevens, "When the Little Ball Moved."

FURTHER READING

Griffin, Nicholas. *Ping-Pong Diplomacy: The Secret History behind the Game That Changed the World*. New York: Scribner, 2014.
Itoh, Maumi. *The Origin of Ping-Pong Diplomacy: The Forgotten Architect of Sino-U.S. Rapprochement*. New York: Palgrave Macmillan, 2011.
Kissinger, Henry. *On China*. New York: Penguin, 2012.

#41 Miami Dolphins Go 17–0

Some teams have come close. Some teams have played superior football. But only the Miami Dolphins have finished a season undefeated and won the Super Bowl.

The perfect Dolphins, as the team is sometimes called, finished the 1972 regular season 17–0. That included 14 regular-season games (before the schedule was expanded to 16 games) and 3 play-off games.

Miami remains acknowledged as one of the greatest teams in National Football League history, and the players from that era of more than 40 years ago still thrive on their unique status.

Although there is some doubt about the story that every year all of the surviving members of the Dolphins toast one another with champagne once the last team in the league loses its first game, there are indications that variations of that do take place. Quarterback Bob Griese has said that he and some teammates toast one another with Diet Coke. Other Dolphins have a toast with champagne.

The achievement of the 1972 Dolphins continues to stand alone.

Hall of Famer Don Shula coached that team. The winningest coach in NFL history, with 328 victories during the regular season and 342 for his career, Shula was the front man for an all-star cast. Among those players were Griese, who suffered a serious injury during the year and was replaced by Earl Morrall, who ironically was the backup for Johnny Unitas when he got hurt and led the Baltimore Colts into Super Bowl III.

More than 40 years after they recorded the accomplishment, the Super Bowl champion Miami Dolphins of 1973, coached by Don Shula, remain the only team in National Football League history to go unbeaten in the modern era. (AP Photo)

Griese broke his ankle and appeared in just six games all season. Things had been going too well. Morrall was 38 years old at the time, pretty much recognizing that as long as Griese was the leader, he was going to be spending more time sitting than throwing. Then, abruptly, the team had an urgent need for his services. He was supposed to be the backup. Next thing he knew, Morrall was just about the most important guy on the team.

The funny thing was that the Dolphins and his old Colts played each other twice that season. That meant going head to head with Unitas. Unitas was a year older and nearing the end of his Hall of Fame career. They met on the field before the game.

Unitas said, "You're getting too old for this, aren't you?" Morrall retaliated with his own zinger: "Well, you're a pretty old buck yourself."[1]

Larry Csonka and Jim Kiick, who were sometimes called "Butch Cassidy and the Sundance Kid," were featured in the backfield, but also had to make room for Mercury Morris. Csonka was a bruising fullback, Kiick the speedier outside runner. They complemented one another perfectly. But then along came Morris, who was faster than Kiick, and he broke up the partnership. That season Csonka rushed for 1,117 yards and Morris for 1,000. Kiick became a backup.

Shula went with the best he had at the moment, though Kiick resisted some of the coach's training methods. Once, when the players were assigned to take a longish run, Kiick was unhappy. "If I wanted to run cross-country," he said, "I would have gone out for it in high school."[2]

Other standouts were linebacker Nick Buoniconti; defensive backs Jake Scott and Dick Anderson; receiver Paul Warfield; and offensive linemen like Jim Langer, Larry Little, and Bob Kuechenberg.

The Dolphins' defense recorded three shutouts during the regular season and held three other teams to 10 points. Miami opened the fall with a victory over the Kansas City Chiefs and then beat, in order, the Houston Oilers, Minnesota Vikings, New York Jets, San Diego Chargers, Buffalo Bills, Colts, Bills again, New England Patriots, Jets again, St. Louis Cardinals, Patriots again, New York Giants, and Colts again.

The closest games were a 24–23 triumph over the Bills in the first encounter and a 16–14 win over Minnesota. The biggest margin of victory was 52–0 over the Patriots in their first meeting. The regular-season excellence propelled Miami to an American Football Conference first-place finish and into the play-offs.

As early as when the team was 3–0 there was considerable optimism in Miami about the outcome of the season, although Shula tried to tamp down some of the giddiness. He was already being asked if he felt that in this season his guys could do no wrong.

"A lot of people can win three games," he said. "We're not letting it go to our heads."[3]

Miami did not crush anyone in the play-offs. All three of the Dolphins' postseason games were close. First they beat the Cleveland Browns, 20–14. Then they took on the Pittsburgh Steelers and won 21–17. In the Super Bowl Miami faced the Washington Redskins and won 14–7. It all added up to 17–0 and a perfect season.

One of the hardest-fought games of the season was against Pittsburgh. Thinking the Dolphins were not showing their usual spark and were in danger of having the season go up in flames, Shula put a healed Griese into the game for his first appearance in weeks. The risky move paid off, and Miami advanced to the Super Bowl.

Linebacker Doug Swift put the Dolphins' situation in perspective on their second consecutive run to the Super Bowl while sporting a 16–0 record. They had to win it, he said, "and if we lose this one people are going to remember us as the biggest bunch of hot air in the world."[4]

The Dolphins gave the people something to remember them by, going 17–0 instead of 16–1.

The closest any team has come since 1972 to pulling together an undefeated regular season capped by a Super Bowl victory is the 2007 Patriots. New England fought through the regular season 16–0 in the expanded schedule, won two play-off games after a bye, and seemed to have the world title wrapped up against the New York Giants when the Giants pulled off a series of somewhat miraculous plays and bested the Patriots. They finished 18–1.

The Dolphins' 17–0 year was set up by the success and then disappointment of its 1971 season. That year Miami finished 10–3–1 in the regular season and advanced to the Super Bowl. But the Dolphins were conquered 24–3 in the Super Bowl by the Dallas Cowboys. They felt they were the better team and were hungry to prove it the next season.

That defeat produced tears in the locker room, including from owner Joe Robbie.

"I can't express how proud I am of this team," Robbie said. "It is unique. It will be here again."[5] Those were brave words at the time, but Robbie was correct, and the Dolphins didn't have to wait long for a second shot at the Super Bowl.

The Dolphins did get back, and as quickly as they possibly could. And the second time around, Miami won it all, with a perfect mark that has stood for excellence ever since.

In 2013 President Barack Obama invited the 1972 Dolphins to visit the White House to bestow special recognition on the squad.

Obama addressed the question "why now" with a joke at the August 20, 2013, meeting. "My answer is simple," he said. "I wanted to be the young guy up here for once."[6]

Larry Little, in Canton, Ohio, spoke for some of his teammates with his summary of their accomplishments.

"I can go no higher," Langer said of being recognized at the White House. "This is it. Hall of Fame, 17 and 0, 32 and 2 over two years, and now being on the White House grounds. Can't beat it."[7]

That was the point. Nobody could beat those 1972 Dolphins.

NOTES

1. Mike Freeman, *Undefeated: Inside the 1972 Miami Dolphins' Perfect Season* (New York: HarperCollins, 2012), 63.

2. Ibid., 40.

3. Ibid., 49.

4. Ibid., 227.

5. Ibid., 9.

6. Jim Kuhnhenn, "1972 Dolphins' White House Visit: Obama Salutes Undefeated Miami Team after 40 Years," *Associated Press*, August 20, 2013.

7. Ibid.

FURTHER READING

Griese, Bob, and Dave Hyde. *Perfection: The Inside Story of the 1972 Miami Dolphins' Perfect Season*. Hoboken, NJ: Wiley, 2012.

Hyde, Dave, and Don Shula. *Still Perfect: The Untold Story of the 1972 Miami Dolphins*. Miami Springs, FL: Dolphin Curtis Publishing, 2002.

Yepremian, Garo, and Skip Clayton. *Tales from the Miami Dolphins Sideline: Reminiscences of the Dolphins Glory Years*. New York: Sports Publishing, 2012.

#42 Frank Robinson, First African American Manager

Jackie Robinson broke the major league color barrier for players in 1947 when he played with the Brooklyn Dodgers. In 1972, in his last public appearance shortly before his death, when he was in failing health and going blind from diabetes, Robinson criticized baseball for being slow to hire an African American manager.

Two years later, in anticipation of the 1975 season, that barrier also fell. On October 31, 1974, the Cleveland Indians hired Frank Robinson to manage the team. This Robinson was a former star player for the Cincinnati Reds and Baltimore Orioles, a Hall of Fame outfielder who remains the only player selected as Most Valuable Player in both the American and National Leagues.

Frank Robinson is no relation to Jackie. He knows Robinson's surviving family members, and to his and Jackie's family's amusement is aware that members of the public sometimes confuse that fact.

Frank Robinson was born in Beaumont, Texas, in 1935, but graduated from high school in Oakland, California, his school being the one that also produced superstar basketball player Bill Russell. Robinson journeyed to Cincinnati to play baseball at Xavier University, but was soon drafted by the Reds, and by age 20, in 1956, Robinson was in the majors and the recipient of the NL rookie of the year award.

A star from the first, the six-foot-one, 183-pound Robinson smacked 38 home runs as a rookie. Although he was solidly built, Robinson was not a behemoth who scared pitchers with his size. Yet in a 21-season career, he blasted 586 home runs. That is in baseball's all-time top 10.

A fierce competitor, Robinson also collected 2,943 hits, drove in 1,812 runs, and batted .294 lifetime. Robinson was a 14-time all-star. He was also an African American in Cincinnati, which was not always warm to black people. He experienced

After authoring a Hall of Fame career as a slugging outfielder for the Cincinnati Reds and the Baltimore Orioles, Frank Robinson made more history. In October of 1974, the Cleveland Indians named him the first African American manager in Major League Baseball. (AP Photo)

his share of discrimination and later in life could give the impression of being gruff and embittered.

Robinson, who was primarily an outfielder, but also played some first base, was hired by Cleveland to be a player-manager. He did not really want to quit the game, and if he had continued to play at a high level for a couple of more seasons, he would have established some even more impressive stats, as long as he stayed healthy.

Although it was doubly demanding and Robinson was under a microscope in his breakthrough role, he did contribute with his bat when he made history on April 8, 1975, managing his first Indians game. He also ripped a memorable home run in his first at-bat in the dual role.

"Of all the pennants, World Series, awards and all-star games I've been in, this is the biggest thrill," Robinson said.[1] The Indians won the game, too.

It might also be said that that was a high point of Robinson's two-plus seasons managing the Indians. He felt he was underpaid and that managing interfered with his playing. Yet he felt obligated to African Americans to accept the chance when it was offered because there was no way to know how long it would take for the opportunity to come around a second time for any African American.

"I wanted to further the cause for African Americans and minorities in baseball," Robinson said. "I thought, 'When will that door open again?' I wanted to be a manager one day. I didn't want to be a player-manager."[2]

In Robinson's first season the Indians finished 79–80. In his second season they went 81–78. In 1977, Robinson was 41 and retired. He was a bench-manager only. And things didn't go so well. With the Indians sitting at 26–31 one-third of the way into the season, the Indians fired Robinson.

Eventually Robinson also managed the San Francisco Giants, Baltimore, Montreal Expos, and Washington Nationals after they moved to the nation's capital from Montreal. In all, Robinson managed for 16 years. His lifetime record was 1,065–1,176. Robinson's teams never won a pennant or played in the postseason.

Judging by the statistics, Robinson was a better player than manager. He did, however, continue to accept administrative jobs in baseball, with teams or the major league front office. In 2012 Robinson became vice president of development for MLB. His task was to boost interest among African American youths in the inner city.

The existence of this post was in itself ironic. In the 1920s, 1930s, and 1940s, when African Americans were locked out of organized baseball by unscrupulous owners applying an unspoken rule, black players would have done anything to get into the sport. Jackie Robinson opened the gates, and numerous African Americans emerged as superstars and Hall of Famers.

In more recent years baseball, once the national pastime, has been supplanted as the most popular team sport in the country by professional football and has been threatened by pro basketball. Baseball has been seeking to reclaim its lost player base.

This was a chore that Robinson embraced. He was a strong believer in wooing inner-city African Americans, teaching them the game, providing equipment, and upgrading fields. It was his passion to generate that interest through U.S.-based academies akin to those set up in foreign countries like the Dominican Republic to develop young talent and to weed out fringe prospects from the real deal.

"Right now the academies are very important to me," Robinson said in 2012 during an appearance at the Negro Leagues Baseball Museum in Kansas City. "They're going up as fast as we can get them up and they are bringing baseball to the youth in the inner cities of this country and giving them an opportunity to come and improve their skills, learn the game of baseball, and the fundamentals of it."[3]

Robinson was thinking back to his own youth and how young boys were so desperate to play baseball that they would commandeer playgrounds in the countryside or in suburbia and even take over city streets with heavy traffic. The desire was there and the hunger to play the most popular sport in the nation.

"It used to be that you were able to get a bat or ball or stick or whatever and get right out on the street and play," Robinson said. "You can't do that anymore. That's the pity of it. But this is the next best thing, giving these kids a chance, a place to go. It doesn't cost them anything but their time and attention. That's all we ask. Be a regular. If they come and join the program, be there."[4]

The white-haired Robinson turned 80 in 2015, and he stepped away from the inner-city program, though his heart was still with it. Even though he is not related to Jackie Robinson, Frank Robinson remained grateful for the way Jackie faced down challenges. Frank Robinson was 11 when Jackie Robinson made his major league debut, and he understood immediately what it meant for African Americans.

"I knew then that if I had the skills and ability to play in the major leagues, I would have the opportunity," Frank Robinson said. "Before that, no chance."[5]

Although he did not say it himself, the same was true for other African Americans aspiring to become managers once Frank Robinson became the first.

Robinson concluded his managing career and his final time wearing a baseball uniform when he was 71 in 2006, as he wrapped up his on-field job with the Nationals.

"It was everything and more than I thought it would be," Robinson said of his career. "It's been a good ride. It's been a good ride."[6]

NOTES

1. Russ Schneider, "(Flashback): Thirty-five Years Ago the Cleveland Indians' Frank Robinson Slugged a Home Run in His Debut as Player-Manager," *Cleveland Plain-Dealer*, April 9, 1975/April 18, 2010.

2. Lew Freedman, "Becoming Manager Was Sacrifice for Frank Robinson," *Call to the Pen*, July 13, 2012.

3. Lew Freedman, "Frank Robinson Still in the Game," *Call to the Pen*, August 7, 2012.

4. Ibid.

5. Ibid.

6. Dave Sheinin, "Nats' Robinson Bids a Fond Farewell," *Washington Post*, October 2, 2006.

FURTHER READING

Robinson, Frank, and Dave Anderson. *Frank Robinson: The First Year*. Concord, CA: Holt, Rinehart and Winston, 1976.

Robinson, Frank, and Al Silverman. *My Life Is Baseball*. New York: Doubleday, 1975.

Robinson, Frank, and Barry Stainback. *Extra Innings*. New York: McGraw-Hill, 1988.

Skipper, John C. *Frank Robinson: A Baseball Biography*. Jefferson, NC: McFarland, 2014.

#43 Althea Gibson

Tennis players were as white as the clothing they wore on the court to play the game when Althea Gibson came along and shattered preconceptions, making her mark as a pioneer in the sport.

Born in South Carolina in 1927, Gibson was the first African American, or person of color from any nation, to make a breakthrough at the top level of international tennis in the 1950s.

In 1956, when the five-foot-eleven, right-hand-hitting Gibson won the French Open, she became the first player of color to win a Grand Slam title. Over the next two years Gibson added the rest of the Grand Slam titles to her resume. She won Wimbledon in 1957 and 1958. She won the Australian Open in 1957 and the U.S. Open in 1957 and 1958.

Gibson also won three doubles crowns at Wimbledon and one each at the other three majors and added three mixed-doubles titles at Wimbledon and one at the U.S. Open. In all, Gibson, who was the best player in the world over that stretch, won 16 Grand Slam titles.

Gibson was an inspirational and transcendent figure in tennis who fought prejudice at every step and refused to back down when people sought to intimidate her. Some people compared her role as a pioneer in tennis to that of Jackie Robinson in baseball.

Born into poverty in Silver, South Carolina, Gibson's parents were sharecroppers on a cotton farm. During the Great Depression the family moved to Harlem, where Gibson spent most of her childhood. Her playgrounds were concrete, and she first excelled at paddle tennis. Gibson was so good at it that she became New York City champion by the age of 12. Paddle tennis is played on a smaller court with a lower net, and the implement of hitting is a paddle instead of a racquet.

Gibson never had it easy on her life path, but she was a driven woman, hungry to prove herself against the best competition in the toughest of forums.

"I always wanted to be somebody," were the first words she penned in her autobiography. "If I've made it, it's half because I was game to take a wicked amount of punishment along the way and half because of an awful lot of people who cared enough to help me. It has been a bewildering, challenging, exhausting experience, often more painful than pleasurable, more sad than happy. But I wouldn't have missed it for the world."[1]

Tennis was generally a game of the country club set, and Gibson's life was far removed from such environs. But she was so popular in her neighborhood and so good at paddle tennis that friends raised money to pay for tennis lessons. She quickly adapted from paddle tennis and began winning tournaments.

Gibson worked her way into prominence with repeated victories and came to the attention of an African American patron, who helped her financially. She attended high school in Wilmington, North Carolina, though she was wary of moving to the South. The discrimination, at least in tennis, was not as bad as she at first feared and when she played on public courts there was often a mix of white and black players around, if not competing against one another.

"I often heard some of them (the whites) criticize the stupidity of the segregation laws that kept them from playing together on the public courts," Gibson said. "I remember one white man grumbling, 'No sense in it at all.' I'll never forget my first bus ride into the downtown shopping area. The first thing I saw when I got on the bus and paid my fare was the sign, 'White in front, colored in rear.' I was burned up that I had to conform to such an ignorant law. It disgusted me and it made me feel ashamed in a way I'd never been ashamed back in New York."[2]

In 1949 Gibson enrolled as a student at Florida A&M in Tallahassee, Florida, on an athletic scholarship. Also in that year Gibson became the first African American woman to compete in the U.S. Tennis Association's national indoor championships.

However, she was still shut out of the U.S. Open because of prejudice. Gibson was cynical about the odds of it ever opening up. It took the backing of premier tennis star Alice Marble, who won 18 Grand Slam titles, mostly in the 1930s, and some other influential authorities to shame the U.S. Open into granting Gibson an invitation to compete in 1950. Marble wrote a lengthy, scathing letter to the editor of *Tennis* magazine in support of Gibson and attacking those standing in her way. It was a loud commentary from a tremendously respected tennis player.

Although Gibson did not win the tournament that year, the exposure and attention lavished on her as a barrier breaker at the event did open doors for her, and she rose to her dominating peak of play a few years later. Gibson was grateful enough to Marble to reprint that letter in its entirety in her autobiography.

Gibson said she just wanted to be treated like everyone else, but realized that because she was an African American in a basically white tennis world, things would not be quite so simple. She toyed with the idea of leaving tennis and joining the army. But she persevered in her tennis goals.

"I have never regarded myself as a crusader," Gibson said. "I try to be the best I can in every situation I find myself in, and naturally I'm always glad when something I do turns out to be helpful and important to all Negroes, or for that matter, to all Americans, or maybe to all tennis players."[3]

Gibson gained a national profile. She graduated from Florida A&M and was sent on an overseas goodwill tour by the U.S. State Department. Even though she began a teaching career in Missouri, she did not abandon tennis and kept improving. When she got her chance to compete in Grand Slam tournaments in the mid-1950s, she began winning them. Gibson became one of the most famous and successful players of her era, and her achievements as an African American crashing through barriers enhanced her reputation as time passed.

The year 1956 was Gibson's coming-out party on the world stage. She captured the French Open singles crown with a 6–0, 12–10 victory over Angela Mortimer Barrett. She also won the doubles championship in Paris with Angela Buxton. Later that season Gibson and Buxton won the Wimbledon doubles. Buxton, who was Jewish, was hardly more welcomed on the tennis circuit than Gibson, and the two women became fast friends as well as doubles partners.

Pioneer Althea Gibson, born in South Carolina and a graduate of Florida A&M, became the first African American to win major tennis titles during the late 1950s and early 1960s and won 11 Grand Slam championships. (AP Photo)

Winning Wimbledon singles in 1957 over Darlene Hard, 6–3, 6–2, was a crowning personal achievement for Gibson.

"I felt all along that it was my day," Gibson said of the final, played in exceptional heat. She won the match in 50 minutes and shouted, "At last! At last!" Queen Elizabeth II presented the trophy, and Gibson bantered with her about the hot weather.[4]

It was a different time in tennis, and there was not much money to be made. The amateur game predominated. Although Gibson won 56 events, she retired in 1958 at age 31. Fifteen years passed before another woman of color, Australian Evonne Goolagong, won a Grand Slam championship, in 1971. It was not until 43 years after Gibson's first success that another African American woman won a Grand Slam. That was Serena Williams in 1999. Williams consulted with Gibson about her experiences long distance before she won her title.

Remarkably, after her great Grand Slam success Gibson turned to professional golf in the 1960s. This was another sport not very hospitable to African Americans, and she once again faced prejudice. In 1964, when she was 37, Gibson became the first African American to compete on the Ladies Professional Golf Association tour. Gibson never won a tournament, but she finished second once and was ranked as high as 27th in her secondary athletic pursuit.

Later in life, while living in New Jersey, Gibson regularly held tennis clinics for inner-city African American children in Newark. After she died in 2003, the city erected a statue in her honor to commemorate her contributions.

NOTES

1. Althea Gibson, *I Always Wanted to Be Somebody*, ed. Ed Fitzgerald (New York: Pyramid Books, 1958), 5–6.
2. Ibid., 44.
3. Ibid., 57.
4. Ibid., 123.

FURTHER READING

Gray, Frances Clayton, and Yanick Rice Lamb. *Born to Win: The Authorized Biography of Althea Gibson*. Hoboken, NJ: Wiley, 2004.

Harris, Cecil, and Larryette Kyle-DeBose. *Charging the Net: A History of Blacks in Tennis from Althea Gibson and Arthur Ashe to the Williams Sisters*. Chicago: Ivan R. Dee, 2007.

Schoenfeld, Bruce. *The Match: Althea Gibson & Angela Buxton; How Two Outsiders— One Black, the Other Jewish—Forged a Friendship and Made Sports History*. New York: HarperCollins, 2004.

#44 Women's Pro Basketball

It was demonstrated that the time for women's professional basketball had come in the United States when the 1996 U.S. Olympic team blitzed the competition at the Atlanta Summer Games after a brilliant year-long tour that won over a legion of fans.

USA Basketball conceived of the idea of pulling together the best female basketball players in the country and having them work together for an entire year leading up to the Games. The women had not lived up to expectations during the 1992 Olympics or at the 1994 World Championships, and it was felt that if they had time to grow together and play together, the cohesive unit that would emerge would earn its payoff with a gold medal at the '96 Olympics.

The plan was perfectly carried out. The talents of the women blended beautifully. And with famed Stanford coach Tara Vanderveer running the show, the team performed with precision and power. Following on the heels of the men's 1992 Dream Team at the Barcelona Games, this women's squad filled the role of a female hoops dream team for the United States.

This was probably the most talented women's team of all time, even though the players did not have the same international stature as the men. The roster consisted of Lisa Leslie, Sheryl Swoopes, Dawn Staley, Katrina McClain, Carla McGhee, Rebecca Lobo, Venus Lacy, Jennifer Azzi, Teresa Edwards, Nikki McCray, Ruthie Bolton, and Katy Steding.

After a wildly popular tour, the women defeated Cuba, the Ukraine, Zaire, Australia, Zaire again, and South Korea in the preliminary rounds. In the championship bracket the Americans bested Japan, Australia again, and Brazil. The closest any team came to the United States was Japan, in a 15-point loss.

Up until then women's professional basketball opportunities for American women were limited to overseas competition. There had been an attempt to start a women's pro league—the Women's Basketball League—in 1978, but that faded out after three seasons. The three most famous players in that ill-fated league were Nancy Lieberman, Ann Meyers, and Carol "The Blaze" Blazjowski. Current Notre Dame coach Muffet McGraw also played in the WBL.

There had been a 1984 start-up of a Women's American Basketball Association, but it didn't last for even one season.

After the 1996 Games, building on the successful tour and the gold medal victory, two professional leagues were founded in the United States.

"That team was probably the primary piece of the foundation that led to the WNBA," said then WNBA president Val Ackerman of the gold medal squad. "That particular team at that particular time, with the top players at the time . . . all came together. That momentum generated the strongest push we could have imagined going into the first season of the WNBA."[1]

The American Basketball Association went head to head with the Women's National Basketball Association. It was a time of peak interest in the women's game, and there were high-quality players in both leagues. Five of the gold medalists played in the ABA.

There was still more money to be made playing in Europe, and many players hooked up with teams both at home and overseas, maximizing their earning power and lengthening their seasons. They were wary about foregoing foreign opportunities, because it was difficult to predict how the new American leagues would fare. Those players were right to be cautious.

Inevitably, it was shown that the U.S. basketball landscape was not big enough to accommodate two women's pro leagues. The WNBA was better funded, had the

Inspired by the popularity of the undefeated women's 1996 Olympic gold medal basketball team, entrepreneurs decided that the time was ripe to bring women's pro basketball to the American sports scene. Two leagues were founded, and the Women's National Basketball Association survived and remains in business. Former teammates Lisa Leslie (left) and Rebecca Lobo fight for a rebound in a 1997 game. (AP Photo/Kevork Djansezian)

security blanket of NBA money and ownership behind it, and won the war. The Women's Basketball League folded after three seasons, and the best players were absorbed by the WNBA.

Play began in 1997. The WNBA focused on a spring-summer season that permitted players to compete overseas during the traditional basketball season. There are currently 12 teams in the league, though some franchises have come and gone.

Some fascinating figures took on head coaching positions in the WNBA. They included Bill Laimbeer, a world champion with the Detroit Pistons, who spent most of his NBA career being accused of dirty play; Paul Westhead, who had introduced super-speed offense to the NBA; Boston Celtics Hall of Famer Dave Cowens; and outstanding women players such as Anne Donovan, Cynthia Cooper, and Nancy Lieberman.

Over the years, from starting as primarily a U.S.-only league, the WNBA has greatly expanded its reach, and many foreigners have taken the plunge and signed with American teams. Lauren Jackson, Penny Taylor, and Sophie Young are among the most prominent.

Recent champions have been the Seattle Storm (2010), Minnesota Lynx (2011), Indiana Fever (2012), Minnesota Lynx (2013), and Phoenix Mercury (2014).

A critical aspect of long-term survival for the WNBA is growth. To date, the league's attendance has been stagnant. There is hardcore support for each team in its market, but regardless of on-court success or marketing programs, the average league attendance number barely budges.

The lowest single-season mark recorded since the WNBA began operating was 7,457 in 2012. League attendance was 7,531 fans per game in 2013. In 2014, it was 7,578. In the 1990s, at times the WNBA topped 10,000 per game, but it has been unable to regain that peak.

The attendance in most cities has been steady, though owners would love to see increases that put the mark over 10,000 per game for every game in every city. One strength of the WNBA has been its regular television coverage. The league is readily accessible through that medium and is on the air in the less-busy summer months, when the only competition is Major League Baseball. The audiences may or may not overlap for the two sports.

Currently the WNBA's contract with ESPN runs through 2019. That provides some stability and a way to keep increasing interest. Besides the national coverage, WNBA teams have cut deals with local radio stations in some markets for regular coverage, as well as with some local TV stations.

The WNBA has never quite attracted the number of hardcore men's fans it hoped to do, but it does, as is appropriate, appeal to little girls developing the aspiration to play the game.

However, the fact that the WNBA has survived for as long as it has—the American sporting landscape is littered with such failed ventures—is a plus. Long-term success does rely on continued growth, finding and holding on to the new fan, getting the message out to basketball fans, and keeping the flow of top players coming.

Replenishing the talent has been an objective, with steady success, as those original Olympians grew older and retired. Retaining season-ticket holders has been a goal and is also seeing increasing success.

"I feel very good about the level of play in the United States, and we've had a very solid year in terms of very key metrics," said league president Laurel Richie in 2012. "This is a process; it takes time to build a following. There are strong signs we're headed in the right direction."[2]

It would have been wonderful for the WNBA if the 1996 gold medal winners could have gone on and on, but the law of physics declined to cooperate. No one from that group made a bigger splash than Lisa Leslie. The six-foot-five Leslie, who in 2007 was the author of the WNBA's first in-game dunk, won three Most Valuable Player awards, was on two Los Angeles Sparks championship teams, was an eight-time all-star, and won four Olympic gold medals during her career, which ended in 2009.

Leslie retired after 11 WNBA seasons believing that the women had truly made a mark and their game was still changing for the better.

"I think we've just truly evolved," Leslie said, "by players individually, our individual talent level has risen, as well as our numbers and our fan support, as well as our corporate sponsorship. It's always been important to me to show the young girls that it's OK to maintain their femininity and play sports."[3]

NOTES

1. "Celebrating the 1995–96 Olympic Team Ten Years Later," WNBA, 2005, http://www.wnba.com/features/tenyears_olympics96.html.
2. William Rhoden, "Amid Successes, WNBA Is Still Facing Challenges," *New York Times*, October 7, 2012.
3. Brian Heyman, "Lisa Leslie, the Face of the WNBA, Prepares for Life after Basketball," *New York Times*, August 22, 2009.

FURTHER READING

Corbett, Sara. *Venus to the Hoop: A Gold Medal Year in Women's Basketball*. New York: Anchor Books, 1997.
Drysdale, Ann Meyers. *You Let Some Girl Beat You? The Story of Ann Meyers Drysdale*. Lake Forest, CA: Behler Publications, 2012.
Porter, Karra. *Mad Seasons: The Story of the First Women's Professional Basketball League, 1978–81*. Lincoln, NE: Bison Books, 2006.

#45 Johnny Vander Meer's Two No-Hitters

It is sometimes too glibly stated that a record set will last forever. No one is around forever to test that theory, but in the case of Johnny Vander Meer's throwing two no-hitters in a row for the Cincinnati Reds in 1938, it would take something on the lines of a major miracle for this record to be broken.

Cincinnati Reds hurler Johnny Vander Meer became the only pitcher in Major League history in 1938 to throw no-hitters in back-to-back starts. He shut down the Boston Bees and Brooklyn Dodgers in two consecutive games in June of that season. No one else has ever matched the feat. (AP Photo)

To break Vander Meer's record, a pitcher would have to throw a no-hitter in three consecutive starts. Vander Meer is the only pitcher to throw two no-hitters in a row in the history of Major League Baseball dating back to 1876. The odds against a pitcher throwing three no-hitters in a row might not equal the odds of filling out a perfect NCAA basketball tournament bracket (calculated as 9.2 quintillion, a number 19 figures long), but it might be in the ballpark.

Entering the 2015 major league season, there had been 287 no-hitters thrown since big-league ball began. The most thrown by any one pitcher is seven, by Hall of Famer Nolan Ryan. Sandy Koufax threw four no-hitters. Bob Feller, Larry Corcoran, and Cy Young each threw three no-hitters.

Vander Meer is one of 22 pitchers who tossed two no-hitters during their careers. None of the other 21 (or of the five others with more than two no-hitters) pitched two no-hitters in a row.

Johnny Vander Meer was born in 1914 in New Jersey and lived 82 years. He threw left-handed, but was a switch-hitter. Vander Meer played a role among Cincinnati's 1940 World Series champions and was chosen as a four-time all-star. He led the National League in strikeouts three times. While his career earned run average was a solid 3.44, his lifetime won-loss mark was just 119–121 in a career that spanned 1937 to 1951.

He retired at age 36. After spending the majority of his career with the Reds, Vander Meer finished up with short stints for the Chicago Cubs and Cleveland Indians. His best all-around season was 1942, when he won 18 games, posted a 2.43 earned run average, and led the league in strikeouts.

But Vander Meer's fame stems from the 1938 season, his second in the big leagues. He went 15–10 with a 3.12 ERA, but for a week in the middle of the season he was untouchable.

On June 11, Vander Meer took the mound against the Boston Bees (better known later as the Braves) and helped by catcher Ernie Lombardi's home run, won the contest 3–0, without surrendering a hit. The Reds scored one run in the fourth inning and two in the sixth, and that was all Vander Meer needed.

Boston was not a great team and did not have many famous players populating the lineup. One well-known player who faced Vander Meer that day was Vince DiMaggio. The center fielder went zero-for-two. Vander Meer allowed just three base runners, and none of them advanced beyond first base.

Four days later, on June 15, before the celebrating had completely died down from Vander Meer's first no-hitter, he did it again. Taking the mound against the Brooklyn Dodgers, different lineup, different day, Vander Meer understood that nothing carried over from his previous gem. Yet he duplicated the feat for the first and only time in big-league history.

Cincinnati won the game, 6–0. The Dodgers tried four pitchers against Vander Meer, but nobody had the necessary stuff. Frank McCormick backed Vander Meer's effort with a home run. While throwing another no-hitter was a surprise, Vander Meer was hot during that stretch of the summer and won nine games in a row.

Although the scoreboard did not reflect it, Vander Meer needed more offense from his Reds teammates against Brooklyn and some defensive help. He somehow went the distance on a day when his control was not fine. He walked eight men, and at different times the Reds made smooth stops in the field that prevented hits.

Cincinnati recorded an 11-hit attack, with 3 hits each from Harry Craft, the future manager, and Wally Berger, who was nearing the end of his career. Vander Meer didn't have to worry about losing the game, but he did have to hold up his end. This was not one of the best Dodgers teams of all time, but Hall of Famers Kiki Cuyler and Leo Durocher were in the lineup.

"I was quick that night," Vander Meer said of his stuff. But he also almost didn't make it out of the ninth inning because of wildness. After he walked two men, manager Bill McKechnie and catcher Ernie Lombardi, along with the infielders, huddled with him on the mound for a pep talk, in one of those mass meetings common to baseball. "Take your time, Johnny," McKechnie said. "Quit pitching so fast and pitch the way you know how to pitch."[1]

Even then Vander Meer needed a sharp play at third base by Lew Riggs to survive. The last out of the second no-hitter was made by Durocher on a pop fly.

"John just came along and did something so brilliant that nobody will ever forget it," said player Birdie Tebbetts, a contemporary of Vander Meer's and later a big-league manager. "I would have done anything to catch those games. On any given day there was no better pitcher."[2]

In 2013 a Johnny Vander Meer Web site was set up to commemorate the 75th anniversary of his back-to-back no-hitters. In Vander Meer's world a Web site would have been as difficult to digest as someone pitching two straight no-hitters is for the rest of the modern world.

"Johnny Vander Meer's accomplishment . . . is one of those amazing feats in the sport of baseball," said one-time New York Yankee star pitcher Andy Pettitte, who won 256 games between 1995 and 2013. "I have pitched against and played alongside of some of the greatest pitchers of our times, watching them never be able to throw one no-hitter, much less back-to-back. Heck, I've been a pretty good pitcher over the years and have never been able to carry a no-hitter past the seventh inning."[3]

When Vander Meer pitched his second straight no-hitter, his big celebration was going fishing with his father. But even though the direct fanfare quickly subsided, he was hailed for the achievement for the rest of his life.

Perhaps Vander Meer's best-known comment on his two no-hitters was, "Kids are always chasing rainbows, but baseball is where you can catch them."[4]

NOTES

1. "Double No-Hit Johnny Vander Meer Is Dead at 82," *Associated Press*, October 7, 1997.
2. Ibid.
3. "The Unbreakable Record: Johnny Vander Meer's Back to Back No Hitters!" 2013, http://www.johnnyvandermeer.com/.
4. Ibid.

FURTHER READING

Green, Ernest J. "Johnny Vander Meer's Third No-Hitter." *The Baseball Research Journal* 41 (Spring 2012).

Johnson, James W. *Double No-Hit: The Story of Johnny Vander Meer's Historic Night under the Lights*. Lincoln, NE: Bison Books, 2012.

#46 The Houston Astrodome

The idea of the Houston Astrodome being proclaimed the Eighth Wonder of the World seems quaint now. Domed stadiums are common, but a half century ago the idea of playing football or baseball indoors was revolutionary.

With 20–20 hindsight the notion shouldn't have been that outrageous, since sports teams of other sorts, like basketball and hockey, had been playing indoors for decades. The Astrodome was just bigger than all of those arenas, and something about the roof gave it a space-age feel.

Construction called for breaking ground on January 3, 1962, and the Astrodome (it was trying to really sound space age, and NASA was in the neighborhood) opened April 9, 1965, for the Major League Baseball season as the home of the Houston Astros. The local baseball team had begun life as the Colt .45s, but switched to the Astros as a nice fit with the stadium.

The original name of the building was the considerably less catchy Harris County Domed Stadium, but that didn't last long. The idea to build a covered stadium came from Roy Hofheinz, who had previously been mayor of Houston, but now owned the baseball club. Hofheinz and his daughter used to complain about the frequent game rainouts when they followed the city's minor league baseball team, and Hofheinz later found himself in the rare position of being able to do something about the weather.

Houston is known for its dense humidity and frequent thunderstorms in the summer, and Hofheinz believed he could eliminate the National Weather Service's role in the Astros' attendance. Building a domed stadium was a major part of the cornerstone of Hofheinz's bid to bring major league ball to Houston, and he considered it not a flighty idea, but something he very much wanted to make happen.

When asked where he got the idea that a domed stadium could work out, Hofheinz cited Buckminster Fuller, a renowned "futurist" who was a repository of far-thinking ideas. "Fuller convinced me it was possible to cover any size space if you didn't run out of money," Hofheinz said.[1]

Construction costs hit $35 million for the project more than a half century ago. More recently, baseball or football stadiums have cost hundreds of millions of dollars to build, and some bills, such as the one for the recently constructed pro

Until the Houston Astrodome opened in 1965 as the home for the Houston Oilers football team and the Houston Astros baseball team, no one envisioned an indoor, domed stadium. It turned into the wave of the future for many innovative stadiums in other communities. (Library of Congress)

football stadium in northern New Jersey for the New York Giants and New York Jets, have topped $1 billion.

The Astrodome is a large building, especially by sports standards. It stands 18 stories high and covers 9.5 acres of ground. The roof is 208 feet above the baseball or football field. The Dome is also air conditioned, and a test to see how air-conditioning might affect the curve ball was conducted by the Astros two months before the season opened. Of all people, Satchel Paige, the venerated and venerable pitching sensation of the past, was the thrower.

The first baseball game at the Dome for which tickets were sold didn't count. It was an exhibition contest between the Astros and the New York Yankees, a sort of Broadway preview of the show to come. Attendance indicated a fascination with the new building, though, with a sellout crowd of 47,879 fans on hand. Among those spectators were President Lyndon Johnson and First Lady Lady Bird Johnson, who were from Texas. The Astros won the game, 2–1.

From the beginning the Astrodome was intended to be the home of the Astros and the football Oilers. The building was virtually round in shape. It also soon became a popular concert venue for big-name acts. Being the first of a kind domed stadium for professional sports, the Astrodome also earned considerable ink, not just in Houston, in Texas, and in the United States, but everywhere. It was looked upon as an architectural marvel and hence earned the appellation "Eighth Wonder of the World."

Many domed stadiums have followed the construction of the Astrodome, from the Super Dome in New Orleans to the Pontiac Dome in Michigan, from the Kingdome in Seattle to the RCA Dome in Indianapolis.

One of the strangest single days in the history of the Astrodome was June 15, 1976. An event transpired that the initiators of the domed stadium idea and the builders never anticipated. A baseball game was called off on account of rain. Not because the rain was falling indoors, but because so much rain fell outdoors that the area around the Astrodome became flooded. The Astros were scheduled to play the Pittsburgh Pirates, but transportation in the city was snarled. Fans could not get to the game. Although the teams made it, the umpires didn't. Hours after the scheduled start time, the game was postponed.

The Astrodome made it onto the U.S. Register of Historic Places, but as time passed the stadium began fraying at the edges, and some areas fell into disrepair. It had passed beyond the novelty stage. Eventually the Oilers moved to Tennessee and were replaced by the Houston Texans. The football team and baseball team wanted their own stadiums to play in, and as has become common in the pro sports era of the last 15 years or so, clamored to have local communities contribute heavily to building them.

In 2000 Minute Maid Park opened for the new baseball season and as the new home of the Astros, at a cost of $250 million. In addition, a flashier $352 million NRG Stadium opened in 2002 for pro football. That glittering new building has a retractable roof, luxury suites, and other amenities more prevalent in modern stadiums.

In 2005 the Astrodome performed one of the most important functions of its lifespan. Following the devastation wrought by Hurricane Katrina in New Orleans, residents of the Louisiana city were bused to Houston, and the Astrodome was used as an emergency shelter.

With the city's two professional franchises that had been the main tenants of the Astrodome moving to new digs, the question arose of just what to do with the Astrodome. There was a proposal put to voters in 2013 asking for $213 million to renovate the Astrodome and keep it going, but the electorate said no.

The Astrodome had hosted United States Football League play, World Football League play, professional soccer, University of Houston football, some bowl games, rodeo, and Wrestlemania. But it was gradually being phased out. It was erroneously reported in some places that the Astrodome had been demolished, following in the paths of the Kingdome and the RCA Dome.

Some consideration has been given to a tear-down. Some serious discussions have taken place about investing millions of dollars in converting the Astrodome into a visitor and convention center, but they were also rejected in a referendum by the public. Three pedestrian ramp towers were demolished, and ramp bridges were disconnected. Ticket booths were removed.

As a last-gasp measure, those who wish to preserve some of the Astrodome's identity and its special history advanced a proposal to remodel the remainder of the structure while leaving intact the roof and having it cover a city park. That was pretty much a final suggestion short of demolition.

Still, there was sentiment for keeping the Astrodome alive from longtime residents of the city. "If the Astrodome wasn't around anymore, I'd think I was living in some other universe," said city councilwoman Jolanda Jones.[2]

There is no doubt that the Astrodome was a special building, ahead of its time, and brought Houston a tremendous amount of attention worldwide. But it seems unlikely it will ever again be used as a regular facility hosting big events.

NOTES

1. Bruce Nichols, "Prototype Astrodome Celebrates 20th," *Dallas Morning News*, April 10, 1985.
2. Dale Robertston, "Prominent Houstonians' Ideas on What to Do with Dome," *Houston Chronicle*, April 4, 2011.

FURTHER READING

Freedman, Lew. *Football Stadiums: A Guide to Professional and Top College Stadiums.* Richmond Hill, ON: Firefly, 2013.
Gast, James. *The Astrodome: Building an American Spectacle.* Boston: Aspinwall Press, 2014.

#47 U.S. Soccer World Cup Champs

For most of the 20th century women's sports was limited by men's ideas. More specifically, men's sexist ideas. In short, it was not deemed ladylike for women to sweat in public. So women were held back from participating in most sports, especially at a high level.

An early exception was track and field in the Olympic Games, but even there women were regarded as too fragile to compete in long-distance running events.

Eventually the world changed, Title IX took hold in America, and sports opportunities for women expanded hugely.

For a long time the international governing body of soccer, however, declined to make women full-fledged partners in the World Cup scene. That changed in 1991. The first women's World Cup was contested in China that year, and the U.S. women made a statement to their fellow citizens and won legions of fans with their breakthrough triumph.

It was the first time that women's soccer had taken center stage in the United States, and the reverberations were powerful and far-reaching. Girls began saying, "Why not me?" Teams sprang up for girls and women. The U.S. women's international soccer players were the heroines of the moment.

The Fédération Internationale de Football Association (FIFA), the governing body of international soccer, yielded to pressure and sanctioned the inaugural women's World Cup competition between November 16 and November 30, 1991, in Guangdong, China. Twelve teams from different countries qualified for the championship rounds in China, including the host People's Republic of China, Japan, Nigeria, Germany, Norway, and Brazil, among others.

Unlike the men's World Cup, for which tickets sell out months in advance, and the host country typically divides matches among its largest cities, this World Cup stayed in one place and averaged just about 20,000 fans per game, or a total of 510,000 fans in attendance.

Some of the most famous women's soccer players in U.S. history were members of the American team, including Mia Hamm, then 19; Michelle Akers; Brandi Chastain; Kristine Lilly; Carin Jennings; Julie Foudy; and April Heinrichs. One common denominator among many of the players was their connection to the University of North Carolina, the collegiate soccer power. Nine of the players had attended that school.

That was no coincidence. Anson Dorrance was the coach of both North Carolina and the national team. Over time Dorrance has amassed a record that includes winning 23 national championships with the Tar Heels.

Dorrance was an innovator, and to him that meant tampering with accepted, deeply rooted precepts in order to build winners.

"We played a 3–4–3 which was like sacrilegious," Dorrance said. "People thought, 'you're not playing a 4–4–2, what kind of tactical midgets are you? You're going to high-pressure? You can't high-pressure in an event where you have a game every three days. . . .' We were great duelers. We were gritty. We were to some extent irreverent because we didn't worship at the altar of the 4–4–2 and we didn't play the ball around in the back for half an hour to show we could possess it. We were different and we scared teams because we were different."[1]

When FIFA started a Women's World Cup in 1991, the United States set a goal of capturing the championship. The USA women's squad, sparked by Mia Hamm, electrified Americans and especially young women who aspired to follow in their footsteps. (Tommy Cheng/AFP/Getty Images)

The 1991 team, later called the "91ers" as they wrote history, formed the core of U.S. women's soccer for years. The players announced their presence in the first World Cup by showing they were the best in the world against the rest of the best in the world.

The United States was placed in Group B for the preliminary round and defeated Sweden, 3–2; Brazil, 5–0; and Japan, 3–0 to advance to the knockout round. That was the one-and-done stage. In the first game of the finals round the Americans crushed Chinese Taipei, 7–0, in the quarterfinals. Next they overpowered Germany, 5–2, in the semifinals, and then edged Norway, 2–1, in the gold medal game.

Heinrichs, the captain, was on a line with Akers and Jennings. Akers, who scored 10 goals, won the Golden Shoe award for her scoring brilliance. Jennings won the Golden Ball award as the player of the tournament.

Beyond winning the championship and etching their names in bright letters into U.S. soccer history, the women's 1991 World Cup players were opening a new chapter for women's soccer in their home country. For many of the younger players on the squad, this was the beginning of long international careers and victories in several other world-caliber events. They became admired role models, with girls growing to womanhood aspiring to be just like them and to win places on the national team.

"The standard they set, we want to keep up, because they epitomize women's soccer and women's sports in general," said Cat Reddick, a younger member of the 2004 Olympic team, about her older, venerated teammates.[2]

Abby Wambach, at the time another of the younger players, who emerged as a star, said, "Thinking about the '91ers' we need to give them something to smile about at the end of their careers. It isn't pressure, but an added sense of responsibility. We are doing what those women taught us from all their years on the national team."[3]

Heinrichs, who was a three-time all-American in college, eventually moved from captain to national team coach, and the United States won silver at the Sydney Olympics in 2000 and gold in Athens in 2004, with her as the boss.

Akers had a glittering career, scoring 105 goals and being a member not only of the 1991 World Cup champs, but one of the 1999 titlists as well. Akers was also part of the 1996 gold medal winning team at the Atlanta Olympics. Akers has had to battle chronic fatigue syndrome, making her success that much more impressive.

While many of the women's soccer players on the 1991 World Cup team gained fame in the United States and around the world in soccer circles, Hamm seemed to stand first among equals as a high scorer. When she retired she owned the record for most international goals, with 158. Ironically Wambach, nearly a decade after uttering her remarks about the group from '91, broke Hamm's record in 2013.

Hamm, who also played for the Washington Freedom in the Women's United Soccer Association, tried to help that group follow the path established by the Women's National Basketball Association. The league only lasted from 2001 to 2003.

One of the most high-profile women's athletes in the country, Hamm had a multitude of endorsements, contributed to soccer in off-field ventures, and gained a rabid following among young women as a role model for soccer play and beyond.

NOTES

1. John D. Halloran, "The Rise and Fall of the United States National Team," *Bleacher Report*, April 23, 2013.

2. Phil Hersh, "Women's Soccer Steps Up as '91ers' Prepare to Exit," *Chicago Tribune*, August 11, 2004.

3. Ibid.

FURTHER READING

Hamm, Mia, and Aaron Heifetz. *Go for the Goal: A Champion's Guide to Winning in Soccer and Life*. New York: HarperCollins, 2000.

Lisi, Clemente A. *The U.S. Women's Soccer Team: An American Success Story*. Lanham, MD: Scarecrow Press, 2010.

Longman, Jere. *The Girls of Summer: The U.S. Women's Soccer Team and How It Changed the World*. New York: Harper Perennial, 2001.

#48 Wilt Chamberlain Scores 100 Points in a Game

In retrospect, given everything else he accomplished on a basketball court, it's almost surprising that Wilt Chamberlain did not score 100 points in a National Basketball Association game more than once. Apparently once was enough, even for Wilt.

Although in the decades since Chamberlain's retirement some players have eclipsed his point totals for a career, many scoring marks that the seven-foot-one, muscular center set remain in the league record book.

While some say it is impossible for anyone to top Chamberlain's single-game record, a flukey situation in any given game could produce a scenario in which the unlikely becomes reality. The circumstances surrounding Chamberlain reaching the century mark on March 2, 1962, were peculiar enough.

Chamberlain was playing for his hometown Philadelphia Warriors against the New York Knicks, but the game was not played in either team's home arena. In those days the NBA, which was still seeking to spread the message of the caliber of its play, scheduled neutral-site contests in communities so they could see the best players in the world up close.

That's why the game was played in Hershey, Pennsylvania, the city 95 miles from Philadelphia best known for its manufacture of chocolate bars, inside the Hershey Sports Arena. While that would sound like an unlikely location for a regular-season game in today's NBA, it was a commonplace occurrence for a team to try to expand its "home" territory in the early 1960s.

It is difficult to believe that if a Wilt Chamberlain was playing on an NBA team today, all of his home games would not be sold out. Chamberlain was a drawing card, a unique individual talent, and one of the most famous athletes in the country during his career. He was easily recognizable, not only because his

Wilt Chamberlain, the most dominating scorer in NBA history, who once averaged 50 points a game for a season, is the only player in history to score 100 points in a game. The Philadelphia Warrior hit the century mark in 1962 in a game against the New York Knicks. (AP Photo/Paul Vathis)

face appeared in newspapers, in magazines, and on television so often, but because he was so tall and towered over much of the populace.

Chamberlain was born in Philadelphia in 1936 (and died at 63 in 1999), and though standing more than seven feet tall never weighed more than 275 pounds, none of it fat. He was always referred to as the strongest player in the league. The thing that set Chamberlain apart from the previous small number of pro basketball seven-footers was his agility. He was no flat-footed player, but possessed great leaping ability and quickness. Combining, height, dexterity, and speed made Chamberlain unstoppable near the basket.

During Chamberlain's career between 1959 and 1973, only one opposing center could begin to cover him defensively. That was Bill Russell of the Boston Celtics. Russell was every bit the defensive genius that Chamberlain was offensively, and although Russell was four inches shorter, he also possessed great jumping ability. Russell was by no means the offensive weapon that Chamberlain was, but for most of his career he was surrounded by better talent, and as a rule the Celtics won the challenges against Chamberlain's teams.

Theirs was one of the greatest one-on-one rivalries in sports history.

Prior to joining the NBA, Chamberlain played college basketball at Kansas and then spent a year touring with the Harlem Globetrotters. Once being unleashed in the NBA with its 48-minute games, Chamberlain overpowered foes and astonished fans with his prowess near the hoop.

Chamberlain was a big-time dunker before the dunk was commonly used. He featured a finger-tip roll as a fancy layup. His size and play engendered nicknames like "Wilt the Stilt" and "The Big Dipper," but he did not like them.

Above all, Chamberlain dazzled with his scoring, rebounding, and shooting percentage. At a time in the NBA when accuracy was not nearly what it is now, Chamberlain made more than 50 percent of his shots. His Achilles heel was free-throw shooting, and that was one area in which he was vulnerable to defensive strategy.

As a rookie, Chamberlain blew away all projections of what he was capable of, averaging 37.6 points a game during the 1959–1960 season and rebounding at a rate of 27 per game. Chamberlain led the NBA in scoring his first six straight seasons and seven times in all. He led the league in rebounding 11 times. His career scoring average was 30.1, and his career rebounding average was 22.9. His lifetime shooting percentage was .540.

Sometimes Chamberlain was criticized for shooting too much and passing too little; sensitive to those comments, he wanted to prove he could generate assists with the best of them. During the 1965–1966 season Chamberlain averaged 33.5 points, 24.6 rebounds, and 5.2 assists per game. Two seasons later he averaged 8.6 assists a game. The province of point guards, that made him the only center to ever lead the league in assists in a season.

Chamberlain was a four-time Most Valuable Player and a 13-time all-star, and in no season did his star shine brighter than the 1961–1962 season. He averaged a stupendous 50.4 points a game. Only a tiny percentage of NBA players ever score 50 points in a game once. Chamberlain averaged that number across an 80-game season.

His showcase performance of the season was the 100-point game.

That season the Warriors were a pretty solid team—not a great one, and not one that could challenge the Boston Celtics for first place in the Eastern Division standings. Boston finished 60–20, Philadelphia 49–31, or 11 games behind. The New York Knicks played in the same division and finished last with a mark of 29–51.

So the Warrior-Knicks encounter of March 2 should have been a fairly nondescript, regular-season game as the play-offs loomed (earlier in the spring then than now). Despite the attraction of a Wilt Chamberlain coming to their small town, the people of Hershey really did not embrace the game at the box office. Attendance was 4,124 in the 8,000-seat building. The game was not televised, but Bill Campbell did play-by-play for WCAU radio in Philadelphia.

Philadelphia's starting lineup featured Chamberlain at center, Guy Rodgers and Al Attles at guard, and Paul Arizin and Tom Meschery at forward. New York's starting lineup was Darrall Imhoff at center, Willie Naulls and Johnny Green at the forwards, and Richie Guerin and Al Butler at the guards.

For the Warriors, Chamberlain, Arizin, and Rodgers were all future Hall of Famers. Attles became a longtime NBA executive. Guerin is in the Hall of Fame, and many believe Naulls should be.

It was a high-scoring game. After one period the Warriors led, 42–26. It was 79–68 at the half and 125–106 after three quarters. The final was 169–147 Philadelphia.

Even by Wilt's standards, he got off to a fast start, scoring 23 points in the first period. Chamberlain had 41 points at the half and 69 after three quarters. He only accelerated the pace after that, with teammates feeding him. During the 12-minute fourth quarter, Chamberlain scored 31 points to finish the game on the dot of 100. As an aside, Chamberlain also grabbed 25 rebounds.

Normally a lousy foul shooter, Chamberlain picked this night to excel at that discipline, making 28 out of 32 tries. He attempted 63 field goals and made 36 of them. The three-point shot was not in effect at the time, but that didn't matter, because Chamberlain never shot from the 22-foot-plus distance anyway.

Philadelphia put four other guys into double figures, Attles with 17, Arizin and Meschery with 16 each, and Rodgers with 11 points, with the bench contributing little. Rodgers totaled 20 assists; Chamberlain made it easy for him on this night. Guerin scored 39 points for the Knicks, Cleveland Buckner notched 33, and Naulls fired in 31 points.

As the game was winding down and Chamberlain was stuck on 98 points, announcer Campbell was gushing into the microphone.

"He has 98 points in professional basketball," Campbell said. "I'll tell you, that's a lot of points if you are playing grammar school kids, isn't it?"[1]

While it was an occasion worthy of note and worthy of celebration, few were hugely surprised that Chamberlain actually scored 100 points in a game. There had been talk of the possibility for a year or more, and in another game Chamberlain had netted 78. But when it happened a jolt of electricity shot through the sport. Man, 100 points!

Chamberlain did not get the last two points until 46 seconds remained in the game, on a dunk.

Some Knicks players were angry that Chamberlain went to town on them. Some Knicks fans dismissed the achievement because the Warriors just repeatedly passed the ball to Chamberlain instead of looking for their own shots. That definitely occurred in the latter stages of the fourth quarter as he inched closer to the milestone. But that was just a little boost to put him over the top. Chamberlain had the wherewithal to get himself into the 80s or so without unusual assistance, if he wanted to do so.

It was bedlam after the game. Philadelphia's famous public relations man Harvey Pollack wrote the number "100" on a piece of paper and asked Chamberlain to pose with it. That is the most famous photograph from the event.

"I never thought I would ever see it happen when I broke into this league," said Arizin, who had been playing for 12 years. "But when Wilt came along I knew he would do it some day. It's a fantastic thing."[2]

Chamberlain recognized that the other Warriors had played a large role in his being able to make it to 100. Although some said he was being a ball-hog, Chamberlain said team work got him the record.

"It wouldn't have even been close to possible without them," he said. "They wanted me to get it as much as I did.[3]

Anyone who was part of that game, or witnessed it (as opposed to people who later said they were there, even if they weren't), never forgot it.

Imhoff, the opposing center, who covered Chamberlain for 20 minutes before fouling out, joked that every March 1 (the day before the anniversary), "I break out into a rash."[4]

There was a sense on that night that everyone had seen a once-in-a-lifetime performance. But no one was quite sure that Wilt Chamberlain wouldn't be able to duplicate it in another game.

NOTES

1. Gary M. Pomerantz, *Wilt, 1962* (New York: Crown Publishers, 2005), 174.
2. Ibid., 182.
3. Ibid.
4. Ibid., 194.

FURTHER READING

Chamberlain, Wilt. *A View from Above*. New York: Villard, 1991.
Cherry, Robert. *Wilt: Larger Than Life*. Chicago: Triumph Books, 2004.
Lynch, Wayne. *Season of the 76ers: The Story of Wilt Chamberlain and the 1967 NBA Champion Philadelphia 76ers*. New York: Thomas Dunne Books, 2002.
Taylor, John. *The Rivalry: Bill Russell, Wilt Chamberlain, and the Golden Age of Basketball*. New York: Ballantine Books, 2006.

#49 Cy Young Wins 511 Games

There is a reason Major League Baseball named the award for the best pitcher each season the Cy Young Award. It's because Cy Young won more games than anyone in history, and all of the evidence accumulated since the award was first presented indicates that is a record that will never be broken.

Cy Young was a right-hand pitcher whose real name was Denton True Young. When others caught wind of his fastball, and he broke some fencing with his pitch

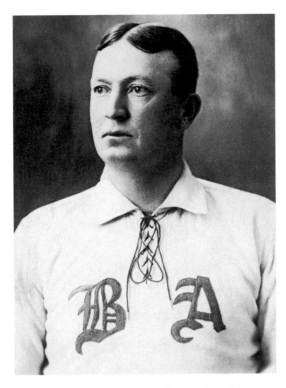

The pitcher born in Ohio as Denton True Young and nicknamed "Cy" set numerous baseball records that will never be broken, but the most glamorous was his record for the most wins—511. After his death in 1955, Major League Baseball created the Cy Young Award to honor the best pitchers in the game each season. (Library of Congress)

during a tryout, it was said that he threw like a cyclone. He did. Over the course of a 22-season career that began in 1890 and culminated in 1911, Young won 511 games. That was just one of his notable achievements on the diamond, but it stands out in neon lights.

The closest Hall of Fame great pitcher on the all-time list of baseball's winningest pitchers (if you can call it close) is Walter Johnson. Johnson, who pitched solely with the Washington Senators between 1907 and 1927, won 417 games. He needed a telescope to see Young over the mountains.

After that come Grover Cleveland Alexander and Christy Mathewson, each with 373 victories, and Warren Spahn with 363. That's the top five. Given the changing nature of the way baseball is played and how managers use their starting pitching staffs and bullpens, nobody believes those marks will ever be challenged again.

Even among the greats Young reigns supreme. He has the most wins, and the most losses: 316. He made the most starts: 815. He has the record for the most complete games: 749. He also threw the most innings (7,356) and gave up the most hits (7,092) and the most earned runs (2,147), despite an earned run average of 2.63. Young made it through his entire career doing all of that throwing while never having Tommy John surgery, or as it might have been called at the time if such a thing existed, Jack Chesboro surgery. Basically, he did not have any major arm trouble.

Young was born in Gilmore, Ohio, in 1867. After retiring from baseball Young remained on his Ohio farm until he passed away at age 88 in 1955. The Cy Young Award was introduced to major league ball in 1956 to honor the best pitcher in baseball each year. Only one Cy Young was given per year until 1967. Since then the American League and National League have honored their best pitchers by league.

A big man for the late 1800s and early 1900s, Young stood six-foot-two and weighed in at about 210 pounds. Photographs show him to be less chiseled than portly, and he had power behind that fastball. Although he did not look as trim and firm as many athletes of the 2000s, Young did adjourn to Arkansas to soak in the Hot Springs as part of his preseason preparation each year.

From the time he was a youth, Young played baseball wherever and whenever he could. He played just one season in the minors, in 1889, before going up to the majors with the Cleveland Spiders (before they were known as the Indians) the next year. Young pitched a three-hit shutout in his first game.

Young also spent a productive chunk of his career with the Boston Red Sox. In 1903, while with Boston, Young pitched the first game of the first World Series against the Pittsburgh Pirates. That year, before the format permanently shifted to best four out of seven games, it was five out of nine. Boston won five games to three, and Young won two of the games.

Years later Young said he had been approached by gamblers on the field trying to buy his allegiance before the first game for $20,000, but he shooed them away. He said he told them, "If you put any value on your money, you'd better bet it on me to win."[1]

Young won at least 20 games in a season 15 different times. He also topped the 30-win mark five times, winning between 32 and 36 games in a season. Four times he led his league in wins. Young's finest single-season earned run average was 1.62 with Boston in 1901, one of six times his ERA was lower than 2.00. Nine times Young reached 40 or more complete games in a year, with 48 his high. He didn't like to come out before going nine innings.

The fireballer also topped 400 innings in a season five times and ended his career with 2,803 strikeouts.

Young also pitched three no-hitters in the majors. In the first one he was on the mound for the Spiders in 1897. The second time Young topped the Philadelphia Athletics for Boston in 1904. His third no-hitter was recorded in 1908 against the New York Highlanders, before they were called the Yankees.

The second no-hitter was a perfect game. Young blitzed the A's on eight strike-outs in the 3–0 win at Boston's Huntington Avenue Grounds. The attendance was just 10,267, though in those days before concrete and steel stadiums went up, that was a very good crowd. The fans turned out that day because the contest was advertised as being between Young and Rude Waddell, the A's ace.

Young's pitching opponent was the esteemed Waddell, who gave up 10 hits and the three runs in eight innings while also hurling a complete game. That was also much more typical of the times; a pitcher finished what he started rather than being routinely relieved by a parade of throwers out of the bullpen as is seen today.

Also common for the time, but not for the modern era, the game took just one hour and 25 minutes to play. Waddell made the last out of the game. One outstanding aspect of Young's showing was that he was already 37 years old. Teammate Duke Farrell tweaked anyone who questioned whether advancing age was slowing down the master. "He fooled them, didn't he?" Farrell said.[2]

Spectators reveled in the greatness they had witnessed, and Young was mobbed by teammates after the game.

"I think the hullabaloo that broke loose after that game was probably the biggest thrill I had in my career," Young said during the last years of his life. "That [the perfect game] always has to be my biggest thrill."[3]

After he stopped pitching, Young only briefly stayed connected to baseball, spending most of his time farming. He did attend Cleveland Indians games, the closest professional team to him and one he had ties to, but mostly just visited or participated in special events when invited.

In 1947, when the creative Bill Veeck owned the Indians, he invited Young and the entire town of Newcomerstown to a Cleveland home game and chartered a train that brought about 1,000 people to the big city. Many others drove themselves.

When Young became ill and was hospitalized with hepatitis in 1950, he was pleasantly surprised to learn how well remembered he was.

"I think I got cards and letters from people in about every state," Young said.[4]

Although several of Young's records are indeed unapproachable, such as his complete-games mark, the 511 wins stands alone as an impressive feat. Later in life Young was asked by a boy who had heard that Cy had once pitched in the majors if he had been any good. Young said, "Son, I've won more games than you'll ever see played."[5]

It was a good quip, and also probably true for most people.

NOTES

1. Reed Browning, *Cy Young: A Baseball Life* (Amherst: University of Massachusetts Press, 2000), 137.
2. Ibid., 144.
3. Ibid., 143.
4. Ibid., 207.
5. Ralph Longo, "Why Cy Young's Win Record Is the Most Unbreakable in All of Sports," *Bleacher Report*, July 13, 2011.

FURTHER READING

Ryan, Bob. *When Boston Won the World Series: A Chronicle of Boston's Remarkable Victory in the First Modern World Series of 1903*. Philadelphia: Running Press, 2003.

Stout, Glenn, and Dick Johnson. *Red Sox Century: One Hundred Years of Red Sox Baseball.* Boston: Houghton Mifflin Harcourt, 2000.

#50 The Jack Dempsey–Gene Tunney Long Count

During his reign as heavyweight champion of the world, Jack Dempsey was viewed as invincible. He was the face of boxing when boxing mattered more to Americans than almost any other sport except baseball.

He was also one of the sports faces of the Roaring Twenties, one of a coterie of big-name athletes who were living large during Prohibition as the nation's psyche bounced back from World War I. In what is referred to by many as "the Golden Age of Sport," Dempsey, Babe Ruth, football player Red Grange, tennis player Bill Tilden, and golfer Bobby Jones were some of the most popular athletes of the time.

Known as "The Manassa Mauler," Dempsey gave the public what it craved in the ring, a big man (for the time) bringing the fight to foes and overpowering them with his fists. Dempsey provided action and walked away with victories. The fans did love him, and Dempsey is considered to be one of the most popular boxers in the sport's history.

During Dempsey's era boxers fought more frequently than they do now. They worked their way up through the crowds of veterans in front of them, obtaining world rankings, and then got their shot at the title. The heavyweight crown was one of the most precious baubles in sport, and it was symbolic of being the toughest man in the world.

Dempsey was born William Harrison Dempsey in Manassa, Colorado (hence the origins of his nickname), in 1895. Though he stood six-foot-one, Dempsey fought at under 190 pounds. With thick, wavy dark hair, Dempsey was attractive to women and with a sneer on his face appeared rakish to men. He impressed people both bare-chested and while wearing a tuxedo.

Dempsey turned pro in 1914 in Colorado Springs and began building his re-sume in western states such as Colorado, Utah, and Nevada. He made his eastern debut in the Bronx, New York, in 1916.

After a couple of fights he returned to the hinterlands, once again plying his trade in the West. It was far more difficult to get noticed by big-time promoters outside of the Northeast or the major cities of the Midwest at that time.

In November 1918 Dempsey toppled Batting Levinsky in Philadelphia in a breakthrough fight. Big wins followed over Billy Miske (twice) and Gunboat Smith. On July 4, 1919, in Toledo, Ohio, Dempsey dismantled former champ Jess Willard, knocking him down seven times in the first round and claiming the heavyweight crown. Willard outweighed Dempsey by 50 pounds, but it did not matter.

The thoroughness of Dempsey's power led some to suggest that he fought with "loaded" gloves, his regular boxing gloves built up by a hard substance enclosed in them. Many years later Dempsey's manager at the time of the fight stated that he filled his man's gloves with plaster of paris, which hardened and enabled Dempsey to do devastating work with his fists.

However, the fierce style of the victory at the time brought Dempsey popularity, and as his reputation grew he sometimes fought in front of massive crowds exceeding 80,000 fans. One was his 1921 match against Frenchman Georges Carpentier; that bout produced boxing's first $1 million gate.

Dempsey ruled the sport and ate up the acclaim, defending the title only periodically. In 1923 Dempsey engaged in one of the wildest championship bouts of all against Luis Firpo. The scheduled 15-rounder packed a full-length bout's worth of action into two rounds. Dempsey knocked down Firpo seven times in the first round, but with one tremendous swing, Firpo smashed Dempsey through the ropes and out of the ring altogether.

It was miraculous that Dempsey beat the count, and later famed artist George Bellows painted a well-known picture of one of the most memorable moments in boxing history. There were 11 knockdowns before Dempsey KO'd Firpo in the second, three-minute round.

Dempsey was only living up to his credo of toughness. What later became a cliché in the fight world, but was first uttered by Dempsey, was both clever and meaningful advice to a young prospect on what to do when he got clocked, but was still standing: "Some night you'll catch a punch between the eyes and all of a sudden you'll see three guys in the ring against you. Pick out the one in the middle and hit him, because he's the one who hit you."[1]

Dempsey went almost three years after the Firpo bout before defending the title again, this time against Gene Tunney on September 23, 1926, in Philadelphia. The bout was part of the city's 150th celebration of the country and was staged in the aptly named (if only temporarily so) Sesquicentennial Stadium. The largest paying crowd—120,557—in American boxing history poured into the stadium. They witnessed one of the most famous transfers of the heavyweight crown.

Born James Joseph Tunney in 1897 in New York City, the challenger had just one loss on his record, stemming from his time spent as a light-heavyweight, or the 175-pound limit. As he gained pounds, the six-footer jumped to heavyweight. Tunney fought in World War I and gained the nickname "The Fighting Marine." A movie of that name was made about his life. Tunney brought a record of 62–1–1 into the Philadelphia fight.

Tunney had been much more active in recent years than Dempsey and was sharper from the opening bell. He consistently beat Dempsey to the punch and easily handled him, lifting the heavyweight title in the process, in what the venerable *The Ring* magazine named its "Fight of the Year." While Dempsey was a slugger, Tunney was a boxer, and he picked Dempsey apart.

By the time the fight ended Dempsey was bleeding from so many cuts he basically could not see clearly. When Tunney was announced as the new champion, Dempsey asked his manager, Jack Kearns, "to lead me out there" because "I want to shake his hand."[2] Dempsey was nobler in defeat than many imagined he would be.

Dempsey recognized he was licked and did not make excuses. When he got home his wife asked what had happened, and Dempsey replied, "Honey, I forgot to duck."[3] That comment was reprinted in newspapers and enhanced Dempsey's reputation further.

The sport cried out for a rematch, and Tunney's first defense of the title was set for almost exactly a year later, September 22, 1927, at Soldier Field in Chicago. Dempsey fought once in between, disposing of future champ Jack Sharkey.

The gate for this fight topped $2.6 million. It was the first $2 million gate. Dempsey was hungry to regain glory and take back the title. Tunney wished to prove his first win was no fluke.

Dempsey had a habit of standing over knockdown victims, poised to rip them again as soon as they beat a 10-count. Forgotten by Dempsey in the heat of battle was a new rule that ordered fighters to go to a neutral corner before the referee could begin his count. Dempsey's seconds had actually asked for the rule to be applied to this fight before it had been universally installed in the sport.

This was Dempsey's undoing and made the fight one of the best-remembered boxing matches, and sporting events, in American history. The long count occurred in the seventh round when Dempsey decked Tunney. Rather than retreat to a neutral corner, Dempsey hovered in the vicinity as he had done in past fights.

Referee Dave Barry urged Dempsey to move into a corner. While he addressed Dempsey, Tunney had free time to recover on the canvas. Barry did not begin counting right away. By the time Dempsey did move away, Tunney beat a 10-count to his feet. It was later shown that Tunney was on the canvas for 14 seconds, basically escaping disqualification by knockout because of 5 extra seconds.

Tunney made it to his feet, lasted through the round, cleared his head, and then bounced back, capturing the victory and retaining the title. It was the greatest blunder of Dempsey's career and one of the biggest of all time in the boxing world.

Tunney fought just one more time, won, and retired with a record of 65–1–1. He died in 1978 at age 81.

Heavyweight Jack Dempsey, heavily favored for his defense against Gene Tunney in Chicago in 1927, failed to follow the rules when he knocked Tunney down. His mistake in not going to a neutral corner promptly resulted in giving the challenger longer than 10 seconds to rise and the error cost Dempsey his title when Tunney prevailed. (AP Photo)

Dempsey never fought again, retiring with a mark of 54–6–9. He remained in the limelight, operating a popular restaurant with his name on it in New York City before passing away at age 87 in 1983.

NOTES

1. Red Smith, "Jack Dempsey, 87, Is Dead: Boxing Champion of 1920s," *New York Times*, June 1, 1983.
2. Ibid.
3. Ibid.

FURTHER READING

Cavanaugh, Jack. *Tunney: Boxing's Brainiest Champ and His Upset of the Great Jack Dempsey*. New York: Ballantine Books, 2009.
Dempsey, Jack. *Dempsey*. New York: Harper & Row, 1977.

Dempsey, Jack. *How to Fight Tough*. Boulder, CO: Paladin Press, 2002.

Kahn, Roger. *A Flame of Pure Fire: Jack Dempsey and the Roaring Twenties*. Orlando, FL: Harcourt, 1999.

Roberts, Randy. *Jack Dempsey: The Manassa Mauler*. Urbana: University of Illinois Press, 2003.

#51 Baseball's All-Star Game

The founding of the annual Major League Baseball all-star game accomplished much more than was first anticipated when it made its debut in Chicago in 1933.

For one thing, it wasn't supposed to be an annual event. It was not expected to begin a wave of professional team sport all-star games, either. And as the first and only, it was not supposed to hold on as the most popular all-star game for decades.

The invention of the all-star game was the brainstorm of one man, even though he needed the cooperation of many to get it going. Arch Ward was the sports editor of the *Chicago Tribune* and was asked by legendary owner and publisher Colonel Robert R. McCormick to dream up some catchy sporting event that would resonate with the public during the upcoming Chicago World's Fair. That was suggested to McCormick by then Chicago mayor Ed Kelly.

The proper name for the World's Fair of 1933 was "A Century of Progress International Exposition." Ward was as much an entrepreneur as a sports journalist, and given carte blanche to provide legs for an idea he had harbored for some time, he approached team owners and league presidents to get them on board before the plan went to commissioner Kenesaw Mountain Landis for final approval. It did not hurt that the *Tribune* had an answer for those owners worried about taking a financial bath. McCormick stepped up to the plate and offered to cover any losses. It was a generous commitment, but unnecessary.

Ward was ingenious in ferreting out allies and siccing them on holdouts, and he managed to pull together enough support to gain approval for the venture. Unlike in modern-day baseball, in which the all-star game is a regular part of the July schedule, complete with a few-day break, there was no interval in the schedule to plug in a new all-star game. That was worked around.

Major League Baseball has been famous for relying on fan input in the selection of the all-star clubs for years, though it has varied in method over time and even been a revoked privilege. But right from the start fan participation was welcomed. Since it was his game and his paper was fronting the ink to promote the

The baseball all-star game was invented in 1933 by *Chicago Tribune* sports editor Arch Ward in conjunction with the World's Fair. Conceived as a one-time event, it became an institution and led to the creation of other major sports' all-star competitions. Famed managers Connie Mack (left), American League, and John J. McGraw, National League, were the field bosses. (AP Photo)

game and was willing to spend as much money as it took, Ward wanted readers of the *Tribune* to be the ones voting for the starting players.

In that he was overruled. Baseball administrators opened the balloting to readers of sports pages in numerous other cities as well. They clipped out ballots, and mailed them to the *Tribune*. Ward presided over the counting.

The game's creation was a dream come true for Ward, who would later lend his hand to the start-up of other sporting ventures, from a charity football all-star game to the development of the All-America Football Conference. But it also turned into a marvelous public relations coup for baseball.

Once baseball authorities had given their approval, Ward understood that his continuing role was to hype the heck out of the game. There were two choices in the City of Big Shoulders for placement of a Major League Baseball all-star game. It could be held at the Chicago Cubs' north side Wrigley Field, or it could be held at the Chicago White Sox's south side Comiskey Park. There was not much debate. Comiskey Park won out because its capacity was much greater.

The date of the game was set for July 6, 1933, and immediately Ward began promoting the contest as "The Game of the Century." His hyperbole took hold, and fans swooned. As soon as the ballots appeared, baseball fans filled them out and sent them in. As soon as tickets became available for the game, they began purchasing them. Box seats went for $1.65 and bleachers for 55 cents, although some were held out for later sale. Not to worry, attendance topped 47,000.

In what turned out to be a wise move, John J. McGraw, who had just retired as manager of the New York Giants after three decades as team boss, but was widely regarded as one of the kings of early 20th-century baseball, was designated manager of the National League squad. Connie Mack, who had been running things for the Philadelphia Athletics for just about the same length of time, was tabbed as the American League manager. The appointments represented smart baseball. Since the game was supposed to be a one-time thing, it was a gesture of respect to two pillars of the sport who would probably never have another chance like this.

Players were excited to be part of an event that was flattering simply in its name. They all wanted to be part of it. They also believed that being designated an all-star was going to be a one-time thing.

"America's response has been overwhelming," Ward wrote about the country's positive reaction to the announcement that the game was forthcoming.[1]

When the final 2,250 tickets went on sale, they were scooped up in 45 minutes. Ward had to write a story telling fans not to besiege him or the White Sox for tickets. If they hadn't already bought some, they were out of luck.

"The last ticket to the Game of the Century has been sold," Ward said. "There will be no more tickets on sale before the game. That's all there is. There isn't any more."[2]

Plenty of future Hall of Famers (an idea that did not come around until the end of the decade) were chosen as members of the first all-stars. In all, about 500,000 votes were cast, and they rolled into Chicago from other big-league towns.

The National League roster included Bill Terry, Paul Waner, Pie Traynor, Chuck Klein, Frankie Frisch, Carl Hubbell, Gabby Hartnett, and Chick Hafey. The American League roster included Lefty Gomez, Lou Gehrig, Al Simmons, Joe Cronin, Rick Ferrell, Jimmie Foxx, Tony Lazzeri, Charlie Gehringer, Lefty Grove, Bill Dickey, Earl Averill, and some fella by the name of Babe Ruth. That was out of 18 players per team, some of whom had to make creative railroad arrangements to reach Chicago for the game a day after their teams played elsewhere.

At the start of the game, in tune with the occasion, Mack and McGraw, both wearing suits and straw hats, posed for a picture gripping a bat, as if they were choosing up to see which team got last at-bats. This was McGraw's final game as a field boss. Already ill, he died in February 1934.

Gomez, a mainstay of the Yankees on the mound, was a terrible hitting pitcher, but drove in the first run in all-star game history with a single that scored Jimmie Dykes. Even Gomez, a naturally funny man who later made his living telling stories on the banquet circuit, made fun of his hitting. He never hit either a home run or a triple regular-season action in his entire career.

Once Gomez hit a double but was picked off. When his manager asked what went wrong, Gomez said, "How would I know? I've never been there before."[3]

Afterward the all-star game reporters asked Gomez some of the standard questions about what kind of pitch he had hit thrown by the opposing pitcher. He said he did not have a clue.

"Don't ask me what the pitch was," Gomez said. "It could have been a fastball down the pipe. With a bat in my hands I couldn't tell a curve from a Cuban palm ball. I do recall that only one of my eyes was closed when I swung."[4]

Fittingly, Ruth hit the first home run in all-star history in the 4–2 American League victory. It came in the third inning. He drove in two runs and hit safely twice. It was one of Ruth's last hurrahs. He was 38 and would be out of the game in two years.

Detroit second baseman Charlie Gehringer was on base when Ruth came to the plate to face "Wild Bill" Hallahan. Hallahan had two strikes on Ruth when the Bambino swung, his usual lefty, level swoop with the bat. The ball was deposited over the right-field fence.

The crowd went crazy. What could be better than this: Babe Ruth, the home-run king, bashing a home run in the all-star game?

Later Ruth said, "I knew it was gone," when he swung.[5]

Not only was Ruth's a great hit, but so was the all-star game. More than 80 years later the baseball all-star game is a fixture in the middle of the long season.

NOTES

1. Lew Freedman, *The Day All the Stars Came Out* (Jefferson, NC: McFarland, 2010), 26.
2. Ibid., 29.
3. Ibid., 77.
4. Ibid.
5. Ibid., 86.

FURTHER READING

Nelson, Murry R. *American Sports: A History of Icons, Idols, and Ideas*. Santa Barbara, CA: Greenwood Press, 2013.
Obojski, Robert. *All-Star Baseball since 1933*. New York: Stein & Day, 1980.
Vincent, David W., and Lyle Spatz. *The Midsummer Classic: The Complete History of Baseball's All-Star Game*. Lincoln, NE: Bison Books, 2001.

#52 Bill Mazeroski's Amazing Home Run

Anyone from Pittsburgh will vote for Bill Mazeroski's home run to win the World Series in the bottom of the ninth inning over the New York Yankees in 1960 as the most famous home run of all time.

They will get arguments about the 1951 home run that won the National League pennant for the New York Giants over the Brooklyn Dodgers, and they might get some feedback on Babe Ruth's called shot home run in the 1932 World Series against the Chicago Cubs.

Perhaps the most famous home run in baseball history, Bill Mazeroski's game-winning shot in the ninth inning of the seventh game of the World Series gave the Pittsburgh Pirates a World Series title over the New York Yankees in 1960. (AP Photo/Harry Harris)

But it is not merely hometown prejudice that those Pittsburghers speak from. They do have a case.

In 1960 the Yankees were a juggernaut. They had dominated post–World War II baseball, and as was common at the time, New York captured the American League pennant. It was not common for the Pirates to win the National League pennant.

The last time the Pirates had appeared in the World Series was 1927. The last time the Pirates had won the World Series was 1925. In the early 1950s the Pirates were not only the worst team in the NL; they also had some of the worst records in history. Pittsburgh's claiming the pennant in 1960 represented the culmination of a slow rebuilding plan over a decade. They had transitioned from terrible to mediocre to good to a champion.

More than a half century later those Pirates have a special niche in local history. The players who populated the roster that season are well remembered and continue to be admired. Among the stars that season were Hall of Fame outfielder Roberto Clemente; pitchers like Bob Friend, Roy Face, Harvey Haddix, and Cy Young award winner Vernon Law; catcher Smokey Burgess; and outfielders Bob Skinner and Bill Virdon. Infielders were Don Hoak; Mazeroski, who also made the Hall of Fame; and Dick Groat, who won the National League batting title with a .325 average and was named NL Most Valuable Player.

The Pirates finished 95–59 that season under manager Danny Murtaugh, another beloved figure in Pittsburgh. The Yankees, who had the same type of impact on society in the 1950s as Elvis Presley, if not greater, won the American League pennant with a mark of 97–57 under Casey Stengel.

Whitey Ford, also on his way to the Hall of Fame, anchored the pitching rotation, but the Yankees were more sluggers than anything, with a lineup that included Mickey Mantle, Roger Maris, Yogi Berra, Elston Howard, and Bill Skowron and such dashing fielders as Bobby Richardson, Tony Kubek, and Clete Boyer. The Yankees had a habit of brushing away most of even the best competition as if they were so many high schoolers.

Mazeroski, a five-foot-eleven second baseman, was a brilliant fielder whose glove work carried him to the Hall of Fame. In 1960 he batted .273 with 11 home runs and 64 runs batted in, made the National League all-star team (one of his seven selections), and won the Gold Glove Award (one of eight times).

"Maz," as the player was often called for short, played 17 years in the majors, breaking in for the 1956 season and retiring at the end of the 1972 season. His lifetime average was .260. At no time did Mazeroski shine brighter than he did in 1960 when his teammates needed him most.

The 1960 World Series was one of the most peculiar of all. At times it seemed as if the Yankees would simply blow the Pirates out of the stadium. To reach Mazeroski's climactic moment, the teams struggled through six games that they split.

The Series opened on October 5 at cavernous Forbes Field in Pittsburgh. The Pirates went with their best, Law, who won 20 games that year. New York started Art Ditmar. Although Law was not at his finest, he got the win (with relief help from Face), in a 6–4 decision.

Game 2 was where the Series started to get a little wacky. New York started Bob Turley against Pittsburgh's Bob Friend. Friend did not have his good stuff, and the Yankees routed the Pirates, 16–3. Mantle, another future Hall of Famer, stroked two home runs. New York batted out 19 hits.

The Series shifted to Yankee Stadium in the Bronx for game 3, and the Yankees, feeding off their momentum from the second game, whipped the Pirates 10–0. Things were beginning to look dire for Pittsburgh. Ford pitched a four-hit shutout. Pittsburgh's Vinegar Bend Mizell took a beating. The Yankees built a demoralizing 6–0 lead by the end of the first inning.

It was a pivotal point in the Series. If the Yankees won game 4 at home, their championship seemed assured. This was a tense, low-scoring game. Law came back for the Pirates and this time pitched at his best. Law left leading after seven innings, but Face kept the Yankees off the board over the last two innings, and Pittsburgh won, 3–2. That tied the Series.

Employing the 2–3–2 World Series home-game schedule, game 5 was also in New York. Only a few days earlier the Pirates seemed in jeopardy of imploding. Instead, they came out of New York with a 3–2 lead in games after winning 5–2. Harvey "The Kitten" Haddix, who in 1959 had pitched 12 perfect games in an outing, only to lose it in the 13th, was the victor. The Yankees only managed five hits. Face came out of the bullpen again and recorded his third save, all three of Pittsburgh's victories.

The Series traveled back to Pittsburgh for game 6. The Pirates had a chance to wrap up the championship, but instead the Series reverted to its earlier form. The Yankees pummeled Pittsburgh, crushing Friend for a second time while Ford cruised for a second time. New York won 12–0 to put doubts in the heads of Pittsburgh fans.

"They beat the heck out of us," Murtaugh said of the day's result. But he also reminded the world that it was only one game and the next one counted the most. "If I'm not mistaken, I believe the score is 3–3 right now."[1]

That Yankees shutout set up a seventh game, one of the most remarkable in World Series history. But the Pirates did not act intimidated, even if they had been on the short end of some of the most one-sided results in Series history.

"They murder mediocre pitching, but they can be stopped," Groat said. "I think we've shown the world that much."[2]

In game 7 the Pirates worked their way to a 4–0 lead before the Yankees scored a single run in the fifth inning. During their dynasty years the Yankees had a way of repeatedly coming back and stealing games in the late innings. It was 4–1 Pittsburgh entering the sixth inning and 5–4 Yankees by the time it ended.

New York added to its lead in the eighth inning, stretching the margin to 7–4. There were many nervous fans at Forbes Field. Then came the bottom of the eighth, Pirates batting, and another of the most famous plays in Series history. Murtaugh pinch-hit Gino Cimoli for Face, and he singled. Virdon was the next man up, and he drove a pitch into the ground to shortstop Kubek. It looked like a routine double-play for New York. But the ball struck a rock, caroming into Kubek's throat, and the injury forced him out of the game.

From there the Pirates scored five runs and took a 9–7 lead into the ninth inning. Pittsburgh couldn't hold it. The Yanks scored two and sent the suspenseful, knotted game into the bottom of the ninth inning for the Pirates' at-bat.

Right-hander Ralph Terry was on the mound for New York. The goal was to set the Pirates down and force extra innings. The first batter of the ninth for Pittsburgh was the right-handed swinging Mazeroski.

Mazeroski gave himself a pep talk as he walked to the plate, reminding himself not to overswing. When asked if he was nervous because of the high-stakes situation, he said no.

"I thought I'd be more nervous this time, but I wasn't a bit," he said, comparing this at-bat with his last one two innings earlier.[3]

With the count 1–0, Maz swung and lofted a ball deep to left. Berra, playing the position, turned around and watched the ball sail over his head.

That was it. A walk-off home run, Pirates win 10–9, Pittsburgh erupts in delirium. Mazeroski was mobbed by his teammates at home plate after his stunning shot, and the Pirates were world champions.

"Yeah, I was swinging for the fence," Mazeroski told sportswriters after the game. "What did I think? I was too happy to think."[4]

Some 33 years later, Joe Carter ended the World Series for the Toronto Blue Jays with a home run, but that was game 6. That is the only other time a Series has ended on a homer, and no other Series has been won on a game 7 home run.

Although he had a very worthy career, Mazeroski is forever adored in Pittsburgh because of that one hit.

NOTES

1. Jim Reisler, *The Best Game Ever: Pirates vs. Yankees, October 13, 1960* (Cambridge, MA: Carroll & Graf, 2007), 7.

2. Ibid.

3. Ibid., 210.

4. Ibid., 222.

FURTHER READING

Finoli, David. *The Pittsburgh Pirates 1960 Season*. Mt. Pleasant, SC: Arcadia Publishing, 2015.

Maraniss, Robert. *Clemente: The Passion and Grace of Baseball's Last Hero*. New York: Simon & Schuster, 2007.

Mumau, Thad. *Had 'Em All the Way: The 1960 Pittsburgh Pirates*. Jefferson, NC: McFarland, 2015.

#53 Michael Phelps

When it comes to an achievement list, Michael Phelps's is longer than the distance from the tips of his fingers to the tips of his toes, the extreme appendages that help him to swim so fast.

He has won the incomprehensible record of 22 Olympic medals during his career in the pool, a preposterous total since even the best of athletes can barely hope to dream of winning one in their careers.

Born in Towson, Maryland, in 1985, Phelps, whose nicknames are "The Baltimore Bullet" and "The Flying Fish," had won 77 medals in international competition as of 2015. He has more than once indicated he is retired, but has come back for a few more swims, and it is even possible that he will seek to represent the United States in one more Olympics in 2016, which would be his fourth.

Those international medals were earned in long-course competition at Pan Pacific, World Championships, and Olympic Games.

Phelps's swimming accomplishments are so voluminous that their true impact is felt only when reviewing his lifetime body of work, starting with the fact that he has been named world swimmer of the year seven times and American swimmer of the year nine times. If there is a signature moment for the man who has been the face of U.S. and worldwide swimming almost since the start of the 2000s, it was in 2008 at the Summer Olympics in Beijing.

To that point in swimming history, the single most dominant and decorated swimmer was the American Mark Spitz. At the 1972 Games in Munich, Spitz won seven gold medals, a standard that had never been approached.

That changed in 2008. Phelps possessed the skills to swim at a world-class level in several disciplines at various distances and had the will to try to break Spitz's record. Phelps may as well have been a torpedo in the pool, the way he sliced through the water. Not only was Phelps the biggest star in the water, the

The most decorated Olympian ever, American swimmer Michael Phelps has earned 22 medals in his career spanning the 2004, 2008, and 2012 Olympics. Phelps set a record in 2008 in China when he won eight gold medals in a single Game. (AP Photo/Itsuo Inouye)

biggest star in his events, but his monumental challenge and achievement eclipsed the accomplishments of anyone else at Beijing.

Phelps made his stay in China worthwhile, breaking Spitz's record by winning eight gold medals in a single Olympics in the pool. He captured gold in the 200-meter freestyle, the 100-meter butterfly, the 200-meter butterfly, the 200-meter individual medley, the 400-meter individual medley, and for being part of three American relay teams: the 4 × 100 meters, the 4 × 200 meters, and the 4 × 100 medley relay.

He set new world records in seven of the eight events. The only event in which Phelps did not establish a new world record was the 100-meter fly, in which he set an Olympic record.

In all it was nearly a surreal performance.

"This is all a dream come true," Phelps said after capturing his eighth gold in 2008 after the United States won the 400-meter medley relay. "Every day it seems like I'm in sort of a dream world. Sometimes you have to pinch yourself to see if it's really real. I'm just happy I'm in the real world."[1]

Little of what Phelps did was that much of a shock. In 2004, at the Athens Olympics, Phelps won six gold medals and two bronze medals. That was quite the impressive Olympic warm-up for 2008. There was considerable doubt about whether Phelps would continue competing through the 2012 Olympics, but after taking some time off, he did.

While acknowledging that he could not match his 2008 performance in eight events, Phelps was still able to win four more gold medals and two silver medals in London four years later.

Phelps was not just the best in the pool, but also the best of all time, much of the time he was competing. By the time he completed his third Olympics in 2012, Phelps had set 39 world records. After the London Games he retired, and the swimming world thought it had seen the last of him in the water. However, in 2014 Phelps indicated he was going to come out of retirement and return to competition.

What neither Phelps nor his fans expected, however, was that the six-foot-four swimmer, who was approaching his 30th birthday, would get into trouble away from his sport. When he was much younger Phelps was charged with driving while impaired and fined. Phelps, 19 at the time, admitted he had let people down. Later, a photograph circulated of him using a water pipe typically employed for smoking marijuana, and he was slapped with a three-month suspension by USA Swimming.

About a decade after Phelps's first run-in with the law over driving while drinking, in the fall of 2014 he was arrested again for driving under the influence and speeding and was suspended from competition for six months by USA Swimming.

"I understand the severity of my actions and take full responsibility. . . . I am deeply sorry," Phelps said on his Twitter account and was quoted elsewhere.[2]

It was unclear if Phelps, who was comparatively ancient for worldwide competition as he was passing another birthday, would mount a serious attempt to make one more Olympic team or if he still had the necessary speed and zest to do so.

He has regularly made public appearances and has worked at becoming a public speaker, often addressing schoolchildren to encourage them to follow whatever path they would like, while explaining that it will take hard work to succeed.

"Everybody has a dream as a child," Phelps said. "We have something we really want to do, really want to accomplish, no matter what it is. I wanted to become an Olympic champion, a world-record holder and a professional athlete."[3]

Phelps said he had to work out every day for years to get ahead, and there has never been an indication that his swimming prowess has translated into any other endurance sport like running or bicycling. He has referred to himself as klutzy when he is out of the pool. But he is in his own world while swimming.

"If you want to be the best, you have to do things others won't do," he has said.[4]

One of Phelps's stated life goals is to promote swimming and overall fitness, and he established the Michael Phelps Foundation in 2008 to those ends. He spoke to young people as part of an outreach program at a Boys and Girls Club while he was in Fort Wayne, Indiana, as part of his mission.

At that point Phelps was still considering a return to the pool, with a possible eye toward seeking a spot on the American team in Rio de Janeiro for the 2016 Games. An early step in that direction would be Phelps trying to swim for the U.S. world championship team.

There is still a chance that Phelps, the greatest swimmer of all time, is not finished on the world stage.

NOTES

1. Phil Hersh, "The Greatest," *Chicago Tribune*, August 24, 2008.
2. "Michael Phelps 'Deeply Sorry' after Arrest for DUI in Maryland," *CBS-4*, October 1, 2014.
3. Dave Gong, "Phelps: No Harm in Asking for Help," *Fort Wayne Journal-Gazette*, March 27, 2015.
4. Ibid.

FURTHER READING

Phelps, Michael, and Alan Abrahamson. *No Limits: The Will to Succeed*. New York: Free Press, 2009.
Phelps, Michael, and Brian Cazenueve. *Beneath the Surface: My Story*. New York: Sports Publishing, 2012.
Schaller, Bob, and Rowdy Gaines. *Michael Phelps: The Untold Story of a Champion*. New York: St. Martin's Press, 2008.

#54 Martina Navratilova Wins and Comes Out

Recognized as probably the greatest women's tennis player of all time, Martina Navratilova not only won a record 167 singles titles and 177 doubles titles, but she was a pioneer athlete in terms of standing up for gay rights when she came out in 1981.

Born in Czechoslovakia, Martina Navratilova became a United States citizen, won 18 Grand Slam titles, and became one of the greatest female tennis players ever. Navratilova became the highest profile gay athlete in the world. (AP Photo/Carol Newsom)

Some 35 years later Navratilova, who was born in Czechoslovakia but became an American citizen, is probably still the most prominent openly gay athlete in the United States.

During the open tennis era, Navratilova was ranked number 1 in the world in singles for 332 weeks and number 1 in doubles for 237 weeks. Partially known for her great rivalry with Chris Evert, Navratilova won just under 87 percent of her singles matches in a career that spanned more than 20 years.

In the four Grand Slam singles tournaments, Navratilova won the U.S. Open four times, Wimbledon nine times, the French Open twice, and the Australian Open three times. In doubles Navratilova won the U.S. Open nine times, Wimbledon seven times, the French Open seven times, and the Australian Open eight times. Over one stretch in doubles, Navratilova and partner Pam Shriver won 109 straight matches. During her career Navratilova won about 84 percent of her doubles matches.

In addition, Navratilova was part of 10 major mixed doubles titles. She either won outright or shared in 59 Grand Slam titles. She won 18 Grand Slam singles finals, but also was runner-up in 14 others. Four of those times Evert won. Another four of those times Steffi Graf won. Navratilova won about $21.6 million in prize money during her career.

Born in Czechoslovakia in 1956, Navratilova turned pro in 1975. That same year she asked for political asylum in the United States, which was granted.

Navratilova, whose parents divorced when she was three, began swinging a tennis racket at age four and began playing tennis at seven. During her earliest days on tour she was viewed as being slightly chubby. But when she embraced a sophisticated training and nutrition program, she emerged as the fittest and strongest player on the women's tour.

Navratilova became a U.S. citizen in 1981. During that process she wondered whether if she were publicly identified as gay she would be refused citizenship and have to leave the country.

"I was sure that any hint of scandal would hurt me financially and maybe worse," she said. "I had applied for American citizenship and my final hearing was scheduled for later that summer. There are some states where homosexuality is a crime and I was afraid my sex life would prevent me from becoming an American."[1]

She said in a newspaper interview that year that she was bisexual and afterward identified as a lesbian, at different times having relationships with basketball star Nancy Lieberman and author Rita Mae Brown. Navratilova has spoken out for gay rights, made speeches, and participated in public marches supporting efforts to provide equal rights and opportunities to gays and lesbians.

However, at the time Navratilova was worried that her candor would hurt her situation with the U.S. government. As much as she was outspoken—and has been since—against communism, Navratilova was concerned she might have to find a new country to live in.

"[P]eople get nervous about anybody who is controversial," Navratilova said. "At the time I didn't care so much about the endorsements, but travel was a pain in the neck without a U.S. passport. My green card, which allowed me to live and work in the U.S., reminded me I was still not a citizen and I always had to carry a re-entry card when I left the States."[2]

Navratilova was so conscious of being essentially an escapee from a communist country that she used to check her airline flight paths when competing overseas to avoid even flying over communist nations. If the plane landed in an Eastern Bloc nation, she feared being returned to Czechoslovakia.

Navratilova worried that she might fail to gain citizenship because of her homosexual relationships. She noted that when she lived in Virginia homosexuality was a crime, and that the U.S. government stance against homosexuality seemed to be based on the fear that a homosexual in the military could be blackmailed into turning over sensitive information to a foreign government.

"In a better world, where you could be open about your sexuality, there'd be no question of blackmail," she said.[3]

When Navratilova was sworn in as an American citizen on July 20, 1981, she wanted to shout and clap, she said, and soon afterward cried. She immediately obtained a passport and realized how precious that was to her when she promptly flew to Australia on it to play tennis.

At the time Navratilova was one of the finest women's tennis players in the world, and she had a handful of Grand Slam championships on her resumé. But most of her best tennis lay ahead, and her preeminence in the sport was still to come. Over the next several years Navratilova emerged as a titan of the sport, almost unbeatable. The matches with Chris Evert were highly anticipated and often very tight. Gradually, however, Navratilova began to pull away in the one-on-ones with Evert.

For 12 years, between 1975 and 1987, either Navratilova or Evert was ranked number 1 in the world for all but about six months. In all, their rivalry, one of the most heralded in American sport, encompassed 80 tournament matches over 15 years between 1973 and 1988. Sixty-one of those meetings took place in championship finals. Navratilova held the edge, 36–25, including 10–4 in Grand Slam finals. The one area where Evert had a clear edge was on clay courts, where her winning margin was 11–3.

Outside of the lines, outside of the tense on-court rivalry, though, Navratilova and Evert warmed to one another personally and developed a lasting friendship. They remained in touch long after their playing days were finished. They bonded over their sport at first, when Billie Jean King, the Queen Mother of women's open tennis, who fought for equal paydays and helped lift the sport from secondary status behind the men, gave them advice to always boost the women's game as ambassadors. They heeded that suggestion.

Evert was always portrayed as more of a feminine ideal, and Navratilova said she was always grateful for the way Evert was open-minded about Navratilova's homosexuality and never let competition get in the way of their common ground and friendship.

"Before I even met her, she stood for everything I admired in this country, poise, ability, sportsmanship, money, style," said Navratilova.[4]

Later, after her tennis career was over, Navratilova coauthored three mystery novels and battled breast cancer. Whenever provided the opportunity, she was firm and outspoken in her views.

When Jason Collins, the NBA player, set off seismic rumbles by admitting in 2013 that he was gay, Navratilova penned an opinion piece for *Sports Illustrated*, discussing her own life as a gay athlete in the 1970s and 1980s compared to the present.

"We've come a long way," Navratilova said in part. "Now that Jason Collins has come out, he is the proverbial 'game-changer.' One of the last bastions of homophobia has been challenged (the locker room). Collins has led the way to freedom. Yes, freedom, because that closet is completely and utterly suffocating. It's only when you come out that you can be exactly who you are. Collins' action will save lives."[5]

An illustration of how things had changed in the United States, as gay marriage became legal in more and more states, Navratilova and her longtime partner Julia Lemigova were married in December 2014.

NOTES

1. Martina Navratilova and George Vecsey, *Martina* (New York: Ballantine Books/ Fawcett Crest, 1985), 219.
2. Ibid., 230.
3. Ibid., 231.
4. George Vecsey, "The Best of Rivals and the Best of Friends, Then and Always," *New York Times*, August 29, 2010.
5. Martina Navratilova, "Jason Collins a Game-Changer," *Sports Illustrated*, April 29, 2013.

FURTHER READING

Blue, Adrienne. *Martina: The Lives and Times of Martina Navratilova*. New York: Birch Lane Press, 1995.
Howard, Johnette. *The Rivals: Chris Evert vs. Martina Navratilova—Their Rivalry, Their Friendship, Their Legacy*. New York: Yellow Jersey Press, 2005.
Navratilova, Martina, and Mary Carillo. *Tennis My Way*. New York: Penguin, 1984.

#55 Magic Johnson Shows You Can Live with AIDS

Almost as much as for his no-look passes, Magic Johnson was famous for his 1,000-watt smile. One of the most famous athletes in the country and one of the most popular basketball players in the world, Earvin Johnson Jr. shocked the world with an announcement that no one saw coming and no one wanted to believe when they heard it.

Johnson held a press conference on November 7, 1991, and told the world that he had tested HIV positive during a routine examination for a life insurance policy. This was at a time when much of the universe considered the contraction of the HIV virus a certain precursor to suffering from the full-blown AIDS virus and put bluntly, was tantamount to a death sentence.

Beloved Los Angeles Lakers guard Magic Johnson, who previously led Michigan State to an NCAA basketball title, shocked the world with his announcement in 1991 that he had tested positive for the AIDS virus. Until that time AIDS was regarded as a "gay disease" and was considered to be a death sentence. In the quarter century since, Johnson has lived positively, publicly, and gracefully. (AP Photo/Mark J. Terrill)

AIDS was seen as an incurable epidemic, but also one that was considered to be mostly limited to homosexuals or in some cases intravenous drug users. Although the test and the announcement led to the termination of Johnson's glittering pro basketball career with the Los Angeles Lakers, it also led to better understanding of the illness. Also, a quarter of a century later Johnson is alive, seemingly well, and in addition has proven to be one of the savviest and creative businessmen among all professional athletes.

At that shocking press conference, Johnson appeared calmer than his listeners.

"We sometimes think only gay people can get it," he said, "that it's not going to happen to me. And here I am saying it can happen to anybody, even me, Magic Johnson. I'm going to go on. I'm going to beat this. And I'm going to have fun."[1]

Johnson was born in Lansing, Michigan, in 1959 and was such a transcendent high school basketball player that a sportswriter nicknamed him "Magic." The appellation has so thoroughly stuck that few recall his given first name.

Although Johnson had the skills to play at almost any college in the country, he chose to stay home and compete for Michigan State. He played just one season before he jumped to the NBA, where he immediately became a star. Johnson stood six-foot-nine and weighed 220 pounds. Players of that size almost exclusively played forward in the pros. However, Johnson broke the mold and introduced a new era of the tall man lining up at point guard.

Unlike most players of that size, who excelled at shooting from outside or elbowing for rebounds, Johnson's brilliance was rooted in his court sense and his passing ability.

Magic really exploded on the national scene in 1979 when he led the Spartans to the NCAA championship game. There they faced Indiana State led by Larry Bird. Michigan State prevailed. In the years immediately following, the two stars emerged as the face of the NBA, Bird with the Boston Celtics, Johnson with the Lakers. Year after year they vied for supremacy. Initially fierce rivals, and always fierce competitors, the duo developed an unlikely friendship born of mutual respect.

Johnson was part of five Laker world championship teams and won three Most Valuable Player awards. He was a 12-time all-star during his career and was hailed as one of the greatest playmakers of all time. He also was named the MVP of the all-star game twice and MVP of the NBA Finals three times.

During his Hall of Fame pro career Johnson averaged 19.5 points a game, 11.2 assists, and 7.2 rebounds a game as an all-around star. Johnson proved his value as a rookie and played a major role in leading the Lakers to the 1980 championship. A year later he signed a 25-year, $25 million contract with the team.

Magic was just 31 and about to begin the 1991–1992 season with the Lakers when he took the physical examination that altered the course of his life. Johnson, who admittedly had lived a wild sexual life, partying with many women for years, almost immediately pledged to use his newfound platform to educate people about AIDS. There were many misconceptions about the illness at the time, including the persistent belief that it was a "gay disease" and that sexually promiscuous hetero-sexuals wouldn't catch it.

Essentially, a low T-cell count was an indicator of HIV (human immunodefi-ciency virus) being present, which could lead to AIDS infecting a person's system and gradually lead to death through reduced immune protection and secondary causes such as pneumonia, tuberculosis, infections, and tumors.

AIDS (acquired immunodeficiency syndrome) was first identified in the United States in 1981, and HIV soon afterward. Originally believed to have no cure, the swift development of counteractive drugs stemmed the spread of the illness among many. AIDS can be transmitted through sexual contact and the transfer of bodily fluids such as blood transfusions.

At the time Magic Johnson turned up HIV positive, there was an erroneous yet strong belief that primarily homosexual interaction caused the disease. Johnson retired from the Lakers immediately after his positive test, and when he said at his farewell press conference that he would beat the disease and continue to fight it on any front, many thought it was just bravado.

Later that winter the fans voted Johnson into the NBA all-star game. Consistent with his upbeat nature, Johnson stated his pleasure at the respect shown and indi-cated he wanted to play. To his chagrin, several other players said that he should not. They feared their own risk of catching AIDS if Johnson were to be injured and bleed on them. While discouraged by that reception, Johnson accepted the invita-tion, suited up, and turned in a startling performance for someone whom others felt was on his deathbed and at the least hadn't played all season.

In the game played in Orlando, Johnson led the West to an easy 153–113 vic-tory by scoring 25 points and gathering 9 assists and 5 rebounds. In a capstone to the event, Magic was named Most Valuable Player.

That might have been Johnson's final appearance on a major basketball stage, but in 1992, when USA Basketball was selecting the greatest NBA players to represent the country in the Barcelona Olympics, the first time pros were able to participate, Johnson was included on the roster. The group came to be known as the Dream Team. Although he was not in top physical shape because of knee prob-lems, Johnson did average 8 points and 5.5 assists a game during the Games as the United States went undefeated and won a gold medal.

Johnson was easing into a new stage of his life as someone afflicted with HIV, yet coping with it. He worked out to build muscle and strength, took care with his nutrition, and looked even stronger than in his playing days. He felt so good that prior to the 1992–1993 season he planned a comeback with the

Lakers. However, there was so much controversy over the same kind of issues he had faced before the Olympics that he did not believe he could resume his career normally.

Near the end of the 1993–1994 season, Johnson served as Lakers interim coach, though it was only for two games. Astonishingly, Johnson gave basketball one more whirl, at age 36. He suited up again for the Lakers. In his first game back Magic scored 19 points, grabbed 8 rebounds, and passed off for 10 assists. He played in 32 games and averaged 14.6 points per game before retiring from the NBA for good.

Proving he was as healthy as could be, Johnson then headed a traveling squad of basketball players named the Magic Johnson All-Stars. He also played a season in Sweden and tried basketball in Denmark for awhile.

Though watchful of his health, Johnson lived a very active lifestyle. He became a spokesman for organizations that sought to educate people about AIDS and became an entrepreneur under the auspices of Magic Johnson Enterprises, with numerous business ventures, a major one helping bring companies to inner-city black neighborhoods with the goal of revitalizing local economies. Johnson was part of the partnership group that in 2012 bought the Los Angeles Dodgers.

At times people have wondered how Johnson has managed to have such a long, fulfilling, and active life with HIV, as if it is somehow easy for him. During a radio appearance in 2014, Johnson stressed that he has not undergone miracle treatments, but takes the same drugs available to other people.

"I do have it and I have had it for 22 years," Johnson said. "It's just laying asleep in my body."[2]

Johnson, whose business empire worth was estimated to be $700 million, continued to make donations of cash and time to charitable causes and speak out for helping those with HIV and AIDS and for research into both. And he also continues to take drugs that keep his illness in remission.

NOTES

1. Rick Weinberg, "7: Magic Johnson Announces He's HIV-Positive," ESPN.com, September 1, 2004, http://sports.espn.go.com/espn/espn25/story?page=moments/7.

2. "Magic Johnson Calls BS on HIV Myths: I Don't Have a Magic Cure," *TMZ Sports*, February 11, 2014, http://www.tmz.com/videos/0_es6dz1cj/.

FURTHER READING

Bird, Larry, Earvin "Magic" Johnson, and Jackie MacMullen. *When the Game Was Ours.* Boston: Houghton Mifflin Harcourt, 2009.

Johnson, Earvin "Magic." *32 Ways to Be a Champion in Business*. New York: Crown Publishing Group, 2009.

Johnson, Earvin "Magic," and Roy S. Johnson. *Magic's Touch*. New York: Perseus Books, 1990.

Johnson, Earvin "Magic," and William Novak. *My Life*. Robbinsdale, MN: Fawcett, 1993.

#56 John Wooden's 10 NCAA Titles

Considered the greatest coach in college basketball history, John Wooden won his 10th NCAA championship in 12 years at UCLA in 1975 and retired to a life of being an elder statesman of the game.

Wooden coached Lew Alcindor (aka Kareem Abdul-Jabbar) and Bill Walton, two big men who were the most dominant players in America during their time in Southern California. He won more men's basketball championships than anyone else (still double the total of any other single coach), led UCLA to undefeated seasons, and dispensed his wisdom about the sport in books. He called his coaching philosophy the "Pyramid of Success."

Forty years after his retirement and not long after his death at nearly 100 years of age, Wooden's record is unmatched.

John Wooden was born in tiny Hall, Indiana, in 1910, but is often described as being from the somewhat larger small community of Martinsville, south of Indianapolis, where he played high school basketball. Wooden's team won a state championship, and he was three times selected as an all-state guard before enrolling at Purdue University.

During his years playing for the Boilermakers, Wooden was a three-time all-American. Although his career predated the NBA, Wooden did play on some lesser-known professional teams. He began his coaching career at Kentucky and Indiana high schools before serving in the navy for three years during World War II. In 1961 Wooden was inducted into the Naismith Memorial Basketball Hall of Fame in Springfield, Massachusetts, in recognition of his playing accomplishments. At that point Wooden had not won any national titles as a coach.

Wooden began his college coaching career in 1946 at Indiana State in Terre Haute and spent two seasons there; the second year the Sycamores finished 27–7. That showing put Wooden on the map.

In a development that changed college basketball history, Wooden was simultaneously being lured west to Los Angeles to take over UCLA's program and to Minneapolis to run the University of Minnesota team. Wooden's wife Nell wanted to stay in the Midwest. At the appointed time, when Wooden was supposed to hear from Minnesota, his phone stayed silent. He thought the school had lost interest, and he accepted the UCLA offer. Only afterward did he learn that communications had been knocked out at Minnesota because of bad weather. Too late. Wooden had given his word, and he stuck to it.

Wooden and his wife did not particularly enjoy the first years at UCLA, and when the head coaching job came open at his alma mater, he was ready to jump to Purdue. It was not as if UCLA was doing badly, either. Records for UCLA's first two seasons were 22–7 and 24–7. However, UCLA officials would not let him out of his contract, so he stayed in Los Angeles and ended up building a dynasty.

Throughout the 1950s UCLA won steadily under Wooden, picking off a conference championship here and there, and somewhat regularly the Bruins were ranked in the Associated Press top 20, or sometimes in the top 10. So it wasn't as if nobody in the basketball world heard of UCLA.

In 1962 UCLA lost in the NCAA semifinals. The Bruins were close. Assistant coach Jerry Norman talked the boss into instituting a zone press and that transformed UCLA. The Bruins became the most feared defensive team in the land, employing a hounding, pincer defense all over the court that intimidated foes and set the high-speed pace for games.

At the end of the 1963–1964 season UCLA had its first NCAA crown in hand, and the Bruins won it all while going 30–0.

"Our club is hard to figure out," Wooden said. "I'll say this for the boys. They meet every challenge with courage."[1]

The Bruins defeated Duke, 98–83, in the title game in Kansas City. It was obvious that Wooden had a special crop of players.

"Duke has plenty of speed, but they couldn't run with us," said UCLA's point guard Walt Hazzard, who was chosen as the National Player of the Year.[2]

The next year UCLA repeated as champs with a 28–2 mark. Guard Gail Goodrich fired in 42 points with his deadly left-handed jump shot. The Bruins topped Michigan, 91–80. Although Goodrich played with fire and confidence, he later admitted he wasn't certain the Bruins could top the Wolverines.

"I honestly wasn't sure when we went out there on the floor if we could win," Goodrich said. "But after three minutes I knew we were going to take it."[3]

This was an era when the NCAA prohibited freshmen from playing varsity ball (the rule came and went), so unlike in present-day schools, Wooden could not simply reload with recruiting. Although it was believed that the UCLA frosh, which featured Alcindor, might have been the best team in the nation, those Bruins could not play for the varsity.

A year later Wooden unveiled what had been lurking in the practice gym. The seven-foot-two Alcindor (he did not change his name to Abdul-Jabbar until 1971,

The UCLA-led Bruins of the 1960s and 1970s won 10 NCAA basketball titles in 12 seasons under legendary coach John Wooden, still the record for men's college basketball. Some of Wooden's greatest stars are (left) Lew Alcindor (Kareem Abdul-Jabbar) and Sidney Wicks. Admired for his leadership, Wooden became an elder statesman of the game before passing away at 99 in 2010. (AP Photo)

when he was in the pros), with his devastating sky hook that could not be blocked, was even better than expected. The reconstituted Bruins went unbeaten and 30–0 again for the 1966–1967 season. The Bruins, with Alcindor in the middle, won two more titles in a row, going 29–1 each year.

It was the most fabulous run in NCAA history. UCLA had won five out of six titles under Wooden. Alcindor was the best player in the country, though as many college students were, he was still finding himself during a tumultuous time in the nation's history, with civil rights battles being fought.

Years later Alcindor reflected on his stay at UCLA beyond just the wins (and not many losses).

"Truly, it was all the games, practices, classes, teammates and friends that comprise my UCLA experience," he said. "Of the many factors that influenced my choice of UCLA, the most significant was its tradition of excellence among black athletes. That, along with the particular genius of John Wooden."[4]

During Alcindor's era UCLA's biggest rival was the University of Houston, led by Elvin Hayes. When UCLA and the Cougars met in the Astrodome in 1968, the event was billed as "The Game of the Century." The attendance of 52,693 set a record. It was also the first nationally televised regular-season college basketball game, and Houston upset UCLA, 71–68.

"There were so many firsts involved, people cannot put it out of their minds," Don Chaney, one of Houston's other stars, said three decades later.[5]

There was a gap in time between the two truly great centers Wooden coached at UCLA, but as the basketball world salivated, relieved that Alcindor was gone, Wooden still had a complement of supremely talented guys.

Burly forwards Sidney Wicks and Curtis Rowe took center stage as the UCLA juggernaut continued rolling, before a six-foot-eleven Californian with decidedly more liberal politics in his head than Wooden's swooped in and came as close as anyone could to filling Alcindor's shoes.

In the early 1970s, UCLA, with Walton spearheading the success and forward Jamal Wilkes by his side, recorded two straight 30–0 seasons and put together an 88-game winning streak that was eventually busted by Notre Dame. When he spoke at all to sportswriters, Walton could be intriguing about subjects outside the court, but also on basketball matters. People usually knew how Walton thought.

"We like pressure," Walton said before one game. "I know I thrive on it. And I like hostile crowds. They make me want to play better."[6]

So did Wooden. As the Walton years passed, Wooden was in his sixties. He was thinking of stepping away and spending more time with his wife. He felt the fans he had pleased for so long had become a bit spoiled, as if failing to win a national title meant the season was a waste.

UCLA's championship string was broken at the end of the 1973–1974 season when the Bruins finished 26–4. As UCLA geared up for the 1974–1975 season, Wooden was thinking it was going to be his last, but he did not tell players or university officials.

UCLA made do without an Alcindor or Walton, but front-court players like David Meyers, Richard Washington, and Marques Johnson were plenty potent. The Bruins did it again, sweeping to a 28–3 record and a 10th national championship as a going-away present for Wooden.

Wooden did not tell people this was going to be it for him until after the Bruins bested Louisville in the semifinals. That gave the players two days for the shock to wear off and to channel their energy into one last win. UCLA beat Kentucky, 92–85.

"We wanted to win it bad for The Man," said Bruins guard Pete Trgovich.[7]

The players did it, and Wooden rode off into a Pacific Coast sunset 27 years after arriving from Indiana. His final college coaching record was 664–162. He had won more than 80 percent of his games.

John Wooden remained in Los Angeles for the rest of his life. He traveled for basketball appearances promoting the game, attended the NCAA Final Four as long as he was able, and was a great and available resource for sportswriters interested in history. Wooden was a few months shy of his 100th birthday when he died in 2010.

NOTES

1. Scott Howard-Cooper, *The Bruin 100* (Lenexa, KS: Addax Publishing Group, 1999), 31.
2. Ibid., 20.
3. Ibid., 32.
4. Ibid., 11.
5. Ibid., 12.
6. Bill Libby, *The Walton Gang* (New York: Coward, McCann & Geoghegan, 1974), 19.
7. Howard-Cooper, *The Bruin 100*, 14.

FURTHER READING

Davis, Seth. *Wooden: A Coach's Life*. New York: Times Books, 2014.
Wooden, John, and Jay Cart. *Coach Wooden's Pyramid of Success*. Ventura, CA: Regal Books, 2005.
Wooden, John, and Steve Jamison. *My Personal Best: Life Lessons from an All-American Journey*. New York: McGraw-Hill, 2004.
Wooden, John, and Steve Jamison. *Wooden on Leadership: How to Create a Winning Organization*. New York: McGraw-Hill, 2005.
Wooden, John, and Jack Tobin. *They Call Me Coach*. New York: McGraw-Hill, 2003.

#57 University of Connecticut Women's Basketball

One of the most consistent and remarkably great sports programs in America is the University of Connecticut women's basketball team. Year after year the Huskies contend for the NCAA championship, and year after year they win more than their share.

Under long-time coach Geno Auriemma, the University of Connecticut women's basketball team has become the gold standard of the sport. In 2015, Auriemma tied John Wooden by winning his 10th NCAA crown and the Huskies have shown no indications of slowing down. (AP Photo/Jeff Roberson)

The Huskies won their 10th national title under longtime coach Geno Auriemma in 2015, and they also held one of the more unassailable records in their sport. Between the beginning of the 2008–2009 season and into the 2010–2011 season, the Huskies won 90 games in a row.

Connecticut finished 39–0 as it won the 2009 NCAA crown. Then the Huskies duplicated that feat by going 39–0 again the next season. They opened the 2010–2011 season strong, winning 12 more games in a row before falling to Stanford at the very end of the calendar year.

Auriemma, who was born in Montella, Italy, in 1954, is the architect of the program. Going into the 2014–2015 season, his all-time record read 914–134. He was moving within shouting distance of 1,000 victories, which would make him the second coach in women's college basketball to obtain that many wins. The first was Pat Summit at Tennessee, Auriemma's archrival.

Auriemma took over the UConn program in 1985 after seven years of stints as an assistant coach and supervised the Huskies' ascent into an elite program. It is difficult for fans to remember, but before Auriemma arrived in Storrs, Connecticut, the team had had just one winning season. It took Auriemma just one year to change the culture. He endured a 12–15 season during his rookie head coaching year and has never had another losing season.

A decade into Auriemma's tenure, in 1995, the Huskies won their first national title. In the years following UConn has only gotten better and better, dominating the Big East Conference with 19 league championships and two additional titles in the new American Athletic Conference, but almost always showing the potential capability of recording an unbeaten year. UConn has 20 times won at least 30 games in a season. Auriemma's 2013–2014 team went 40–0. That was Auriemma's fifth undefeated national championship.

Under Auriemma's guidance, the United States has won gold medals at the 2012 Olympics in London, at the 2010 World Championships in the Czech Republic, and in the 2014 World Championships in Turkey. Now in his early sixties, but as active as always, Auriemma has already been elected to the Basketball Hall of Fame.

It took until Auriemma's fourth season at Connecticut for the Huskies to earn an invitation to the NCAA tournament, but they have never been left out since. UConn has featured such stars as Nykesha Sales, Kerry Bascom, Diana Taurasi, Sue Bird, Brianna Stewart, Shea Ralph, Jessica Moore, Swin Cash, Svetlana Abrosimova, and Kaleena Mosqueda-Lewis.

Connecticut's breakthrough on the national level came in 1995. The star of that 35–0 Huskies team was all-American center Rebecca Lobo, at the time the preeminent player in the country. The year before Lobo, Jennifer Rizzotti, and Kara Wolters led UConn to a 30–3 season. They became the idols of little girls across Connecticut and laid the foundation for the spectacular success that has followed.

The rivalry with longtime power Tennessee revved up that season, and the breath-of-fresh-air, Connecticut based team (rather than "home" teams from Boston or New York being rooted for) touched a chord with locals. When the Huskies won that first title, they were thrown a parade in Hartford, where an estimated 100,000 people turned out. That was a milestone for women's team sports.

Connecticut basketball was here to stay, although it took six seasons to win another NCAA crown. But what Auriemma provided was high-level, fast-placed, winning basketball year after year. His recruiting became almost machinelike, luring elite players from all over who aspired to play for him and UConn.

The leaders of the group that kicked off the 90-game winning streak were Maya Moore, Rene Montgomery, and Tina Charles. The signing of Moore was a major coup. She was the 2007 national high school player of the year, for a school in Georgia. She had no connection to Connecticut, but was attracted by the Huskies' excellence. In 2009 Moore was the national college player of the year.

After the Huskies completed that undefeated championship season, they were invited to the White House by President Barack Obama, who took the players over to an on-premises court to do a little shooting.

The Huskies went out and had an instant-replay season the next year, winning the NCAA title again and increasing their winning streak to 78 straight. Moore remained the top threat and was aided by Charles, Kalana Greene, Tiffany Hayes, and Kelly Faris, all of whom received some kind of postseason honors.

Charles, a senior, eclipsed Moore to win national player of the year honors, and she became a Women's National Basketball Association number 1 pick.

"Coach always says to chase perfection, and you will catch excellence," Charles said.[1]

Although Charles was off to the Connecticut Sun, the Huskies were still loaded in 2010–2011. The Huskies started the year by besting Holy Cross, Baylor (the number 2 ranked team in the country, by just one point), Georgia Tech, Howard, Lehigh, Louisiana State, South Florida, Sacred Heart, Marquette, Ohio State, Florida State, and Pacific. Then UConn took on another power, Stanford, on December 30, 2010. The Cardinal prevailed, 71–59, to end the Huskies' winning streak.

The streak is the longest in women's or men's college basketball. UCLA owns the men's streak of 88 straight wins.

Connecticut finished the season 36–2, but lost to Notre Dame in the title game, despite Maya Moore's 36 points. During Moore's four seasons at UConn the team went 150–4. Moore scored a school-record 3,036 points. She was the number 1 pick in the WNBA draft in 2011 and still plays for the Minnesota Lynx, in addition to playing overseas.

Auriemma shed tears in public after his 2014 team completed its 40–0 run to give UConn and Auriemma its record ninth women's basketball title, surpassing Tennessee's old record of eight.

"I don't usually get this emotional, but this one got me," Auriemma said as he bid farewell to seniors.[2]

While the Connecticut women are as modern as any other sports team, Auriemma and his longtime associate head coach Chris Dailey dreamed up one way to hold their players' attention during the season. They are forbidden to tweet. The Huskies must sign off Twitter for the duration of the season.

Dailey said the idea came to her and Auriemma in 2011 when the team made a tour of Italy and the players had no cell phone service.

"And they survived," Dailey said. "Can you imagine? Ten days without anything."[3]

If that rule represented a simple recipe as a smooth route to a national title, every other team in the NCAA would apply it. Their opponents probably agreed there was more to it, especially when the Huskies demolished Texas 105–54 to set an NCAA regionals or finals plurality record in the 2015 tournament. The game was Auriemma's 100th win in NCAA play.

With his 10th title, Auriemma tied UCLA's John Wooden for the most college basketball championships. That's a ring for each finger.

NOTES

1. Elizabeth Merrill, "Charles Rides Tall Tale to Fairy-Tale Finish," ESPN.com, April 9, 2010, http://m.espn.go.com/ncw/story?storyId=5068769&wjb=&pg=0&lang=ES.
2. Mike Singer, "UConn Women Finish 40–0, Win Record 9th Championship," *CBSSports.com*, April 8, 2014. http://www.cbssports.com/collegebasketball/eye -on-college-basketball/24519390/uconn-finishes-40-0-wins-record-ninth-ncaa -championship.
3. Tim Casey, "Is There Anything UConn Can't Do? Tweet, for One," *New York Times*, March 27, 2015.

FURTHER READING

Auriemma, Geno, and Jackie MacMullan. *Geno: In Pursuit of Perfection*. New York: Grand Central Publishing, 2009.

Goldberg, Jeff. *Unrivaled: UConn, Tennessee and the Twelve Years That Transcended Women's Basketball*. Lincoln: University of Nebraska Press, 2015.

Thomas, Mel, and Geno Auriemma. *Heart of A Husky: Determination, Perseverance, and a Quest for a National Championship*. Covington, KY: Clerisy Press, 2009.

Walters, John. *The Same River Twice: A Season with Geno Auriemma and the Connecticut Huskies*. New York: Author, 2002.

#58 The Cal Ripken Streak

Cal Ripken Jr., son of a major league manager and brother of Billy, another major leaguer, was an esteemed player who starred for the Baltimore Orioles for 21 seasons, but was most famous for coming to work every day.

That's how Ripken always portrayed his best-known feat of playing 2,632 games in a row. He showed up. Ripken, as a shortstop and third baseman for the Orioles, broke one of baseball's so-called unbreakable records, a mark that many believed would last forever. Now he owns the record that people are sure will last forever.

New York Yankee first baseman Lou Gehrig earned the nickname "Iron Horse" during the 1920s and 1930s because he never missed a game. Gehrig held down the first-base job for the Yankees for 14 years without sitting out a game because

When Yankee Lou Gehrig benched himself after playing in 2,130 straight games, no one believed his record would ever be broken. Orioles star Cal Ripken shot past that mark with a new record of 2,632 consecutive games played. (AP Photo/Denis Paquin)

of a head cold, a hang nail, or anything more serious. Between 1925 and 1939, Gehrig played in 2,130 straight games.

Before Ripken came along and began his own consecutive games streak, the second longest major league games streak on record belonged to shortstop Everett Scott, who played in 1,307 straight games ending in 1925. Scott's streak ended three weeks before Gehrig's began. Scott's total remains third on the all-time list, and only seven players in baseball history have played in as many as 1,000 straight games without a miss. The others are Steve Garvey (1,207), Miguel Tejada (1,152), Billy Williams (1,117), and Joe Sewell (1,103).

Gehrig is still pretty much regarded as the greatest first baseman of all time. He batted .340 lifetime with 2,721 hits, including 493 home runs, and with 1,995 runs batted in. He played on six Yankee World Series champion teams and was chosen for seven all-star teams, somewhat remarkable since the all-star game didn't even exist until several years into his career. Gehrig won two Most Valuable Player awards and won a Triple Crown in 1934.

Lou Gehrig would probably have accomplished much more if he had not been struck down by amyotrophic lateral sclerosis. The fatal illness first ended his baseball career and then ended his life when he was just 37, in 1941, when he might still have been playing. The disease struck Gehrig hard, and he went from being one of the finest players in the world to warming the bench and then retirement in a very short time. Gehrig was remembered for the noble manner in which he accepted and fought his fate. The difficult-to-pronounce disease, which destroyed his motor system and led to paralysis, has come to be known as Lou Gehrig's disease.

The most famous statistic associated with Gehrig's name long after he retired was the consecutive games streak total of 2,130. It began with a pinch-hitting appearance and ended because Gehrig pulled himself from the lineup and was on his way to the Mayo Clinic for a diagnosis. Babe Dahlgren replaced Gehrig at first.

"I hated to break his streak," Dahlgren said. "I remember Lou taking the lineup card up to the plate that day. When he came back to the dugout he went over to the water fountain and took a drink. He started to cry."[1]

Cal Ripken was born in 1960 in Maryland and was 20 when he broke into the majors with the Orioles, his only major league team. He was a shortstop initially, an unusually large one at six-foot-four and 200-plus pounds, but eventually a third baseman.

Ripken appeared in 3,001 games, collected 3,184 hits, slugged 431 home runs, drove in 1,695 runs, and had a .276 batting average. He won the American League rookie of the year award and two Most Valuable Player awards. Ripken was a 19-time all-star who won two Gold Gloves.

Much like Gehrig, Ripken was cherished for his consecutive games streak, yet said all he was doing was keeping up attendance at work. He was paid to play and was healthy, so he played every day. When Ripken surpassed Gehrig, the late Yankee had held the record for 56 years. Ripken's streak began on May 30, 1982, and he broke the mark on September 6, 1995, in his 2,131st game in a row.

Since the record involved could be charted by the schedule and not by mounting hits or home runs, it was easy for the Orioles to anticipate when Ripken would catch Gehrig, and they made elaborate plans for the occasion. President Clinton, Vice President Al Gore, and their families were in the house, taking the short ride from Washington, D.C., to the ballpark. Ripken met with the dignitaries in the Orioles clubhouse before the game.

No acknowledgment of the occasion was planned until the fifth inning, when the game, which could have been rained out, became official. Play was stopped at the start of the bottom of the fifth inning. A banner was updated from 2,130 to 2,131, fireworks were shot off, and players and fans cheered. Ripken took eight curtain calls responding to the applause. Then teammates forced him onto the field to run a victory lap. As Ripken circled the park on the run for 12 minutes, he high-fived many fans leaning over the fences.

Baltimore won 4–2, and more formal ceremonies commenced. The festivities at Camden Yards honored both Ripken and Gehrig. The Orioles were playing the Angels, but the baseball seemed almost secondary. Anytime Ripken twitched, it seemed, flashbulbs went off in the stands, documenting his tiniest moves. A microphone was set up on the pitcher's mound, and Ripken praised Gehrig.

"Tonight, I stand here overwhelmed as my name is linked with the great and courageous Lou Gehrig," Ripken said. "I'm truly humbled to have our names spoken in the same breath."[2]

In an impressive bit of organizing, the Orioles had invited Joe DiMaggio, the great Yankee star, and a teammate of Gehrig's during the latter's final days with the club, to Baltimore, and DiMaggio came onto the field to speak.

"Wherever my former teammate, Lou Gehrig, is today, he's tipping his cap to you, Cal," DiMaggio said. "He's looking down on you, Cal, with appreciation."[3]

Not only did Ripken play through minor annoyances such as headaches, but in 1985 he came close to resting because of a sprained ankle; he played through the pain.

Ripken's pursuit and breaking of the record was followed nationally. He kept right on playing, staying in the Orioles lineup for another 500 games in a row. Also like Gehrig, Ripken made the choice to sit one day, ending his streak in 1998, roughly three years after cracking Gehrig's mark.

Ripken went to manager Ray Miller and told him not to include him in the Orioles' starting lineup.

"It was time," Ripken said. "Baseball has always been a team game. I talked to my wife [Kelly] and decided, 'Let's end it in the same place it started. In my home state. In front of friends and family. In front of the best fans in the world.'"[4]

When it was clear Ripken wasn't going to play, the Orioles played a video tribute on the scoreboard. He emerged from the dugout and tipped his cap to fans and to the opposing Yankees, who as a team tipped their hats to Ripken.

Ripken displayed a sense of humor after the game on what life as a spectator had been like.

"So that's what a day off feels like," he said. "Now that I know what it feels like to take a day off, I don't want to watch many games. I tried to do what others do. But I was antsy. I was fidgety."[5]

During the streak not only did Ripken not take any days off, he rarely took an inning off. Out of 19,330 possible innings, Ripken played for Baltimore in 19,163 of them.

Ripken retired after the 2001 season when he was 40, but he has stayed connected to baseball in a number of ways. He has cowritten baseball books for children. He has been a broadcaster and has become the owner of several minor league teams. Believing strongly in baseball opportunities for young people, Ripken also started Cal Ripken Baseball, a program for youths.

NOTES

1. Richard Goldstein, "Babe Dahlgren, 84, Successor to Gehrig when Streak Ended," *New York Times*, September 6, 1996.

2. Rick Weinberg, "13: Ripken Tops Gehrig, Takes Lap around Camden," ESPN.com, http://sports.espn.go.com/espn/espn25/story?page=moments/13.

3. Ibid.

4. Roch Kubatko, "Calling His Own Number, Ripken Ends the Streak," *Baltimore Sun*, September 27, 2001.

5. Richard Justice, "It's Over: Ripken Sits Out after 2,632 Games," *Washington Post*, September 21, 1998.

FURTHER READING

Ripken, Cal, Jr., and Mike Bryan. *The Only Way I Know*. New York: Penguin, 1998.
Seidel, Jeff. *Baseball's Iron Man: Cal Ripken Jr., a Tribute*. New York: Sports Publishing, 2007.

#59 Wayne Gretzky Changes Hockey

If your nickname is "The Great One," the odds are you are pretty special at what you do. No one played hockey the way Wayne Gretzky played hockey, and no one did more to popularize the National Hockey League in parts of the United States that had little background in the sport.

While some might argue that Gordie Howe was the greatest all-around hockey player ever, or that Bobby Orr fit that description, a legion of fans will differ and give the nod to Gretzky. There is no debate about who the greatest scorer of all time is. It was almost as if Gretzky invented the goal.

Gretzky was born in 1961 in Brantford, Ontario, and he was swiftly identified as a hockey prodigy who was a brilliant scorer even as a youth. Some of his foes might have still been coping with learning how to skate without double runners, but Gretzky had a nose for the puck and an instinct for finding the net.

The player later said his childhood differed quite a bit from the average Canadian boy's because of his early stardom in the national sport.

"I could skate at two," Gretzky said. "I was nationally known at six. I was signing autographs at 10. I had a national magazine article written about me at 11 and a 30-minute national television show done on me at 15. I turned pro and kept going to high school."[1]

It would be difficult to suggest that Gretzky ever flew under the publicity radar. Hockey made Gretzky tick, and it wasn't because his parents pushed him. He pushed them.

"I had a serious addiction to hockey," Gretzky said of his youth. "I'd drag my dad [Walter] over to the park every day and make him sit out there freezing his buns until bedtime. He finally got so cold he did something crazy. He turned our backyard into a hockey rink. The Wally Coliseum. The first time he did it I was four."[2]

Through his stick handling, skating, and sense of anticipation Gretzky was such a magnificent scorer that he changed the view of what was possible on the ice. He could thread the needle with passes and his body, find teammates with blind passes, guess with uncanny accuracy where they would be when he spun around, and sense vulnerabilities in goalies that they did not even realize they possessed.

While most Canadian players his age were adjusting to junior hockey, Gretzky at 17 turned pro to skate in the World Hockey Association. The NHL wouldn't have him because of his youth, but for a time in the early 1970s the upstart WHA was an alternative.

Gretzky, who grew to six feet and 185 pounds while always appearing slender, broke in with the Indianapolis Racers and swiftly was moved to the Edmonton Oilers in the 1978–1979 season. Before he even skated a minute in Edmonton, coach Glen Sather told Gretzky, "One day we're going to be in the NHL and one day you're going to be captain of this hockey team. Remember I told you that."[3]

Gretzky didn't believe that at first; he was too young to see the future. But that season he scored 46 goals with 64 assists for 110 points, was chosen second-team all league, and won the rookie of the year award.

A year later Edmonton was part of the NHL, and Gretzky was even more explosive, scoring 51 goals, accompanied by 86 assists for 137 points. He made his first NHL all-star team; won the Lady Byng Trophy, the Hart Memorial Trophy, and his first Most Valuable Player award. He was still just 19.

Wearing his iconic "99" on his jersey, Gretzky won seven scoring titles and 10 in all. Gretzky is the only NHL player to score 200 points in a season, and he did that four times, the first time during the 1981–1982 season, when he totaled 212 points. That year he also scored a still-standing record of 92 goals. Gretzky topped his points record with 215 during the 1985–1986 season.

Gretzky scored more than 100 points in a season 16 times. He won the Hart Trophy nine times, the Ross Trophy as top scorer 10 times, and the Lady Byng Trophy for sportsmanship five times.

As Sather had predicted, the NHL absorbed the Oilers, and Gretzky became the face of and leader of the franchise. In the five seasons encompassing 1984 to 1988, the Oilers captured four Stanley Cups, with Sather as coach and Gretzky as the dominant on-ice presence. He also became captain of the talented Oilers for the 1983–1984 season. That year Gretzky began the season by scoring at least one point in each of Edmonton's first 51 games. That record for opening a season and consecutive-game scoring still stands.

"For the fans, it was paradise," Gretzky said of winning the first Cup. "They swarmed the ice and smothered us. And there I was in the middle of it all, holding that Cup. You know, I've held women and babies and jewels and money, but nothing will ever feel as good as holding that Cup."[4]

There has never been a hockey player with the flair and scoring instincts of Wayne Gretzky. The superstar scorer lifted the Edmonton Oilers to four Stanley Cups and set numerous records while spreading excitement around the National Hockey League. (AP Photo)

Edmonton won two Stanley Cups in a row, missed out for a year, and then won two in a row again. By then Gretzky was a Canadian hero and a North American institution. Even Americans who lived in warm-weather climates without professional hockey knew who he was. Those fans who lived in areas with NHL teams couldn't wait to see him play when the Oilers came to town. He was the sport's greatest drawing card.

One of the most shocking trades in sports history smashed Gretzky's belief that he would be an Edmonton Oiler for his entire career. It was like the Boston Red Sox trading Ted Williams or the Chicago Bulls trading Michael Jordan. The idea was unfathomable. But after the 1988 season, when the Oilers captured their fourth Stanley Cup, Edmonton owner Peter Pocklington swapped Gretzky to the Los Angeles Kings.

It was hard to tell who was more stunned by the switch, Gretzky or hockey fans. People close to Gretzky knew he was on the market before he did, but didn't want to disturb his concentration during the play-offs. Although in the dark, Gretzky, who did not want to change cities, had previously learned that Pocklington had financial difficulties. Gretzky had a personal services contract with Pocklington, not a deal with the Oilers.

Eventually Gretzky played a role in the negotiations that opened the channels for him to be traded to Los Angeles, though it was with regret, and he felt more Stanley Cups were to be had in Edmonton. The trade went through on August 9, 1988. Gretzky had tears in his eyes at his farewell press conference. In all, five players changed teams, and Edmonton got $15 million as well.

Besides playing the best he could and trying to lead the Los Angeles Kings to a Stanley Cup, Gretzky was charged, at least unofficially, with inducing his new warm-weather environment to fall for hockey.

For his first seasons in L.A., Gretzky worked his magic. He scored 168 points during the 1988–1989 season, which did not lead the league, but he did top the NHL in points three more times while with the Kings. He led the league in assists five times in six years with L.A., missing out only when injured. Gretzky did help Los Angeles to a Stanley Cup final in 1993, but could not bring a Cup to town.

What Gretzky did was raise the profile of NHL hockey in one of the largest cities in the country and also around the United States. He might have been Canadian, but he was American by proxy through his sport.

"All of a sudden, hockey was getting chic in LA," Gretzky said of his stay in California. "Celebrities that rivaled the famous Lakers followers started coming to our games. Overnight, season ticket sales went from 4,000 to 13,000."[5]

In his late thirties Gretzky moved on, briefly to the St. Louis Blues, then for his three final seasons to the New York Rangers. He retired at 38 in 1999, the owner of 61 National Hockey League records, including most goals, 894, and most assists, 1,963. Those totals do not count Gretzky's year in the WHA.

Gretzky's lifetime points total of 2,857 is 970 ahead of second place on the all-time list. There is no denying Gretzky is "The Great One."

NOTES

1. Wayne Gretzky and Rick Reilly, *Gretzky* (New York: Harper Paperbacks, 1991), 6.
2. Ibid., 17.
3. Ibid., 38.
4. Ibid., 85.
5. Ibid., 210.

FURTHER READING

Kennedy, Brian. *Facing Wayne Gretzky: Players Recall the Greatest Hockey Player Who Ever Lived*. New York: Sports Publishing, 2014.
Podnieks, Andrew. *The Great One: The Life and Times of Wayne Gretzky*. Chicago: Triumph Books, 1999.

Sports Illustrated, ed. *The Great One: The Complete Wayne Gretzky Collection*. Toronto: Fenn/McClelland & Stewart, 2012.

Strachan, Al. *99: Gretzky, His Game, His Story*. Toronto: Fenn/McClelland & Stewart, 2013.

#60 Pat Summitt Wins Big and Inspires

A pioneer in the evolution of women's college basketball, Pat Summitt is the all-time leader in coaching wins, with 1,098 victories. Her winning percentage was 84 percent, and she presided over eight national champion teams at the University of Tennessee.

Summitt chose to retire after the 2012 season after she began suffering from a type of early onset Alzheimer's disease, a diagnosis that saddened the college basketball world. Summitt has continued to stay close to the Lady Volunteers' program and has become a major figure speaking out and lobbying for Alzheimer's awareness and a cure.

Pat Summitt was born in Clarksville, Tennessee, in 1952, and during her playing career and before her marriage was known as Pat Head.

Though she was always active in basketball, Summitt's high school generation predated Title IX, and initially she did not have a place to play. The family moved to another town so Summitt, who excelled at the game, could continue to play. She improved and attended the University of Tennessee-Martin, where she earned all-America notice. In 1976 Summitt was co-captain of the U.S. team at the Montreal Olympics, a squad that won the silver medal.

Summitt wanted to stay involved with basketball, but opportunities were limited for women. When the federal Title IX legislation was passed requiring colleges to expand sports opportunities for women, Summitt seized her chance to coach. At first she was a graduate assistant at Tennessee, but she became head coach before her 23rd birthday. It was a job with little financial reward or status at the time. Summitt made $250 a month and had to wash her players' uniforms.

With few resources, but gaining experience on the job (Summitt was an Olympian while she was Tennessee's coach), Summitt slowly but steadily built Tennessee into a national power. Tennessee was already a major player in women's college basketball in the Association for Intercollegiate Athletics for Women before the NCAA even sanctioned the sport. Tennessee reached the Final Four three times while the AIAW ran the championships. The Lady Volunteers lost in the championship game in 1980 and 1981.

Long-time University of Tennessee women's basketball coach Pat Summitt led the Lady Volunteers to eight NCAA titles and won more than 1,000 games. Yet Summitt proved even more inspirational when she was forced to retire young to confront early-onset Alzheimer's disease. (AP Photo/Wade Payne)

The NCAA supervision of women's college basketball took hold for the 1981–1982 season, and Tennessee was invited into the field for the first postseason championship conducted by the organization. The Lady Vols advanced to the Final Four, something that would become a regular occurrence under Summitt.

Summitt coached Tennessee to 16 Southeastern Conference regular-season crowns and 16 SEC tournament crowns. For all of its early success, it took the Tennessee team until 1987 to win its first NCAA championship. Tennessee topped Louisiana Tech, 67–44, to win it all.

From then on Tennessee began piling up the national championships under Summitt's guidance, swiftly adding the 1989 and 1991 titles. Sheila Frost, Deadra Charles, and Dena Head excelled during that stretch.

The 1987–1988 team finished 31–3, but lost in the Final Four. The 1988–1989 team roared back and finished 35–3 while grabbing the second title. The 1990–1991 team ended up 30–5.

In moments of candor Summitt admitted that she was a big control freak and kind of thought that's what the job of coaching entailed.

"I'm a coach so I take the issue of control personally," she said. "I've always seen the movements of players on the court as an extension of myself, like puppets on a string. Their failures were my fault, their successes my responsibility. I demanded that they act like Pat and think like Pat. A row of little Patlings."[1]

Eventually Summitt did loosen up a bit in certain ways, though the Lady Vols were always going to play her way. A recruiter par excellence, Summitt was often able to ferret out the best talent in the country, sweet-talk the players into coming to Knoxville with her record as an excellent argument, and then mold each new group into winners.

Not only did the Lady Volunteers always qualify for the NCAA tournament, they almost always went deep into the tournament. If you played for Tennessee you had a standard to uphold, and Summitt convinced the necessary high quality of players to come to Tennessee so that standard was in reach every March.

After those first three championships, there was a little bit of a title lull, even though Tennessee ripped off seasons that included 28–3, 29-3, 31–2, and 34–3 finishes. It was the 1995–1996 squad that plucked the fourth national title with a 32–4 record. Chamique Holdsclaw was a freshman on that squad, and she was soon praised as one of the greatest female basketball players of all time.

The six-foot-two Holdsclaw, from New York, led the Lady Vols to three straight NCAA crowns, was a four-time all-American, and concluded her Tennessee career as the leading scorer and rebounder in program history. Despite all of the stern discipline imparted to Summitt's players, they almost all called her "Pat" rather than "Coach." The one player who refrained from that familiarity was Holdsclaw, who said she called Summitt "Coach" on purpose.

"Just out of respect," Holdsclaw said. "She's not one of my peers, you know. I'm not going to call her Pat. Doesn't sound right."[2]

During the season after Tennessee claimed that fourth crown, the Volunteers tumbled to a 29–10 record and a mark of just 8–4 in the Southeastern Conference. By Tennessee standards that was an off year. However, to everyone's surprise, the team rallied late in the year and rode emotion to an unlikely fifth NCAA title.

"Of all our runs to a championship, this really is the most unexpected," Summitt said. "It came from a team with tremendous heart and desire."[3]

Compared to that season the next campaign, the 1997–1998 season, was a breeze. The Volunteers finished 39–0, the best record in Summitt's career, with one of the best teams in NCAA history, taking the school's sixth NCAA crown. Only three teams came within 10 points of winning against Tennessee that season, and the Lady Vols won the championship 93–75 over Louisiana Tech.

Besides Holdsclaw, Tamika Catchings, another all-time Tennessee great, was honored as an all-American, the first of four selections for her. Semeka Randall was another star on that club.

Summitt grew up in a tightly knit family, yet she was often bringing in players who came from single-parent homes. It was important for her Vols to be close, to trust one another, care about one another, and treat each other as family. It was good for the players and optimum for the team.

"Small intimacies form a team," Summitt said. "You measure them for their uniforms and ask them if they prefer blue or orange practice shorts. You distribute their Adidas sneakers and tease them about their less-than-delicate shoe sizes. You go over their physicals and examine the scars from old injuries. These are the tiny, but vital stitches of personal knowledge that draw you together. If you're the coach, you just hope they don't unravel on you by halftime."[4]

At halftime of the 1998 title game, the contest that would wrap up the 39–0 year, Tennessee led Louisiana Tech, 55–32, after shooting 62 percent from the floor. In essence the game was over, but Summitt did not want her team thinking that way. At all costs, the players had to forestall a comeback. Tech did play better in the second half, but never really threatened.

Summitt recognized how special that accomplishment was, praising the Lady Vols in the locker room.

"That was some of the best basketball ever played," Summitt said. "I am so proud for you and so happy for you. You are the most exciting team I've ever seen."[5]

Summitt won two more NCAA championships, in 2007 and 2008.

When Summitt went public with her announcement in August 2011 that she was suffering from early onset dementia, diagnosed at age 59, a spontaneous movement of support grew up. The phrase "We Back Pat" became part of the lexicon. T-shirts with the phrase were printed and sold. Proceeds were donated to charitable organizations oriented to battling Alzheimer's. The SEC made a $100,000 donation to Summitt's new foundation.

Summitt coached one final season, leading the Volunteers to a 27–9 record, an SEC Tournament title, and a spot in the NCAA Elite Eight. Following the 2011–2012 season she retired, with a 1,098–208 record.

The U.S. Sports Academy presented Summitt with its Mildred "Babe" Dickinson Zaharias Award for Courage in 2011. In 2012 Summitt was honored with the Presidential Medal of Freedom and took part in a presentation at the White House on May 29.

Summitt said that the first person to donate to her Pat Summitt Foundation was Connecticut coach Gene Auriemma, her longtime rival, who gave $10,000. In early 2015 Summitt, with her son Tyler, announced the creation of the Pat Summitt Alzheimer's Clinic at the University of Tennessee Medical Center. Her foundation donated $100,000 toward the effort.

NOTES

1. Pat Summitt and Sally Jenkins, *Raise the Roof* (New York: Broadway Books, 1998), 3.
2. Ibid., 43.

3. "Pat Summitt," UTsports.com., University of Tennessee Women's Basketball, http://www.utsports.com/sports/w-baskbl/mtt/Summitt_pat00.html.

4. Summitt and Jenkins, *Raise the Roof*, 65.

5. Ibid., 272.

FURTHER READING

Goldberg, Jeff. *Unrivaled: UConn, Tennessee and the Twelve Years That Transcended Women's Basketball*. Lincoln: University of Nebraska Press, 2015.

Summitt, Pat, and Sally Jenkins. *Reach for the Summitt*. New York: Broadway Books, 1998.

Summitt, Pat, and Sally Jenkins. *Sum It Up: A Thousand and Ninety Eight Victories, a Couple of Irrelevant Losses, and a Life In Perspective*. New York: Crown Publishing Group, 2013.

#61 Jack Johnson Is Hated for Being Black and Good

Jack Johnson was the heavyweight champion when boxing wasn't ready to have an African American heavyweight champion and became perhaps the most hated big-time athlete in American history through little fault of his own.

Born in Galveston, Texas, in 1878 and nicknamed "The Galveston Giant," Johnson became the first African American heavyweight champ when he won the crown in 1908, but was victimized by so much discrimination that he was hounded out of the country and tormented into poverty, as well as being convicted under a specious law.

Johnson was the son of a dedicated mother and father who were former slaves and worked hard as a janitor and dishwasher to feed a family of nine children. Despite receiving limited formal schooling growing up in Texas, he was known to be intelligent and witty. He also didn't want to remain anonymous and very much wanted to better himself financially.

Even though he lived in Texas, Johnson later said that he did not suffer discrimination early in life, and as a youth many of his friends were white. The discrimination would come later.

Johnson turned to boxing to try to make a living at a time when the professional game was illegal in Texas. After an early pro bout he and his opponent, Joe Choynski

The flamboyant and skilled Jack Johnson was the first African American to win the heavyweight title when it was the most coveted individual sporting prize in the world—and was hounded and persecuted for it. Johnson was loved and hated, but persevered at the peak of his profession. (Library of Congress)

of Chicago, were arrested and jailed. Their shared fate brought them closer together out of the ring than they were in it, and Johnson benefited by boxing lessons from his more experienced foe. Later he said it was invaluable training.

What Choynski recognized in Johnson was a natural quickness and innate ability to duck punches, which would be developed if he gained some sophistication. Choynski's tutoring helped make Johnson hard to hit.

Indeed, Johnson seemed more interested in gaining ring experience and piling up points in some of his fights than in fighting to knock opponents out.

In the earliest years of the 20th century, there was a generally accepted title of "Black Heavyweight Champ." That was because top-flight African American fighters were squeezed out of the top levels of the fight game and could not get title matches against the best white boxers.

In 1902 Johnson bested Frank Childs, who had once held the title of Black Heavyweight Champion. Johnson was only vaguely interested in counting that as a great achievement, but it was the logical extension of what was available to him at the time.

That year Joe Gans became the first universally recognized African American to hold a world championship when he won the lightweight crown.

In 1903 Johnson won the "The World Colored Heavyweight Championship." Some terrific earlier African American fighters who were closed out of the ranks of the overall heavyweight championship had held that crown before Johnson, notably Peter Jackson and Harry Wills.

Johnson kept that crown for five years, defending it 17 times, but eventually maneuvered his way into a shot at the genuine heavyweight title by leaving the country for the match.

On many occasions Johnson challenged heavyweight champ James J. Jeffries, but Jeffries would not fight him. (In 1907 Johnson bested former champ Bob Fitzsimmons.) Jeffries held the title for six years between 1899 and 1905, but then retired. Marvin Hart beat Jack Root to claim the crown, but lost it after a year to Canadian Tommy Burns.

On December 26, 1908, Johnson met Burns in the ring in Australia. For two years Johnson had done everything he could to goad Burns into fighting him, issuing inflammatory statements in newspapers. When they met in Sydney, Johnson got the best of it, and the fight was stopped after 14 rounds.

Leading up to the fight even the most so-called responsible newspapers wrote stories tinged with racism about how horrible it would be if Johnson were victorious. At that time, and even to some degree today, the myth and symbol of the holder of the world's heavyweight boxing crown earned him the right to be called the toughest man in the world.

American boxing interests were dismayed that a black man had won the crown. How could an inferior African American be the toughest man in the world? Immediately after Johnson won the title, a cry went out across the sport seeking "a Great White Hope" to appear and defeat Johnson. This is how that ugly label originated, although many decades later a theatrical play and movie about the abuse Johnson took borrowed that phrase for its title. Promoters were looking for volunteers, for anyone, to step up and pummel Johnson.

Johnson, emboldened by his victory, dressed to the nines, partied constantly, and made the then-heinous mistake of publicly dating white women. He was vilified by many, even upsetting his natural allies, other African Americans.

The six-foot-tall and heavily muscled Johnson, who would not kowtow to anyone, lived a dashing and public lifestyle, building up enmity in many camps. He held the heavyweight title from 1908 to 1915 and periodically defended it. Sometimes the defending fights were against lesser known foes like Tony Ross, Al Kaufman, Jim Flynn, Jim Johnson, Frank Moran, and Jack Murray.

But he also took on Jack O'Brien, Stanley Ketchel, and Jeffries, who was persuaded to come out of retirement, only to take a brutal beating. Some of Johnson's defending fights took place in Paris, France. It was easier for him to fight there than at home.

"I was constantly harassed and criticized," Johnson said. "Those who conceded, but resented my rightful claim to the title, started a turmoil by hunting a 'white hope' or one who would regain the title for the white race. This hunt was a long and bitter one."[1]

White promoters were confident that by talking Jeffries back into the ring after a six-year absence they would at least wrest the crown from Johnson. Hyped as "The Fight of the Century," before it Jeffries ridiculously stated that he was fighting Johnson to prove that the white man was superior to the black man.

Johnson noted that Jeffries did not want to fight and was entrenched in retirement. He thought it absurd that Jeffries had come back to fight.

"One of the greatest fighters in the history of pugilism had been coaxed back to contend for the title in order to satisfy jealousy, hatred, and prejudice," Johnson said.[2]

On a 110-degree day in Reno, Nevada, Johnson carved up Jeffries, at one point knocking him through the ropes with a left hook. It was not a close fight.

"I hit Jeff at will," Johnson said later. "There was no place that was beyond my reach. The cheering for Jeff never ceased. But their cheering turned to moans and groans when they saw that he was suffering as he was."[3]

By crushing Jeffries, Johnson triggered some of the worst inner fears and disgusting behavior of whites, who believed he would be defeated. Ruffians rioted all over the country in anger over Jeffries's beating. There were said to be riots in 25 states and 20 deaths as a result.

Johnson made members of the black community uncomfortable with his garish lifestyle and by marrying three white women over the course of his life. In 1912 Johnson was charged with violation of the 1910 Mann Act, which made it illegal to transport a single woman across state lines for prostitution, debauchery, or immoral purposes. Although he was convicted of a felony, most right-thinking people believed these were trumped-up accusations motivated by racial prejudice, since Johnson was with the girlfriend he later married.

Sentenced to a year and a day in prison, Johnson fled the country through Montreal and went on to France, where he lived in exile until 1920, then surrendered to U.S. authorities and served his prison sentence.

In between the conviction and his return Johnson met Jess Willard in a defense of his heavyweight title in Havana, Cuba, in 1915. Willard was six foot six and at 235 pounds outweighed Johnson by about 35 pounds. He proved to be the great white hope the establishment had been looking for, lifting the crown from Johnson. Although Johnson ended the day flat on his back, his arm shielding his face from the hot sun, many believe he could have risen to continue, but chose not to, ending his long ordeal of battling with the boxing powers as much as with boxers.

A year after the Willard fight, Johnson confessed that he had taken a dive in the 26th round after leading for 20 rounds. He said he was told that his conviction under the Mann Act would be vacated and he could return to the United States if he lost the fight, that $50,000 in large bills was given to his wife at ringside during the bout, and that she flashed him the high sign to show that she had counted it. Johnson's tale was generally disbelieved, and he did not return to the United States for five more years, whereupon he was incarcerated.

Johnson, who died in 1946, won 80 fights and was enshrined in various boxing halls of fame starting in 1954. Long after his death, Johnson received new fame, respect, and acclaim based on his accomplishments, and public opinion turned in his favor in response to the disgraceful way he had been treated.

NOTES

1. Jack Johnson, *In The Ring—And Out* (New York: Citadel Press, 1992), 169.
2. Ibid., 170.
3. Ibid., 185.

FURTHER READING

Johnson, Jack. *Jack Johnson Is a Dandy*. New York: Chelsea House, 1969.
Johnson, Jack. *My Life and Battles*. Edited and translated by Christopher Rivers. Westport, CT: Praeger, 2007.
Roberts, Randy. *Papa Jack: Jack Johnson and the Era of White Hopes*. New York: Free Press, 1985.
Ward, Geoffrey. *Unforgiveable Blackness: The Rise and Fall of Jack Johnson*. New York: Vintage Books, 2006.

#62 Fernandomania

Probably the last time a rookie baseball player was treated like a rock star was in 1981, when Mexican pitcher Fernando Valenzuela surfaced with the Los Angeles Dodgers and exploded onto the American scene during the heart of the season.

Looking back, the excitement, the frenzy, and the extreme reaction that Valenzuela provoked seem flabbergasting. One minute he was an unknown, and the next he was practically a cult figure, everyone's favorite pitcher.

It was the summer of 1981, and the southpaw astonishingly lit up the major league landscape during his first blush of touring National League cities and anchoring the Dodgers in L.A.

Seemingly naïve, with limited English-speaking capability, Valenzuela was just 20 years old when he took the game by storm. He morphed from a player whose name some people had difficulty saying to the NL rookie of the year, the league's

A sensation with his stunning results and his quirky, eye-rolling delivery, Los Angeles Dodgers southpaw Fernando Valenzuela took the baseball world by storm in 1981. The instant star jump-started "Fernandomania" in the fan base and that season was chosen National League rookie of the year and Cy Young winner. (AP Photo)

Cy Young Award winner, and the cornerstone of a Dodgers rotation that won the World Series.

Valenzuela did not ease into major leagues stardom, but burst upon the scene, winning his first eight decisions in a row. He was charming in a soft-spoken way and had an unusual delivery to the plate. The left-hander tilted his head way back, and as he went into motion, his eyes seemed to roll back in his head, implying that if they were seeing anything, it was the sky above.

Standing five foot eleven and weighing 180 pounds, Valenzuela did not have a chiseled body. He seemed pudgy, with a bit of a bulging belly, so his appearance belied his success. He was shaggy haired, too, so his cap did not always fit snugly on his head. Perhaps a few intense Dodger fans recognized Valenzuela's previous season contributions in 1980, when he went 2–0. But few really pay detailed attention to September call-ups. Also, not much is read into their success, because a few games represent only a limited sample.

So even though Valenzuela had been showcased briefly with the Dodgers, in 1981 it was as if he had come from nowhere. To a certain degree, by American sporting standards, he had. Born in 1960 as one of 12 children into a family in Etchohuaquila in Mexico's Sonora state, Valenzuela grew up in a family of limited means. Pitching was his entrée to a new life.

"It is incredible. It is fantastic. It is Fernando Valenzuela," longtime Dodgers broadcaster Vince Scully said at one point.[1]

Fate seemed to tap Valenzuela on the shoulder at the start of the 1981 season. Starting pitchers who figured to get the nod for the opener ahead of Valenzuela were injured and unable to take the ball. So Fernando got the assignment. He pitched a shutout over the Houston Astros.

What transformed Valenzuela into a phenomenon overnight was not that one game, nice start though it was. As Valenzuela pushed his record to 8–0, he notched five shutouts along the way. He practically never gave up a run, holding still with an earned run average of 0.50 at that point.

That brilliant stretch, coupled with Valenzuela's demeanor, ignited the firestorm of hero worship. Valenzuela was so good, so soon, it was almost as if he were a fictional character. Baseball had been steadily becoming more accepting of Hispanic ballplayers, from Cuba to the Dominican Republic, from Nicaragua to Mexico, for a few decades, although the numbers were much lower than they are today. Valenzuela was not a novelty in those terms.

Yet his limited facility with English, coupled with his almost superhuman pitching feats, set him apart from previous Hispanic stars. He was refreshing, seemed innocent, and got fans' juices going. It was fun to watch Valenzuela pitch because of his style, and it was fun to watch his shooting star arrival in the majors, getting off to the kind of start reserved only for Hall of Famers.

Almost as soon as Valenzuela had built up a few terrific performances, he was surrounded at his locker by reporters begging for his story, and the most intrepid invaded Mexico and sought out his home. It must have been like aliens landing from Mars when the scribes reached Etchohuaquila. Of all things, Valenzuela's out pitch was the screwball. The screwball did screwy things to pitchers' arms, so not many embraced it or succeeded with it before they blew their elbows out or something. Everyone remembered "King" Carl Hubbell, but not many fans could name many subsequent stars who had used the screwball.

Tug McGraw, Mike Cuellar, and Mike Marshall had success with the screwball, which breaks in the opposite direction of a curveball. Before Hubbell, Christy Mathewson was a great. After Hubbell wrapped up, Warren Spahn became a great when he adapted to lost speed on his fastball.

Something about Valenzuela's manner and successful pitching touched the happy gene in fans. Overnight, Valenzuela became a hero in Los Angeles, a city with a large Mexican American population. But he was just as big in the heartland. People just loved the guy. Almost immediately, Fernando souvenirs became available for sale.

Valenzuela took baseball fans on a joy ride, until a labor dispute grounded the season from June 12 to August 9. A total of 713 games were wiped out, owners lost $72 million, and players lost $4 million a week in salary.

When the season resumed after the unscheduled intermission, an all-star game was played. Valenzuela, the unknown of only a few months earlier, pitched for the National League. During the break Valenzuela was nicknamed "El Toro," the bull.

Valenzuela ended the messy split season with a 13–7 record and a 2.48 earned run average, 11 complete games, 8 shutouts, and a league-leading 180 strikeouts. In later seasons, Valenzuela won 19, 17, and 21 games for the Dodgers and was chosen for six all-star games. In the 1986 all-star game Valenzuela struck out five straight American League hitters, tying a record set in 1934. In 1990 Valenzuela pitched a no-hitter against the St. Louis Cardinals.

During his big-league career Valenzuela won 173 games. There was something magical about his rookie season, and Fernando never matched his superiority, leading the league in so many key categories. He remained a popular figure in Los Angeles, where he won the vast majority of his games, and pitched for the Dodgers for 11 years, but Fernandomania itself was pretty much a one-year wonder.

Between 1991 and 1997 Valenzeula pitched for the Angels, Orioles, Phillies, Padres, and Cardinals, though he really had only one more good year, going 13–8 for the Padres in 1996. Valenzuela departed the majors after 17 years in 1997, but he did not retire from baseball.

Out of the limelight, back in Mexico, Valenzuela kept throwing in the Mexican League for a while, even playing in games in his midforties. Although Valenzuela returned to his Dodgers roots in 2003, it was in a less visible role than pitching. He joined the club's Spanish broadcasting team. He has since shifted jobs, but continues to broadcast in Los Angeles.

Also, Valenzuela has three times served as a coach for Team Mexico in the World Baseball Classic, in 2006, 2009, and 2013.

"Fernandomania surprised me a lot," Valenzuela said. He didn't expect the attention and had difficulty fathoming it. "Because the Dodgers had in those years so many great players with long careers, to be so focused on one player was strange to me."[2]

The crazed reception Fernando Valenzuela received from the public would have seemed strange to anyone.

NOTES

1. Chris Erskine, "Fan's Collection Is a Key Component of 'Fernando Nation' Documentary," *Los Angeles Times,* October 20, 2010.
2. Ibid.

FURTHER READING

Haddad, Paul, and Jon Weisman. *High Fives, Pennant Drives, and Fernandomania: A Fan's History of the Los Angeles Dodgers' Glory Years (1977–1981).* Solana Beach, CA: Santa Monica Press, 2012.

Katz, Jeff. *Split Season, 1981: Fernandomania, the Bronx Zoo, and the Strike That Saved Baseball.* New York: Thomas Dunne Books, 2015.

#63 Frank Shorter Is Golden

Never has one man's toil produced so much sweat in others. Frank Shorter, the slender Yale University graduate who in 1972 won the gold medal in the Olympic marathon in Munich, is credited with kicking off the running boom that seemed to set half of America off jogging.

Rarely has any single event initiated so much pain from people who said they were having fun as Shorter's brilliant run in the Summer Olympics.

Not so long before an individual out on the streets of his neighborhood running from block to block might have found himself being taunted by drivers passing by, or at the least stared at by those whose houses and lawns he ran by.

Running was something criminals did from the police and members of track teams did going around in circles. Something in Shorter's magnificent victory, however, inspired Americans to get off the couch in front of the television set and go out exploring on foot, fast or slow, in a shuffle or a long stride.

Shorter was born in Munich in 1947 when his father was serving in the U.S. Army. He grew up in Middletown, New York; graduated from a private high school in Massachusetts; and enrolled at Yale, where he competed on the cross-country running team and track team as a distance runner. He also earned a law degree from the University of Florida.

Shorter improved as a runner and in 1969, his senior year in college, he won the NCAA cross-country championship. Shorter had the endurance to excel as a cross-country man, winning the national open championship four times, and enough speed to withstand the kicks of runners on the track, and he began winning track national titles in the 1970s as well.

During that era amateurism ruled, and a runner could not make money from his sport. It was difficult to continue training sufficiently to compete on a world-class level while also pursuing a career.

Few remember that in 1972, when Shorter won the signature race of his career by capturing the 26.2-mile marathon, he also finished fifth in the 10,000 meters on the track in Germany. Shorter had advertised his form and talent to the world in the 1971 Pan American Games when he triumphed in the 10,000 meters and marathon. In 1972 he won the Sullivan Award as the top amateur athlete in the United States.

One bizarre thing that occurred in the 1972 Olympic marathon, as Shorter wended his way through the streets toward the last short run inside the Olympic Stadium on the track, was the discomfiting entrance of another runner ahead of him. It was an imposter, a German man seeking to soak up glory in front of the home crowd.

When American Frank Shorter, a Yale University graduate who trained at altitude in New Mexico at the time, won the gold medal in the Olympic marathon in 1972 the results were unforeseen. Shorter's stunning triumph set off an unprecedented long-distance running boom across the United States. (AP Photo)

Shorter's victory was hailed in the United States as an outstanding accomplishment, particularly one for Americans. Only twice before, and not since 1908, had an American won the gold medal in that endurance contest. Over the decades between, any marathon contested on American soil that did not come with the prefix Boston was a rarity.

Within a short time of Shorter's gold medal triumph, more Americans knew the lore of the origin of the marathon than probably knew the name of their local congressional representative. The marathon's roots date to 490 BC. In the days long before cell phones or communication of any sophistication whatsoever, a Greek messenger named Pheidippides was sent to Athens on foot to report that the Persians had been defeated in battle on the Plains of Marathon. The legend goes that Pheidippides hustled as fast as he could, delivered the message, then keeled over and died.

That was an inauspicious tale for anyone who hoped to enter a marathon, but eventually millions upon millions of Americans who had watched Shorter win or read about it did so.

The modern marathon, with its distance of 26 miles, 385 yards, was introduced with the revival of the Olympic Games in Athens in 1896. The Boston Marathon was established a year later as a spring ritual. For years only a couple of hundred people entered each April. By 1970 the race had become popular enough, with roughly 1,000 entries, that a qualifying standard was set to both satisfy the demand and try to ensure that those entering had the needed experience to run so far. The standards have been tweaked and stiffened many times in the decades since.

Boston's marathon goes on as the gem of the sport, with its point-to-point course leading runners from the community of Hopkinton through Ashland, Framingham, Natick, Wellesley, Newton, Brookline, and on into Boston for the finish. About 30,000 runners sign up each year now.

Dozens of other marathons are conducted each year across the United States, with the New York Marathon and Chicago Marathon being among the most prestigious.

Shorter's Olympic gold was the spark for an unprecedented running boom in the United States, one that focused more attention than ever before on health and fitness. Friends convinced friends to come out and run with them. Husbands and wives ran around their subdivisions. Running became a social activity. Clubs were formed, and buses were chartered for groups wishing to enjoy new running experiences in new places and throw in a little sightseeing at the same time.

There are estimates that some 25 million Americans took up running competitively, for fun, or for their health, in the first decade or so after Shorter's triumph. Setting a good example was President Jimmy Carter, who was photographed running in races with Secret Service agents around him.

Shorter could never have imagined what he wrought, though he was also a beneficiary. He became an iconic figure to runners, a symbol of what the best could achieve on foot. Other long-distance running stars emerged and also became widely admired, from Bill Rodgers and Alberto Salazar to Grete Weitz, the Norwegian woman who seemed to take personal ownership of the New York Marathon for a while, and Joan Benoit Samuelson, the diminutive Maine runner. Samuelson, the best American female marathoner, stunned fans by running the 1984 Olympic Trials Marathon just 17 days after undergoing arthroscopic knee surgery and then won the gold medal at the Los Angeles Summer Games later that year.

Boston, which was once operated with as much sexism as any sporting event, eventually enthusiastically welcomed women and also became one of the earliest and most prestigious marathons to welcome wheelchair racers. Everyone wanted to do a marathon, and everyone wanted to compete in Boston.

One of the most coveted titles to gain in an overseas marathon was the Fukuoka race in Japan, which Shorter won four times in the 1970s. Shorter went after an Olympic repeat in 1976 in the marathon at the Montreal Games. He came close, but won a silver medal. Shorter is still the only American to win two Olympic marathon medals.

Shorter spoke later about the fact that he ran that marathon with a minor fracture, incurred right before qualifying.

"I finished second despite a hairline fracture in my left ankle that I suffered right before the Olympic trials marathon two months before," he said. "There was no time to let it heal, so I had no choice. I never thought about it during the race, nor did I let the constant rain bother me, and I hate running in the rain. The feeling I had when I crossed the line was pride. I had not given up on two counts."[1]

Shorter, a longtime resident of Boulder, Colorado, played a role in establishing the popular Bolder Boulder road race in that community and is so well-regarded there that a statue of him was erected outside the University of Colorado football field.

Long retired from competition, Shorter, who owned an athletic supply company, said he still tried to run for an hour daily at an easy pace.

Nearly 40 years after Shorter won the gold medal, he made headlines in 2011 as he revealed the painful story of his past. He said he grew up with an abusive father who hit him often and was a terror in the home even while appearing to be a saintly doctor in public. Shorter had tried to go public in 1991, but for many years he felt that no one would believe him if he talked about his father in such a way.

Shorter visited his father on the 86-year-old man's death bed and said: "What I felt looking into his eyes was an enormous sense of relief. Now he couldn't hurt me anymore. He couldn't hurt my mother, and he couldn't hurt my sisters or brothers. He couldn't hurt anyone."[2]

Shorter spontaneously went public at a running speaking forum, with fellow running friends present who had never heard about his tribulations.

Always a supporter of the running world, Shorter took on a new cause, speaking out against domestic violence and child abuse. It will take a lot of energy and effort for Shorter to become half as influential in that realm as he was in instigating the running boom. After all, millions followed in his footsteps.

NOTES

1. "Frank Shorter: Bolder Boulder Co-Founder Talks about Life on the Run," Sports Fan Mail, *Denver Post*, May 30, 2011.
2. John Brant, "Frank's Story," *Runner's World*, August 31, 2011.

FURTHER READING

Shorter, Frank. *Olympic Gold: A Runner's Life and Times*. Boston: Houghton Mifflin Harcourt, 1984.
Stracher, Cameron. *Kings of the Road: How Frank Shorter, Bill Rodgers, and Alberto Salazar Made Running Go Boom*. Boston: Houghton Mifflin Harcourt, 2013.

#64 Wilma Rudolph

One of the greatest of American track stars overcame poverty, health problems, and prejudice to excel in sprints and become the first woman to win three gold medals in a single Summer Olympics, in Rome in 1960.

Wilma Rudolph became a pioneer athlete and a symbol of success to the African American community with her inspirational story. Born prematurely at only four and one-half pounds, Rudolph grew up as one of 22 children in a merged household and overcame childhood polio, scarlet fever, and a susceptibility to illness to become the fastest woman in the world.

Born in Saint Bethlehem, Tennessee, in 1940, there was little in Rudolph's youth that would indicate she would grow up to be such a fast runner that Italians nicknamed her "The Black Gazelle" because they admired her achievements. It was not the only nickname the speedy Rudolph acquired. In France she was called "The Black Pearl." Others called her "The Tornado, the fastest woman on earth." They represented a potpourri of descriptions of a woman who as a little girl had to limp through life for a time.

"All of those years being sick left a lot of scars on me mentally," Rudolph said. "Those years left me very insecure. I lived in mortal fear of being disliked."[1]

Rudolph was just a youngster, although one with great promise, when she ran as part of the U.S. 4-by-100-meter relay team in Melbourne, Australia, in 1956 and won a bronze medal. If Rudolph had never taken another step on a track after that, her story still would be acclaimed a virtual miracle. Four years later, though, Rudolph became the toast of the Games, winning gold medals in the individual 100 meters and 200 meters and by leading the American squad to gold in the 4-by-100 relay.

The slender, five-foot-eleven, 130-pound Rudolph's timing was impeccable. The Rome Olympics was the first one to receive widespread international television coverage. That meant millions of people viewed her brilliant accomplishments.

Amazingly for a woman who obtained fame from her speed afoot, Rudolph had contracted infantile paralysis at age four. Her affliction was not as devastating as it might have been, but she had a twisted left leg and wore a brace on it until she was nine, plus a corrective orthopedic shoe for two more years. She could only dream of track spikes.

Rudolph overcame her affliction and matured into a superb athlete, first as a basketball player. Then she was scouted by Tennessee State's famed track coach Ed Temple, who coached the Tigerbelles team for 44 years and coached with three U.S. Olympic teams, including the 1960 group that Rudolph was on.

Born into poverty and afflicted with polio as a youth, Wilma Rudolph became one of the most inspirational track and field athletes of all time. Rudolph won three gold medals while participating in the 1956 and 1960 Summer Olympics. (AP Photo)

As part of a high school state champion basketball team, Rudolph took time out at age 16 to earn her bronze medal in Melbourne.

Going to college was not something talked about in the Rudolph household. No one had ever done it, and Rudolph was the 20th of 22 siblings. When Temple sought her out to attend Tennessee State, Wilma received encouragement from her mother, Blanche.

"You're the first one in this house who ever had the chance to go to college," Blanche Rudolph said. "If running's going to do that, I want you to set your mind to be the best."[2]

When Mrs. Rudolph said that, there was really no reason for her to foresee what the implications would be. But in only a few years her daughter, who had endured so many troubles, was being toasted as the best: not just the best at her school, but the best in the world.

Wilma got her sneak preview of the Olympics as a teenager in 1956.

Women's sports ranked far behind men's sports in acceptance and popularity in the mid-20th century, and there were no opportunities to compete in many sports. Running the sprints in track and field was one area in which it was possible to shine. There were no distance races for women yet, and high-level intercollegiate team sport competition lay two decades in the future.

Although Rudolph was an all-around athlete who might well have continued to play basketball if there had been a chance, she was fortunate that her best skill—speed—could be showcased as part of the Olympic program.

Of the 17 women on the 1956 U.S. track team, nine were African American. Before heading to Australia the group had the chance to shop in Los Angeles, where they were denigrated by a white woman even though they were representing their country.

When Rudolph returned to Burt High School, she was greeted by a banner reading, "Welcome Home, Wilma." She had a pretty nifty item to bring to show and tell, and she did pass her bronze medal around at school. So many classmates took an up-close-and-personal look at the medal that Rudolph was surprised to see fingerprints all over it when she brought it home. Her attempt to restore some of the luster was only partially successful.

"I discovered that bronze doesn't shine," she said. "So I decided, 'I'm going to try this one more time. I'm going to go for the gold.'"[3]

The 1960 Games was Rudolph's tour de force, but she might have lost out. While practicing leading up to the competition, she sprained an ankle. It wasn't as much of a hindrance as it could have been, and icing the ankle was therapeutic, so the injury didn't hold her back.

Rudolph won the 100 meters in 11.0 seconds and the 200 meters in 23.2, and the all-Tennessee State relay team won the gold in a world-record time of 44.5 seconds. The latter, the cooperative effort involving four teammates, came with a bit of extra difficulty. Although Rudolph was calm before the race, noticeably free of nerves, Coach Temple almost got heartburn during it.

"The baton was bobbled when Lucinda [Williams] passed off to Rudolph," Temple said. "My heart sank to my feet."[4] But Rudolph recovered smoothly and sprinted through the finish tape for the victory.

Rudolph was just 20 years old. Foreshadowing her future endeavors, upon returning to Clarksville, Tennessee, where authorities wanted to throw a parade in her honor, Rudolph insisted it be an integrated event, the first in the community's history.

Unlike today's track and field landscape, in which runners continue competing long after they graduate from college, in the days when amateurism ruled, continued competition was equal to a vow of poverty. Rudolph competed for just two more years internationally, retiring at 22.

Later, Rudolph made a living as a teacher and also ran a community center. She received a multitude of honors, including winning the Sullivan Award, emblematic of the nation's top amateur athlete, and over the years she was enshrined in several halls of fame. Rudolph also hosted a television show in Indianapolis.

A portion of a highway near Rudolph's childhood home in Clarksville, Tennessee, is named after her. There is also a statue of her in Clarksville. A Women's Sports Foundation award for courage is also named after Rudolph. She died at age 54 in 1994 from throat cancer and a brain tumor. In 2004 she appeared on a U.S. stamp.

During her life, and with her achievements living on in record books, Rudolph was and has been a role model for women, especially African American women.

Anita DeFranz, a black woman athlete who later served as a U.S. representative on the International Olympic Committee, recalled what it was like to see Rudolph when she was the best sprinter in the world.

"There she was, with the whole world focused on her," DeFrantz said. "And wasn't it wonderful? Here was somebody that looked like me and she'd done something that everybody celebrated."[5]

NOTES

1. Maureen M. Smith, *Wilma Rudolph* (Westport, CT: Greenwood Press, 2006), 3–4.
2. Ibid., 18.
3. Ibid., 41.
4. Ibid., 59.
5. Ibid., 103

FURTHER READING

Nelson, Murry R. "Wilma Glodean Rudolph." In *American Sports: A History of Icons, Idols, and Ideas*, edited by Murry R. Nelson. Santa Barbara, CA: Greenwood Press, 2013.

Rudolph, Wilma, and Martin Ralbovsky. *Wilma: The Story of Wilma Rudolph*. New York: Signet, 1977.

Smith, Maureen Margaret. *Wilma Rudolph: A Biography*. Westport, CT: Greenwood, 2006.

#65 Tiger Woods Tries to Be the Greatest

Emerging as one of the best golfers of all time and chasing the record for winning the most majors, Tiger Woods made a splash from the beginning of his career.

It was not only because of his brilliant play, but because he didn't look like anyone else on the tour. Golf had long been accused of being discriminatory toward African Americans, consigning them to the role of caddy more often than not and prohibiting country-club membership in general.

Woods broke down barrier after barrier, becoming the most popular golfer in the world, demonstrating that it did not matter what color a man's skin was in terms of being superb at hitting the little white ball.

Raised almost from birth to become a golfing prodigy, Woods marched through every level of play, year after year, as someone ahead of his class.

Born in Cypress, California, in 1975, the son of an African American father (with a mix of other nationalities) named Earl, who was his motivator and coach for much of his youth, and an Asian mother, Kultida, from Thailand, Woods's given name is Eldrick, but he is universally known as Tiger.

Earl Woods, who had been a pretty good golfer, joked that he introduced his son to golf when he was "in vitro," when his wife was pregnant with the boy.[1] In reality, Papa Woods introduced Tiger to golf by the time he was two years old. He took to it at once. At that age he appeared on *The Mike Douglas Show*. A year later he putted against Bob Hope.

Golf was Woods's passion and raison d'être. As a 15-year-old high school student, Woods became the youngest U.S. Junior Amateur champion. He won that title three straight years, stamping him as a player to watch, though for the most part the golfing world was already on the alert.

Still 19 and an amateur, Woods played in the Masters in Augusta, Georgia, in 1995. Before giving up his amateur status, Woods won an NCAA championship for Stanford. He was 20 when he turned pro and joined the PGA Tour. He was lanky at six foot one, but has filled out to a muscular 185 pounds, giving him plenty of power to drive the ball.

Woods was so well known and such a superb career was predicted for him that as soon as he turned professional he obtained numerous high-dollar endorsement deals, particularly with Nike, the athletic shoe manufacturer.

After one year of play Woods was named *Sports Illustrated*'s Sportsman of the Year and he was anointed the PGA's rookie of the year. His career took off like a rocket, leaving everyone on Earth behind. Woods won his first Masters championship in 1997; not long into his career, as he pocketed titles in the most prestigious of tournaments, he stated that his career goal was to set a new record for most major tournaments won.

For the most part Woods, who mostly gives pro forma answers about golf at his press conferences, has guarded his privacy zealously and rarely talks about himself in detail. He mostly avoids political stands or controversies. When he was younger he admitted to thinking about how the African American players who had come before him had been shut out of tournament golf or had battled to open doors. Augusta was probably the least welcoming of major golf sites to blacks, but there weren't a whole lot of wide-open-arms invitations anywhere.

It took until 1961 for the PGA to open its fields to African Americans. Nobody was fighting to keep Tiger Woods outside the fence. He was one of the biggest athletic stars in the world, and he was good for business. Where Woods played, the crowds followed.

The emergence of Tiger Woods in 1996 thrust a new star on the professional golf scene and opened the sport to more interest by African Americans. Woods has won more than 100 tournaments around the world, including 14 major championships, and hopes to add to his total before retirement. (AP Photo/Dave Martin)

When he was turning pro and the issue of country-club courses closed to African Americans was raised, Woods demonstrated tremendous self-confidence and comfort over his impending career.

"I shot in the 70s when I was eight," Woods said. "I shot in the 60s when I was 12. I am the only man to win three consecutive U.S. Amateur titles. There are still golf courses in the United States that I cannot play because of the color of my skin. I'm told that I'm not ready for you. Are you ready for me?"[2]

It was a bold and direct statement, and soon enough Woods proved he belonged with the elite of the sport and anyone who didn't recognize that had better get on board.

After Woods captured his first Masters title, he said he couldn't help but think of those who had been banned before him.

"I have a great deal of reverence for the Masters tradition, especially since my victory in 1997," he said. "But I must admit the first time I drove down Magnolia Lane I was not thinking about Bobby Jones or all the Masters stood for: I was thinking of all the great African American players who never got a chance to play there. That I was able to win there, I believe, brought a little bit of vindication."[3]

Jack Nicklaus, the record holder with 18 majors, is often called the greatest golfer of all. During the early stages of his career Tiger seemed a threat to zoom past Nicklaus in major wins and be proclaimed the best golfer. For years he reigned supreme, raking in awards, shooting the lowest scores, making the most money, and edging closer to Nicklaus's total. He dominated the tour so thoroughly that it was a given he would be in contention if he showed up for an event, and he was always the favorite. Sometimes it was a surprise if Woods did not win a tournament. He was that good and that consistent for years.

By 2013 Woods had been selected the PGA Player of the Year 11 times and had topped the money list 10 times. The majors are the tournaments that Woods focuses on, and he gained his greatest pleasure winning the Masters, the U.S. Open, the British Open, and the PGA Championship. Between 1997 and 2008 Woods won 14 majors. He seemed to be on a clear path to surpass Nicklaus.

By 2015 Woods had also amassed 79 tour victories, the second most in golf history behind Sam Snead's 82. Woods also had 40 wins on the European Tour and 2 wins in Japan. He has won the World Golf Championship 18 times.

Due to turn 40 at the very end of 2015, Woods had, however, endured many bumps in his once smooth road in recent years. He endured injuries to his knee and back; went through a humiliating, highly publicized breakup with his wife; and stopped winning major tournaments.

It was distressing to watch as so many aspects of Woods's life seemed to be unraveling. Younger players were creeping up on him at the course and surpassing him. First the stresses of his personal life were distractions, and then physical ailments began mounting up. He took leaves of absence from the tour to recover and to reconstruct his game, but every time he came back, some part of his body failed him.

For a good portion of his career Woods was the number 1 ranked player in the world. However, in the spring of 2015, because he had been inactive due to a constant battle with injuries, the man ranked number 1 for 683 weeks fell out of the top 100. He was last ranked number 1 in May 2014.

As Woods approached 40, when golfers' skills diminish anyway, there was open speculation that he would never play first-rate, competitive golf again; that his quest to pass Nicklaus's majors total would never happen; and that the Tiger

Woods who had been such a terrific player might never be on view again. It was a difficult thing to predict.

It would be more satisfying to all golf fans if Woods went out on his own terms, but even if he never played top-level golf again, he could walk away from the sport knowing he was one of the greatest ever and that he had served as an important pioneer in bridging golf's unfortunate discriminatory past into a more open-minded present.

NOTES

1. Lawrence J. Londino, *Tiger Woods* (Westport, CT: Greenwood Press, 2010), 2–3.
2. Ibid., 74.
3. Ibid., 39.

FURTHER READING

Barbie, Donna J. *The Tiger Woods Phenomenon: Essays on the Cultural Impact of Golf's Fallible Superman.* Jefferson, NC: McFarland, 2012.
Callahan, Tom. *In Search of Tiger: A Journey through Golf with Tiger Woods.* New York: Three Rivers Press, 2004.
Helling, Steve. *Tiger: The Real Story.* Boston: Da Capo Press, 2010.

#66 Honus Wagner and Baseball Cards

The kids who flipped their little pieces of cardboard with baseball players' faces on the front didn't know they were gambling with a fortune. Neither did those reckless souls who attached the cards to the spokes of their bicycles so they would make a cool sound when the wheels turned.

Baseball cards were for young baseball fans who loved the sport and collected the cardboard for kicks (and may well have been more devoted to the pink chewing gum than the miniature sports souvenirs). They outgrew them about the same time they discovered girls and left them behind when they headed off to college, giving mom the chance to clean the closet and dump the cards in the trash.

Only later, when a casual hobby morphed into a pricey collectors' world, and experts began valuing old baseball cards the way some people do their jewels, did grown-up versions of those kids groan about how they could have started a college trust fund for junior, if they had only known.

The first baseball cards predated the 20th century. Early cards were promotions of tobacco companies, not Bazooka gum. They were sought after by young fans and viewed basically as toys. Although the biggest stars were always coveted, condition didn't always matter, nor rookie cards, nor collecting the whole set.

It might be said that Honus Wagner changed the landscape. That was true when he played for the Pittsburgh Pirates during his Hall of Fame career as a shortstop, but also when his face popped up on a baseball card as part of the T206 set issued between 1909 and 1911.

"The Flying Dutchman" has taken better pictures, but none so enduring. The card in question shows Wagner staring into space, his thick brown hair parted in the middle, against an orange backdrop. He is wearing a gray Pittsburgh uniform top buttoned to his neck. The "white border" card set was issued over a three-season period, with 524 different cards printed, and the cards were inserted into cigarette packs.

Those cards were smaller than the size of future cards, measuring just $1^7/_{16}$ by $2^5/_8$ inches.

Wagner's card was one of

WAGNER, PITTSBURG

To many, Hall of Famer Honus Wagner of the Pittsburgh Pirates was the greatest shortstop of all time. His 1909 baseball card is the most coveted of all time. Wagner asked for the card to be removed from sale because he didn't want youngsters to have to buy tobacco to obtain it. Over the years it has become increasingly valuable, selling once for more than $2 million. (AP Photo/Kathy Willens)

these, but it did not stay on the market as long as the other cards. It was withdrawn, thus creating a shortage and ultimately, tremendous value. Wagner informed the card company—American Tobacco Company—that he did not want to be part of its set because he thought it bad form that children had to buy tobacco to possess the card.

The Hall of Fame baseball star was from Carnegie, Pennsylvania, and an image of the card that Wagner made famous adorns the local American Legion Hall of him there.

"It is hardly surprising that Wagner's hometown would honor him with a mural of his baseball card," authors of a book about baseball cards once observed. "Although Honus looks stiff and not quite real in the picture, like the portraits of saints that hang in old Byzantine churches."[1]

The number of cards of Wagner generally believed to be produced before his run was terminated is a matter of speculation. At times the total was estimated to be as low as 40. Then it was upped to 50. Acknowledging that some perished from wear and tear and that some logically disappeared over time, the number has been rounded off at 200 at the most.

The Wagner card is the most coveted and expensive of all time. A value was first placed on the Wagner card in 1933: $50. In April 2013 a Wagner card sold for more than $2 million. Long before that it was obvious that the collecting of old baseball cards was not for kids anymore. Other Wagner cards have sold for six figures, the total depending on condition. Ironically, exact duplicates (except for the back) can be bought for $1.

Demand grew for other old cards, notably those depicting Babe Ruth, Ty Cobb, Cy Young, and other long-deceased Hall of Famers. The 1952 Mickey Mantle, his rookie card, exploded in interest and value, selling for as much as $282,500. In 2010 a high-quality Mantle rookie sold for $130,000. In April 2015 a Mantle rookie card was listed on eBay with a buy-it-now price of $5,999. It was definitely not in pristine condition, but that was a whole lot cheaper than $130,000.

The Wagner card came to symbolize a revolution in baseball card collecting, which by the 1990s had become a billion-dollar industry that included football, basketball, and hockey cards, as well as baseball cards, although baseball cards still drove the marketplace. While the manufacturer Topps still represented the backbone of the industry, it faced many challenges from other companies. The market became flooded with product. The main producers created competing sets and colorful sets beyond the basics.

Baseball cards were not mass-marketed every year in the decades following the T206 set. The modern era of card production stems from 1948 and includes a small period of time ending in 1955 when both Topps and Bowman manufactured baseball card sets. Topps had a monopoly after that until 1981, but eventually lost a lawsuit to keep competitors out of the market.

For decades young baseball players felt validated when the card company came to them, offered a tiny payment for pictures of them, and then printed their very own cards. Later, Marvin Miller, executive director of the players' union, sought to have players compensated more for the rights to their pictures. Player involvement shifted from being more of a fun thing to a business thing.

During the 1980s, a period some might consider the heyday of card production, an eager collector could purchase three complete baseball card sets per year made by Topps, Fleer, and Donruss. The companies, soon joined by others like Upper Deck and Score, began making subsets and offshoots. It was impossible for youngsters to collect everything because that would cost too much.

Kids still bought their packs, for $1 or more, the nickel price having gone the way of the nickel candy bar.

"There is a magic to opening a fresh pack of cards," said Mike Berkus, the founder of the annual National Sports Collectors Convention.[2]

Almost out of nowhere, star players' rookie cards became especially valuable. Sets with scarce higher numbers became more valuable. Card collecting was no longer just for kids, and it was no longer play. It became as profitable as dealing in coins or stamps or a few other traditional collecting media. Speculators would buy a dozen of a rookie card of a budding star, planning to keep them in safe deposit boxes and remove them a decade later when they had matured in value.

Cards once carelessly stuffed into pockets were preserved in plastic, because even the tiniest nick or crease diminished their value. They were handled like the best China, mostly to be taken out and admired only on special occasions.

Some analysts suggested nostalgia as part of the reason for the increased interest in baseball cards, Baby boomers could return to the pleasure of their youth, only with deeper pockets, allowing them to scramble for the cards they couldn't obtain when they only cost a nickel. For them, collecting baseball or other sports cards was more fun than playing the stock market. It was also easier to get their children involved in watching a hometown hero like Albert Pujols smack the ball out of the ballpark than in how Microsoft stock was doing.

Money was spent. Money was made. Money was wasted. The marketplace became glutted.

Ultimately, Topps's competitors mostly died off. The value of star cards that had shot into the hundreds of dollars collapsed. To a large extent, baseball cards went back to being baseball cards for the majority of collectors. Collecting also shifted back to being more of a hobby than an investment opportunity.

Speculators abandoned baseball cards, leaving behind a hobby in upheaval, but mostly a hobby again. Baseball cards did not go away and are unlikely to do so.

But except for the wealthy, collecting baseball cards pretty much returned to the hands of youngsters and the average Joe.

NOTES

1. Michael O'Keefe and Terri Thompson, *The Card: Collectors, Con Men, and the True Story of History's Most Desired Baseball Card* (New York: William Morrow, 2007), 49.
2. Mike Tierney, "Fewer Are Investing Hearts and Minds into Baseball Cards," *New York Times*, June 30, 2013.

FURTHER READING

Beckett Media. *Baseball Card Price Guide*. Dallas, TX: Beckett, 2015.
Hwang, Jeff. *The Modern Baseball Card Investor*. Duluth, GA: Dimat Enterprises Inc., 2014.
Jamieson, Dave. *Mint Condition: How Baseball Cards Became an American Obsession*. New York: Grove Press, 2011.
Waldo, Ronald T. *Honus Wagner and His Pittsburgh Pirates: Scenes from a Golden Era*. Jefferson, NC: McFarland, 2015.

#67 Pittsburgh's Immaculate Reception

Even now, more than 40 years later, when Franco Harris is old enough to collect Social Security, the former Pittsburgh Steelers' fullback is best remembered for the single most dazzling and important play in his old National Football League team's Super Bowl dynasty years.

Harris may be a Hall of Fame player who won four Super Bowl rings, was a nine-time NFL all-star, and rushed for 12,120 yards, but any time his name is mentioned among football fans, one particular play is sure to come up.

On December 23, 1972, Harris was on the receiving end of "The Immaculate Reception," even though he was not the intended receiver. The amazing catch and run gave Harris's Steelers the winning touchdown in a play-off game against the Oakland Raiders when all looked hopeless.

Harris, one of the most popular and productive players in Steelers history, won the 1972 league rookie of the year award after joining Pittsburgh as a number 1 draft pick out of Penn State. Not everyone felt Harris would be a star pro player, but he proved them wrong immediately, rushing for 1,055 yards and scoring 10 touchdowns his first year in the league. He was on his way to scoring 100 NFL

Regarded as the most remarkable single play in NFL history, Franco Harris's so-called "Immaculate Reception" catch on a deflected ball gave his Steelers a playoffs victory over the Oakland Raiders and helped propel the Steelers to a Super Bowl title. (AP Photo/ Harry Cabluck)

touchdowns and his later induction into the Pro Football Hall of Fame in Canton, Ohio, in 1990 after a career spanning 1972 to 1983.

Born in Fort Dix, New Jersey, Harris was the son of an African American military man and a mother of Italian heritage. When he became a star NFL player fans formed "Franco's Italian Army" as a fan club. Harris's style of wearing a beard at the time was unusual for an NFL player.

The Pittsburgh Steelers were a heartbreak NFL franchise. They were born in 1933, but never finished in first place over the next 40 years. Art Rooney was an admired owner whose teams just could not win the big one. That began to change in 1972. After going 6–8 during the 1971 season the Steelers began emerging from the wilderness.

That season the Steelers finished 11–3 and won the American Football Conference Central Division. That advanced Pittsburgh to a play-off game for the first time since 1947.

Late in the game, however, Pittsburgh looked doomed to defeat against the 10–3–1 Raiders coached by John Madden. The clock was ticking down to the game's closing seconds and Pittsburgh trailed, 7–6. Oakland's Kenny Stabler had just scored to give the Raiders the lead with 1:17 to go.

But the Steelers had the ball, and quarterback Terry Bradshaw was trying to orchestrate a miracle in the passing game. Pittsburgh had the ball, but it was fourth down and 10 yards to go for a first down, and just 22 seconds were left in the game when he faded back to throw. Bradshaw saw John "Frenchy" Fuqua, the stylish dresser who was one of the most flamboyant players on the team, in possible position to catch a desperation pass at the Raiders' 35-yard line. As Fuqua reached for the ball, Oakland defensive back Jack Tatum arrived on the scene to intervene, make a play, and prevent a catch.

Tatum, Fuqua, and the football collided in a perfect storm of contact, the two humans falling to the wayside and the football floating through the air, on its way down to the ground for an incompletion, a result that would have turned the ball over to Oakland and ended the Steelers' playoff hopes.

Harris had begun the play in the Pittsburgh backfield, blocking against the first wave of Raiders defenders. But then he drifted downfield in the hopes of being an open man as a safety valve receiver if Bradshaw needed him. He was in the vicinity when Tatum and Fuqua collided and the ball squirted free. Before the ball could hit the field and be whistled dead, Harris lunged forward, got two hands on the ball, gathered it in for a catch and ran for daylight.

Fending off nearby Raiders seeking a last-ditch tackle, Harris ran all of the way to the end zone for a touchdown. The play went for a 60-yard score and gave Pittsburgh the lead in the waning seconds and the play-off win by a 13–7 margin, all amid controversy.

While there was no question that Harris made the catch before the ball fell to the ground and ran to the end zone without any infraction, the issue was whether or not it was a legal catch for another reason. Under the rules, one offensive player could not catch a ball if it bounced off another offensive player without being touched by a defensive player. If both offensive and defensive players touched the ball, Harris's catch would also be good.

The officials huddled for a discussion before making a final decision. Not all of the officials had seen the play, though, and they felt they could not make a call. Referee Fred Swearingen placed a phone call to NFL supervisor of officials Art McNally in the press box. McNally reportedly had seen an instant replay demonstrating that the ball hit Tatum. Supposedly the conversation was not complicated. Swearingen told McNally he had two officials who saw a touchdown, and McNally told him to go ahead and make the ruling.

That clinched it. Harris's catch for the winning points counted. "The Immaculate Reception" went into the books and is ranked as the most famous play in NFL history.

However, even 40 years later, tapes of the bang-bang play seem inconclusive about who touched the ball in the collision. Casting some doubt about what occurred are firsthand accounts of several players involved or nearby, which differ. Not as many camera angles were at work at the time as are used from in televised games today.

Oakland players felt they got cheated. Steelers players felt they deserved the victory.

"Franco made that play because he never quit on the play," said Pittsburgh coach Chuck Noll. "He kept running. He kept hustling. Good things happen to those who hustle."[1]

The phrase "The Immaculate Reception," entered the NFL lexicon later that night. A Steelers fan telephoned a Pittsburgh TV station and spoke to prominent broadcaster Myron Cope, who used it on the air in his story about the game. The words stuck to the play.

The jubilant Steelers advanced to the next round of the play-offs, losing 21–17 to the Miami Dolphins. The Dolphins were on their 17–0 perfect season run.

However, with the core of the team intact and built up from the days of losing, the Steelers emerged as the team of the decade. Harris, Bradshaw, "Mean" Joe Greene, Rocky Bleier, Jack Lambert, Jack Ham, John Stallworth, Lynn Swann, and others formed the cornerstone of a dynasty under Chuck Knoll.

The Steelers won Super Bowls in 1975, 1976, 1979, and 1980, and those teams are revered in Pittsburgh. Yet none ever produced a more dramatic or memorable play than "The Immaculate Reception."

Later in life Harris and his old backfield running mate from Penn State, Lydell Mitchell, another NFL star, formed a business partnership to found SuperBakery, a company devoted to providing better nutrition for schoolchildren. Harris also became the owner of a women's football team. A statue of Harris catching the ball in the famous play was erected at Pittsburgh International Airport in 2006.

As proof that Pittsburghers can never get enough of "The Immaculate Reception," a monument of Franco Harris commemorating the play was erected in 2012 at the old Three Rivers Stadium site where he did it.

"Isn't this beautiful, guys?" Harris said to the crowd at the unveiling. "That play really represents our teams of the '70s."[2]

NOTES

1. "History: Immaculate Reception Notes," Steelers.com, http://www.steelers.com/history/three-rivers/immaculate-reception.html.

2. "Immaculate Reception Honored," *Associated Press,* December 22, 2012.

FURTHER READING

Garner, Joe. *100 Yards of Glory: The Greatest Moments in NFL History.* Boston: Houghton Mifflin Harcourt, 2011.

Pomerantz, Gary M. *Their Life's Work: The Brotherhood of the 1970s Pittsburgh Steelers.* New York: Simon & Schuster, 2013.

#68 Babe Didrikson Zaharias

Back in the dark ages of women's sports in the United States, when high schools barely fielded any teams at all for female students, and colleges' sports menus were at least as ill-funded, one woman and her accomplishments stood out as a shining beacon.

Babe Didrikson Zaharias is the greatest female athlete of all time. She excelled where and when she was not supposed to and was a role model for any female athlete who battled long odds. She enjoyed a sports career that was not supposed to happen, because American society was mostly a series of closed doors for women with aspirations in sport.

Didrikson, whose given first name was Mildred, was born in Port Arthur, Texas, in 1911 and became a star performer in golf, track and field, and basketball in a life cut short at age 45 in 1956 by cancer. Zaharias was her married name.

Perhaps not quite as famous as another Babe, Babe Ruth, when she became a national celebrity Didrikson claimed she was nicknamed for the slugger after she hit a slew of home runs in a cluster. She kept that story alive, but apparently her mother referred to her as Babe from the time she was tiny.

Didrikson was athletic enough to do anything. She was a superb basketball player, could dive at the pool, and was an excellent bowler. In 1931 Didrikson competed for a women's basketball team, and the squad won a national championship in Amateur Athletic Union play.

In an almost surreal performance, the 1932 AAU track and field championships were an illustration of how far ahead of her time Babe was compared to most female athletes. She entered eight events in that national competition and won five of them, with a tie for a sixth title. Six gold medals in one meet made Didrikson the Jim Thorpe of her sex. She set four world records.

Later that year Didrikson represented the United States in the Summer Olympics in Los Angeles, winning two gold medals and a silver medal at the Games in the new Los Angeles Coliseum. Didrikson captured gold in the 80-meter hurdles and the javelin throw and earned silver in the high jump. The trio of successes showed that Didrikson possessed speed, strength, and leaping ability.

Didrikson was once asked if there was anything she didn't play, and she said, "Yeah, dolls." They didn't interest her, especially since as a teenager she knew what she wanted to be when she grew up. "My goal was to be the greatest athlete who ever lived," she said.[1] Few would challenge the assertion that she succeeded in that ambition among women athletes.

If competition was involved, Didrikson, who also performed in vaudeville and did some acting, was attracted to the game. She played on a touring basketball team and entered billiards events, though that was far from her best sport. Didrikson stood five foot seven, but despite weighing just 115 pounds she was exceptionally strong, and that aided her in her competitions.

Many consider Babe Didrikson Zaharias the world's greatest female athlete. She excelled in golf, track and field, and basketball after growing up in Port Arthur, Texas. Among her achievements were winning two Olympic gold medals and one silver medal in the Summer Games of 1932. (AP Photo)

Looking for a new outlet, Didrikson hooked up with golf in 1935. In 1938 she tried something no one had ever thought of doing before: she entered a men's golf tournament. Although she shot 81 and 84, she did not make the cut, but she did end up marrying her partner on the course, George Zaharias, who was a wrestler.

Didrikson, who began going by Zaharias, was considered a professional because of her basketball days. Authorities told her that she would be able to regain her amateur status if she did not compete in any other sport for three years. She put herself through the ordeal, being labeled an amateur again in 1942, but emerged as the top female golfer.

Asked how she did so well at golf, Zaharias was straightforward with her reply, although it was not particularly profound.

"The formula for success is simple," she said. "Practice and concentration and then more practice and concentration."[2]

Zaharias won the 1946 U.S. Women's Amateur and the 1947 British Ladies Amateur. Soon enough she realized being an amateur wasn't really worth it after all. Later in 1947 Zaharias turned pro in golf. Nationally famous for her sports achievements, Zaharias drew big crowds who cheered her on as she played her 18 holes during tournaments.

Even as Zaharias gained fame for her recurring athletic successes, many male sportswriters of her era felt a woman's place was in the home cooking and cleaning and not competing at all. They were out of step then and would be more out of step now.

Why wouldn't Zaharias think she could play excellent golf, given the attributes she felt it took to be good at the game?

"Golf is a game of coordination, rhythm, and grace," she said. "Women have these to a high degree."[3]

In 1950 Zaharias was one of the founders of the LPGA, the Ladies Professional Golf Association, which endures today as the governing body of women's professional golf. As player-administrator Zaharias spent three years as president of the fledgling organization in the early 1950s.

Zaharias, who won 41 events on the pro tour, earned titles in 10 majors. She was named Associated Press women's athlete of the year six times, the first time for her track and field accomplishments in 1932 and in 1945, 1946, 1947, 1950, and 1954 for her golf exploits. As for any comparison with Jim Thorpe, when the AP conducted a poll in 1950 to determine the greatest athletes of the first half of the 20th century, Thorpe won the male honor, and Zaharias had the female honor bestowed on her.

To many Zaharias seemed invincible, a tower of strength in any sporting endeavor she involved herself in, yet her golfing career and life were cut short by illness. She was diagnosed with colon cancer in 1953, but after undergoing surgery she rallied to make a comeback in 1954. She and her husband founded the Babe Didrikson Cancer Clinics.

Not completely cured, Zaharias entered eight golf tournaments in 1954 and won two of them. However, a complete recurrence of the cancer led to her death on September 27, 1955, in Galveston, Texas. Certainly, Zaharias did not envision an early death for herself. She pictured herself playing golf for the rest of her life, but a life that would last twice as long.

"I expect to play golf until I am 90," she said. "Even longer if anyone figures out how to swing a club from a rocking chair."[4]

In 1977, when the LPGA Hall of Fame opened, Zaharias was a member of the charter class.

NOTES

1. Larry Schwartz, "Didrikson Was a Woman Ahead of Her Time," *ESPN's Sports Century*, ESPN.com, https://espn.go.com/sportscentury/features/00014147.html.
2. Ross Atkin, "12 Quotes from Babe Didrikson Zaharias," *Christian Science Monitor*, June 22, 2012.
3. Ibid.
4. Ibid.

FURTHER READING

Cayleff, Susan E. *Babe: The Life and Legend of Babe Didrikson Zaharias*. Champaign: University of Illinois Press, 1996.
Johnson, William Oscar, and Nancy P. Williamson. *Whatta Gal! The Babe Didrikson Story*. New York: Little Brown, 1977.
Van Natta, Don, Jr. *Wonder Girl: The Magnificent Sporting Life of Babe Didrikson Zaharias*. New York: Little Brown, 2011.
Zaharias, Babe Didrikson. *The Life I've Led: My Autobiography*. Taylorville, IL: Oak Tree Publications, 1955.

#69 Indiana State versus Michigan State

They were just becoming famous. Larry Bird and Magic Johnson were two of the best-known college basketball players in the United States during the 1978–1979 season. It was very early in their careers, but there was universal acknowledgment that they were two special players.

Bird was a tall blond dude, a country boy from Indiana, who led his Indiana State team to an undefeated season leading up to the NCAA championship game. He seemed shy and was labeled "The Hick from French Lick." He played forward in a manner that few fans had ever witnessed.

Johnson was from Lansing, Michigan, and stayed home to turn Michigan State into a national contender. His given name was Earvin, but everyone called him Magic because of his slick skills handling the ball. He played point guard in a manner that few fans had ever seen.

They were on a collision course to reach the NCAA championship game during March 1979, the excitement intensifying by the weekend during March

When Indiana State's Larry Bird and Michigan State's Magic Johnson met for the NCAA crown in 1979, it became the most watched game in college basketball history and set the tone for their NBA rivalry to come. (AP Photo)

Madness as each team kept winning.

Bird was born in 1956 and grew to six foot nine and 220 pounds. He looked slow, but played fast. He had fabulous court vision and was a lights-out shooter from the perimeter. Indiana State had a limited history of basketball success until he arrived on the Terre Haute campus, a refugee from Indiana University in Bloomington, where he felt out of place.

Johnson was born in 1959 and also grew to six foot nine and 220 pounds. He too looked slow on the court, but slowed down the action in his head to know where best to pass the ball. He was not a good outside shooter, but was an adept scorer.

For Bird and Johnson, although they could not know it at the time, this was the beginning of an enduring on-court rivalry and eventually a solid friendship. They played the sport the same way, as leaders of their teams, but also both had the capacity to make their teammates better. They both won multiple NBA championships and shared the experience of being part of the Dream Team gold medal squad in the 1992 Summer Olympics in Barcelona. That all lay in the future in 1979.

In 1979 college basketball was not nearly as popular as it became in the ensuing decades. Nor was the NCAA tournament an all-consuming passion for that many Americans, although it was an anticipated stopover on the annual sports calendar.

Bird, a senior and a future multiple Most Valuable Player for the Boston Celtics, was not a hugely recognized player at the start of the season, but his brilliant play brought Indiana State national attention. The Sycamores, coached by Bill Hodges, rolled to a 33–0 record and their scheduled meeting with the Spartans. Carried by Bird, Indiana State soared to number 1 in the Associated Press rankings.

Rarely recalled, but notable at the time, was an 83–79 exhibition game victory over the Soviet Union that served as a clue to how good Indiana State could be.

Michigan State was ranked number 3 with its 25–6 record by the time the teams met. The Spartans, coached by Jud Heathcoate, had a rugged time of it in the Big Ten Conference, going 13–5. But Johnson, who was a sophomore, helped the team jell as the season wore on, and the Spartans were playing at their peak in the tournament.

Indiana State beat Virginia Tech, Oklahoma, Arkansas, and DePaul to reach the championship game. Michigan State beat Lamar, Louisiana State, Notre Dame, and Penn to reach the championship game. Their parallel courses completed, the teams converged for the NCAA title on the night of March 26, 1979, in Salt Lake City.

Eagerly anticipated, the game became the most-watched NCAA televised game of all time and increased the popularity of the sport. More than 35 million people tuned in, and the rating was the highest ever.

Johnson guided Michigan State to the victory, 75–64, ending Indiana State's unbeaten season and providing the Spartans with their first NCAA men's basketball crown. Magic scored 24 points and collected 7 rebounds. Forward Greg Kelser scored 19 points for Michigan State. Guard Terry Donnelly added 15 more points.

Johnson, chosen for all all-American teams, was selected as the most outstanding player of the Final Four. He also left college at age 19 to move directly to the pros and the Los Angeles Lakers after gaining the title.

Bird scored 19 points and gathered 13 rebounds for the losing Sycamores. At a time before the NCAA's increased popularity led the governing body of college sports to only schedule the Final Four in large domed stadiums, the attendance was 15,410. Indiana State guard Carl Nicks scored 17 points. Bird missed 14 of 21 shots that night. Yet the beginning of Johnson's admiration for Bird's game began there.

"We've never seen a player like Larry Bird, and there's never been a player since like Larry Bird that could go inside, outside, make the pass, get the rebound, make the steal, make the block, take it the length of the court himself and make a play," Johnson said. "He's still, to me, the most amazing player that's ever played and the most unique player that's ever played."[1]

Although both players were gone from their respective schools after that season, Bird and Magic's showdown was a pivotal moment for the NCAA tournament. That year 40 teams were invited, but the field expanded over the next few years, first growing to 48 teams and now to 68 teams.

The showcase of great players and teams from all over the country and the belief that the underdog always has a chance and that even the most powerful programs can go down to defeat unexpectedly each March, have given the tournament a special cachet. Fans think that nothing can surprise them, yet each tournament they *are* surprised by the results. March Madness has become so big that workplaces halt in their tracks as workers follow the games. Employees in the largest and smallest of businesses fill out brackets predicting how the games will go, even if they are not really fans and don't really follow the sport the rest of the winter. Networks bid for long-term TV contracts worth billions of dollars for the right to televise the games.

The Indiana State–Michigan game and the Bird-Magic showdown are credited with leading to a boom in college basketball. Some call it "the most important" game in college basketball history because it led to the expansion of the tournament, new levels of attention from fans, and the true jumping off point for March Madness.

As basketball players, Bird and Magic's careers went on. Michigan State evolved into a perennial college power. Indiana State has never been back to the NCAA tournament and never has fielded a team quite so good. In 2015 Bird, then president of the Indiana Pacers of the NBA, was asked about his memory of the near-miss.

"That was the toughest defeat I've ever taken," Bird said. "That was hard, and it's still hard. We were not expected to get there, and then to get there and have that one opportunity, and then not play well, it's disappointing."[2]

Everyone knew Bird played hard and took losing hard. This was one defeat he could never shake and could never get back. There was no "wait till next year" for him in college basketball.

"It was such a wonderful ride, but with such a letdown at the end, it's physically just draining," Bird said, "and it was tough to take because when you go that far and you have an opportunity to win a national championship and you don't do it, it's really unbearable. It's heartbreaking."[3]

NOTES

1. Dick Jeradi, "Larry Bird, Magic Johnson Share Memories from 1979 NCAA Matchup," *Philadelphia Daily News*, April 7, 2009.

2. Sam Gardner, "Larry Bird Still Feels Sting of Losing Perfect Record in Title Game with Indiana State," *Fox Sports*, March 30, 2015.

3. Ibid.

FURTHER READING

Bird, Larry, Magic Johnson, and Jackie MacMullen. *When the Game Was Ours*. Boston: Houghton Mifflin Harcourt, 2009.

Davis, Seth. *When March Went Mad: The Game That Transformed Basketball*. New York: Times Books, 2009.

Einhorn, Eddie, and Ron Rappaport. *How March Became Madness: How the NCAA Tournament Became the Greatest Sporting Event in America*. Chicago: Triumph Books, 2006.

#70 A Basketball Sisterhood

For those who saw it happen in the interview area behind the scenes at the Atlanta Olympics in 1996, it was an unforgettable sight. Venus Lacy, a center for the U.S. women's basketball team, lifted the gold medal hanging around her neck up to her mouth. Mischief in her eyes, Lacy bit down on the medal as if it was a chocolate coin that kids love. Then she admitted it was the real thing, not a fake coin but genuine gold.

The American women earned it. They had devoted a year of their lives to preparing for and competing in the Olympics representing their country, and in the end the reward justified their effort.

Stanford coach Tara VanDerveer had taken a leave of absence from her job, although she was regarded as one of the finest coaches leading one of the best programs in NCAA women's college basketball. A dozen women were selected to play for Team USA, all of them stars. They were asked to invest a full year of preparation by playing as a team, touring the country and the world to face the stiffest competition, and all of it worked out.

What that group did was to sell the sport. Playing at a superior level and simultaneously showing fans that they were first-class people, that USA team was a breakthrough ambassador for women's basketball, unified in a 10-month international tour that showcased their skills while bonding the players.

Americans have always been possessive of basketball played against other countries. The game was invented in Springfield, Massachusetts, in 1891, and there has always been a belief that U.S. teams should win when engaged in international competition. This high standard was always applied to the men and began to be applied to the women as well.

The feeling was that they should win. Only they didn't in 1994, losing the world championships to Brazil. That spawned the idea of forming a standing national team with players who would play together like a true team, learning one another's habits.

The 1996 U.S. women's Olympic basketball team, featuring such players as (left to right) Rebecca Lobo (13), Katy Steding (11), Venus Lacy (14), and Dawn Staley (5), not only won the gold medal but went undefeated over a year of prep play and created such excitement that it led to the creation of a women's professional league. (AP Photo/Elise Amendola)

So planning for the Atlanta Games—it did not hurt that the Olympics were to be held on American soil and the country wanted to make a good impression—began early. A U.S. team was selected and spent 10 months playing games, honing teamwork. The Americans won 52 straight games, in the process beating the national teams of 25 countries. It might be argued that the achievement of going unbeaten for a year against that competition was good enough for a gold medal right there.

Twelve women were selected for the United States, and not only was this an all-star team then, but the roster remains an all-star team from the perspective of terrific and well-known players populating it.

The team was made up of Dawn Staley, Katy Steding, Sheryl Swoopes, Katrina McClain, Nikki McCray, Carla McGhee, Venus Lacy, Lisa Leslie, Rebecca Lobo, Jennifer Azzi, Ruthie Bolton, and Teresa Edwards.

"I look back and see that the '95–96 National Team experience was the beginning of greatness," McGhee said. "Great friends, great bonds, great memories, great opportunities, great fan support and awareness, and, of course, great basketball. I am very thankful and blessed for everything associated with that team."[1]

The phenomenal play and lively personality of the team jump-started the creation of women's professional basketball in the United States, as personified by the Women's National Basketball Association today. The players themselves, in most cases, moved on from the Olympics to pro ball in the United States, though many had already been playing overseas.

A major legacy of the 1996 team was being the impetus for the start-up of pro ball for women in their home country, an achievement that has provided opportunities for future generations of female players.

The most accomplished of that group of players on the court was six-foot-five center Lisa Leslie, who stuck with the program and won four Olympic gold medals. That was in addition to being part of two WNBA championship squads.

Teresa Edwards was right up there for special mention. Edwards, a five-foot eleven guard, was on four gold medal–winning U.S. Olympic teams, plus a bronze-medal winning team. She chose to sign with the Women's Basketball League over the WNBA as a player-coach, but when that league folded she shifted to the WNBA. Edwards is still an assistant coach in the WNBA for the Atlanta Dream.

Swoopes was a superstar in college at Texas Tech and was the first player signed by the WNBA when the league was formed. A three-time Olympic gold medalist, Swoopes also won three Most Valuable Player awards in the WNBA and was a renowned creator on offense and an intense performer on defense. She also coached at Texas Tech.

Lobo was the star of the University of Connecticut's 35–0 NCAA champion team and remains in the limelight as a WNBA broadcaster for ESPN. A member of the Women's Basketball Hall of Fame, Lobo said when her four-year-old daughter wandered into a room and saw daddy watching a UConn men's game, the girl said she did not know that boys played basketball.

Azzi and Bolton have been women's college head coaches. Steding coaches Boston University.

Staley, a three-time gold medalist and a six-time WNBA all-star, has gained fresh fame for her coaching. She lifted the Temple women's program to the NCAA tournament, but departed for South Carolina and the herculean task of building from scratch a program that had never had success.

It took three seasons to post a winning record. The fourth year South Carolina won 25 games. In 2013 Staley was inducted into the Naismith Memorial Basketball Hall of Fame. In 2015 she eclipsed her previous college coaching accomplishments, leading South Carolina to a 30-plus-win season, a top-five national ranking, and the Final Four.

Lacy, who learned swiftly that her gold medal tasted better than chocolate, is from Chattanooga, Tennessee. In addition to winning a national title at Louisiana Tech and the gold medal with the U.S. team, Lacy played professionally in Greece, Italy, and Japan and won a European title with her Greek team. Lacy was inducted into the Louisiana Sports Hall of Fame in 2014.

Lacy overcame childhood leg problems that required her to wear braces, inspired by the running success of track star Wilma Rudolph, who suffered from polio, and the fictional character Forrest Gump, played by Tom Hanks in the movie of the same name.

"My knees were almost turned backwards," Lacy said. "I couldn't run like the rest of the kids. I wore braces, even at night. My mom and my grandfather would massage my knees for me. Then one day I was watching TV and saw a show on Wilma Rudolph. I said, 'I want to be like that.'"[2] Lacy did not turn out exactly like Rudolph, but she did win a gold medal in another sport.

The players knew they were part of something special and something enduring. They were pioneers and leaders for women's basketball at the right time.

"To me it was the light on my professional career," Bolton said. "My experience with USA Basketball was great not just because of the winning, but because of the friendships I've developed. Of course, winning always makes it better."[3]

NOTES

1. "Celebrating the '95–96 Olympic Team Ten Years Later," WNBA.com, http://www.wnba.com/features/tenyears_olympics96.html.

2. Jim McClain, "Former Louisiana Tech Star Powers into Louisiana Sports Hall of Fame," *New Orleans Advocate*, July 20, 2014.

3. "Celebrating the '95–96 Olympic Team Ten Years Later."

FURTHER READING

Corbett, Sara. *Venus to the Hoop: A Gold Medal Year in Women's Basketball.* New York: Anchor Books, 1998.

Leslie, Lisa, and Larry Burnett. *Don't Let the Lipstick Fool You.* New York: Dafina Books, 2009.

VanDerveer, Tara, and Joan Ryan. *Shooting from the Outside.* New York: Harper Perennial, 1998.

#71 Marshall University's Plane Crash

One of the most devastating tragedies to hit the sports world was the 1970 plane crash that killed the Marshall University football team and others in its traveling party following a road game.

The death toll from the accident was 75, including 37 members of the Thundering Herd football team. Also killed were eight members of the coaching staff, boosters traveling with the team to the game at East Carolina, and the jet plane's crew.

The horrific crash of chartered Southern Airways Flight 932 occurred just after 7:30 p.m. on November 14, 1970, hours after the team lost 17–14 to the Pirates in Greenville, North Carolina. The plane was about two miles shy of landing at the Huntington, West Virginia, Tri-State Airport when it crashed into a hill.

Given how many millions of miles of travel American sports teams engage in, accidents with airplanes have been very rare. A transportation accident such as this

The crash of an airplane in 1970 wiping out the Marshall University football team is one of the dramatic tragedies in the history of college sports. The program was rebuilt and later a movie named *We Are Marshall* told the story of the program's saddest and most uplifting chapter. (AP Photo)

one is the ultimate nightmare for schools and professional teams that travel constantly for away games.

In 1961 the entire U.S. Figure Skating team was killed on its way to the world championships in Prague, Czechoslovakia. On October 2, 1970, only six weeks before the Marshall squad was destroyed in its crash, the Wichita State football team was racked by a similar incident. The team was traveling in two planes, however, and just one of the two crashed, causing the deaths of 14 players and head coach Ben Wilson on their way to a game at Utah State.

The entire men's basketball team at the University of Evansville was killed on takeoff on December 13, 1977, while headed to a game at Middle Tennessee State. Other casualties of the chartered plane crash were members of the press, boosters, coaches, and crew members.

On March 14, 1980, the 14-member U.S. boxing team was killed in a plane crash while flying on Polish Airlines. Two Oklahoma State basketball team plane crashes, one involving the men's team, the other the women's team, have occurred, killing coaches, players, and staff members. One crash happened in 2001, the other in 2011.

There has never been a fatal plane crash involving an American major professional sports team. Quietly, professional sports leagues have put in place procedures for replenishing a franchise in case of emergency and tragedy.

All of the accidents that took the lives of members of those U.S. amateur or college teams are tragedies that deeply affected families and communities. But perhaps no plane crash that involved a sports team is better remembered or was more dramatically felt than that of the Marshall football team. That may have been because more people perished in that crash than any of the others and because of Hollywood's role in telling the story of the disaster and its aftermath.

That 1970 season opened with great promise at Marshall. The team was on a five-season losing streak epitomized by a 27-game losing streak in the middle. Yet the Thundering Herd had won its first game of the season, and the program seemed to be on an upswing.

Improvement was still being shown, even in close defeats, when the plane carrying the hopes of a community crashed in the fog and erupted into flames that burned intensely even as a search for signs of life and then bodies took place.

One day after the crash, more than 7,000 shocked people attended a memorial service in Huntington at the Marshall Fieldhouse.

Red Dawson, one of the assistant coaches, had not been on the plane. He had driven to the East Carolina game, making recruiting stops, but on his way home he had heard about the plane crash on the radio and sped back to Huntington. Once there he participated in a body search, and as a representative of the football program he later met with families. It was a daunting task, one Dawson did not relish, and he was bothered by it for years as he sought to come to terms with the terrible event. Decades later Dawson said something happens every day in his life to remind him of the crash and the loss of so many people dear to him.

Determined to carry on, hopeful of a brighter future after a horrific experience, Marshall chose to field a football team in 1971, one that it counted on the community of 80,000 to support as it rebuilt its program and morale. The school received a special exemption to use freshman players for that season (at a time when freshmen were ineligible for sports).

Coach Rick Tolley was among those killed, so Marshall truly had a blank slate, with nothing more than empty offices where the football coaches worked. It would have been easy to drop football at that time, and there were some advocates of that position. Some of the youngest players still on campus, who had not made the traveling squad and did not fly to East Carolina, pleaded to continue, and the administration agreed.

Jack Lengyel was hired to try to rebuild, starting in 1971. That season Lengyel fielded a team of freshmen, walk-ons, and players recruited from other teams on campus.

Touched by Marshall's effort, like so many other football fans, President Nixon sent Lengyel a letter of encouragement. In part, he wrote: "Friends across the land will be rooting for you, but whatever the season brings, you have already won your greatest victory by putting the 1971 varsity on the field."[1]

On September 25, 1971, Marshall defeated Xavier, 15–13, at Fairfield Stadium in Huntington, Lengyel's first victory with the youthful team he called the "Young Thundering Herd." Marshall won on the last play of the game. Marshall finished the emotional season 2–8. Lengyel could not raise Marshall's level of play and departed after three seasons with a 9–33 record. Lengyel later spent 14 years as athletic director for Navy.

It took until 1984 for the Thundering Herd to field a winning team in football again. But after the NCAA created a Division I-AA, a step below Division I, Marshall became a power. Some of the stars produced were receiver Randy Moss, Chad Pennington, Ahmad Bradshaw, and Byron Leftwich, all of whom played for the Thundering Herd in the years after the tragedy. They were the living legacy of that squad, players of later generations who in their own way helped vindicate the school's decision to keep football going.

"Seventy-five people would have died in vain," said Keith Morehouse, the team's play-by-play announcer. His father, Gene, was Marshall's radio announcer back then and was killed in the plane wreck. "I was nine years old at the time and all I knew was that I had lost my father."[2]

In the late 1980s Marshall football began reaching new heights. During the 1990s the Thundering Herd went 114–25. Marshall was regularly ranked in

Division I-AA, competed in that division's play-offs, and was invited to bowl games.

In 2006 a movie called *We Are Marshall* appeared, starring Matthew McConaughey as Lengyel, telling the story of the plane crash and of the rebuilding of the program. It also served as a historical reminder for younger people who did not remember the accident.

The title of the film was the battle cry adopted by Marshall football teams that succeeded the sadly doomed team and by Huntington fans. The real Red Dawson and Jack Lengyel had small parts in the movie.

Neither the school nor the community has ever let the coaches, players, and other victims of the plane crash be forgotten. A memorial monument was erected at the entrance to the campus student center.

Every year, on November 14, a memorial service to honor those who lost their lives is conducted at the site of the monument. In 2014 Tom Shoebridge, a New Jersey high school coach, whose brother Ted was the quarterback on the team and lost his life in the crash, was a guest speaker.

"You guys down here in Huntington, you just could have stood by the wayside and forgot about it," he said. "You didn't. You stood and said, 'You know what? We're going to be better. We're going to honor them. We're going to be bigger We're going to be stronger. We're going to be Marshall University.'"[3]

NOTES

1. Lou Sahadi, "Marshall Football: From Tragedy to Triumph," ESPN.com, November 19, 2003, http://espn.go.com/classic/s/Classic_Marshall.html.
2. Ibid.
3. "Lives Remembered at 2014 Memorial Service," *Herald-Dispatch*, November 14, 2014.

FURTHER READING

Casto, James E. *Marshall University*. Mt. Pleasant, SC: Arcadia Publishing, 2005.
Nolte, Rick, Dave Wellman, Tim Stephens, and Mickey Johnson. *The Marshall Story: College Football's Greatest Comeback*. Macon, GA: Henchard Press, 2007.

#72 Oklahoma Football's 47-Game Winning Streak

The longest major college football winning streak in the history of the sport occurred in the 1950s and is now about 60 years old. No other school has come within binocular viewing of Oklahoma's 47-game consecutive win streak under coach Bud Wilkinson, and as time passes it seems to be a smaller and smaller speck on the horizon.

This feat has not only stood the test of time, it is difficult to imagine it being vulnerable to another team breaking it any time soon.

The winning streak began in 1953 and covered parts of five seasons, ending in 1957. The second-longest football win streak in modern major college play is 35 straight, a mark established by Toledo between 1969 and 1971. Miami won 34 straight games between 2000 and 2003. Southern Cal won 34 straight between 2003 and 2005, but victories were vacated because of NCAA penalties.

Much earlier, during the era of leather helmets or no helmets, when forward passing was a foreign concept, a couple of programs put together long undefeated streaks. The University of Washington won 40 straight games between 1908 and 1914, and twice Yale won 37 straight, going unbeaten for years two times by 1893. Both times Princeton ended the winning streak.

Between 2000 and 2003, Mount Union, playing in NCAA Division III, won 55 straight games. Memorably, Mount Union also owned the old record of 54 straight wins, ending in 1999. Those are the longest NCAA college football win streaks at any level of play.

Born in 1916 in Minneapolis, Charles Burnham Wilkinson played quarterback at the University of Minnesota in the 1930s. Wilkinson picked up his habit for winning there when the Golden Gophers won three straight national titles between 1934 and 1936. He then entered college coaching. He was an assistant at Syracuse and Minnesota and during World War II at Iowa Pre-Flight while part of the navy. Wilkinson became an assistant coach at Oklahoma in 1946 and the head coach in 1947.

No one could deny that Wilkinson was ready. That season the Sooners finished 7–2–1 and shared the conference title. That was the first of 13 straight league crowns Oklahoma won under Wilkinson as the league name changed from Big Six to Big Seven to Big Eight. These days that league is known as the Big 12.

Starting in 1948 Oklahoma won 31 games in a row, and in 1950 the Sooners captured Wilkinson's first national title. Wilkinson's early all-Americans during that stretch included guard Buddy Burris, quarterback Jack Mitchell, tackle Wade Walker, tackle Jim Weatherall, safety Buddy Jones, and end Frankie Anderson. A 1949 all-American was quarterback Darrell Royal, who went on to become a famed coach while leading Texas, the Sooners' archrival.

A running back named Billy Vessels also distinguished himself under Wilkinson's guidance, scoring 15 touchdowns in the 1950 national championship year and winning the Heisman Trophy in 1952. Startlingly, Oklahoma's major winning streak began after Vessels graduated. There is a Billy Vessels statue in Norman, Oklahoma, next to the football stadium.

The Wilkinson-led Sooners finished 10–1 in 1948, his second season on the job. In 1949 they went 11–0. In 1950 they were 10–1. Following that championship season Oklahoma slumped to 8–2, Wilkinson's weakest season until 1959.

What transpired in-between stunned college football fans nationwide. Oklahoma could not lose. The Sooners began their 1953 season with a loss and a tie, but ended it 9–1–1 season while capturing the Orange Bowl, 7–0, over Maryland. It was a happy New Year and a herald of the following fall. Although voters in the national polls seemed skeptical of Oklahoma's strength, only voting the team up to third, the Sooners were unbeaten at 10–0 in 1954.

They were believers by 1955 when Oklahoma finished 11–0, winning another Orange Bowl, 20–6 over the Terrapins, who finished third in the rankings. In 1956 Oklahoma did not play in a bowl game (there were many fewer in those days, and more emphasis was placed on the regular season), but finished 10–0, and the polls proclaimed them champs again.

Over the first several weeks of the 1957 season Oklahoma was rolling again. The Sooners handled all foes—Pittsburgh, Iowa State, Texas, Kansas, Colorado, Kansas State, and Missouri—to start 7–0. Oklahoma did best Colorado by only one point.

On November 16 Notre Dame came to Norman for a contest at Oklahoma Memorial Stadium and escaped with a 7–0 victory, shutting down the Sooners' winning streak at 47 games. *Sports Illustrated*, then only a few years old, got an early jump on its "cover jinx." As the Fighting Irish traveled to Oklahoma, SI went to press with a cover emblazoned with the phrase, "Why Oklahoma Is Unbeatable." Bud Wilkinson should have known right then it was all over.

Notre Dame coach Terry Brennan devised a special defense for Oklahoma that he hoped would slow down the more athletic Sooners.

"I knew that Oklahoma had a little more talent," Brennan said. "We thought, well, we have a chance. I came up with a defense, how crazy it was, but it worked. Why not? We were outgunned. It worked. It worked all day."[1]

The Fighting Irish players carried Brennan off the field on their shoulders after the victory.

The Oklahoma Sooners have long been a power in college football, spanning decades and eras. But the Sooners' greatest achievement was winning 47 straight games between 1953 and 1957 under coach Bud Wilkinson. That remains an NCAA Division I record. (AP Photo)

Notre Dame had been terrible the year before, but was improving. Among the notable budding stars were Nick Pietrosante, later a fullback for the Detroit Lions, and Dick Lynch, later a standout defensive back for the New York Giants. Pietrosante, who played both ways in the game, scored the only touchdown—on defense. He sacked the quarterback, causing a fumble, picked up the loose ball, and scored on a 19-yard touchdown run. Pietrosante also rushed, for 169 yards. His was the only score in the game.

Oklahoma had not lost in more than 1,500 days and had not been shut out in 120 games.

"Just stunned silence," said Jay Wilkinson, Bud's son, of the mood inside the stadium when the final gun sounded.[2]

That was the only game that Oklahoma lost that season, finishing 10–1. The Sooners finished 10–1 again in 1958. Among the best Sooners of the time were receiver Tommy McDonald and center Jerry Tubbs, later a middle linebacker in the pros.

Oklahoma's dominance vanished after that. The Sooners went 7–3 in 1959 and then in a shocking reversal, Wilkinson-coached Oklahoma recorded a losing record in 1960. The Sooners did not come out of the tailspin. Wilkinson led Oklahoma to 8–3 and 8–2 records in 1962 and 1963 and then left college coaching with a mark of 145–29–4.

From 1961 to 1964, while still coaching, Wilkinson served on the new President's Council on Physical Fitness created by President John F. Kennedy. When Wilkinson's teams were rolling along undefeated, people used to joke that he was so popular he should run for president. In 1964, running as a Republican, Wilkinson ran for the U.S. Senate from Oklahoma, but lost.

Wilkinson was inducted into the College Football Hall of Fame in 1969.

For years after that Wilkinson worked in college football broadcasting, but in the late 1970s he was summoned back to the sideline by the St. Louis Cardinals to give NFL coaching a whirl. He lasted two years, and his teams did not fare very well.

Wilkinson died at age 77 in 1994.

NOTES

1. Berry Tramel, "OU-Notre Dame: Terry Brennan, 85, Can Still Draw Out the Defense That Helped Notre Dame End OU's 47-Game Win Streak," *NewsOK.com*, NewsOK.com, September 25, 2013, http://newsok.com/ou-notre-dame-terry-brennan-85-can-still-draw-out -the-defense-that-helped-notre-dame-end-ous-47-game-win-streak/article/3886688.

2. Jake Trotter, "Reliving the End of the Streak," ESPN.com, October 26, 2012, http://espn .go.com/colleges/oklahoma/football/story/_/id/8552757/reliving-1957-oklahoma -sooners-loss-notre-dame-fighting-irish-snapped-ou-47-game-win-streak.

FURTHER READING

Keith, Harold, and Berry Tramel. *Forty-Seven Straight: The Wilkinson Era at Oklahoma.* Norman: University of Oklahoma Press, 2003.

Towle, Mike. *I Remember Bud Wilkinson: Personal Memories and Anecdotes about an Oklahoma Sooners Legend.* Nashville, TN: Cumberland House Publishing, 2002.

Wilkinson, Jay. *Dear Jay, Love Dad: Bud Wilkinson's Letters to His Son.* Norman: University of Oklahoma Press, 2014.

Wilkinson, Jay, and Gretchen Hirsch. *Bud Wilkinson: An Intimate Portrait of an American Legend.* Urbana, IL: Sagamore Publishing, 1994.

#73 Tommie Smith's and John Carlos's Gloved Fists

It was the 1960s and the United States and other parts of the world swirled with the turmoil of political protests. Amid these demonstrations agitating for advancements in human rights and for economic progress, Mexico City sought to stage the 1968 Summer Olympics.

This was the peak of Vietnam War protests in the United States, but civil rights activists had been at the forefront of political demonstrations for their worthy cause for more than a decade. Rosa Parks had refused to leave her seat on the bus, marchers had filled the streets of cities in Alabama and Mississippi, Martin Luther King Jr. had tried to rally the fair-minded, and violence against African Americans spilled onto television screens to educate a nation about what discrimination really meant.

In Mexico demonstrations of a different sort were taking place. Although it was reported in American newspapers, the level of impact for sports fans in the months during the run-up to the October 12 start of the Games was minimal.

It was a summer of discontent in Mexico. The Mexican Student Movement of 1968 was underway. Increasing anger at government repression and economic disadvantage led thousands to demonstrate in the streets. On August 27 a demonstration that attracted approximately 500,000 people agitated Mexico City.

Despite warnings from the government, protestors refused to settle down, and 10 days before the scheduled start of the opening ceremony a confrontation between soldiers and protestors took place, with an estimated several dozen demonstrators killed and 1,000 arrested. Politically savvy individuals wondered if the Olympic Games, always touted as a respite of peace and cessation of hostilities between foreign lands, could be conducted in that type of atmosphere.

Internally, the United States was politically divided as it had not been since the Civil War. The nation was fighting an unpopular war in Vietnam, with the situation in Southeast Asia becoming gradually more perilous with each passing day and more anger spilling out of protestors with each passing month.

In April 1968 the murder of King inflamed the country, drove African Americans who revered him to despair, and set off riots in big cities nationwide. King's assassination was a gaping wound. It seemed to be a shocking illustration of the depths to which white people would go to keep black people down and out of the mainstream of daily life. To many it was as if the Civil War had never been won, as if repressors had never gotten the message that slavery was dead and that equal rights were guaranteed under the law.

Shortly thereafter, Robert F. Kennedy, the former attorney general, brother of slain president John F. Kennedy and the front-runner for the Democratic nomination for president, was assassinated while campaigning in Los Angeles. A seething nation was distraught and furious.

The idea of a boycott of the Games by African American athletes originated with Harry Edwards. Edwards was born in East St. Louis, Illinois, in 1942. A track athlete who migrated to San Jose State in 1960, Edwards was one of several African Americans dismayed to encounter housing discrimination and social segregation at the school.

Edwards earned his bachelor's degree there and a graduate degree at Cornell, then returned to San Jose as a visiting professor between 1966 and 1968. Determined to effect social change, he was the cofounder of a group called United Black Students For Action. The organization, looking for ways to make its dissatisfaction with campus life for African Americans known, threatened to hold a racial protest at a football game. The school responded, calling off the game, and began addressing the group's concerns.

Working off that success and operating under a new name, the Olympic Project For Human Rights, Edwards and others called for black athletes to try to draw attention to the cause of improving conditions for African Americans.

"For years we have participated in the Olympic Games, carrying the United States on our backs with our victories, and race relations are now worse than ever," Edwards said. "We're not trying to lose the Olympics for Americans. What happens to them is immaterial. . . . But it's time for the black people to stand up as men and women and refuse to be utilized as performing animals for a little extra dog food."[1]

Edwards was blunt, and he had many sympathizers in the black community, but there were not as many followers as he might have hoped. Athletes who had been training for years were not inclined to retreat from this opportunity on the world stage. They had put in the sweat and training and were optimistic that there would be rewards. One of the believers, before it was deemed that a boycott did not have much traction, was world-class sprinter Tommie Smith.

Despite the conflicts in Mexico and the roiling sentiments in the United States, the Games did begin on schedule.

The men's American track team was probably one of the best ever. Jim Hines and Charlie Greene went gold-bronze in the 100 meters, Lee Evans, Larry James, and Ron Freeman swept the 400, Tom Farrell took bronze in the 800, world record-holder Jim Ryun tripped in the 1,500 but still won silver, Willie Davenport and Erv Hall went 1–2 in the 110-meter hurdles, and George Young won an unexpected bronze in the steeplechase. The U.S. won gold in both the 4 by 100 and 4 by 400 relays.

In the field events Bob Seagren won the pole vault; Randy Matson won the shot put, with George Woods second; and Al Oerter won the discus. Ralph Beamon set an astounding world record in the long jump, Dick Fosbury introduced a new style of high jumping while taking gold in that event, and Bill Toomey won the decathlon.

Then there was the 200 meters on October 16, in which American Tommie Smith won gold with a world-record run of 19.83 seconds; taking bronze behind him was John Carlos in 20.10. Both men wore black socks as part of their uniforms. Their performances earned them a trip to the medals podium, where the National Anthem of the winner is played after medals are draped around the winners' necks.

As the "Star-Spangled Banner" played, Smith and Carlos, each wearing one black glove, each raised one clenched fist skyward and bowed their heads. Smith, Carlos, and silver medalist Peter Norman of Australia all wore human rights patches on their sweat suit jackets. Norman stood staring straight ahead during the ceremony. Photographs of the medal trio were transmitted around the world and displayed in newspapers in multitudes of countries.

In 1968, efforts were made to boycott the Summer Olympics in Mexico City with the goal of bringing attention to certain difficult circumstances affecting black athletes. While the boycott fizzled, African American 200-meter medalists Tommie Smith and John Carlos took the podium with clenched fists to support the cause. (AP Photo)

Interestingly, it was later revealed that Smith and Carlos intended to each wear a pair of black gloves, but Carlos accidentally left his in the Olympic Village. It was Norman, who was white, who suggested that they divide up the single pair and each wear one. Smith wore the right one and Carlos the left one.

Gradually, fans in the Olympic stadium reacted with boos and insults. The men's protests were understood, if not appreciated.

"It was not a gesture of hate," Smith told sportscaster Howard Cosell. "It was a gesture of frustration. This was going to be a silent gesture that everyone in the world could hear."[2]

Carlos was less measured and less diplomatic in his comments.

"We feel that white people just think we are animals to do the job," Carlos said. "We saw white people in the stands putting thumbs down at us. We want to let them know we are not roaches, ants, or rats. I've heard, 'Boy, boy, boy' all through the Olympics."[3]

Before they even said a word, the gestures of Smith and Carlos were interpreted as Black Power salutes. Indeed, both members of the San Jose State track team had been influenced by the ideas and suggestions of Harry Edwards, although later Smith said their actions were not about black power, but about human rights.

International Olympic Committee President Avery Brundage, an American accused of being out of touch with the modern world, felt the spirit of the Games, supposedly free of politics, had been desecrated. Reacting with fury, Brundage expelled Smith and Carlos from the Games.

Those were not the only repercussions. Smith and Carlos were heavily criticized in newspapers and magazines back in the United States. Even Norman paid a price. He was reprimanded by Australian Olympic authorities and was left off his country's 1972 team despite top qualifying times and his 1968 silver medal.

Initially, Smith and Carlos were pariahs in their own land, but with the passage of time public opinion changed, and Smith and Carlos came to be seen as heroic, speaking up at great cost for a cause they believed in at a time when it was unfashionable. The photograph of their protest is famous, and murals have been painted of them making their gesture.

One of those murals was painted in 2000 in a suburb of Sydney, Australia. Norman traveled to see it and posed for a picture next to the mural. When Norman died in 2006, Smith and Carlos were pallbearers at his funeral.

As the 50th anniversary of Smith's and Carlos's brazen salute approaches, their protest is better remembered than their success on the track. One would not have been possible without the other, but the combination meant that Smith and Carlos recorded two of the most impressive Olympic moments of their generation, and perhaps of all time.

NOTES

1. Kareem Abdul-Jabbar, "Boycott Questions: 1968 vs. 2008," *Los Angeles Times*, May 5, 2008.

2. Richard Hoffer, *Something in the Air: American Passion and Defiance in the 1968 Mexico City Olympics* (New York: Free Press Books, 2009), 161.

3. Ibid., 162.

FURTHER READING

Carlos, John, and Dave Zirin. *The John Carlos Story: The Sports Moment That Changed the World*. Chicago: Haymarket Books, 2011.

Smith, Tommie, Delois Smith, and David Steele. *Silent Gesture, The Autobiography of Tommie Smith*. Philadelphia: Temple University Press, 2008.

#74 Jim Brown's Stunning Career and Departure

He was one of a kind. Jim Brown was broad-shouldered with a thin waist, and he hit the line of scrimmage like a sledgehammer blow when he ran the ball for the Cleveland Browns. Those in the know saw greatness in Brown from the moment he broke into the Browns' backfield in 1957, and unless a fan has seen him play live or studied the tapes of his movements, he cannot dismiss Brown from the discussion as the greatest football player of all.

Sometimes Brown carried entire defensive lines on his back, his 230-pound chiseled body exceptionally large for a running back during his era. They couldn't count the yards fast enough when Brown ran. He was the National Football League's rookie of the year in 1957 and was a nine-time Pro Bowl selection in all nine seasons that he played in the league.

Brown led the NFL in rushing eight times. The only time he missed out was when he played injured, with a battered wrist. Brown did not need a trophy case to catalog all of his honors; he needed a permanently rented hotel suite to house them all.

Brown could be sneakily dramatic in the way he slowly rose, as if he was an old man coping with arthritis, after being tackled. He was outspoken about civil rights. He was a leader just by being Jim Brown, the baddest man in the game, who could not be taken down by solo tacklers.

He made some people uneasy in an era when African Americans were agitating for a fair deal, and nobody was going to short Brown on anything. He was a marvel to watch, the cornerstone of the Cleveland Browns, the finest player in the league.

And then all of a sudden he was gone, vanished from the scene as if kidnapped in mid-stride. So abruptly did he skip out that it was as if he had never been around the NFL at all.

Four decades after his retirement as a superstar running back for the Cleveland Browns, many still consider Jim Brown to be the best player in National Football League history. Brown set numerous records before leaving the sport young to become a movie actor and later a social activist. (AP Photo)

In 1965, after nine seasons, Brown quit football to make movies. He had already jetted out of the country to go on location for the filming of *The Dirty Dozen* when he sent word he wasn't coming back.

When he stepped away from pro football Brown was just 29 years old. He had already amassed 12,312 rushing yards, a mark so far ahead of others that it seemed unlikely it would be broken in his lifetime (things change). He averaged 5.2 yards per carry and scored 126 touchdowns. It should be noted that Brown played during the era of the 12-game regular season, and the top running backs who have surpassed his yardage total have had the advantage of competing in longer regular seasons.

"When you have a thoroughbred," coach Paul Brown said early in the fullback's career, "you run him."[1]

For the first half of Brown's career the NFL played 12-game regular seasons. That changed to 14 for the second half of his career, in 1961, and then jumped to

16 games a year in 1978, long after his retirement. The top challengers to his rushing totals certainly had more cracks at carrying the ball if their teams wanted to use them that way.

Brown was born in St. Simons, Georgia, in 1936. Until the age of eight he was raised by a grandmother. But he attended high school in Manhasset, New York, on Long Island, where his mother worked as a domestic. Brown was a remarkable all-around athlete, earning 13 letters. One of his achievements was averaging 38 points a game for the school's basketball team.

Brown went to Syracuse University, where he not only starred in football, but was a spectacular lacrosse player. Some say he was the greatest lacrosse player of all time. Unlike today's specialist athletes, while Brown was earning first-team all-American status in football, he also played not only lacrosse, but also basketball, and competed for the track team. In his best season in hoops he averaged 15 points a game. He also scored 43 goals in a 10-game lacrosse season.

A number 1 draft pick of the Browns, Brown measured six foot two and weighed 232 pounds as an NFL player. Although Brown did not play as many games as many other rushers and did not stay in the sport as long as they did, he is the only back in NFL history to average 100 yards per game for his entire career. Six times Brown scored at least four touchdowns in a game.

One code that Brown lived by was to hit would-be tacklers as hard as they tried to hit him.

"He told me, 'Make sure when anyone tackles you he remembers how much it hurts,' Hall of Fame tight end John Mackey said Brown told him. "He lived by that philosophy and I always followed that advice."[2]

In 1964 Brown, who possessed a devastating straight arm, was the star of the last Browns team to win an NFL championship. In fact, that was the most recent Cleveland professional team to win a title.

Brown became interested in pursuing an acting career while he was still an active player, filming a role in a Western called *Rio Conchos* in 1964. Many athletes have been lured to Hollywood and appeared in films during their playing days or after they retired. The Browns believed that Brown would be returning to the lineup for the 1966 season.

The player indicated that he planned to play that year and then retire. However, off-season filming ran long for *The Dirty Dozen* in London because of weather problems, and Brown was going to be late to the Browns' training camp. Browns owner Art Modell was irked that Brown would not be reporting on time and made the mistake of threatening him with a $1,500 a week fine if he didn't show up. Brown said fine and quit football right then, a year ahead of time, short of his 30th birthday. It was a serious miscalculation by Modell, driving away the greatest football player of all time.

Brown launched himself into filmmaking full blast. *The Dirty Dozen*, with its ensemble cast, was a hit and remains a widely watched movie. Brown never became an all-star actor, but he did acquire a large body of credits in film and television work. One well-known movie in which he played a significant role was *100 Rifles*, with Raquel Welch and Burt Reynolds. Brown also acted in *Ice Station Zebra*. He appeared in 32 movies.

The respected filmmaker Spike Lee made a documentary in 2002 about Brown, *Jim Brown, All-American*. A review of the film called Brown "one of the greatest natural sportsmen of modern times."[3]

Over time Brown, who was enshrined in the Pro Football Hall of Fame in 1971, was recognized as one of the most prominent civil rights activists among pro athletes. Concerned about inner-city youths and gang activity, Brown in 1988 founded an organization called Amer-I-Can to deal with such problems.

Brown had some domestic problems and served a six-month jail term in 2002 for vandalizing his wife's car.

In 2008 *The Sporting News* selected the top 100 NFL players in league history and ranked Brown number 1. In 2010, when NFL Films selected a 100-best list of pro football players, Brown came in second to receiver Jerry Rice. In 2014 the *New York Daily News* picked an NFL top 50 and Brown was number 1.

"He was a beast," said Hall of Fame linebacker Lawrence Taylor, ranked number 2 on the *Daily News* list. "He's all man. Fast and strong."[4]

NOTES

1. Larry Schwartz, "Brown Was Hard to Bring Down," ESPN.com, https://espn.go.com/sportscentury/features/00014125.html.
2. "No. 1 Jim Brown," *The Sporting News Archive*, April 1, 2008.
3. Stephen Holden, "Jim Brown, All American," *New York Times*, March 22, 2002.
4. Gary Myers, "NFL Top 50: Jim Brown Is Best Player in League History," *New York Daily News*, December 3, 2014.

FURTHER READING

Brown, Jimmy, and Myron Cope. *Off My Chest*. New York: Doubleday, 1964.
Freeman, Mike. *Jim Brown: A Hero's Life*. New York: HarperCollins, 2009.

#75 Willie Mays's World Series Gem

One of the greatest baseball players of all time because he could do anything on the diamond, Willie Mays holds an iconic place in the heart of the game.

It is said that a scout's dream is coming across a ballplayer who has five tools: the abilities to run, throw, field, hit, and hit with power. Mays was one of those players who made baseball count to five.

Fleet-footed and devastating at the plate, Mays, who was born in 1931 in Westfield, Alabama, batted .302 lifetime, with 3,283 hits, 660 home runs, and 1,905 runs batted in; scored 2,062 runs; and won 12 Gold Gloves for his fielding, even though the Gold Glove wasn't invented yet when he broke in with the New York Giants in 1951.

Mays won the rookie of the year award and two Most Valuable Player awards. He won a batting title and stole 338 bases. In his younger days Mays dashed around the bases so swiftly, or ran so hard after fly balls, that his cap frequently flew off. He had trouble remembering names, so in greeting he often said, "Say, hey." That earned him the nickname "The Say-Hey Kid."

Chosen an all-star in 20 different years, Mays was technically a 24-time all-star because for a period of time in the middle of his career the big leagues played two all-star games per season.

Mays stood just five foot ten and weighed 170 pounds, but packed a surprising amount of power into his frame and seemed bigger. Perhaps that was because he was a larger-than-life player.

The list of Mays's baseball achievements is lengthy, but one single play has come to symbolize his career and talent. It took place on the largest of stages, in the World Series of 1954. That season was a rare one for the 1950s in the American League, in that the New York Yankees did not win the pennant. Although New York won 103 games, the Yankees were still smoked in the AL standings by the Cleveland Indians, who put together a stupendous year. The Indians finished eight games ahead with 111 victories.

In the National League the Giants, who typically had their own difficulties outlasting the Brooklyn Dodgers, had their turn. The Giants won 97 games, 5 more than the Dodgers. Cleveland's fabulous year made the Indians heavy favorites to win the World Series.

Game 1 was scheduled for September 29, 1954, at the Polo Grounds, home of the Giants. It was a tense ball game, and in the top of the eighth inning, with Cleveland at the plate, the score stood 2–2. Giants starter Sal "The Barber" Maglie, a right-hander, was still throwing. But Maglie was courting trouble. He walked

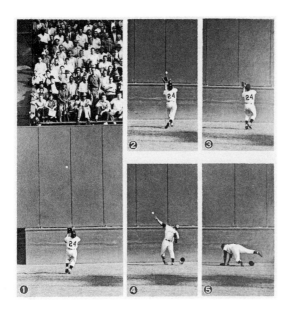

Although Willie Mays never made the claim, almost all other baseball observers and historians have labeled his over-the-shoulder catch in the 1954 World Series the greatest grab in the sport's history. Mays robbed Cleveland's Vic Wertz of a critical hit and turned the tide of the Series at its start. (NY Daily News Archive via Getty Images)

Larry Doby and then allowed a single to Al Rosen. This was the heart of the Cleveland order. Runners were at first and second when New York manager Leo Durocher called to the bullpen for reliever Don Liddle.

Once Liddle took his warm-ups, Cleveland's Vic Wertz stepped into the batter's box. Wertz, a left-handed swinger, was playing first base, and his bat was afire. He smacked four hits that day. The count was two balls and one strike, and Wertz liked the look of Liddle's next offering. He swung and connected. At first the ball seemed destined for outer space.

However, one thing the Polo Grounds had in centerfield where Mays roamed was space. At its deepest point the distance from home plate to the wall was 483 feet, a ridiculously long way. This incredible field gave Mays the belief that he could catch up with Wertz's shot on the open plain. Mays took off after the ball like a gazelle, pursuing a ball it seemed impossible to reach. Even worse, Mays had been playing fairly shallow, giving him an even longer chase than might ordinarily be involved.

The ball kept flying, and Mays's legs kept churning. With fans disturbed because Wertz's blast clearly meant that Cleveland was about to take the lead, Mays miraculously caught up to the ball on the warning track, his back to the field. He thrust the glove on his left hand up and made an over-the-shoulder grab, snaring the ball on the fly, with himself on the fly.

Jack Brickhouse, most famous in Chicago for his on-air presence for the Cubs, was handling the national broadcast for NBC and recognized the hit for the danger it presented right away.

"There's a long drive, way back at center field," Brickhouse called the shot off of Wertz's bat. "Way back, way back. It is a—Oh, my! Caught by Mays! Willie Mays just brought this crowd to its feet with a catch which must have been an optical illusion to a lot of people. Boy!"[1]

Then, aware of the circumstances, Mays enhanced the greatness of a play that in some quarters came to be known as "The Catch" by spinning around, and as his baseball cap naturally flew off the back of his head, zipping a throw back to the infield to try to hold the runners.

Since the base runners were confident Wertz's hit was going to fall, they were running at the same time Mays was running. When it became clear Mays had made the catch, Doby, the lead runner, had to scamper back to second base or risk being doubled off. There was an unlikely chance that what seconds earlier seemed like a possible game-winning hit could turn into a double play.

The ball was hit so deeply that Doby still had time to go back to second base, tag up, and make it to third. Rosen stayed put on first. The Giants got out of the inning without giving up a run. New York scored in the 10th inning to win the opener and go up 1–0 in games.

It has been said that Mays's dazzling play not only broke Cleveland's momentum, but took the starch out of the Indians. Although that is supposition, the Giants swept the favored Indians 4–0, in one of the biggest World Series upsets of all. Mays's brilliant catch may have been the catalyst.

"We had Hall of Famers on that pitching staff and we were swept in four games," said Al Lopez, the manager of the club, who is also a Hall of Famer.[2]

Watched by millions on television and with awestruck broadcasters giving it a push, Mays's play took on tremendous stature and has often been referred to as baseball's best catch. Mays, who had different standards, used to say that it wasn't even his own best catch, but just received more exposure on a bigger stage because it happened during the World Series.

Even as Mays jogged off the field alongside fellow Giants outfielder Monte Irvin, a Hall of Famer who was agog over the catch, Mays said, "I had it all the way."[3]

Few others have seen the catch as such a sure thing, crediting the 1954 Series grab as the best catch in the annals of the sport. At the least, it would be difficult to argue against this being Mays's most important catch.

NOTES

1. James S. Hirsch, *Willie Mays: The Life, the Legend*. New York: Scribner, 2010.
2. Terry Pluto, "It's Still Hard to Believe the Cleveland Indians Lost the 1954 World Series," *Cleveland Plain Dealer*, October 22, 2014.
3. Hirsch, *Willie Mays*.

FURTHER READING

Eisenstein, Charles. *Willie's Time: Baseball's Golden Age*. Champaign: Southern Illinois University Press, 2004.

Hirsch, James S. *Willie Mays: The Life, the Legend*. New York: Scribner, 2010.

Linge, Mary K. *Willie Mays: A Biography*. Westport, CT: Greenwood, 2005.

Madden, Bill. *1954: The Year Willie Mays and the First Generation of Black Superstars Changed Major League Baseball Forever*. Boston: Da Capo Press, 2014.

Mays, Willie, and Lou Sahadi. *Say Hey: The Autobiography of Willie Mays*. New York: Simon & Schuster, 1998.

#76 The Ice Bowl

How cold was it? That's the first question people ask when TV sportscasters refer back to the times nearly 50 years ago when nobody had heard the phrase "global warming" and instead talked about "the Ice Bowl." This was a case of frigid fingers.

The Ice Bowl, a label often used as a joke when people talk about being outdoors at an event too long in the winter, was actually a football game that was pretty much played in weather conditions equal to hanging out in a meat locker for three hours.

This was the 1967 National Football League championship game between the Green Bay Packers and the Dallas Cowboys. It doesn't take Albert Einstein's IQ to figure out where the game was played. Wisconsin in late December is not a vacation destination for people who like beaches.

The game was contested at Lambeau Field on December 31 (Happy New Year!) to determine which team would advance to the Super Bowl to play the American Football League champion. This was the second season of an interleague title play-off, and it was scheduled to be played at the Orange Bowl in Miami two weeks later. Presumably, the winner of this game would be thawed out by then.

These were very good football teams, and including coaches and front office personnel, 17 men involved with the two teams were later elected to the Pro Football Hall of Fame in Canton, Ohio.

Four divisions, named the Capitol, Century, Coastal, and Central, comprised the NFL that year. The first two were in the Eastern Conference and the latter two were in the Western Conference. Dallas won the Capitol Division with a 9–5 record and then beat the Cleveland Browns to advance to the league title game. The Packers won the Central Division with a 9–4–1 mark and topped the Los Angeles Rams to advance to meet Dallas.

As a rule, Green Bay was not only the smallest city in the league, but usually the coldest, and that dated back to the beginnings of the NFL in 1920. Still, no one

Nearly 40 years after The Ice Bowl was played in Green Bay between the host Packers and the Dallas Cowboys, the coldest game in NFL history lives on in lore. It was −13 degrees on the thermometer with a windchill reading of −36 on that December day in 1967. (AP Photo)

anticipated the meteorological phenomenon, with Green Bay having home-field advantage.

It truly was frosty on the last day of the year. Game-time temperature registered at −13 degrees, and the windchill factor was calculated at −48. Nearly a half century later the NFL still regards the Ice Bowl as the coldest game played in league history. A January 10, 1982, game between the Cincinnati Bengals and the San Diego Chargers at Riverfront Stadium in Cincinnati is ranked second. That is based on the −9 kickoff temperature, although the windchill was listed as −58.

"It was like the North Pole," Cowboys coach Tom Landry said years later of the Ice Bowl. "You can imagine the shock. I think we were in shock most of the game."[1]

Attendance at Lambeau was 50,826, and photographs of the scene indicate how warmly people were dressed. There were parkas galore, gloves on every hand, and hoods pulled up over hats; thick, foggy breath was being expelled as fans sought to follow the action. Legendary Green Bay coach Vince Lombardi wore an overcoat that did not button all of the way to the neck. Through the V space at his neck layers of sweatshirts and shirts could be glimpsed. Lombardi also wore a heavy fur hat with the earflaps down. It was so cold that the officials suspended the use of whistles to stop plays because the first time one was blown it stuck to the referee's lip and made it bleed.

Yet for all of those handicaps, when one might think the weather would be a distraction, or that football players might be busy rubbing their hands together instead of catching the ball, it was a cleanly played game.

Green Bay scored first on an 8-yard pass from quarterback Bart Starr to Boyd Dowler, and Don Chandler kicked the extra point for a 7–0 lead. The same combination connected on a 46-yard touchdown pass, with Chandler converting for a 14–0 lead. But Dallas came back to get on the scoreboard before halftime when George Andrie scooped up a Starr fumble and ran seven yards for a critical TD. Pat Villanueva made the extra point. With 32 seconds remaining in the second period, Villanueva booted a 21-yard field goal. So it was 14–10 Packers at the half.

There was no scoring in the third quarter, but the fourth period was action packed. The Cowboys took the lead for the first time when Dan Reeves tossed a 50-yard halfback option pass to Lance Rentzel. After Villanueva's kick Dallas was up 17–14. Now the hordes at Lambeau were not only shivering, they were worried.

It looked as if Reeves might be the hero, but he had his own problems.

"I got hit in the face and my facemask was gone," Reeves said. "I felt to see if any teeth were missing. I went to feel with my tongue and I couldn't get my tongue up there. Two teeth on the left-hand side had knocked through my upper lip. When I got my facemask fixed, I stood in front of the heater on the sidelines and blood came pouring out. I've got a scar where the tooth went through and when I shave, I have no feeling there. Every morning, I'm reminded of the Ice Bowl."[2]

There was less than five minutes to play when the Packers got the ball back on their own 32-yard line.

"In the huddle, Bart [Starr] just settled us all down," said Packer fullback Chuck Mercein. "He said, 'All right, this is it, let's get it done.' And I think everyone knew it was our last chance. The drive began."[3]

The Packers marched down the field and were positioned at the one yard line with 13 seconds to go when Starr rushed over for a TD on a quarterback sneak. Chandler added the extra point, and Green Bay won, 21–17.

Suddenly it wasn't quite so cold in Green Bay, Wisconsin, anymore. But the Packers also knew they had escaped.

"We felt elation, but more than that, we felt relief," said all-star guard Forrest Gregg. "We knew that the next game we played was the Super Bowl in Miami, and we knew that we would be in the sunshine."[4]

NOTES

1. Hank Gola, "The Ice Bowl between the Cowboys and Packers Is a Game Frozen in Time," *New York Daily News*, January 10, 2015.
2. Ibid.
3. Ibid.
4. Mike Shropshire, *The Ice Bowl* (New York: Donald I. Fine Books, 1997), 195.

FURTHER READING

Gruver, Ed. *The Ice Bowl: The Cold Truth about Football's Most Unforgettable Game.* New York: McBooks Press, 1998.

Gulbrandsen, Don. *Green Bay Packers: The Complete Illustrated History.* Minneapolis, MN: MVP Books, 2011.

Maraniss, David. *When Pride Still Mattered: A Life of Vince Lombardi.* New York: Simon & Schuster, 2000.

#77 Rocky Marciano, Undefeated Champion

They always come back. That is a boxing adage applied to great fighters who retire and then decide they miss the fight game and want to return. Sometimes they lose, and after recovering from a beating, decide they don't want to go out that way. Sometimes they retire as champion and decide maybe they were too hasty.

One of the few greats who walked away from boxing at the peak of his game was Rocky Marciano. Marciano is the only heavyweight champion to retire unbeaten. On September 21, 1955, he stopped challenger Archie Moore in the ninth round of a scheduled 15-round title bout at Yankee Stadium, and he never fought again.

Marciano walked away from the sport that made him rich and famous with a record of 49–0. Unlike so many big-time fighters over the generations, once Marciano quit he stayed retired. He was never seriously tempted to return to the ring. He was 32 years old when he bested Moore.

The champ did not make a rash call. He took time to ponder his circumstances and his future. Marciano announced his retirement on April 27, 1956. The slugger who excited the masses with his aggressive, hard-punching style hung up his gloves after making six title defenses.

Marciano was from an Italian family in Brockton, Massachusetts, a suburb of Boston. He was born in 1923 as Rocco Francis Marchegiano. Marciano first played baseball, then got into weightlifting, and then discovered the heavy bag. Punching the inanimate object led to him trying the real thing, punching other people, though not right away, although ultimately that worked out well for him. Marciano played some football, too. After working as a laborer in a variety of jobs, he served in the U.S. Army during World War II.

As an amateur boxer with a minimum of experience, Marciano won the Armed Forces championships in 1946. Before he gave up baseball for good, Marciano took a shot with a Chicago Cubs minor league team. He didn't last, and when he returned to Brockton headed to the gym.

Marciano's handlers, managers Al Weill and Allie Columbo, and trainer Charlie Goldman, taught him and guided him well from the time the five-foot-eleven slugger began his pro career in 1948. Marciano, who was 25 and didn't have a deep background in the sport, was hurried along by keeping busy. The Marciano team put one heavyweight after another in front of him, and Marciano either knocked them down or knocked them out. He was a devastating puncher with fists of steel even if he was not very large for the weight class. Although heavyweight had no weight limit, Marciano fought at under 200 pounds, at weights that today would classify him as a cruiserweight, a nonexistent class during his career.

The exercise was good for "The Rock." He stopped his first 16 opponents and by his 26th fight moved up in class against the difficult Roland La Starza. It was a close call for the man from Brockton. He prevailed in a split decision, though a loss at that point could have changed history.

Marciano ripped off 12 more wins and was considered a factor in the heavyweight division when he met former champion Joe Louis in a scheduled 10-rounder in Madison Square Garden in New York. Louis, who had the longest reign in history, was one of those ex-champs who came back when he shouldn't have after voluntarily surrendering the crown. Marciano took no pleasure in pummeling a man he admired, but stopped Louis on an eighth-round technical knockout for his 38th straight win.

Louis returned to the ring because he needed money. The IRS was pursuing him for back taxes. Marciano represented the biggest fight money option, and if he could top Marciano, Louis would have been in line for another title shot. Marciano did not know which Louis he was facing: the old, reliable champ, or someone over the hill.

Nearly a half century after his career ended, Rocky Marciano remains the only heavyweight champion to retire undefeated. He left the sport with a mark of 49–0 and he solidified his reputation by stopping former champ Joe Louis at Madison Square Garden in 1951. (AP Photo)

"Louis really had me worried in advance," Marciano said. "Everyone kept talking about the wonderful shape he was in during his training. He was knocking down sparring partners right and left."[1]

It was an illusion, though. Louis could not stand up to Marciano's power.

On September 23, 1952, Marciano got the chance he had been waiting for. He was the challenger for Jersey Joe Walcott's heavyweight title at Municipal Stadium in Philadelphia.

Walcott, who ordinarily was a gentleman, for some reason insulted Marciano before the bout. It was not his best strategy.

"Marciano is an amateur," Walcott said. "He wouldn't have qualified for Joe Louis' bum of the month tour. I'll knock him out."[2]

The bout was scheduled for 15 rounds, but Marciano stopped Walcott in the 13th to lift the crown. The fight was later chosen as the best of the year by *The Ring* magazine. That made The Rock 43–0.

A rematch at Chicago Stadium was hardly a replay. Marciano, heavily favored after what experts had seen the first time around, blasted Walcott out in one round. A left hook and a right cross put Walcott down, which was satisfying to the champ, but not a combination he believed would end the fight. By the time the referee reached an eight-count, Marciano realized he was going to win with a minimum of sweat.

"This guy's not getting up," he told himself.[3] Walcott did, but alas for him, it was at the equivalent of a count of 11, when 10 terminated the bout.

Marciano held the prized title for three years, stopping Walcott in the first round of a rematch, La Starza, ex-champ Ezzard Charles twice, Don Cockell, and finally Moore. Marciano retired with his 49–0 mark, 43 of the victories by knock-out. He is the first and last heavyweight champ to retire unbeaten.

Actually, for one very short period of time in 1959 Marciano toyed with the idea of a comeback. He trained for four months but realized fighting again was not the right move.

Marciano did some acting and was a referee for wrestling bouts.

On August 31, 1969, the day before his 46th birthday, Marciano was traveling in a small plane in Iowa that crashed into a field. He was killed on impact. Rocky Marciano was the partial inspiration, in name and otherwise, for the *Rocky* movie and its sequels.

On the 60th anniversary of Marciano's stopping Jersey Joe to win the heavyweight championship, the city of Brockton unveiled a 20-foot-tall, two-ton statue of him throwing a punch. The statue stands on the lawn at Brockton High School.

NOTES

1. Russell Sullivan, *Rocky Marciano: The Rock of His Times* (Urbana: University of Illinois Press, 2002), 99.
2. Ibid., 121.
3. Ibid., 132.

FURTHER READING

Skehan, Everett M. *Rocky Marciano: Biography of a First Son*. Boston: Houghton Mifflin Harcourt, 1977.
Sullivan, Russell. *Rocky Marciano: The Rock of His Times*. Urbana: University of Illinois Press, 2005.

#78 A. J. Foyt

As the 20th century drew to an end and a new millennium beckoned, newspapers, magazines, broadcasters, and anyone who got the notion selected "bests" lists. Some observers disagreed with various lists, but there was no outcry, only agreement, when A. J. Foyt was anointed the automobile racing world's driver of the century.

An irascible Texan who not only wished everyone in his way would get out of his way, but often possessed the wherewithal to shove them out of the way, Foyt was a pedal-to-the-metal guy in cars of any shape or design. But he was best known for his dominance of IndyCar racing.

That wasn't true when Anthony Joseph Foyt Jr. was a young driver, though, growing up in the Houston area, where he was learning and trying to make it on circuits with cars his father designed. He got his start racing midget cars in Texas when he was 18 in 1953.

The partnership with his father didn't work immediately, and Foyt stewed when others teased him. He was not the type to let affronts roll off his back.

"If I heard, 'Whatsamatter, kid, can't your daddy build race cars? once I heard it a thousand times,'" Foyt wrote in an autobiography. "If I could pick one thing that made me a winner, that would be it. I wonder how many kids have made it in life—I mean really got to the top because some SOB made fun of their daddy. If I had been big enough, I would have punched out every one of them right there on the spot."[1]

In 1977 Foyt became the first driver to win the Indianapolis 500 four times. He was the face of the world's most famous automobile race, and even as he passed 80 years of age in 2015 he remained an icon of the sport. Foyt won the big one at the Indianapolis Motor Speedway in 1961, 1964, 1967, and 1977.

Two others have equaled his record of four victories since then: Al Unser and Rick Mears.

In all, Foyt won 67 IndyCar events, but did not confine his racing to the insect-shaped, low-slung, buzzing cars. He tried just about every kind of race there was and did well wherever he drove. Most racing fans likely don't even know that Foyt ever entered stock car races, but he won seven NASCAR races and scored top-10 placings 36 times.

One of those victories was at the Daytona 500, the stock-car world's most prestigious event. Foyt also won the 24 Hours of Daytona and the 24 Hours of Le Mans. He was versatile as well as fast and is the only driver to record triumphs in all four events.

A. J. Foyt became the first driver to win the world's most prestigious automobile race four times in 1977. Many experts consider Foyt the greatest racer in history. (AP Photo)

Between 1960 and 1979 Foyt won 12 U.S. Auto Club championships, and he holds the record for most USAC wins, 159. He also won two IROC (International Race of Champions) titles. Just put Foyt in a car and turn him loose, and there was a pretty good chance he would take the checkered flag.

Foyt made his first appearance at the 500 in May 1958. He was so anxious to get in his car, so excited to be at the Indianapolis Motor Speedway, that he showed up early. He beat both his car and his owner to the track, and when he went to pick up his pass he was told he was too early and to come back later. He had to wait two more days, but when Foyt got inside the sprawling track, he drank in the sights at the famous oval and everything that made the Speedway special.

"The first thing I did was walk up and down through the garage area, very slowly," he said, "trying to take in everything, but at the same time trying not to look too impressed. But I was so impressed I almost couldn't stand it."[2]

Foyt had to pay some dues, but he had a natural affinity for Indy. He also discovered early on that simply being one of the 33 drivers in the field carried power. Indianapolis was the one auto race every year that everyone watched, whether they were a fan of automobile racing, a sports fan, or neither. It was a happening.

"It was amazing what driving in the Indianapolis 500 did for my image," Foyt said. "I was asked to speak at women's club luncheons, both Houston newspapers interviewed me, the television stations sent cameramen over, and I even got fan mail. I heard from relatives I never knew I had. I wonder what it would have been like if I had won."[3]

He found out soon enough with that first triumph in 1961.

If it had been up to Foyt alone, he probably never would have climbed out of the driver's seat. He competed in the Indianapolis 500 for 35 straight years.

Foyt is a member of five motorsports halls of fame, but despite all of his accomplishments, he is most renowned for his victories and staying power in Indianapolis. He has remained active in the sport by funding cars under the auspices of A. J. Foyt Enterprises and entering them in a variety of automobile racing disciplines, but he always makes it to Indianapolis for Memorial Day Weekend.

Another reason Foyt remains so popular is his durability. During the height of his career, Foyt did not always have it easy. He was involved in at least four major crashes and incurred a mix of serious injuries. He always battled back from the broken bones and setbacks, however, and fans admired his gumption.

In 2011, for the 100th anniversary of the Indianapolis 500, Speedway officials chose the fancy-haired businessman Donald Trump to drive the pace car at the start of the race. The backlash was severe, and Trump withdrew. The second time around the choice to drive the pace car for the special anniversary was Foyt, the person many believed should have been chosen from the get-go.

"I never knew officially who was going to drive it," Foyt said. "I knew they said Donald Trump, but, you know No. 2 can wind up winning the race and I've done that before. So if I out-dueled him, I'm very happy about it. I'll be leading the race again is all I can say.

"I'm just very honored I can do something back for the speedway because the speedway is what made A. J. Foyt and my whole racing career."[4]

NOTES

1. A. J. Foyt and William Neely, *A.J.: My Life as America's Greatest Car Driver* (New York: Times Books, 1983), 3.

2. Ibid., 64.

3. Ibid., 80.

4. "Foyt Agrees to Drive Pace Car for Indianapolis 500," *Associated Press*, May 15, 2011.

FURTHER READING

Arute, Jack. *Tales from the Indianapolis 500*. New York: Sports Publishing, 2012.
Libby, Bill. *A.J. Foyt Racing Champion*. New York: Putnam, 1978.

#79 Bobby Thomson Wins the Pennant

The home run that gave the New York Giants the National League pennant in 1951 was called "the shot heard around the world."

Given the fact that Major League Baseball was grounded in the United States in 1951, that was a bit of an exaggeration, but it certainly was a loud blast heard around the sport. The shocking homer to decide the NL representative for the World Series came off the bat of outfielder Bobby Thomson after his Giants stunned the Brooklyn Dodgers by catching and passing them in the standings in the closing days of the season.

The Dodgers built a big early lead over the summer in the pennant race. On August 10 Brooklyn led New York by 12½ games in the standings. The Dodgers seemed to have things sewn up. But the Giants kept coming and coming, gaining a game here and a game there throughout a superb month of September. As late as September 20, the Dodgers were in first by four and one-half games.

New York won its final seven straight games and actually forced Brooklyn to win its last game to tie for first. At the end of the regular season the archrivals owned the same record, 96–58. To determine the National League representative in the World Series, a tie-breaker was needed, and the teams engaged in a three-game playoff series.

It was a best-two-out-of-three series, with the Dodgers winning a coin flip to obtain game 1 at home in Ebbetts Field. The payback was that the Giants would host games 2 and 3, if necessary, at the Polo Grounds. The Yankees had clinched the American League pennant and were waiting to see who their opponent would be.

The strategy backfired on Brooklyn when the Giants won game 1, 3–1. Jim Hearn got the win, besting Ralph Branca. Thomson hit a home run, his 31st of the season. The play-off statistics counted in regular-season totals.

Already angered because they hadn't sealed the pennant earlier, and smarting from the home defeat, the Dodgers jumped on New York pitching early and blasted the Giants 10–0 in Game 2. In a bold choice, Brooklyn started rookie Clem Labine, who shut down the Giants on six hits as his teammates slugged four home runs, including one by Jackie Robinson.

So the play-off was going the distance. Game 3 was played on October 3. New York started Sal Maglie and Brooklyn countered with Don Newcombe. The Dodgers scored one run in the first inning, and no one else scored until the Giants scored one run in the seventh. Dodgers tacked on three runs in the eighth inning. Things appeared bleak for the Giants, trailing 4–1 when they came to bat in the bottom of the ninth inning.

Singles by Alvin Dark and Don Mueller and a double by Whitey Lockman helped New York creep closer. Brooklyn manager Chuck Dressen made the fatal choice of going to his bullpen for Branca, who had had only one day's rest after his game 1 start.

The righty swinging Thomson was due up. That year Thomson batted .293 with 32 homers and 101 runs batted in. It took just two pitches for Thomson's waving bat to connect with a Branca pitch. It was 0–1, Branca ahead, after the first one. It would be the last time for a long while. The ball soared to left field for the game-winning smash, producing a 5–4 result that left Dodger fans devastated and Giants fans ecstatic.

Larry Jansen won his 23rd game of the season. Branca lost his 12th.

The sudden clout, on the heels of the stunning September comeback, was labeled "The

Labeled "the shot heard around the world" by announcer Russ Hodges, New York Giants outfielder Bobby Thomson's legendary home-run swat in the ninth inning of an October 3, 1951, game against the Brooklyn Dodgers won his team the National League pennant. (AP Photo)

Miracle at Coogan's Bluff," the headline on famed sports columnist Red Smith's piece about the game. Smith continued: "The art of fiction is dead. Reality has strangled invention."[1]

Fans at the Polo Grounds hadn't been so happy since New Year's Eve. Winners like Thomson drank champagne. Losers like Branca trudged off the field to the visiting clubhouse.

Thomson knew he got good wood on the ball. "Right away after I hit it," he said, "I thought it was a home run. Going around the bases, I could hardly breathe. I was starting to hyperventilate."[2]

Some rank Thomson's homer as the most significant in major league history. At the least it rates in the top three, with Bill Mazeroski's bottom-of-the-ninth shot to win the 1960 World Series for the Pittsburgh Pirates and Babe Ruth's called shot for the Yankees against the Cubs in the World Series of 1932.

"Bobby Thomson will always hold a special place in our game for hitting one of the signature home runs in baseball history," said Commissioner Bud Selig when Thomson died in 2010.[3]

Thomson played 15 seasons, hit 264 home runs, and made three all-star teams. Branca won 88 games in a 12-year career.

The blow forever linked Thomson the hitter with Branca the pitcher as hero and goat. They eventually were in demand at sports collectors shows, together, made many appearances, and remained friends until Thomson's death.

In 2003 reports were issued that the Giants had been guilty of sign stealing, and Thomson admitted as much to Branca. He did say at other times that he did not know what pitch was coming. The revelation did not disrupt the men's friendship, but it seemed to ease Branca's mind.

"It wasn't illegal, it was just immoral," Branca said. "I don't care whether he had the sign or not on that pitch. It's irrelevant. He hit a good pitch. But I would like to know: without the sign stealing, could they have won?"

Thomson's actual hit was immortalized in the radio call by Giants announcer Russ Hodges, who breathlessly informed listeners, "The Giants win the pennant. The Giants win the pennant."[4]

It was hard to believe after the 2–13 dark days of spring and the 50–22 brilliant days of summer and autumn, but yes, the Giants had won the pennant.

NOTES

1. Red Smith, "The Miracle of Coogan's Bluff," *New York Herald Tribune*, October 4, 1951.

2. John Schlegel, "Thomson Hit Famous '51 Playoff Homer, Dies," MLB.com, August 17, 2010, http://m.mlb.com/news/article/13548902/.

3. Ibid.

4. "Private Talk a Cleansing for Branca, Thomson," *Associated Press*, November 19, 2003.

FURTHER READING

Branca, Ralph, and David Ritz. *A Moment in Time: An American Story of Baseball, Heartbreak, and Grace*. New York: Scribner, 2011.

Prager, Joshua. *The Echoing Green: The Untold Story of Bobby Thomson, Ralph Branca, and the Shot Heard Round the World*. New York: Vintage Books, 2008.

Robinson, Ray. *The Home Run Heard 'Round the World: The Dramatic Story of the 1951 Giants-Dodgers Pennant Race*. New York: Dover Publications, 2011.

#80 Red Sox at Last

There used to be a saying tinged with despair for baseball fans growing up in New England. It went like this: The Red Sox will win the World Series in my lifetime.

Those were the believers talking, the live-and-die with the Boston Red Sox fans in the six-state area. The Red Sox owned those millions of hearts, but had done nothing to earn them.

The American League was formed in 1901. Boston was a charter member. When the first World Series was played, Boston met Pittsburgh and the Bostonians won. Over the first two decades of the 20th century the Red Sox were just about the best team around. By 1918 the Boston Americans had won five world championships.

There was no reason to predict the imminent demise of the franchise's on-field health, but for the next 86 years the Red Sox did not win another World Series. Sometimes the team won pennants, only to frustrate fans by coming close and losing in the play-offs against the best of the National League in heartbreaking ways.

Things started to go bad in 1919, and they got worse soon after when despised owner Harry Frazee shipped Babe Ruth to the New York Yankees. The Red Sox knew what a special property Ruth was because he had been a brilliant starting pitcher, and in 1919, when he eased into hitting full time, he led the NL in home runs. That didn't matter. Off to New York went Ruth in exchange for cash and some ballplayers whom nobody remembers. Between his power hitting and popularity, Ruth launched the Yankees' dynasty.

After the triumph in the 1918 Series, the Red Sox did not win another pennant until 1946. They won another one in 1967, another in 1975, and another in 1986. Flags waved over Fenway Park, but championship rings were never sized.

By 2004 the Red Sox drought had reached 86 years, and that was long enough that the old adage no longer applied. Many fans could no longer hope that they would see a Boston champ in their lifetimes, especially those who had died.

The Red Sox appeared to be potential pennant-winners in 2004, but in the end their nemesis, the Yankees, caught them and won the American League's Eastern Division with 101 victories, three more than Boston. The four AL teams advancing to the play-offs were the Red Sox, Yankees, Anaheim Angels, and Minnesota Twins. New York topped Minnesota in one division series, and Boston topped the Angels in the other.

This set up an American League Championship Series between the Yankees and Red Sox, and the best-of-seven encounter shaped up as a swift one once New York powered to a 3–0 lead. Even worse, the Yankees won game 3, 19–8, while pounding Boston pitching for 22 hits. Fans at Fenway Park were almost frozen in disappointment and assumed game 4 would be a formality.

What followed was the greatest comeback in major league history. Boston did what no other team ever has. The Red Sox bounced back from the 3–0 deficit to win four consecutive games and capture a play-off series.

The Red Sox won game 4 by a 6–4 score in Boston. Game 5 was tense, but the Red Sox won again, 5–4. Designated hitter David Ortiz homered in both games. The season was on the line at Yankee Stadium on October 19 in game 6, and starting right-hander Curt Schilling, who had joined Boston in free agency for just such a big-game moment, was the hurler.

However, Schilling was injured and not supposed to be playing. But he wasn't sitting this one out. A torn right ankle sheath needed between-game care, stitches, and stabilizing. When Schilling threw, some of the stitching tore loose, and his ankle began to bleed. Television cameras spotted the blood coming through his sock as Schilling pitched on and beat the Yankees 4–2. Guts and determination carried Schilling through in a remarkable performance for the ages that tied the ACLS 3–3.

The setting for game 7 could not have been more dramatic. There was a packed Yankee Stadium with 56,129 spectators for the October 20 contest. Yankee fans had no doubt their team would beat the Red Sox, because they always had in the past when they needed to do it. Red Sox fans feared their hearts would be broken once more.

They needn't have worried. This time the fates chose Boston. The Red Sox bashed out 13 hits, Derek Lowe cruised on the mound, and Boston won 10–3. Hungry as they were for the ultimate prize, Boston fans so reveled in this rousing destruction of the Yankees in the comeback stretch that they might have been satisfied with that turn.

But finally, this was one year the Red Sox didn't have to settle for almosts. Boston swept the St. Louis Cardinals in the World Series, brushing the National League champs aside as effortlessly as if they were swatting flies, as slugger Manny Ramirez won the Series' Most Valuable Player Award.

The World Series trophy was headed to Boston, where the smiles did not fade from baseball fans' faces for a year and a celebratory parade virtually overwhelmed the city. It was estimated that 3.2 million people crammed the seven-mile parade route.

"All is Forgiven," read one banner. "Now we just have to wait for the other six signs of the Apocalypse," said another. And others said, "Thank You."[1]

The perpetrators of the Red Sox miracle were impressed by the devotion fans showed, coming out to stand and wave and cheer on a cold and damp day.

"And the people didn't even care," pitcher hero Derek Lowe said. "They've waited a long time. You'll never see a parade like that with so many people, no matter what sport or what city."[2]

The 2004 Boston Red Sox ended an 86-year world championship drought when they captured the World Series, putting an end to what some referred to as a longstanding "Curse of the Bambino." That phrase was affixed to the team after Babe Ruth was ill-advisedly traded to the New York Yankees before the 1920 season. (AP Photo)

Mercifully, Boston baseball fans did not have to wait another 86 years for a glimpse of a fresh World Series trophy. The Red Sox won it all again in 2007 and 2013.

NOTES

1. Charles Krupa, "Millions Turn Out for Red Sox Victory Parade," *Associated Press*, October 29, 2004.

2. Ibid.

FURTHER READING

The Boston Globe, *Finally! The Red Sox Are Champions after 86 Years*. Chicago: Triumph Books, 2004.

O'Nan, Stewart, and Stephen King. *Faithful: Two Boston Red Sox Fans Chronicle the Historic 2004 Season*. New York: Scribner, 2005.

Prime, Jim. *Amazing Tales from the 2004 Boston Red Sox Dugout: The Greatest Stories from a Championship Team.* New York: Sports Publishing, 2014.

Wisnia, Saul. *Miracle at Fenway: The Inside Story of the Boston Red Sox 2004 Championship Season.* New York: St. Martin's Press, 2014.

#81 Dan Jansen's Challenges

The greatest speed skater in the world couldn't stay on his feet. It was as if he were a child learning the sport in need of double runners. The Olympic Games always have the power to impress and inspire, but Dan Jansen's story was unique, at times heartrending.

Born in 1965 in West Allis, Wisconsin, one of the few U.S. speed skating meccas, Jansen turned to the sport at a young age, encouraged by his sister Jane. He made his first American Olympic team in 1984. While he was still learning and improving, Jansen came close to winning a medal that year with a fourth-place finish in the 500 meters.

The speed skating oval at Sarajevo was outdoors. Not long before Jansen's 500 it began to snow. While more recent converts to speed skating might think that weird, the Games went on, and Jansen didn't mind at all because he had skated in snow many times.

Jansen held third for a while during the competition and was beginning to think he might claim the bronze medal. In the end he was surpassed, but as an 18-year-old mostly just absorbing the Olympic experience, he was content with his finish.

"I wasn't crushed," he said. "There would be other medal chances for Dan Jansen."[1]

By the next go-around, the 1988 Winter Olympics in Canada, the experienced Jansen seemed at the peak of his game. That year, leading up to the Games in February, Jansen became the world champion sprint racer. In Calgary he was favored to win gold medals in the 500 meters and 1,000 meters.

Dan and Jane were two of nine children, but these two were particularly close. Dan was the youngest and Jane was five years older. Just before Jansen was scheduled to race in the 500 meters on the oval, he learned that Jane was dying of leukemia. He telephoned her, but she could not respond to his voice. She died within hours at age 27.

Emotional and distraught, Jansen questioned himself about going on, whether he should skate or withdraw. He thought it over and chose to compete. But he admitted his mind was a mess. His discussions with himself in no way resembled focused preparation.

"Jane is dead," Jansen later recounted how his thoughts collided. "Should I be here? Jane is dead. What does everybody think about me skating? Jane is dead. How hard must this be for my parents, watching me on TV and facing the prospect of what must be absolutely the worst thing in life, burying a child? Jane is dead."[2]

His mother told him to race. Jansen then had to go out and compete in the biggest race of his life. As he sped out of his start, blades slashing, Jansen fell down heading into the first turn. That ruined his 500 chances.

"The only thing I remember about being at the starting line is that I wasn't focused on the race, a fatal flaw, to say the least," Jansen said. "To a person, my whole family, those at the Games and those watching at home,

For years the United States' finest speed skater, Dan Jansen's failure to win a gold medal in two Olympics because he fell in races wrung the heartstrings of American sports fans. An inspirational victory in 1994 at last gave him gold. (AP Photo/Ron Heflin)

said I looked like a ghost, all the color drained from my face. Everything seemed to be happening as if I was in a dream, and I just couldn't get myself to concentrate."[3]

Jansen had four days to regroup before the 1,000 meters. He said thousands of people from Wisconsin signed and sent him a 96-foot banner of support. He was leading the 1,000 at the 800-meter mark, but the ice got the better of him again and he fell a second time, falling right out of the medals.

The tragedy of his sister dying on the day Jansen was trying to fulfill his Olympic dreams and the misfortune that befell him on the ice made Jansen a sympathetic figure to Americans. He said he hated being that guy identified by the sad connection to his sister's death and falling down. Up until then he had been known as one of the best speed skaters in the world. Now he was known for something very different.

Trying to put his disappointment behind him, Jansen kept skating for the U.S. team and remained a major figure in the world rankings. Prior to the next Winter Games in Albertville, France, in 1992, Jansen's third, he set a world record in the 500 meters. That was still his event, and he was a serious contender at 1,000 meters.

Yet he once again came home empty-handed, with a best finish of fourth. His Olympic career seemed jinxed. The Games seemed to be the only ice he could not conquer. He later second-guessed himself for possibly tapering his training too soon, and he also had the bad luck of having rain fall on his race on the outdoor track accompanied by 50-degree temperatures. Jansen, who described himself as a "long-glide" skater, said the conditions were more conducive for choppier striders.

"My performance absolutely devastated me," Jansen said. "I went into semi-seclusion, thereby dooming myself for the 1,000 three days later."[4]

Almost as bad, Jansen knew he was being discussed as someone who choked in big races. Unlike in the previous Games, when Jane died, there was no built-in explanation for his failure in these races, when he should have been medaling.

"Knowing that people felt that way about me hurt," he said. "It hurt a lot."[5]

Before the 1994 Winter Games in Lillehammer, Norway, Jansen again won the world sprint championship. He knew this was going to be his final Olympics, and after all of these years and tries he still had not won a medal. Once again he was entered in the 500 and the 1,000.

Americans had watched and suffered alongside Jansen for many years, almost physically blanching when something occurred to leave him short of a medal. In Norway he finished eighth in the 500. It was all coming to an end in a hurry. He had one last chance in the 1,000.

Racing well, Jansen put all his speed into the blades. Between 600 and 700 meters Jansen slipped slightly, balancing himself on his left hand. Spectators passed through an "Oh, no" moment. But he righted himself, skated through the finish, and captured the gold medal in world-record time.

As he skated a slow victory lap, Jansen, who had gotten married and had a daughter in the intervening years, carried his year-old baby in his arms, a little girl named Jane. Those who knew the Dan Jansen story shed tears.

NOTES

1. Dan Jansen and Jack McCallum, *Full Circle: An Olympic Champion Shares His Breakthrough Story* (New York: Villard Books, 1994), 82–83.

2. Ibid., 113.
3. Ibid., 114–115.
4. Ibid., 159.
5. Ibid., 161.

FURTHER READING

Jansen, Dan. *Full Circle: An Olympic Champion Shares His Breakthrough Story*. New York: Villard, 1994.

#82 The Fosbury Flop

The Olympic motto is "faster, higher, stronger." The "higher" part of that principle can be narrowed down to the high jump in track and field. The high jump is the original jumping event in sport.

Contestants approach a bar held up by stanchions at increasing heights while getting a running start.

Research indicates that the first time anyone recorded someone attempting to jump over a bar was in Scotland in the 19th century. The high jump was included as part of the track and field program in Athens in 1896 in the first modern Olympics. The U.S. contingent swept the event. Ellery Clark won the first gold medal, and teammates James Connolly and Robert Garrett finished in a tie for second; both were awarded silver medals.

For a time, beginning in 1900 there was also a standing high jump, in which no run-up to the bar was permitted. Ray Ewry of the United States won the first gold medal in that event, in Paris. Ewry dominated the event in the early years of the Games, though it was discontinued in 1912.

Over the decades the method thought to be best for jumping over the bar varied. There were a scissors style, a Western roll style, and a straddle style, though essentially they were all generally approaching the bar head on, even if different takeoff legs (inner or outer) were employed. Others began approaching the bar from an angle.

The first seven-foot high jump was recorded by American Charlie Dumas in 1956. In one of the event's great rivalries, American John Thomas and Russian Valeri Brumel exchanged the world record and went head-to-head at numerous competitions in the early 1960s. In 1960 Brumel took silver and Thomas took bronze in Rome. In 1964 Brumel took gold and Thomas took silver in Tokyo.

When American Dick Fosbury erupted on the scene no one could believe the way he cleared the high-jump bar. Fosbury changed the way high jumpers competed. He replaced the scissors kick with a backwards leap. (AP Photo/Sal J. Veder)

Thomas set a world record of 7 feet, 3¾ inches, and then Brumel broke it, notching a leap of 7 feet, 5¾ inches.

The individual who most transformed the high jump event was American Dick Fosbury, in 1968, demonstrating a technique no jumper had ever thought of using before. Fosbury set the world agog when he dispensed completely with high kicking in any form. He ran up to the bar and twisted his body so that his head, shoulders, and back cleared the height first instead of his legs.

Fosbury, who was born in Oregon in 1947, attended Oregon State University. He was already a high jumper in high school and sought out a new technique for improving his jumping. The scientific advantage to the Fosbury style was that it thrust more body mass over the bar first on the jump.

The reason behind Fosbury's innovation was not complicated. He was lousy at the straddle method, in which the leaper went over the bar head first, but facing down, and had to lift his trailing legs over. As a high school sophomore Fosbury, who liked high jumping, at first couldn't clear the five-foot mark to qualify in dual meets. If he didn't find a way to improve, he was not going to be long for the high-jump world. His method was pretty much born out of desperation.

Fosbury gradually improved as he juggled techniques, and it was not until his senior year of high school that he devoted his efforts to the style that came to be named for him. It was very simple. If Fosbuy went over the bar head first with his face to the sky, he could go higher. This was unorthodox in the extreme. It looked peculiar to anyone who saw Fosbury high jump, but there was no rule against his style.

His high school coaches finally backed off trying to make him practice the standard style because of his continual improvement when doing it his way. They left him alone after he cleared 6 feet 3 inches and then improved to 6 feet 5½ inches, a jump that placed him second in the state meet. Still, astonished reporters outdid themselves in sarcastic comments about the way Fosbury looked as he jumped.

Fosbury faced the same prejudice against the "flop" when he first went out for the team at Oregon State. However, roughly the same pattern emerged. The more Fosbury worked out with the flop, the better he got. After he topped six feet ten inches nobody ever bothered urging him to do what everybody else was doing. Instead, others who saw Fosbury began emulating him, or at least trying to do so. The six foot ten was a new school record, and track people around the country began to notice Fosbury, who only a few years earlier couldn't clear a bar a foot and a half lower.

When Fosbury appeared on the cover of *Track and Field News*, the bible of the sport, in early 1968, he knew he had arrived. It was noted that the lanky lad from Oregon had discovered a new way to defy gravity. This man from nowhere won the NCAA championships.

Ed Caruthers, another top high jumper, first encountered Fosbury at the college championships and gaped at his style. His first thought was that the flop was "a goofball kind of thing."[1]

Fosbury emerged on top at the U.S. Olympic Trials for the 1968 Summer Olympics, leaping seven feet one inch. A second Trials was conducted that year at altitude, and Fosbury was one of the three U.S. qualifiers, at seven feet three inches. There seemed to be no ceiling on his steadily higher jumps.

"Sometimes I see movies," Fosbury said of his own prowess, "and I really wonder how I do it."[2]

Fosbury was ranked 61st in the world a year before the Olympics, and he had never competed internationally until he walked into the stadium in Mexico City. When he took his first jumps, backward, so to speak, fans laughed at him. But their attitude soon changed.

"Psychologically, I was extremely benefited by the actions of the crowd, who began to notice me," Fosbury said. "I felt their focus, and I was able to channel that attention into a high level of intensity, raising but trying to control my level of excitement."[3]

Fosbury won the high jump gold medal, clearing a height of 7 feet 4¼ inches. It was a coming out party for the Fosbury Flop. Fosbury's stupendous rate of improvement and his gold medal conquest changed the mind-set of the world. By the time of the Olympics in Munich in 1972, in less than one four-year Olympiad cycle roughly three-quarters of Olympians were using the flop. Almost all top-class high jumpers in the modern era high jump use Fosbury's style.

Dick Fosbury changed the high jump world for good.

NOTES

1. Richard Hoffer, *Something in the Air: American Passion and Defiance in the 1988 Mexico City Olympics* (New York: Free Press Books, 2009), 208.
2. Joe Durso, "Fearless Fosbury Flops to Glory," *New York Times*, October 20, 1968.
3. Simon Burnton, "Dick Fosbury Introduces the Flop," *The Guardian*, May 8, 2012.

FURTHER READING

Farrow, Damian, and Justin Kemp. *Why Dick Fosbury Flopped and Answers to Other Big Sporting Questions*. Crows Nest, NSW: Allen & Unwin, 2004.
Hoffer, Richard. *Something in the Air: American Passion and Defiance in the 1988 Mexico City Olympics*. New York: Free Press Books, 2009.

#83 Win One for the Gipper

What began as a Notre Dame football rallying cry to honor a dead comrade has been said and used so many times it has become a cliché. But the story behind the phrase, to some lost over time because it occurred so long ago, is one of inspiration and above all of proud lore for the Fighting Irish.

Although he perished in a plane crash at the height of his fame in 1931, Knute Rockne's name lives on in college football history for the brilliance of his teams and his role in establishing Notre Dame in the football firmament.

Rockne was born in Voss, Norway, in 1888, but his family moved to Chicago when the boy was five. He picked up football as a youth, but also competed in track. Rockne's family did not come from wealth, and he worked to save money to obtain a college education. He was 22 when he enrolled as a student at Notre Dame, about 90 miles away.

As a player Rockne was involved in the first regular use of the forward pass. He graduated from Notre Dame in 1914 with plans to become a pharmacist. That idea did not last long. Rockne leapt at the chance to stay in football as a coach at Notre Dame. That sojourn as an assistant covered the years 1914–1917, but Rockne played some professional ball in Akron and in Massillon, Ohio, at the same time.

Rockne, his jaw as pugnacious as his tackling despite not being a large man, took over as Notre Dame's head coach in 1918. It was Rockne who put the program on the map, Rockne who built Notre Dame into a player on the national scene, and Rockne whose glory days with

George Gipper was the first renowned Notre Dame football star, but the shifty all-American halfback died at 25 from an infection. Lore states that on his death bed Gipp told coach Knute Rockne (pictured) to exhort his players to victory by invoking his name at a critical time. (Library of Congress)

the Fighting Irish laid the foundation for the Notre Dame of today. The tradition began with "The Rock."

Coach Rockne led Notre Dame football for 13 seasons, between 1918 and 1930. His teams won 105 games, lost 12, and tied 5. His winning percentage was .881, the best of all time. In five of those seasons Notre Dame finished undefeated, including his last two years. Under Rockne the Irish won four national championships.

Those who wonder how Notre Dame ever became serious about football need only look at Rockne's record and examine the things he said.

"Four years of football are calculated to breed in the average man more of the ingredients of success in life than almost any academic course he takes," Rockne said.[1]

A number of Rockne's players earned "A" grades on the gridiron. One of these young men, whose style and flair differed from many, was a halfback named George Gipp. Gipp was born in Michigan in 1895. At six feet and 175 pounds, he was a star running back and punter and became Notre Dame's first all-American player. He was chosen for Walter Camp's all-American squad shortly before Gipp died.

Gipp came to Notre Dame with the intention of playing baseball for the school (and planned to try out for the Chicago Cubs after graduation). With no high school football background, he was wooed to the football team by Rockne, who saw him on campus drop-kicking the ball 60 yards or more. Gipp led the team in running and passing for three straight years.

Gipp was a party animal who did not especially like adhering to training rules. He was the type of guy who would skip out on curfew for a good time. Late in the 1920 season, Gipp contracted pneumonia and an infection. Legend has it that while hospitalized, knowing he was not going to survive, he talked frankly to Rockne on his deathbed.

The Gipp speech that is in the Notre Dame archives and has been used in movies, with minor variations, goes like this: "I've got to go, Rock. It's all right. I'm not afraid. Some time, Rock, when the team is up against it, when things are wrong and the breaks are beating the boys, ask them to go in there with all they've got and just win one for the Gipper. I don't know where I'll be then, Rock, but I'll know about it and I'll be happy."[2]

Those were supposedly Gipp's dying words. He passed away at age 25 on December 14, 1920. That was real enough, but skeptics believe Gipp never said any such thing and that Rockne made up the whole conversation. However, in 1928, when Notre Dame was playing inspiring football against an Army team that was undefeated, Rockne, a master speechmaker when revving up his squads, pulled out the story at halftime and urged the Irish "to win one for the Gipper." Notre Dame was trailing 6–0 when the speech was delivered, but won 12–6.

Numerous magazine and newspaper stories over the years have questioned the reality of the Rockne-Gipp exchange. Few of them did so more vigorously than the *Philadelphia City Paper* in July 1995, which engaged in an energetic attempt to debunk several aspects of Gipp's life. As is widely known, the Gipp character did say those words in the 1940 film *Knute Rockne, All-American*. In that movie, Ronald Reagan played George Gipp, speaking to Rockne, played by Pat O'Brien. Many years later, when he was running for president, Reagan regularly worked the message into his speeches or campaign appearances. For the rest of his life, Reagan made periodic use of the Gipper speech.

While doubters can be piled neck deep, this is exactly the type of thing movie-goers and sports fans alike love to hear and want to believe.

The Rock was the king of his profession when he died in a plane crash at age 43 on March 31, 1931. He was admired and known throughout the country, and his death made front-page news everywhere.

His memory is honored in monuments and statues in several places. A Rockne statue was erected in Voss, his place of birth in Norway, even though the country has almost no interest in football. Another Rockne statue stands outside Notre Dame Stadium.

Rockne is the one who said "Win one for the Gipper," but Ronald Reagan did much to perpetuate the phrase in the common lexicon. If there were doubts about the authenticity of the message, the spirit was understood very clearly.

NOTES

1. Bob Carter, "Sport Century Biography: Knute Rockne Was Notre Dame's Master Motivator," ESPN Classic, https://espn.go.com/classic/biography/s/Rockne_Knute .html.

2. University of Notre Dame Athletic Archives, UND.com, http://archives.nd.edu /research/texts/rocknespeech.htm.

FURTHER READING

Chelland, Patrick. *One for the Gipper: George Gipp, Knute Rockne, and Notre Dame Football*. New York: Skyhorse Publishing, 2010.

Lefebvre, Jim. *Coach for a Nation: The Life and Times of Knute Rockne*. Minneapolis, MN: Great Day Press, 2015.

Robinson, Ray. *Rockne of Notre Dame: The Making of a Football Legend*. New York: Oxford University Press, 2002.

#84 Kerri Strug

Olympic gymnastics took place in Athens in 1896, but until offbeat events like club juggling were shed over the next 30 years, it did not really begin to resemble the competitions fans watched every four years. And it was not until the early 1950s that the program took on the characteristics of the present-day program.

Gymnastics, as the present-day fan knows the sport, made a huge breakthrough with the televised accomplishments of Nadia Comaneci, a Romanian who won the hearts of the world by standing out at the 1976 Summer Games in Montreal.

Comaneci, age 14, memorably won three gold medals in those Games, but imprinted her performances on the public's mind by earning a perfect 10 score in the uneven bars. That was the first perfect 10 awarded by judges in Olympic gymnastic history. The attention garnered by the score elevated the profile of women's gymnastics in a way that no other event ever had.

From that Olympics onward, gymnastics became one of the popular showcase sports of the Games. While the Soviet Union and eastern bloc countries dominated for a time, the United States sent forth athletes who burst into world prominence periodically, increasing the popularity of the sport among Americans.

In 1984 diminutive Mary Lou Retton, who stood four foot nine and weighed 93 pounds, stole the hearts of U.S. fans by winning the gold medal in the all-around, as well as two silver and two bronze medals in other events.

By 1996 the United States had a team that could go beyond setting forth one star competitor. The Americans had team depth and were anxious to shove the Soviet Union off the top rung of the medals podium, a place occupied by that country for all but one Games since 1952.

Bela Karolyi, who had coached Comaneci to her golds, defected to the United States in 1981 and emerged as the top club coach in the country. Several of the Olympians were under his influence. The U.S. squad of Amanda Borden, Amy Chow, Dominique Dawes, Shannon Miller, Dominique Moceanu, Jaycie Phelps, and Kerri Strug was poised to dethrone the Soviets. Miller was the reigning U.S. champion, but both Dominiques had also won national championships.

The group was nicknamed "The Magnificent Seven," but would not be quite as magnificent if it only won the silver medal. The Americans were hungry for team gold. The world watched. As scores were recorded and the battle for the title remained close, it was apparent that the United States needed a good showing from Kerri Strug in the all-around.

The vault loomed, and Strug faced a difficult situation. She was competing on a badly sprained ankle that barely allowed her to stand. But it was imperative that on her dismount she land cleanly. That involved landing hard, with her full body weight, on the ankle.

Strug had been in gymnastics since she was three, and her first competition was at age eight while living in Tucson, Arizona. Her older sister Lisa had already been competing. Kerri showed so much promise that she moved to Houston, Texas, to train under Karolyi in 1991. In 1992, when Strug was only 14, she was part of the U.S. squad that won the bronze medal in team gymnastics in the Barcelona Games.

Karolyi officially retired after the 1992 competition, so Strug switched to the Dynamo Gymnastics Club in Edmond, Oklahoma, under Steve Nunno. Before the

Overcoming injury at the most critical moment of competition, Kerri Strug's dramatic performance in the vault at the 1996 Summer Olympics in Atlanta gave the United States the team gold medal in gymnastics. Strug had to be carried to the podium by coach Bela Karolyi to receive her medal. (AP Photo/John Gaps III)

1996 Games, Karolyi came out of retirement, and Strug trained under him before the Atlanta meet.

The Americans led the team standings going into the vault, but several weak performances opened the door for a Russian comeback if Strug faltered. Strug was the last American in the rotation, and if she did not succeed cleanly, they might fall out of first place. An excellent Strug vault would clinch the gold medal. So the team's hopes fell on her shoulders.

Karolyi delivered a needed pep talk to Strug before she started her second vault. She asked him how badly the team needed her to do well, and he informed her that the gold medal was within reach, but it was up to her.

"I said to her, 'We need it, we need it,'" said Karolyi. "She said, 'All right, all right.'"[1]

Strug limped to the starting place for her run-up.

"When Dom [Moceanu] fell the first time, I thought, 'No, I can't believe it. She never falls,'" Strug said. "Then she fell a second time, and it was like, 'Forget this. This is a nightmare.' My heart was beating like crazy, knowing that it was now up to me. I thought, 'This is it, Kerri. You've done this vault a thousand times, so just go out and do it.'"[2]

Through her smile at the judges Strug gritted her teeth and then ran for the apparatus. She spun in the air, landed hard on her ankle, kept smiling, but also kept her balance. Strug stuck the landing, fans roared, and the points scored were just what the Americans needed to capture the gold medal in team gymnastics for the first time. The second she could, Strug began hopping on her good foot.

Right after her landing, however, Strug tumbled to her knees and had to be helped from the floor. The injury was bad enough to keep her out of the individual all-around competition, and she was replaced by a teammate.

When the medals were presented, Karolyi, who had often been described as a big bear of a man, scooped up Strug in his arms and carried her to the podium to collect her team gold medal.

The gritty, come-through performance made Strug a national sensation. After the Games Strug made the rounds of television shows, appeared on the cover of *Sports Illustrated*, and met President Bill Clinton. The Magnificent Seven even starred on the cover of a Wheaties box, the cereal makers deciding that they were definitely their kind of athletes.

NOTES

1. George Vecsey, "A Hurting Kerri Strug Wasn't Ready to Stop Yet," *New York Times*, July 24, 1996.

2. Rick Weinberg, "Kerri Strug Fights Off Pain, Helps U.S. Win Gold," ESPN.go.com, July 19, 2004.

FURTHER READING

Strug, Kerri, and John P. Lopez. *Landing on My Feet: A Diary of Dreams*. Kansas City, MO: Andrews McMeel Publishing, 1997.

#85 Loyola's 1963 Iron Men

Prejudice was still pervasive in early 1960s America and the Loyola University men's basketball team did not have to travel far from its home base in Chicago to understand that it still infected sport.

The Ramblers made the mistake of scheduling away games in Louisiana and Houston. On those two eye-opening trips African American players were taunted with racial insults, and they could not stay in a segregated hotel. That was all the proof needed to remind them that skin color in their home country still precluded equal rights.

However, during the 1962–1963 college basketball season Loyola found out that it was more equal than almost anyone else on the court. During these times of upheaval, when Dr. Martin Luther King Jr. was leading marches protesting discrimination against African Americans, Loyola featured four black men in the starting lineup.

Coach George Ireland was more of a risk-taker than most, indifferent to the pressures of the times, when it was considered unacceptable to use more than two African Americans in the five starting slots or to ever play more than three at a time.

Ireland knew that four of his five best players were African Americans, so he started them. For anybody who didn't like it, tough. For the first half of the season, seven of Ireland's top eight players were black. In late December, at a holiday tournament in Utah, the Ramblers became the first major NCAA school to play five black players on the court at once. Unfortunately, at midseason two players became academically ineligible and a third quit the team, so Loyola's depth was not its strong point.

Although never ranked number 1 in the polls that season, Loyola was voted second. An independent program that did not play a conference schedule, the Ramblers needed an at-large invitation to the NCAA tournament, and they got it.

Loyola's style was characterized by superb rebounding and a dominant fast break. Captain Jerry Harkness, who would earn all-American status; Les Hunter, who later played in the NBA; Ron Miller; Vic Rouse; and Johnny Egan were the mainstays, the iron men starters whom Ireland relied on and hated to replace on the floor.

"God put all of the pieces together," Miller said years later.[1]

Playing hard and fast, Loyola had the capacity to overpower teams. By the end of the regular season, following a 21–0 start, the squad's record was 24–2. Five games stood between the Ramblers and a national crown. Teams like defending

In a surprising triumph, Loyola University of Chicago won the 1963 NCAA men's basketball title. Coach George Ireland used four African American starters at a time when most fans considered that to be unacceptable liberalism. In the championship overtime victory over Cincinnati, the five starters played the entire 45 minutes. (AP Photo)

national champion Cincinnati, Duke, Mississippi State, Illinois, Bowling Green, and Oregon State were in the way.

Loyola opened NCAA tournament play against Tennessee Tech, a lesser seed, and recorded an astonishing result. The Ramblers thoroughly demolished Tech, 111–42, the largest margin of victory in NCAA tournament history. The five Loyola starters scored between 17 and 21 points each. The next assignment in the Mideast Region semifinals was facing Mississippi State.

For a few years in the late 1950s and early 1960s, Mississippi State eclipsed Kentucky in the Southeastern Conference. However, with Mississippi's strict segregationist laws, any time the Wildcats qualified for the NCAA tournament, the school declined the invitation because it was not legal for Mississippi teams to compete on the same court as a team with African Americans.

State's players and coaches wanted to go, but they couldn't. At the start of the 1962–1963 season players were told that if they qualified for the NCAA, this time they would go. But when they learned that the all-white Wildcats would have to meet a team so densely populated with African American opponents, the governor and legislators demanded that Mississippi State stay home.

Mississippi State president Dean Colvard took a stand, declaring that the team could go. Legislators sought an injunction to prevent the team from leaving the state for the game in Michigan. Colvard and others in authority made themselves scarce to avoid being served with the injunction, and the players and coaches sneaked across the state border.

In a game that drew national attention because of the racial associations, Loyola prevailed, 61–51. The game was well-played, and there were no racial overtones. Whites and blacks shook hands in front of flashbulbs bursting. The friendly nature of the competition between players and the way Mississippi State fought back against arcane laws led to change on campus and was a step along the civil rights trail. The Loyola-Mississippi State contest eventually was labeled "The game of change" because of its significance.

At that point in the season, with so much at stake, Ireland hardly ever took his iron men out of a game.

"Unless you fouled out, you were playing the whole game," Egan said.[2]

Loyola topped its in-state rival, Illinois, 79–64, to advance to the Final Four, and then handily topped Duke, 94–75, to reach the championship game against Cincinnati, which also had three black starters.

The Ramblers shot poorly, were out-rebounded, and fell behind by 15 points in the second half. They looked like doomed losers to the Bearcats. Things seemed so bleak Harkness remembered thinking, "Please let us make it close."[3]

Abruptly, Loyola began to do all of the things right that the team had executed flawlessly all season. Ireland used no bench, sticking with the five starters for every minute.

With time running out, Loyola shocked the Bearcats by tying the game and sending it into overtime. At the end Loyola was the winner, 60–58, a claimant to the NCAA crown for the first and so far only time. Ireland, Harkness, Hunter, Rouse, Egan, and Miller did it their way. The winning basket came on a tip-in at the buzzer by the late Rouse, who overcame childhood illness but died young.

"Rouse was born with polio," Harkness said. "He wore braces on his legs when he was young. He was told he would never walk. Can you believe the determination and drive? He deserved the last basket."[4]

All of the African American starters (Egan was the one white in the group) had been rejected and faced discrimination, and this was their payback. A few years later Texas Western made noise by defeating all-white Kentucky with an all

African American starting lineup, and history remembers the Miners better as pioneers.

But as the 50th anniversary of Loyola's championship came around in 2013, considerable attention was devoted to the accomplishment. Books were written about the team. President Barack Obama invited the living members of the squad to the White House. Loyola became the first team inducted as a group into the College Basketball Hall of Fame in Kansas City. The Ramblers were better re-membered every day.

NOTES

1. Lew Freedman, "Forever Loyola," *Basketball Times*, March, 2003.
2. Ibid.
3. Ibid.
4. Ibid.

FURTHER READING

Freedman, Lew. *Becoming Iron Men: The Story of the 1963 Loyola Ramblers*. Lubbock: Texas Tech University Press, 2014.
Freedman, Lew. "Loyola Recalls Barrier-Breaking Moment Long Forgotten, Ignored." *Basketball Times*, USBWA, http://www.sportswriters.net/usbwa/awards/writing/2008/column.html (accessed May 6, 2015).
Lenehan, Michael. *Ramblers: Loyola Chicago—The Team That Changed the Color of College Basketball*. Evanston, IL: Agate Midway, 2013.

#86 The Death of Len Bias

A two-time all-American forward for the University of Maryland, and a two-time Atlantic Coast Conference player of the year, Len Bias was one of the premier col-lege basketball players of the mid-1980s.

At six foot eight, he was lithe and powerful with a marvelous shooting touch, and was predicted to become an all-star professional. Taken in the first round (sec-ond pick overall) by the Boston Celtics, Bias was supposed to be a cornerstone of the rebuilding franchise.

That never happened. Two days after the June 17, 1986, draft, the basketball and sports worlds and the world at large were shocked to hear that Bias had died, and drugs were supposed to be the cause.

Bias was from Landover, Maryland, and stayed close to home for college. He was a great jumper, which allowed him to compete for rebounds with taller centers, and he was a tremendous shooter who could hit from outside. When the Terrapins needed him to score, he did so.

Thirty years ago it was common for even the best athletes to stay in college through their senior year rather than making themselves eligible early for the NBA draft. In the modern era Bias would possibly have come out to the NBA after his sophomore year, and certainly by his junior year.

Instead, Bias played right through his college eligibility. He was on the cusp of his big score, about to negotiate what would obviously have been a multiyear, multi-million-dollar contract with the Celtics. He was also talking about a $1.6 million endorsement deal with a Reebok-related company.

Just two days after being drafted as the No. 2 overall selection in the NBA draft by the Boston Celtics in 1986, Maryland's Len Bias died from a cocaine overdose in a dorm room. The untimely demise of one of college basketball's best players spiked a promising career, stunted the improvement of the Celtics, and focused unwanted attention on the Maryland program. (AP Photo)

The feeling is that Bias went out to celebrate his good fortune and overdosed on cocaine. There were some who said that he must have tasted cocaine for the first time that night and that this error in judgment cost him. Others said they had taken cocaine with Bias over a period of time. An autopsy showed that Bias's overdose on cocaine had led to fatal cardiac arrhythmia.

Bias had flown to Boston with his father for the Reebok conversations. When he got back to Maryland he went to his dorm room on the University of Maryland campus, ate dinner with friends, and at 2:00 a.m. drove to a friend's gathering. He was back home within the hour. That is when Bias and his friends began taking cocaine.

Awake and conversing with Terrapin teammate Terry Long at around 6:30 a.m., Bias was struck by a seizure. A 911 call was made, and he was rushed to the hospital. He was pronounced dead at 8:55 a.m. Doctors attributed Bias's death to cocaine aggravating his heart. The ripple effects from Bias's death were powerful. The timing harmed the Boston Celtics team for years, since they lost a potential franchise player with no replacement. But that was the least of the bad effects. Bias was only 22 and lost his life. The University of Maryland basketball program's image was tarnished. So was the image of the University of Maryland.

Terrapin players Long and David Gregg were suspended from the team and indicted for possession of cocaine and obstruction of justice. Brian Tribble, a close friend of Bias's, was indicted for possession of cocaine and possession of cocaine with intent to sell. After charges were dropped against Long and Gregg, Tribble was also accused of obstruction. Tribble went to trial and was acquitted of all charges. However, in 1990, following a sting operation, he pled guilty to unrelated drug dealing charges.

The Bias incident led to university and national soul-searching. Bias had been a superb athlete, and people wondered how he could play at such a high level if he was on drugs. The murkiness of how often Bias had taken cocaine was an issue in the case, never resolved. Few believed that the night of his death was the first time Bias had ever taken cocaine, but not everyone thought he was a regular user, either.

The consequences at Maryland were wide-ranging. Despite being on campus for four years, Bias had not been on track to graduate because he was 21 credits short. This brought out an entirely different set of issues about whether Maryland was taking its educational responsibilities seriously.

Eventually athletic director Dick Dull resigned. So did basketball coach Lefty Driesell, although he did not want to and believed he was a scapegoat for something that was not within his control. The Bias Driesell knew could run fast and jump high. He didn't take cocaine.

"There was nothing I did wrong—what did I do wrong?" Driesell said. "Leonard Bias was a great kid. I loved him. But he was not under my jurisdiction in any shape or form. It wasn't anything I had something to do with. He made a bad decision to try cocaine for the first time."[1]

A grand jury looked into the circumstances of Bias's death, and in 1987 its report criticized the athletic department, the admissions office, and campus police.

Bias had been nationally famous for playing basketball. He became nationally famous for being dead. The high-profile nature of the Bias case, in such proximity to the nation's capital, brought calls for action to crack down even harder on drug users and dealers. Bias's death persuaded Congress to enact an expansion of drug laws giving law enforcement agencies the power to indict suppliers of drugs for reckless homicide. The law kicks in when a user overdoses.

In states where suppliers have been prosecuted for providing drugs that led to deaths, the indictments are called "Len Bias cases."

Len Bias's death also affected his relatives, but it energized his mother Lonise, who became an anti-drug-use activist and makes speeches on the topic. Her target audience seems to be teenagers. Just don't get involved with drugs, she tells them. Look what happened to my son, and my family, she says.

"I am the legacy that was left behind," Lonise Bias has said.[2]

In October 2014 a man with a far more complicated legacy than most was invited into the University of Maryland Athletics Hall of Fame. Len Bias was given a standing ovation when his name was read. He could not be present to accept the honor.

NOTES

1. Michael Weinreb, "The Day Innocence Died," ESPN.com, June 20, 2008, http://sports.espn.go.com/espn/eticket/story?page=bias.
2. Ibid.

FURTHER READING

Cole, Lewis. *Never Too Young to Die: The Death of Len Bias*. New York: Pantheon, 1989.
Harmon, F. Martin. *Charles "Lefty" Driesell: A Basketball Legend*. Macon, GA: Mercer University Press, 2014.
Smith, C. Fraser. *Lenny, Lefty, and the Chancellor: The Len Bias Tragedy and the Search for Reform in Big Time College Basketball*. Baltimore, MD: Bancroft Press, 2002.

#87 Peyton the Great

There has never been a moment's doubt since he entered the National Football League that Peyton Manning is a great quarterback. Not for one minute has that been in dispute. It merely has been a question of degree: How great is he?

Is Peyton Manning the greatest quarterback of all time? Maybe. Will Peyton Manning retire with the best statistics of all time? Maybe. Manning is one of those athletes who made a mark as a rookie and has matured into a finer athlete with experience.

Yet even Manning fans would not have predicted his achievements in the 2013 season, the unbelievable numbers he recorded for the Denver Broncos. Never has any great quarterback rivaled this one-season wonder who astounded football fans.

Manning grew up in New Orleans, where his father, Archie Manning, had been the quarterback for the New Orleans Saints, and where his younger brother Eli would also emerge as a star quarterback.

Peyton grew to six foot five and 230 pounds. He was an all-American for the University of Tennessee and the number 1 draft pick of the Indianapolis Colts in 1998. He has been an NFL starter since he was 22 and built most of his NFL legend while playing for the Colts. That includes leading the club to the 2007 Super Bowl championship, when he was the Most Valuable Player. The Colts beat the Chicago Bears, 29–17.

"Peyton is a tremendous player, a great leader," said Indianapolis coach Tony Dungy. "He prepares, he works, does everything you can do to win games and lead your team. This guy is a Hall of Fame player and one of the greatest ever to play."[1]

Manning had been waiting a long time for a Super Bowl ring, and now he had one.

"It's hard to put into words," said Manning, who completed 25 of 38 passes for 247 yards, with one touchdown. "I'm proud to be part of this team. We stuck together, won this game for our leader, Tony Dungy."[2]

A 14-time Pro Bowl player, Manning has won a record five Most Valuable Player awards, in 2003, 2004, 2008, 2009, and 2013. Jim Brown, Johnny Unitas, and Brett Favre have each won three times.

Manning believed he would play in Indianapolis forever, but after 14 seasons the Colts chose to part ways with him. The split revolved around Manning's health at the same time that he was due millions of dollars from his contract. Manning coped with a series of surgeries on his neck that could have jeopardized his future in the sport, and whether he could continue playing could not be determined before a large payment was due to him and before the next NFL draft.

The result was that Manning joined the Denver Broncos starting with the 2012 season. He proved healthy enough to play at his old level and continue leading a team into contention for the play-offs and Super Bowl. Manning was Manning.

However, in his second season with Denver, Manning more resembled all three Mannings rolled into one. He was like a Manning who never missed his morning Wheaties and a Manning who was 15 years younger.

While leading the Broncos to a Super Bowl appearance, Manning put together the greatest single season any quarterback has compiled in NFL history. It

Future Hall of Fame quarterback Peyton Manning is en route to setting the major NFL passing records through his long career with the Indianapolis Colts and Denver Broncos. He had a record-setting season for the ages in 2013. (AP Photo/David J. Phillip)

was almost as if his game-by-game numbers were kept track of by a pinball machine.

During that 2013 season Manning threw a league-record 55 touchdown passes (against 10 interceptions) and topped out at 5,477 yards gained passing in the regular season. He led the league in pass attempts with 659 and in completions with 440.

Manning's 55 touchdowns eclipsed Tom Brady's old record of 50, thrown in 2007 for New England. Third on that list was Manning, with 49 from the 2004 season. The yardage total was an all-time record, too. Manning has thrown for 4,000 yards or more in a season 14 times.

Manning's career total for passing yards, 69,691, ranks him second behind Favre's 71,838 record total, within easy reach for Manning during his next full, healthy season. After 2013 positioned him, Manning became the all-time league record-holder with 530 touchdown passes. He passed Favre's record of 508 in mid-October 2014.

"I'm very humbled and I'm very honored," Manning said. "I certainly think about how grateful I am for all the teammates and coaches that I've played with and played for throughout my career, not only here in Denver—in Indianapolis and all the people that have helped me along the way."[3]

But there's more. In the middle of Manning's weekly onslaught on defensive backs, he did something else quite special. On September 6, in a Broncos game against the Baltimore Ravens, Manning threw seven touchdown passes in one game, tying an NFL record.

The record dates to Sid Luckman in 1943, and the seven-in-one game has been done a handful of other times. Adrian Burk, George Blanda, Y. A. Tittle, and Joe Kapp are the other members of the seven-touchdown club.

"He's phenomenal. To continue to come out every year and put that kind of performance on for us, it's amazing," said Denver end Julius Thomas.[4]

Only two months later the Philadelphia Eagles' QB Nick Foles also threw for seven touchdowns in a game.

"He's the best that ever played the game," said Broncos receiver Demmaryis Thomas of Manning. "He made me a better player when he first came in [to Denver]. He changed up some things on how we run routes and watch film, and just sitting in the film room and seeing what he does I think made everybody a better player around him."[5]

In a glittering career, 2013 was a signature season. What Manning did seemed impossible, especially for a 37-year-old player.

NOTES

1. "Super Bowl XLI Recap," NFL.com, February 4, 2007, http://www.nfl.com/superbowl/history/recap/sbxli.
2. Ibid.
3. "Peyton First with Seven TDs Since '69," ESPN.go.com, September 6, 2013, http://espn.go.com/nfl/story/_/id/9639918/peyton-manning-denver-broncos-ties-nfl-record-seven-touchdown-passes-baltimore-ravens.
4. "Top Quotes from Peyton Manning's Record Night," *Denver Post*, October 19.
5. Ibid.

FURTHER READING

Freedman, Lew. *Peyton Manning: A Biography*. Santa Barbara, CA: Greenwood Press, 2009.

Manning, Peyton, and Archie Manning, with John Underwood. *Manning*. New York: Harper Entertainment, 2001.

#88 Bob Beamon's Leap

In one of the most electrifying and unanticipated boosts to a track and field record in one gulp, Bob Beamon increased the world long-jump record by so much that he covered his face in disbelief when told the distance.

The scene was Mexico City, during the Summer Olympics of 1968, and the American long jumper, long-legged and with great spring, was a favorite for the gold medal. The native of Jamaica from Queens, New York, had come on strong in the event and had a personal best of 27 feet 4 inches on his résumé.

That was a mark very close to the existing world record of 27 feet 4¾ inches, set by the Soviet Union's Igor Ter-Ovanesyan in 1967. For the last few years

On October 18, 1968, Bob Beamon, a star for the University of Texas at El Paso, unleashed what was considered a miraculous long jump of 29 feet, 2½ inches, setting a new world record for the gold medal at the Mexico City Olympics. The stupendous leap remained the world mark for nearly 23 years. (AP Photo)

Ter-Ovanesyan and the U.S. athlete Ralph Boston had been trading the record back and forth, with upgrades in tiny increments. Since 1960 Boston had set six world marks and Ter-Ovanesyan two.

Beamon had overcome several disadvantages to reach this point in his career and felt that just maybe he could even break the world record on a good day. He was raised by a grandmother from the age of eight, told that his mother had died. He did not learn until later that his mother gave him to his grandmother because his father was abusive to his mom and threatened to kill the child if he lived with them.

The boy had his own problems as he grew up in a tough neighborhood pock-marked by violence and drug use. He was a handful at school and was almost expelled. He was a fatherless kid running with a bad crowd.

Beamon definitely had the hops. He set a national high school record in the triple jump before heading west to the University of Texas at El Paso, an out-of-the-way track team. Things turned sour when Beamon refused to compete in a meet against Brigham Young University because he claimed the school was racist. Beamon was suspended from his team for this.

Boston, the first person to break 27 feet in the event, won a gold medal in the long jump in 1960 in Rome, and a silver medal in Tokyo in 1964. After Beamon was ousted from his team, Boston took the younger man under his wing and tutored him even though Boston was still active. Leading up to the 1968 Games Beamon—who would only be 22 at the time of the Olympic event—won 22 out of 23 meets. He qualified at the U.S. Trials and ironically, so did Boston, his mentor.

During the preliminary rounds in Mexico, Beamon almost lost out, fouling on his first two rounds. But he straightened out his form and advanced. The clutch come-through put him in the medal round against Boston, Ter-Ovanesyan, and England's Lynn Davies, who won gold in 1964.

With that group in the mix, some figured it would take a world-record jump just to win, but when it came to that event, an inch here or an inch there usually was enough.

When Beamon unleashed THE jump, Boston, who knew Beamon's form and capabilities well, turned to Davies and said, "That's over 28 feet."[1] Davies disagreed, mostly because it seemed unlikely.

That was why the thousands of witnesses in the Olympic Stadium, the millions watching on TV, and the competitors near the pit went into collective shock when Beamon's mark was posted. Beamon ran down the approach ramp, pushed off, landed well, and bounded off the sand feeling pretty good about his jump. The mark was posted in meters, 8.90, and Beamon had no idea how that translated to feet and inches.

The officials knew a world record was at stake and wanted to be certain in verifying. They reverted to extra measurement, a delay that seemed to take forever. From the flurry of action, Beamon sensed he might have set a world record, but he didn't know the metric translation. Beamon asked Boston, and Boston told him it was 29 feet. "No, wait," Boston added. He knew his math. "It's more than 29 feet."[2]

When the distance of the jump was announced as 29 feet 2½ inches, Beamon could not even process the information. It was like a verbal typographical error. The verified distance was a new world by more than 21 inches, nearly two feet. When the news penetrated his brain, Beamon was so astounded that he fell to his knees, covered his face with his hands, and gradually tried to cope with the realization he had done the impossible.

The information sank in slowly, and Boston and another U.S. jumper, Charlie Mays, tried to hold Beamon up as he began to sink to the ground. Beamon also said, "I want to vomit. Tell me I'm not dreaming."[3]

What Beamon had done was probably the single most astonishing performance in track and field history. It was amazing to the witnesses, officials, the jumpers— and to Beamon, who never contemplated a jump like that.

Beamon's effort completely demoralized some of the other competitors who had also been dreaming of gold. They knew they couldn't compete. Davies even suggested he couldn't even try anymore.

"We can't go on," he said to Boston. "We'll look silly." Davies turned to Beamon and said, "You have destroyed this event." Ter-Ovaneysan felt the same. "Ralph," he said, also to Boston, "compared to this jump, we are as children."[4]

The news was so stunning that Beamon's body was almost vibrating. Soon after the jump the weather changed and some rain came down. That made it difficult for others in the flight to challenge Beamon for first, as if they were likely to anyway. None of the other favorites or comparative unknowns in the event topped 27 feet. Boston took third for a bronze medal to complete his collection of long-jump medals. Davies and Ter-Ovaneysan were shut out.

That pinnacle of Beamon's career virtually ended his track career. It might be said that he never came back down to Earth. Eventually he earned a college degree from Adelphi on Long Island, and he has spent much of his adulthood working with youths. He is a member of American track halls of fame.

Beamon's jump was so far out there that over time, when other athletic feats bordered on the impossible they were referred to as "Beamonesque." The world record lasted for 23 years, until American Mike Powell surpassed it with a leap of 29 feet 4⅜ inches in 1991. Powell's jump has been the record for longer than Beamon's.

But more than 45 years later, Beamon's leap remains the Olympic record, a goal waiting to be matched by someone from somewhere.

NOTES

1. Richard Hoffer, *Something in the Air: American Passion and Defiance in the 1968 Mexico City Olympics* (New York: Free Press, 2009), 185.
2. Ibid., 186.
3. Ibid.
4. Ibid., 187.

FURTHER READING

Beamon, Bob. *The Man Who Could Fly: The Bob Beamon Story*. Columbus, MS: Genesis Press, 1999.

#89 Roger Maris Tops the Babe

There was only one Babe Ruth, with his devastating swing and power and his flamboyant personality, but from the moment the Bambino hit 60 home runs for the Murderers Row New York Yankees, there were contenders hoping to remove his name from that record in the books.

As the home run became more of a weapon following the Deadball Era, more sluggers came along who could clout with the best of them. Jimmie Foxx hit 58 home runs one year. So did Hank Greenberg. But for the 34 seasons between 1927 and 1961, no one could etch his name alongside the Babe's in the 60-homer category.

In 1961 the linear descendants of Ruth's Yankees, a group of Yankees a couple of generations younger, possessed the same goods as the '27 Yanks. They had power at every position and leaders in the batter's box that could smash home runs with anyone.

As the season unfolded it was obvious that New York was the best team not only in the American League, but in all of baseball. But it was also an exciting season because center fielder Mickey Mantle, the heir to the throne as the power king of the franchise, and his right-field partner Roger Maris were hitting at a spectacular rate.

Mantle was a switch-hitter. Maris swung from the left side. Mantle was the better known of the two, already a New York institution. He broke into the majors in 1951, overlapping with Joe DiMaggio for the final season of Joltin' Joe's career. By 1961 Mantle was a superstar who could run, throw, field, and hit with power, an all-around star. A decade into his career Mantle owned two Most Valuable Player awards and had won four AL home-run titles. In 1956 he slammed 52 home runs.

At that point in baseball history, the 50-homer club was much smaller than it is today. Anyone who made it to 50 was seen as a threat to some day chase down Ruth's 60.

Maris was younger. He broke into the majors in 1957 with the Cleveland Indians and had also played for the Kansas City Athletics. Just how good Maris could be was unclear when he became a Yankee in 1960. Pretty good, it turned out. Maris smashed 39 home runs, drove in 112 runs, and won the Most Valuable Player award.

He was hardly an unknown when the 1961 season opened, though nobody was predicting a milestone season. But as the Yankees began sprinting away from the field in the standings, Maris and Mantle, nicknamed "The M&M Boys," began pulling away from the other top home-run hitters.

They took turns slamming four-baggers, and fans and sportswriters noticed. People did the math and realized they were ahead of Ruth's record-setting pace. It was thrilling to have two guys in the hunt, and they were teammates to boot. One thing that was usually overlooked when people pointed out that a hitter was ahead of Ruth at a certain point in time was how Ruth got to 60. He concluded August with 43 homers and then recorded a smashing September, belting 17. That was the trick that separated the pretenders and contenders from Ruth. They had to labor hard after Labor Day.

Baseball had also been altered somewhat since Ruth's heyday. In 1961 the American League expanded from 8 to 10 teams, and to balance the schedule teams played 162 games instead of the previous 154. Ruth set his mark in a 154-game schedule. During the 1961 season, when Maris and Mantle seemed to have a chance to pass Ruth, Commissioner Ford Frick made a controversial announcement that discombobulated the race.

Ford declared that if a player did not match or exceed Ruth's 60 homers in 154 games and subsequently topped the total, it would carry an asterisk in the record books. Ford was pilloried and accused of making the decision because he was an old friend of Ruth's who had even ghostwritten his biography.

As August 1961 ended, Maris already had 51 homers. That took some of the heat off his September challenge. Meanwhile Mantle, who had been hovering in the chase, began incurring injuries and illnesses. He fell behind, though he eventually did post his career-best 54 homers.

Alone out front, the pressure built on Maris. Rather than be hailed as much as he should have been, he was insulted by fans, who said he was no Babe Ruth. He was haunted by the asterisk threat. Sportswriters picked at him. He dreaded suiting up some days, and his hair began falling out from the stress.

It took 34 years, but a slugger surpassed Babe Ruth's single-season home-run record of 60 blasts. Another Yankee outfielder and left-handed hitter, Roger Maris, accomplished the feat with 61 homers in 1961. (AP Photo)

As days of the regular season dwindled, Maris hit enough home runs to stay within striking distance of the Babe, but did not pass him within the 154-game limit set by Frick. After 154 games Maris had 58 homers. He tied Ruth on September 26, 1961, clouting his 60th shot off Baltimore's Jack Fisher. The record-setting homer (and Frick notwithstanding, it was always viewed as the standard) was a blast off of Boston's Tracy Stallard on October 1.

The big blow for Maris came at Yankee Stadium on a 2–0 count.

"I was ready and connected," Maris said. "As soon as I hit it, I knew it was No. 61."[1]

Maris was a naturally quiet man who did not seek the limelight. He was thrust into his front-and-center position by this feat, but he didn't relish the attention.

Maris won his second MVP award that season, but never hit more than 33 homers in a year again. He died young, at age 51, of cancer, but his record endured. The new single-season home-run record belonged to Roger Maris, and he kept it for 37 years, until the 1998 season when Mark McGwire and Sammy Sosa passed him. It was not Ruth those guys were chasing, but Maris.

"I always come across as being bitter. I'm not bitter," Maris said years after setting the record. "People were very reluctant to give me any credit. I thought hitting 60 home runs was something. But everyone shied off. Why, I don't know. Maybe I wasn't the chosen one, but I was the one who got the record."[2]

Maris retired with 275 lifetime homers. The season of '61 when he hit 61 was the only year he led a league in home runs.

NOTES

1. Lew Freedman, *Going Yard: The Everything Home Run Book* (Chicago: Triumph Books, 2011), 164.
2. Stephen Borelli, "Remember Roger Maris?" *USA Today*, January 17, 2002.

FURTHER READING

Allen, Maury. *Roger Maris: A Man for All Seasons*. New York: Dutton Adult, 1986.
Clavin, Tom, and Danny Peary. *Roger Maris: Baseball's Reluctant Hero*. New York: Touchstone, 2011.
Dreb, Jon. "Maris Hits 61st in Final Game," *New York Times*, October 2, 1961.
Vincent, David. *Home Run: The Definitive History of Baseball's Ultimate Weapon*. Washington, DC: Potomac Books, 2007.

#90 The National Hockey League Expands

No one can ever accuse the National Hockey League of being shy in the 1967–1968 season, when in a bold swoop the half-century-old league doubled its number of franchises across North America from 6 to 12 in a single expansion.

Many said the NHL was ripe for expansion from its "Original Six," the nickname of the half-dozen big city teams. But nobody saw this coming. No major league had ever expanded internally with such enthusiastic abandon.

Other sports had dealt with mergers and absorbing franchises after they had been challenged by upstart leagues. Other sports had meticulously planned steady but gradual expansion. But the NHL took expansion to a new extreme.

The National Hockey League was founded in 1917, partially as an outgrowth of its predecessor National Hockey Association. Actually, "Original Six" is a misnomer, since the six teams referred to in the label were not firmly established in the NHL until the 1920s. But from the mid-1920s through 1967 the teams in the world's best league were the Boston Bruins, New York Rangers, Detroit Red Wings, Chicago Blackhawks, Montreal Canadiens, and Toronto Maple Leafs.

It was a cozy little bunch. Especially in the United States, hockey was a bit of a foreign sport in many regions. Only the Northeast and the upper Midwest could be called hockey hotbeds. In Canada, of course, hockey was the national sport, but French-speaking Montreal and English-speaking Toronto were the main hub cities and seemed to cover the bases for the time being.

One impetus to expand in a grand gesture was the realization that geographically the NHL was confined to a small area. Major League Baseball watched the Giants and Dodgers abandon New York for California in the late 1950s. Pro football was doing fine in the West. The Minneapolis Lakers transferred to Los Angeles.

As early as four years before, expansion discussions had taken place on how to alter the NHL's boundaries, especially in the United States. When the NHL announced its expansion it awarded franchises to Los Angeles, Oakland, St. Louis, Minnesota, Philadelphia, and Pittsburgh. Canadians were angry because they felt Vancouver should have a team.

The creation of the Canucks followed three years later as the NHL continued expanding to receptive cities. In between the World Hockey Association was formed to challenge the established NHL and placed clubs in Calgary, Winnipeg, and Quebec City, among other places.

When the NHL carried out its broad expansion, it gave careful thought to the alignment of the franchises as well. It split into two divisions. The eastern division encompassed all six of the older teams. The western division included all six of the new teams. On the one hand that emphasized old rivalries among the Original Six, and on the other it let the newcomers battle it out among themselves to rank number 1 and then face the eastern winner for the Stanley Cup.

In the East the Canadiens ruled the regular season, and the other three clubs advancing to the play-offs were the Rangers, Bruins, and Blackhawks. While no team in the West compiled a winning record, the top clubs were around .500, OK for beginners. The Philadelphia Flyers were tops in the regular season and were joined in the play-offs by the Los Angeles Kings, St. Louis Blues, and Minnesota North Stars.

Montreal and St. Louis met for the Stanley Cup, and the Canadiens won in four straight games. The Blues set themselves apart with future Hall of Famer Glenn

The largest and single most significant expansion by a U.S. major professional team was undertaken by the National Hockey League in 1967. During that year the NHL doubled the size of the league in one swoop from 6 teams to 12. (AP Photo)

Hall in net. His goals against average was 2.48 in 49 games. He shared net-minding duties with Seth Martin, whose own GA was 2.59.

The Blues had another ace. Their first-year coach was Scotty Bowman. It soon became apparent that Bowman knew what he was doing on the bench. In his long career he led Montreal and Detroit to nine Stanley Cup titles and won a record 1,244 games. Bowman could thank NHL expansion for his first head coaching job.

While the western teams were full and equal partners and had a shot at the Stanley Cup, none of the West's players were chosen for the first or second all-league team in 1967–1968, and none of the scorers made it into the top 10 on a list that was loaded with future Hall of Famers such as Stan Mikita, Gordie Howe, Phil Esposito, Bobby Hull, Johnny Buyck, Jean Ratelle, Rod Gilbert, Norm Ullman, and Alex Delvecchio. The only top-10 scorer that season who did not make the Hall of Fame was 10th-placer Kenny Wharram.

The tandem of Hall and Martin constituted the only two goalies in the top 10 who were from the West.

The first time one of the expansion clubs won a Stanley Cup was 1974, when the Philadelphia Flyers, who were known as the Broad Street Bullies, captured the crown. The Flyers won again the next year.

Of the six teams that entered the league together for the 1967–1968 season, four of them—the Penguins, Blues, Flyers, and Kings—are still playing in the same city where they began. The North Stars would be doing so also if management hadn't performed the unimaginable by alienating the fan base in hockey-mad Minnesota. The North Stars moved to Dallas and became the Stars and were replaced in Minnesota by an expansion team called the Wild.

Only the California Seals, who became the Oakland Seals and then the California Golden Seals, failed, eventually moving to Cleveland to become the Barons, where they failed again.

During the first few years of the western division the Blues were the flagship club. But the Flyers succeeded them and became the first expansion team to go all the way. Coach Fred Shero led the club to the two Cups.

"Everybody loved him," said star goalie Bernie Parent. "Freddy would never challenge a player in front of the group. It was always behind closed doors in his office. We respected him for that."[1]

As their nickname suggests, the Flyers were the toughest team around, and they knew how to make their rugged play pay off with goals and victories. The on-ice leader was feisty captain Bobby Clarke, whose teammates would follow him through a brick wall.

"We were good enough and deep enough to win a Cup if anybody had got injured, except Bernie [Parent]," Clarke said. "If we lost him we wouldn't have won the Cup. Either Cup. He was that good for us and that important to us."[2]

The Flyers had all of the components of a championship team, and that included attitude, a big part of their identity.

"One of our battle cries in the dressing room was, 'We will never be outworked,'" said defenseman Jimmy Watson. "And I love that battle cry."[3]

The Flyers carried the banner for the 1967–1968 expansion teams, the final proof that they belonged. The group expansion was a daring move, but it was a huge success for the NHL.

NOTES

1. Adam Proteau, "An Oral History of the Broad Street Bullies," *The Hockey News*, November 10, 2014.
2. Ibid.
3. Ibid.

FURTHER READING

Laroche, Stephen. *Changing the Game: A History of NHL Expansion*. Toronto: ECW Press, 2014.

#91 College Basketball's Game of the Century

There was a time in American history when college basketball was not on some TV channel every night in the winter. Decision makers did not think there was much market for college basketball on a weekday evening, or even on a heavily scheduled sports weekend. There were also fewer TV channels to carry programming.

Those planners just weren't looking in the right places. When the confluence of circumstances presented itself on a winter's night in 1968, TV officials decided that, yeah, maybe college hoops could make interesting viewing.

On January 20 of that year two programs on a high collided for the right to be ranked number 1 in the nation. UCLA, already into its phenomenal run under coach John Wooden, owned NCAA titles from 1964, 1965, and 1967. The Bruins were the top-ranked team in the country again. At that juncture of the season UCLA was 13–0 and had not lost a game in two and one-half years.

The Houston Cougars, coached by Guy Lewis, had the best team in that program's history and were ranked number 2. The Cougars were 16–0 on the season.

This was UCLA under Lew Alcindor, the seven-foot-two center from New York City who later changed his name to Kareem Abdul-Jabbar. The Bruins were much more than Alcindor, though. They had talent at every position. Lucius Allen, Mike Warren, Mike Lynn, and Lynn Shackelford were some of the other top guys. Also, Wooden was coaching through the stretch that ultimately would see him acclaimed as the best college coach ever.

Houston was led by six-foot-nine Elvin Hayes and guard Don Chaney, future pros; Ken Spain; and George Reynolds. The Cougars hungered to knock UCLA off its perch.

The publicity for the matchup was so hot it was set for the Astrodome, a baseball-football venue, because it was believed no college arena would be

During the 1960s and into the mid-1970s, the UCLA Bruins were college basketball's dynasty under coach John Wooden. The University of Houston, led by star Elvin Hayes, rose up to challenge UCLA and on January 20, 1968, in the sport's first nationally televised regular-season game, Houston upset the Bruins, 71–69, at the Houston Astrodome. (AP Photo)

able to accommodate the demand for tickets. This was long before the NCAA Final Four routinely played its championships in domed stadiums. It was long before there were many domed stadiums.

The buildup resulted in the game being called "The Game of the Century," and its ripple effects and breakthrough aspects warranted it, even if sometimes there is a different "Game of the Century" a month later in another sport.

Besides the domed stadium with its extra-large seating capacity and the opponents being the top two teams in the country, the television angle was important. The NCAA championship game itself had only been televised live for a few years. No one really considered regular-season college games worthy of national exposure. Regionally, yes, teams had followings that would support air time.

One of the visionaries of sports television was Eddie Einhorn. He founded the TVS Television Network in 1960, two years after producing a nationally syndicated radio broadcast of the NCAA championship.

Einhorn, now a part-owner of the Chicago White Sox after running CBS Sports for a while, both saw and created the market for UCLA-Houston. After paying $27,000 for the right to telecast the game (in an era of pittance rights fees), Einhorn syndicated the game to 120 television stations around the country. Dick Enberg, the esteemed broadcaster, handled the play-by-play.

Years later Enberg reflected on Einhorn's early belief that college basketball would play well on TV.

"He was ahead of his time, plain and simple," Enberg said.[1]

The hype was so strong for the game and the suspense was so high that 52,693 fans paid for admission to the Astrodome. For years that was the largest crowd to ever watch a college basketball game.

There was one thing amiss as the teams prepared to take the floor for the showdown. Eight days earlier Alcindor, UCLA's best player, had suffered a scratched cornea in a game. He had missed the two preceding games because of the injury. When a similar injury occurred in the pros, Alcindor/Jabbar took to wearing goggles for the rest of his career to protect his eyes.

Houston led by three points in the first half, so the Bruins, who brought in a 47-game winning streak, knew they were in a battle. Hayes, who was a tremendous player and carried his stardom into the NBA, responded to the nickname "The Big E," and on this night fans chanted it as he played a superb game.

Alcindor finished with 15 points, but shot just 4-of-18 from the floor. He added 12 rebounds. Hayes, who was a forward, dominated the contest with 39 points and 15 rebounds and three times blocked Alcindor's shots. Reynolds, 13 points, and Chaney, 11 points, a future Boston Celtic, complemented him. UCLA was led by Allen with 25 points. Warren contributed 13 points.

The game stayed close. It was 69–69 with less than two minutes to play. Hayes was fouled on a shot and made both free throws for a 71–69 lead. UCLA had the ball, but couldn't convert, and that score was how the game ended.

While many spoke to Wooden as if he had just been through a tragedy, he said essentially that the loss was not a big deal. It didn't count in conference play and didn't change UCLA's goal of winning another national crown.

"People think it was a terrible loss," Wooden said. "Not to me it wasn't. Not more than other losses."[2]

Houston did replace UCLA at the top of the polls, but in a rematch in the NCAA semifinals, the Bruins destroyed Houston, 101–69, for revenge, and then captured the 1968 championship.

Einhorn and his network paid each school $125,000 after the event was over, at a time when the NCAA tournament payoff was slightly more than $31,000.

By 1969 NBC, one of the major networks, was televising NCAA basketball play-off games and paid $500,000 for the opportunity. In the 21st century the rights fees are negotiated in long-term contracts that pay billions of dollars to the NCAA to show the entire tournament. And other networks show regular-season games on seemingly every day of the week.

In 2013 the *New York Times* caught up to Einhorn for his insights on the college game. He said he was skipping the Final Four that weekend to take a grandchild to Disney World instead.

"I've been to enough of 'em anyway," he said. "I never thought it would get this big, but it shows I was right."[3]

NOTES

1. Ben Strauss, "College Games on Television? That Might Work," *New York Times*, April 6, 2013.
2. Scott Howard-Cooper, *The Bruin 100* (Lenexa, KS: Addax Publishing Group, 1999). P. 13.
3. Strauss, "College Games on Television?"

FURTHER READING

Abdul-Jabbar, Kareem, and Peter Knobler. *Giant Steps: The Autobiography of Kareem Abdul-Jabbar*. New York: Bantam Books, 1983.
Davis, Seth. *Wooden: A Coach's Life*. New York: St. Martin's Press, 2015.
Enberg, Dick. *Dick Enberg: Oh My!* New York: Sports Publishing, 2004.

#92 Baseball's Only Fatality

When a batter is struck in the head by a fastball or a pitcher is struck in the head by a line drive, fans hush in fear. They worry they may have witnessed the accidental death of a player in the middle of a game. The sense of joy at being at a ball game is drained from the atmosphere as medical personnel rush to the site of the fallen player and he is either helped to his feet or carried off the diamond on a stretcher.

Major League Baseball dates to 1876 and the founding of the National League. It is a miracle that more players have not been killed by a hurtling baseball in nearly 140 years. In fact, that worst of tragedies has happened just one time on the field in all of the games played over all of those years.

The day hell broke out on the field was August 16, 1920, in a game between the Cleveland Indians and the New York Yankees at the Polo Grounds.

Carl Mays, a submarine-style fastball pitcher for New York, was on the mound in the fifth inning. Coming to the plate was Indians shortstop Ray Chapman. Cleveland brought a 3–0 lead into the inning and was batting in the top half of the fifth.

Chapman was born in Beaver Dam, Kentucky, in 1891 and was 29 on this day. He broke into the majors in 1912 and played his entire career for Cleveland. Chapman had appeared in 111 games, and the versatile right-handed swinging infielder was batting .303.

Mays was born in Liberty, Kentucky, the same year. He made his major league debut in 1915 and was a fine pitcher for the Boston Red Sox, taking a turn in their rotation for three Boston World Series champs in 1915, 1916, and 1918 before being swapped to the Yankees. Mays recorded 21- and 22-win seasons for Boston and was even better for New York.

Mays was known for being cantankerous and for pitching hitters inside, often hitting them if he felt they crowded the plate too much. That was the situation that day. Chapman was hugging the plate. Mays's delivery came in high and hard, and those who saw the game in an era long before televised baseball said that Chapman never moved. It appeared he did not see the pitch coming and more or less froze in the box, bat on his shoulder.

A sickening sound pervaded the stands when the ball struck Chapman on the left side of the head. This was also an era when batters did not wear helmets. The noise was loud, and the ball bounced onto the playing field. Thinking the ball had hit Chapman's bat, Mays threw to first baseman Wally Pipp, thinking he had fielded a short ground ball.

Hit in the head by a pitch on August 17, 1920, thrown by New York's Carl Mays, Cleveland Indians second baseman Ray Chapman died 12 hours later. Chapman is the only Major League player to die from injuries suffered on the field. (Library of Congress)

There are contradictory accounts of what Chapman did. Some say he started to run to first base, as if he had been hit by a pitch, but didn't make it far. He ran a few steps and fell to the ground on the base path. Others said he never moved from the batter's box and slowly slipped to the ground, when the umpires summoned a doctor from the stands. Only then, it was said, did Chapman rise and try to speak. He was unable to do anything but mumble.

Several players on both teams surrounded Chapman, trying to help him, though not Mays, who stayed on the mound. Chapman was taken to a nearby hospital, where doctors quickly discovered he had incurred a skull fracture.

The game was not interrupted, and Mays remained the Yankees' pitcher until the ninth inning when he was relieved. Cleveland won the game, and Mays took the loss.

An account from the *New York Times* spelled out the late evening tension at the hospital as doctors worked on Chapman. It read: "The operation was decided upon at 10 o'clock at a conference of several physicians, manager Tris Speaker, and business manager Walter McNichols of the Cleveland club. Chapman had been growing steadily worse during the evening and it was agreed that it would be unwise to delay the operation. Speaker had talked earlier in the evening over long distance with Chapman's wife Katie in Cleveland, and she left soon afterward for New York. With the injured man growing worse, the decision was made to operate before her arrival.[1]

In the middle of the night, 12 hours after being struck by the pitch, Chapman, who was a newlywed, died in his hospital bed, the only on-field major league fatality in history. After his death, Chapman was transported by train back to Cleveland. Manager Tris Speaker and player Joe Wood accompanied the body with his widow.

Following Chapman's death the local district attorney investigated to determine if any charges should be brought. Mays went to the legal offices without being summoned, and nothing more came of the matter on the police docket or in courtroom proceedings.

While some historical accounts view Mays as remorseless, he did say of Chapman, "I knew that the sight of his silent form would haunt me as long as I live."[2]

The next year was Mays's best. He led the American League with 27 victories, a .750 winning percentage, and 336⅔ innings pitched.

Mays stayed in baseball through 1929, completing a 15-year career with the Cincinnati Reds and New York Giants after his stint with the Yankees. He finished with an exceptional 207–126 mark and an excellent 2.92 earned run average. After he retired from pitching, Mays spent some years as a big-league scout. He died in 1971 at age 79.

To date, no other major league player has been killed by a pitched ball. Adam Greenberg, a Cubs prospect, was hit in the head in his first at-bat in 2005, effectively ending his career. Seven years later Greenberg, still hoping for a comeback, had one more at-bat for the Floridians.

Hall of Fame catcher Mickey Cochrane nearly died from a pitched ball that cut short his career 27 games into the 1937 season when he was playing for the Detroit Tigers. He was in a hospital for 10 days before he regained consciousness.

Red Sox star Tony Conigliaro was hit in the head by a pitch during the 1967 pennant race, and despite intermittent comebacks he periodically suffered headaches and vision problems and was out of baseball by age 30.

Over the last few years at least three big-league pitchers—Aroldis Chapman, Brandon McCarthy, and J. A. Happ—have been smacked in the head by balls hit at about 100 mph. Fractures were suffered, but all regained equilibrium sufficiently to pitch again. The incidents did prompt discussion on ways to develop better equipment for protection.

After Chapman's demise, the Indians inserted Joe Sewell at shortstop. In his 22-game debut Sewell batted .329. It was the beginning of a 14-year career with a lifetime .312 batting average. Sewell was elected to the Baseball Hall of Fame.

In 1920 the Indians finished strong after Chapman was killed. They won the American League pennant and the World Series, one of only two world championships the team has won.

The Indians honored Chapman by creating a plaque commemorating his career and life and hanging it at their home stadium. When the team moved to a bigger ballpark, the plaque followed. Subsequently, it was lost for years before being found in a storage area. It is now on display at Progressive Field, the Indians' current home.

NOTES

1. "The Pitch That Killed Ray Chapman," *New York Times*, August 17, 1920.
2. Vince Guerrieri, "Carl Mays: My Attitude toward the Unfortunate Chapman Matter,"*Baseball Magazine* (November 1920), reprinted at Did the Tribe Win Last Night?, January 2, 2015, http://didthetribewinlastnight.com/blog/2015/01/02/carl-mays-my-attitude -toward-the-unfortunate-chapman-matter/.

FURTHER READING

Lawless, Molly. *Hit by Pitch: Ray Chapman, Carl Mays, and the Fatal Fastball*. Jefferson, NC: McFarland, 2012.
Sowell, Mike. *The Pitch That Killed*. Chicago: Ivan R. Dee, 2003.

#93 The Earthquake World Series

It was going to be a red, white, and blue week in the San Francisco Bay area in October 1989. The World Series was in town, and for the first time in history the National League representative Giants and the American League representative Oakland Athletics were playing for the world championship.

The situation was like hosting the Super Bowl with two home teams. Oakland finished the regular season 99–63 and San Francisco finished 92–70, so fans of both sides had enjoyed a happy summer. The Giants topped the Chicago Cubs in the National League Championship Series, and the Athletics bested the Toronto Blue Jays in the American League Championship Series. Like a Subway Series in New York, this was one World Series that needed no travel time to speak of between ballparks.

One needed an exceptional memory to recall that in the olden days the Giants and Athletics had played each other three other times in a World Series. Of course the Athletics were representing Philadelphia at the time, and the Giants represented New York. Also, the most recent time the teams had met was in 1913.

One player who was particularly excited about the scenario was Oakland third baseman Carney Lansford. He grew up in Santa Clara, a neighboring city.

"I know what it means for the fans for there to be a Bay Bridge World Series," Lansford said. "I grew up as a kid watching the Giants and A's play. One was not more favorite than the other. I pulled for both."[1]

Sportswriters and others had fun trying to come up with an appropriate nickname for the event and toyed with such labels as the "Bay Bridge Series," based on the name of the structure connecting the communities; the "BART Series," based on the name of the commuter rail system connecting the communities; or the more generic "Battle of the Bay."

Alas for all those giddy fans, before the Series ended there was one more candidate for a name applied to the proceedings: "The Earthquake Series."

The Series opened in Oakland's Alameda County Coliseum, and behind the superb pitching of ace Dave Stewart the A's prevailed 5–0. Game 2 also took place at the Coliseum, and the results were similar, with the Athletics winning this one 5–1 to move ahead 2–0 in the best-four-out-of-seven series. Things were looking gloomy for the Giants.

A home-field advantage has never seemed to mean nearly as much in baseball as it does in pro football or basketball, but the Giants were hopeful that playing at Candlestick Park would bring them good luck. The 'Stick was renowned for its all-season turbulent winds, but October 17 was a sunny, pleasant day, prompting Giants hitting coach Dusty Baker to say, "This was probably the time of year they sold the property [to the Giants]."[2]

The teams were in the park, and a large number of fans were inside, too, mingling, finding their seats, excited for the game to start at 5:35 p.m. And then the earth moved. It took a moment or two for even earthquake-hardened Northern Californians to realize what was happening. But at 5:04 p.m. the ground began vibrating. This was no brief shake. The rumbling and violence lasted 17 seconds. People ran for the field first. Then the ballpark was evacuated. The San Andreas

Fault, usually the focal point of earthquake problems in the area, was again the culprit.

It became quickly apparent that the earthquake was pervasive in the vicinity and the damage was major. Large sections of concrete tumbled from buildings, and a chunk of the upper deck of the Bay Bridge above San Francisco Bay collapsed onto the lower deck. Fires broke out in the Marina District, and a section of I-880 buckled. Compounding the situation, it was rush hour so traffic was at its heaviest, yet it was lighter than usual because many people had gone home early to watch the game or had already collected in groups for Series-watching parties.

Pitcher Dennis Eckersley recognized exactly what was occurring.

"When it hit, I knew," he said. "I'm from the Bay Area. It sounded just like a train coming through the door. It scared you to death."[3]

All of the players knew something was going on, but they were not in a position to gauge the severity at first, even in their own small corner of the city, never mind across the region. They knew a dugout in the bowels of a stadium was not a good place to hang out.

"We're watching smoke come out of the air vents," Stewart said. "It was tremors. We got the hell from underneath the stadium."[4]

Although the panicked players and their families could not know it then, the quake would cause $6 billion worth of damage and cost 63 lives. It became known as the Loma Prieta earthquake and registered 6.9 on the Richter scale. Broadcasters Al Michaels, Tim McCarver, and Jim Palmer were in danger, but stayed on the air as long as possible. Cameramen showed scenes of the people milling around on the field and how the camera jumped with the ground's jolt. It was noted that this was the first time a major earthquake was shown on live television.

That was the season of Pete Rose's banishment from baseball for gambling and the death of Commissioner Bart Giamatti soon afterward. Tribute was paid to Giamatti before the first game. His second in command Fay Vincent was now in charge. When the quake hit, Vincent was standing on the field near the Giants' dugout and was talking to Willie Mays. Vincent postponed game 3, and it was also left to him to decide when to resume the Series. The Bay area was grieving and disorganized, with streets closed and buildings damaged. It was obvious the city needed some time to regroup.

The gap was 10 days between games 2 and 3. When play continued the spirit had gone out of the occasion. The Athletics overpowered the Giants, completing the four-game sweep for the championship on October 28. Stewart was the Most Valuable Player.

But this was one championship series that was going to be remembered for more than what happened on the field of play.

The excitement of an all San Francisco Bay World Series in 1989 was ameliorated when the championship showcase of Major League Baseball was interrupted by an earthquake. The Oakland Athletics and San Francisco Giants were preparing to take the field at Candlestick Park for Game 3 of the Series when the damaging earthquake hit, causing death and destruction. (AP Photo)

NOTES

1. Gary Peterson, *The Earthquake World Series: Battle of the Bay* (Chicago: Triumph Books, 2014), 159.
2. Ibid., 163.
3. Ibid., 167.
4. Ibid., 168

FURTHER READING

Nelson, Murry R. "Earthquake World Series: 1989." In *American Sports: A History of Icons, Idols, and Ideas*. Santa Barbara, CA: ABC-CLIO, 2013.
Vincent, Fay. *The Last Commissioner: A Baseball Valentine*. New York: Simon & Schuster, 2007.

#94 Libby Riddles Wins the Iditarod

The 1,000-mile-long Iditarod Trail Sled Dog Race is considered to be one of the most demanding physical challenges in the world. It has been called a tougher physical challenge than climbing the 29,035-foot Mount Everest by those who have faced both obstacles.

It is dogs and musher against the elements and terrain, from Anchorage, Alaska's largest city, to Nome, the once-famous gold-mining community on the Bering Sea Coast. Teams of up to 16 huskies travel over hilly, desolate regions, on frozen rivers, and through blizzards in freeze-the-flesh winds, in temperatures carrying imminent danger of frostbite. For the challenges it presents the Iditarod is called "The Last Great Race on Earth."

The Iditarod was founded in 1973 to commemorate an emergency run from Nenana to Nome in 1925 when mushers delivered life-saving medication to halt a diphtheria outbreak. Airplanes couldn't perform the task because of weather.

Iditarod is the name of an old mining town in Alaska's interior that is currently a ghost town. The National Historic Trail actually is longer than the race route, beginning in Seward, a seaport community on Resurrection Bay that is 120 miles farther away from Nome. That portion of the trail is not part of the race.

Creation of the Iditarod was the brainchild of a crusty musher named Joe Redington Sr., who was dismayed to see that the old ways of relying on dogs for transportation in Alaska's rural communities were dying out in favor of the snowmobile. Redington, with the help of several key volunteers, promoted the idea, raised a $50,000 purse (unheard of at the time for mushers), and somehow supervised the feel-its-way inaugural race.

The race grew from its shaky beginnings in 1973 into Alaska's most popular sporting event and most unifying statewide event. The appeal to the rugged Alaskan psyche was strong. These were real men, went the thinking, men who did not wear loafers or sit in climate-controlled offices. They wore their furs proudly, set out solo in the wild with just their loyal dogs, and took on any obstacle they encountered. The entire affair harkened back to Gold Rush days and the writings of Jack London. To a large degree the Iditarod represented what it meant to be Alaskan and unique.

One theme often heard in a state that was as new as 1959 was, "We don't care how they do it Outside." Outside, in this context, meant the lower 48 states of the United States.

Despite its image, the race called above all for smooth partnering between musher and dogs. It was apparent from the start that a woman could mush 1,000

In 1985, Libby Riddles pulled off a daring and dramatic move in a dangerous storm to become the first woman to win the 1,000-mile Iditarod Trail Sled Dog Race from Anchorage to Nome in Alaska. Her internationally appreciated victory gave fresh cache to female competitors in the grueling race. (AP Photo)

miles, too. By the early 1980s, one woman had emerged from the pack and seemed likely to become the first female to capture the Iditarod title. That was Susan Butcher, who had already placed second by the time the 1985 race began.

However, early on Butcher's race was derailed. Her team ran into an ornery moose that stomped some of her dogs. She scratched. As the race unfolded it was clear that it was going to be a particularly stormy year and that the weather would play a major part in musher strategy, perhaps more than usual.

Less heralded than Butcher at the start of the race was a different female musher named Libby Riddles. Riddles lived in the small Bering Sea Coast community of Teller and shared a kennel with another top competitor named Joe Garnie. They took turns running the team in the Iditarod, and 1985 was Riddles's turn.

Well into the race the weather deteriorated. High winds obliterated the trail, making visibility nonexistent. Snow fell in feet. The temperature plummeted. The lead pack of mushers piled up in the village of Unalakleet, where the trail turns to the Bering Sea. The consensus was that the weather was too harsh and conditions too daunting to break trail. As others debated, Riddles plunged into the storm, plowing on to Shaktoolik on her own and grabbing the race lead. The other mushers felt it was unwise to go ahead. They believed breaking trail was too tough and their dogs would burn out.

This was Riddles's gamble, going for victory, taking a shot at the big prize. She was 28, in her third Iditarod, less experienced than other top mushers, but she was game in the harshest of conditions. Alone in the blizzard at one point Riddles zipped herself into her sled for some rest as the sled rocked in the wind.

Riddles mushed on, later saying, "I was just trying to keep my face out of the wind. It's really hard on the leaders. In January the wind is even worse. You have to crawl on the ground to get anywhere because it's so strong."[1]

But her leaders were tougher than the booties they wore on their feet and they knew the area as well, being from Teller. Neither Riddles nor the dogs flinched. Once she broke away from the lead group and conquered the storm, the race belonged to Riddles.

When she crossed the finish line, Riddles said, "What I feel like is if I die now it's OK."[2]

Riddles won $50,000 and lasting fame in Alaska, where all Iditarod champions are revered. But more than that, her stunning victory was a giant step for women in sport. The sheer act of winning the Iditarod was prestigious enough, but the manner in which Riddles triumphed impressed many. Her mushing into a potentially life-threatening storm when other competitors sat still added to the luster of the triumph. It became a major aspect of the lore in the telling.

Also, because it was won by a woman for the first time, the race received massive additional attention from beyond the state's borders. At the time it could be said that except for limited dog mushing circles the Iditarod was pretty much a race whose reputation halted at the state line. Riddles's high-profile win changed that. Certainly the age of marketing and the Internet contributed, but other factors connected with Riddles, from her appearance as a comely woman to the nerves of steel it took to battle the storm, helped put the Iditarod on the worldwide map.

"How she did it is far more important to the race than that she was the first woman," said Leo Rasmussen, a longtime member of the Iditarod Trail Committee and a past president of the organization. "Was Libby's win important? To tell you that it wasn't would be telling you the greatest lie on earth."[3]

The world did notice. In Alaska, women made a best seller out of a T-shirt decorated with the words, "Alaska: Where Men Are Men and Women Win the Iditarod." All dressed up, not in a snowsuit, Riddles graced the cover of *Sports Illustrated*. The Women's Sports Foundation honored her.

It was a never-to-be-forgotten time for Riddles and the Iditarod.

NOTES

1. "Iditarod 1985, Libby Wins!," *Anchorage Daily News*, March 1985, 75.
2. Ibid., 90.
3. Lew Freedman, "The Return of Libby Riddles," *Anchorage Daily News*, December 11, 1988.

FURTHER READING

Freedman, Lew. *Iditarod Classics*. Kenmore, WA: Epicenter Press, 1992.

Riddles, Libby, and Tim Jones. *Race across Alaska: First Woman to Win the Iditarod Tells Her Story*. Harrisburg, PA: Stackpole Books, 1988.

Salisbury, Gay, and Laney Salisbury. *The Cruelest Miles: The Heroic Story of Dogs and Men in a Race against an Epidemic*. New York: W.W. Norton, 2005.

#95 Baseball Teams Start City Hopping

From 1903 through 1953 there were eight teams in baseball's American League and eight teams in baseball's National League. One thing you could count on each spring was that your hometown would be there, good or bad, but ready to go.

There was franchise stability throughout the game for more than half a century once Baltimore moved to New York in 1903 and became the Highlanders and then the Yankees. This was not true for other major sports that passed through their infancy living through the same type of turbulence Major League Baseball experienced before the turn of the 20th century.

For those 50 years baseball was the rock. Come each April the first pitch was thrown for AL clubs in Boston, New York, Philadelphia, Chicago, Detroit, Cleveland, Washington, and St. Louis. The game began as usual for National League clubs in Boston, New York, Philadelphia, Chicago, Brooklyn, Cincinnati, Pittsburgh, and St. Louis.

By the 1950s, however, demographics were shifting. America may have thought it had completed the era of westward expansion when the West was won, but more people felt the lure of California. The older manufacturing cities of the East were showing wear. Just as was often said by gunfighters in Western movies, those towns were no longer big enough for the good guy and the bad guy. In these cases, the towns were no longer big enough to financially accommodate two teams when one would suffice, and other towns might be friendlier.

Just after World War II, the National Basketball Association was being formed through the merger of two leagues. Cities calling themselves home to pro basketball came and went so quickly they didn't have time to do the laundry for team uniforms. In football, the established National Football League was challenged by the All-America Football Conference. Here, too, one moment a city would be in the league and the next a team would be out of business.

Football went through the entire deal again beginning in 1960, with the creation of the American Football League. While there was not much franchise shifting, the number of cities with pro teams expanded markedly.

Baseball, however, was supposed to be a different animal. It was more rooted in the national psyche. Called the national pastime, baseball held such a position of preeminence in American society that other pro sports looked to the game to learn how to conduct business and for leadership on universal issues. The most vivid example of that was whether to play on during World War II. It was to baseball's leadership that President Franklin D. Roosevelt sent his letter giving the OK to continue. Football and hockey followed that lead.

In 1953 the Boston Braves surveyed the landscape and fled Beantown for Milwaukee (and then Atlanta), leaving behind a Braves Field that was remodeled into a small football stadium for Boston University and memories of the good old days with Warren Spahn, Johnny Sain, and praying for rain, as the short-handed pitching rotation was frequently described.

Bill Veeck, owner of the St. Louis Browns and once operator of the AAA team in Milwaukee, had wanted to move his team there, but American League owners supported Braves owner Lou Pierini for the market instead.

Competition within cities played the major role in uprooting franchises. The Browns faced too much of an underdog fight against the deep-pocket St. Louis Cardinals. Veeck proposed moving the Browns to Baltimore. He was refused and sold the team, and then the other owners let the Browns leave their home to become the Baltimore Orioles for the 1954 season. Now the team has been in Baltimore longer than it was in St. Louis.

Veeck, a famed showman-owner, did everything possible to boost attendance at Browns games, including in his most famous stunt sending three-foot-seven midget Eddie Gaedel up to bat.

"For a minute I felt like Babe Ruth," said Gaedel, who walked on four pitches.[1]

Connie Mack held the Philadelphia Athletics together for more than half a century through his influence, but as Mack finally left managing to others and approached his own death, the A's met their demise, moving to Kansas City in 1955 (and ultimately to Oakland).

While some fans were disgruntled over the loss of the Braves, Browns, and Athletics, the wailing was muted because attendance had been steadily dropping and counterarguments were difficult to mount showing that teams would be better off financially by staying.

In contrast there was significant outrage (and grudges passed on generation to generation) at the abandonment of Brooklyn by the Dodgers in 1958 and of New York by the Giants that year. It was a trashing of tradition in pursuit of the dollar,

For 50 years, Major League Baseball's lineup of American League and National League teams remained the same. Beginning in the early 1950s, teams began changing cities, the most depressing for fans being the abandonment of Brooklyn for Los Angeles after the 1957 season. LA mayor Norris Poulson and Dodger owner Walter O'Malley celebrate the move. (AP Photo)

and not even the owners really tried to dispute the role big money played in the relocation to the West Coast.

One minute New York, with its self-proclaimed confidence that it was the center of everything, was home to three major league teams. The next it retained just one, the Yankees, and there were no National League games to be had in the six boroughs until the New York Mets began play in 1962 as a substitute for the departed franchises.

Leo Durocher, who played for the Yankees and managed the Dodgers and Giants in a Hall of Fame career, once said that if he was told either the Brooklyn Dodgers or the Brooklyn Bridge was leaving, he would bet on the bridge getting out of town first.[2]

The hatred toward departing owner Walter O'Malley was such that it would not be safe for him to walk down Flatbush Avenue.

It was hard to keep up with the Washington Senators. The original club of super pitcher Walter Johnson left D.C. after the 1960 season and transferred its history to the new Minnesota Twins. Feeling heat from majordomos of political power, baseball brought in a new Washington Senators team at the same time to quiet discontent. Those Senators stayed around through 1971 and then became the Texas Rangers.

The nation's capital was without a Major League Baseball team until 2005 (fans could follow the Orioles, 40 miles away), when the city acquired the Montreal Expos. One difference was that the Nationals played in the National League, unlike their predecessors.

Other strange doings were still to come. Baseball granted Seattle an expansion franchise, the Pilots, for 1969, but then allowed the team to flee to Milwaukee to become the Brewers. The Mariners came into existence in 1977.

This type of pattern emerged in other pro sports as well. It takes a knowledgeable NBA fan to be aware of the Sacramento Kings' odyssey. The Kings began play as the Rochester Royals in the late 1940s, became the Cincinnati Royals, and then became the Kansas City-Omaha Kings.

In the NFL, the old Chicago Cardinals became the St. Louis Cardinals, then became the Arizona Cardinals. The Cleveland Browns were uprooted by a determined owner in defiance of extreme local opposition and became the Baltimore Ravens, moving there because the beloved Baltimore Colts had jumped to Indianapolis. The NFL then awarded Cleveland a new Browns team.

Fans of all of these teams were outspoken in expressing their feelings of betrayal, though mostly they felt powerless to halt these shifts, which rebuffed their allegiance. While the franchise moves were always portrayed as being good for the long-term health of the teams, only a limited amount of sympathy was expressed to the team supporters.

It was obvious that in the future there would be no guarantee of a franchise staying put.

NOTES

1. Larry Schwartz, "Midget Gaedel Walks in Only MLB Appearance," ESPN.com, November 19, 2003, http://espn.go.com/classic/s/moment010819-gaedel-midget.html.
2. Patt Morrison, "A Very Good Fit," *Los Angeles Times*, March 29, 2008.

FURTHER READING

D'Antonio, Michael. *Forever Blue: The True Story of Walter O'Malley, Baseball's Most Controversial Owner and the Dodgers of Brooklyn and Los Angeles*. New York: Riverhead Books, 2010.

Heller, David Alan. *As Good As It Got: The 1944 St. Louis Browns*. Mt. Pleasant, SC: Arcadia Publishing, 2003.

Hogan, Kenneth. *The 1969 Seattle Pilots: Major League Baseball's One-Year Team*. Jefferson, NC: McFarland, 2006.

Peterson, John E. *The Kansas City Athletics: A Baseball History, 1954–1967*. Jefferson, NC: McFarland, 2003.

#96 Monica Seles Is Stabbed

Monica Seles was born in Yugoslavia in 1973 and became an American citizen in 1994. She emerged as one of the best female tennis players and then had her accomplishments overshadowed by a bizarre, life-threatening incident.

The area Seles spent her early years in is present-day Serbia. Her family, however, moved to the United States in 1986, and she began training at the famed Nick Bollettieri Tennis Academy in Florida.

Seles played her first professional match at age 14 in 1989 and played professionally until 2008. By the end of her first year on tour her world ranking had climbed to number 6.

During her lengthy career (with interruptions) Seles compiled a record of 595–122, for an 83 percent winning percentage. She won nine Grand Slam singles championships and five Grand Slam doubles titles, finding success at Wimbledon, the U.S. Open, the French Open, and the Australian Open. She also won an Olympic bronze medal at the Sydney Olympics in Australia in 2000.

The winner of 53 career titles, Seles was ranked number 1 in the world in 1991.

Seles's career was off to a brilliant start, and she seemed ready for a lengthy run at the top. Then an appalling incident occurred that defined the rest of her tennis days before she was even 20 years old.

On April 30, 1993, Seles was playing in a tournament in Hamburg, Germany. She was in the midst of a quarterfinal match against Magdalena Maleeva and was ahead in the contest. During a break between games a man later identified as an unemployed German toolmaker named Gunter Parche, 38, a fan obsessed with rooting for Seles's rival Steffi Graf, ran up behind her (as she was bending forward) and stabbed Seles between the shoulder blades with a boning knife.

Fortunately for Seles, when she reached the hospital, it was discovered that although she was having difficulty breathing, the knife had only penetrated slightly more than a half inch into her skin. The event made news worldwide and was met with disbelief about why anyone would wish to harm a professional tennis player.

One of the most bizarre and frightening incidents in sports history occurred in 1993 when Monica Seles, the No. 1 women's tennis player in the world, was stabbed from behind during a match. Although Seles recovered physically, the attack disrupted her psyche and career. (AP Photo)

There was immediate speculation that the attack was politically motivated because of Seles's origins and the unrest there and because she had received death threats based on her Serbian family ties. That motive was investigated, but was quickly dismissed.

It was determined that Parche was stalking Seles to aid Graf and that he was prepared to fly on to Italy for Seles's next tournament. He was categorized as mentally unbalanced. In fact, much to Seles's dismay, Parche never went to jail for his assault. The courts put him on two years' probation and ordered him to undergo psychological treatment.

Seles was so angry about the disposition of the case that she has never visited Germany again.

"Germany is the country where that man attacked me from behind, yet was not sufficiently punished," she said. "I cannot understand why this man did not have to pay for his crime."[1]

It seemed it was Seles who was sentenced to prison rather than the perpetrator. She withdrew from tennis at the height of her game and did not play on tour for two years. It definitely seemed as if her psyche had been harmed more than her body. On a bright note, a band from Australia, paying tribute to Seles and her difficult circumstances, recorded a song named "Fly, Monica, Fly." Seles said later that the song did inspire her. She met the members of the group, and it eventually changed its name to the The Monicas.

Seles did come back and had a long career, but in some ways she was not the same player. She sometimes played brilliantly, but not as consistently. Seles did not seem to have the same hunger for victory or fierceness needed to put players away. She came close, but did not achieve the caliber of results in big tournaments that she had recorded before the stabbing.

"I was stabbed on court, in front of thousands of people," Seles said. "It is not possible to talk about distancing yourself from that. It changed my career and irrevocably damaged my soul. A split second made me a different person."[2]

Other top competitors could see the difference in Seles before and after the stabbing and the way it affected her tennis in the long term.

"Mentally she was just so tough, she was right up there with Chris [Evert]," Martina Navratilova said. "You couldn't crack her, you never got the feeling she was panicked or pissed off. Nothing. You could not read her body language. Up 6–4, 4–0 or down 6–4, 4–0, she was immaculate, and she lost a little bit of that, not hardness, but supreme confidence. . . . She lost her edge."[3]

The stabbing haunted Seles's reputation in the sense that the incident was always attached to her name when she arrived in a city to play a tournament. It appeared that the attack was always lurking in the back of her mind. Seles was not impressed with the security measures taken at tournaments and wondered if they were sufficient to repel another madman.

Some steps were taken to better protect tennis players. Awards ceremonies were shifted from more public areas to more cloistered ones. There were larger police presences at sporting events than there used to be. That became especially true in the United States, but much more because of the terrorist attacks of September 2001 than because of the Seles stabbing.

Still, with the passage of time security levels at sporting events have increased. Every major sporting event that employs security guards seats them with their backs to the action and faces to the crowd to scan people for potential trouble.

Whereas in the earlier days of sport fans mingled more freely with athletes, sometimes even during batting practice in ballparks, the athletes of 2015 were more removed from their cheering public than ever before. No athletic governing body, team, or official specifically has recently stated that they toughened security because of Monica Seles, the attack having occurred so long ago. But each step that has followed over the years to upgrade security stems from the Seles stabbing.

Olympic security, with uniformed troops patrolling, uniformed police on every corner and at every entrance, long ago reached the point of practically frisking everyone who walks in a door that puts them in proximity to an athlete. Terror attacks in Munich in 1972 and the bomb blast in Atlanta in 1996 have heightened awareness to red alert at all times.

There now exists an organization named the National Center for Sports Safety and Security. There also was a time when no sports fan thought such an agency would be necessary. And sports stars frequently travel in entourages that include personal bodyguards.

NOTES

1. "Germany Knife Attack on Monica Seles Changed the Face of Sport," *The Australian*, April 30, 2013.

2. Ibid.

3. Melissa Isaacson, "Stabbing Stole Monica Seles' Career," ESPN.com, May 1, 2013, http://espn.go.com/espnw/news-commentary/article/9226901/espnw-stabbing-stole -monica-seles-tennis-career.

FURTHER READING

Layden, Joseph. *The Monica Seles Story: The Return of a Champion*. New York: St. Martin's Press, 1996.

Seles, Monica. *Getting a Grip on My Body, My Mind, My Self*. New York: Penguin, 2009.

Seles, Monica, and Nancy Ann Richardson. *Monica: From Fear to Victory*. New York: HarperCollins, 1996.

#97 Billie Jean King Steps Up for Women's Tennis

A crusader for equal prize money for women in tennis matches and equal treatment and attention at the grand slam tournaments where they overlap with men, Billie Jean King brought her point home forcefully in the strangest of forums.

Looking back, the challenge was ludicrous. The event was silly. But the consequences were far-reaching. When you are battling for a cause you never know what will tilt public opinion in your favor.

In the early 1970s King was one of the best female tennis players in the world. At times she had been number 1. She was tenacious, fearless, and also outspoken about how women were treated as inferiors to men in the tennis world.

Among singles, doubles, and mixed doubles, King was an all-time all-star at Wimbledon, the U.S. Open, the French Open, and the Australian Open, winner of 41 Grand Slam events. She won 12 singles crowns, 18 doubles titles, and 11 mixed doubles championships. Overall, King won 129 tournaments, and her overall record in competition was 695–155 or an 81 percent winning percentage.

At those major events King knew that spectators came to watch the women as well as the men, yet the men competed for much larger prize purses. The prize money issue was a huge one. It went beyond matching money with the men.

"At some tournaments—at a lot of tournaments—we didn't get a cent unless we reached the quarterfinals, which meant the overwhelming majority of us didn't win anything," King said.[1]

King participated in a combined 16 U.S. victories in the Federation Cup and Wightman Cup. Eventually, because of her battles for equal consideration for women in tennis, she was awarded the Presidential Medal of Freedom and was a Sports Illustrated Sportswoman of the Year.

Still, King, who was born in 1941, is best remembered among some sports fans for her challenge events with the loud-mouthed, baiting, older Bobby Riggs, who purposely personified male chauvinism.

Riggs, who was born in 1918, was a top male player in his youth. He won 11 major titles, including doubles events, although they were defined differently during his career. Always a hustler and a gambler, Riggs plunged into absurd bets at times, but was often creative enough to pull out wins and rake in cash.

In 1973, thinking he could exploit the reverse side of King's efforts seeking equality for women in tennis, Riggs ridiculed the quality of the women's game. He declared that he could beat the best women in the world even at age 55 and that any man could beat any woman. Initially, King ignored his braggadocio and his challenge, but after Riggs took on and defeated Margaret Court Smith, she felt obligated to stand up for women's tennis.

Riggs made short work of Smith, winning 6–2, 6–1. The loudly hyped match, followed by Riggs's triumph, gained Riggs even more attention. He was on the cover of both *Sports Illustrated* and *Time*. The 30-year-old Smith's loss on May 13 was dubbed "The Mother's Day Massacre." Riggs alternated between mischievous humor and sarcastic digs and at no time, consistent with his theme, did he come off as gallant.

When King heard the score of the Smith match, she was appalled.

"I went bananas," she said. "None of us could believe it. No way."[2]

After his win there was no muzzling Riggs. He sought another victim and taunted all women's players. This was all part of his hustle. An irritated King agreed to a match called "The Battle of the Sexes," on September 20, several months later, scheduled for the Astrodome in Houston. At stake, besides reputations and public perception, was a $100,000 winner-take-all prize.

The nationally televised event was as much schmaltzy show business as sport. The entry onto the court by the protagonists owed as much to a Busby

Billie Jean King's 1973 showdown with showboating Bobby Riggs in the so-called "Battle of the Sexes" in the Houston Astrodome—as well as King's entire effort and philosophy—brought attention and ultimately equal prize money to women's tennis. (AP Photo)

Berkeley Hollywood musical spectacular, or a Las Vegas show, as it did to a heavyweight title fight introduction. The scene seemed to have little in common with the average tennis match.

The players' entrances boggled the minds of spectators. Riggs was carried to the court in a rickshaw pulled by scantily dressed female models. King arrived in a chair carried by bare-chested muscle men attired like ancient slaves. This goofy display seemed to have the hand of Riggs behind it more than King, who might just have gone along to be a good sport.

Riggs and King exchanged gifts. Riggs gave King a large lollipop. King gave Riggs a piglet, a clear reference to him being a male chauvinist pig. More than 30,000 people attended the match, and more than 90 million watched on television worldwide.

On the court they looked their ages, King 29 and Riggs 55. King thoroughly outplayed Riggs, dismantling his game and winning 6–4, 6–3, 6–3.

In the aftermath of King's convincing win, rumors began to circulate that Riggs had thrown the match to win large sums of money he had bet on himself.

Sometime later Riggs took a lie detector test, which indicated that he had not fixed the result. Riggs went into seclusion after losing and later challenged King to a rematch. She declined. Her point was proven, and there was nothing to be gained from another match. The two actually became good friends in later years.

King became an icon of women's tennis, women's sports, and the women's movement. She was out front on issues of equal pay for equal work, for women having careers instead of marriages if they wished to, sexuality, and abortion. The world is a very different place now than in the early 1970s, when King was often seen as controversial for her views.

"Liberalized abortion laws? Yes," she said. "An end to job discrimination? Of course. Equal pay for equal work? No question. But those are details. What really counts is for us to be able to fulfill our potential in whatever way we choose."[3]

NOTES

1. Billie Jean King and Kim Chapin, *Billie Jean* (New York: Pocket Books, 1975), 129.
2. Ibid., 202.
3. Ibid., 200.

FURTHER READING

King, Billie Jean, and Christine Brennan, *Pressure Is a Privilege: Lessons I've Learned from Life and the Battle of the Sexes*. New York: LifeTime Media, 2008.

King, Billie Jean, and Frank Deford. *Billie Jean*. New York: Viking, 1982.

King, Billie Jean, and Cynthia Starr. *We Have Come a Long Way: The Story of Women's Tennis*. New York: McGraw-Hill, 1988.

Roberts, Selena. *A Necessary Spectacle: Billie Jean King, Bobby Riggs, and the Tennis Match That Leveled the Game*. New York: Crown, 2005

Ware, Susan. *Game, Set, Match: Billie Jean King and the Revolution in Women's Sports*. Chapel Hill: University of North Carolina Press, 2015.

#98 Tommy John Surgery

Sometimes people forget that Tommy John was a very fine pitcher. Many believe he belongs in the Hall of Fame, although he has not made it yet, despite winning 288 games over a long career.

The other part of Tommy John's legacy, and a bigger one for many people, is how he donated his pitching arm to science. Not quite literally, but close to it. The

What began as experimental surgery in 1974 by Dr. Frank Jobe to rescue the career of pitcher Tommy John by transplanting a tendon from his non-pitching arm to his throwing arm has become probably the best-known sports-related surgery. The operation has saved the careers of many big-league pitchers. (AP Photo/Damian Dovarganes)

surgery that repaired his once-injured arm and enabled him to continue pitching for many years turned out to be the prototype for a procedure that has rescued the careers of uncounted numbers of hurlers.

Born in 1943 in Terre Haute, Indiana, John was a left-handed pitcher who played in the majors for 26 years. When he retired after the 1989 season John was 46. He had 18 seasons in which he won at least 10 games, and three times he won at least 20 games. His career earned run average is an excellent 3.34.

A four-time all-star, John was not the hardest of throwers and finished with 2,245 strikeouts. He specialized in throwing the sinker and inducing batters to hit ground balls to his infielders and preferably into double plays. The bulk of his early career was spent with the Chicago White Sox and Los Angeles Dodgers after he broke into the majors with the Cleveland Indians in 1963.

Although he spent less time with the New York Yankees, two of John's best years came in pinstripes when he won 21 and 22 games back to back in 1979 and 1980. John appeared in the World Series for both the Dodgers and the Yankees and pitched in 14 postseason games in all with a 6–3 record and a playoff earned run average of 2.65.

For most of his career John was either a staff ace or a top-ranked rotation pitcher. He almost never pitched in relief.

Overall, John had a first-rate pitching career and a longer stay in the majors than 95 percent of the players who ever take the mound. Yet, strangely, his greatest fame in baseball, it can be argued, stems from his getting hurt.

John was cruising through the 1974 season with the Dodgers with a 13–3 record when his left pitching elbow went bad. A visit to the doctor confirmed a very negative diagnosis. He had injured the ulnar collateral ligament, and it was not going to heal. John's career was in jeopardy. The only answer was an experimental surgery in which a doctor uses a tendon from another place on the body and implants it to substitute for the ruined ligament.

Dr. Frank Jobe, a renowned sports medicine expert and orthopedic surgeon, performed the surgery on September 25, 1974. Jobe took a tendon from John's right wrist for his fix. John was the first baseball player to have it done. Even after the operation, the chances of John ever pitching again were unknown. He sat out the entire 1975 season rehabilitating his arm. The Dodgers did not expect to see John in uniform again. Part of John's out-of-sight work was done with former Dodger standout relief pitcher Mike Marshall, who had his own ideas about pitching motions that put less stress on the throwing arm. John learned from Marshall and adapted.

When John showed up to pitch for LA again in 1976, everyone was surprised. When he finished 10–10 he was named comeback player of the year for the National League. Some viewed John's return as a miracle. He did not merely make a cameo appearance in his comeback; he stuck around for 14 years after his surgery and won 164 games after his arm had been given up for dead. Jobe was not sure if the surgery would have long-lasting positive effects, so he did not perform another one for two years after John's, waiting to see how that one went.

In the intervening 40 years since John underwent the operation, the surgery has been named after him. More officially the procedure is called ulnar collateral ligament reconstruction. Doctors have far more experience with it, and it has been viewed as a career-saving operation for pitchers who would otherwise have seen their pitching days be ended prematurely. Tommy John surgery has a high success rate, but it is not perfect for every pitcher.

Still, the list of pitchers who have been operated on and bounced back is an impressive one. While no pitcher wants to have his arm surgically repaired, Tommy John surgery has almost become a security blanket, an insurance policy, to provide aid and hope if something does go wrong.

John Smoltz, Stephen Strasburg, Adam Wainwright, A. J. Burnett, Chris Carpenter, John Lackey, Jamie Moyer, and Kerry Wood are some of the most prominent pitchers who have needed Tommy John repair work. Unfortunately for them, some pitchers have even required the operation twice, including Daniel Hudson, Kris Medlen, and Jarrod Parker. Rarely is Tommy John surgery a remedy for a position player, but sometimes a fielder does need work on his arm.

Jobe also introduced innovative shoulder surgery to help baseball players. His most famous success story with that procedure was Orel Hershiser who faced re-tirement without the operation. On the day Hershiser returned to the mound, he signaled a thank-you to Jobe in the stands.

Jobe and Robert Kerlan, another prominent doctor, owned a California clinic for years, and Jobe was a consultant to the Dodgers for decades. As an indication of how significant Jobe's innovation has been, he was honored during the Hall of Fame induction ceremony in the summer of 2013. He died in 2014. Upon Jobe's death Hershiser said, "He gave me back my career" and he "may have touched more wins and saves than anyone in baseball."[1]

When Jobe passed away, commissioner Bud Selig issued a statement of praise. It included the comment that Jobe's "work in baseball revolutionized sports medicine."[2]

John, the first beneficiary of the groundbreaking operation, said, "I think there should be a medical wing in the Hall of Fame, starting with him."[3]

NOTES

1. Richard Goldstein, "Frank Jobe, Surgeon Who Saved Pitchers' Careers, Dies at 88," *New York Times*, March 6, 2014.
2. Rob Gloster, "Frank Jobe, Surgeon Who Repaired Pitchers' Elbows, Dies at 88," *Bloomberg Business*, March 7, 2014. http://www.bloomberg.com/news/articles/2014-03-07/frank-jobe-surgeon-who-repaired-pitchers-elbows-dies-at-88.
3. Goldstein, "Frank Jobe."

FURTHER READING

John, Tommy, and Sally John. *The Sally and Tommy John Story*. New York: Scribner, 1983.
John, Tommy, and Dan Valenti. *T.J.: My 26 Years in Baseball*. New York: Bantam Books, 1991.

#99 Fantasy Sports

Not everyone can be a star athlete in the pros, college, or high school. But just about anyone with an interest can pretend to be.

A fascinating phenomenon of recent years has been the mass indulgence of armchair quarterbacks and living-room couch managers in fantasy sports. They couldn't lick or join 'em, so they dreamed up a method to parallel them.

The definition of fantasy is that it is make-believe. It is all in your head, not real life. According to Webster's dictionary, fantasy is "unrestrained imagination" or "an illusory mental image."

Typically in fantasy sports a participant acts as an owner of a team competing in a fictional league against another team owner after "drafting" players from a pool of real-life individuals. How the teams fare depends on how these real-life players fare in real games.

While a fabulous boom in participation in fantasy sports has taken hold in recent years, the origins of people (overwhelmingly boys and men) playing fantasy sport pretty much date to the 1950s. Although today's participants probably wouldn't think so, one of the first fantasy leagues was devoted to golf. You take Arnold Palmer, I have Jack Nicklaus.

A Harvard University sociologist named William Gamson was credited with creating something called "Baseball Seminar" in 1960, in which participants could score points based on how real-life players fared. That game was transplanted to the University of Michigan, where a student named Daniel Okrent picked it up. Okrent later invented "Rotisserie Baseball."

Meanwhile, a fantasy baseball league began at Glassboro State College in New Jersey in 1976. That was after The Greater Oakland Professional Pigskin Prognosticators League was founded, a fantasy pro football league that dated to the early 1960s.

Okrent, a writer and editor, gets the credit for developing Rotisserie League Baseball in 1980, which differed in rules from its predecessors. In his fantasy league, competitors drafted players from current major league rosters to form their own teams and used their daily statistics to plot their fake teams' progress. The name Rotisserie was adopted because Okrent and his friends met at a New York restaurant named La Rotisserie Française to play.

Rotisserie League fantasy baseball took off in the early 1980s during the real Major League Baseball labor strike and when Okrent wrote about the game for a national sports publication, *Inside Sports*, which is now defunct.

In the years since then fantasy sports participation has mushroomed. Players group together with like-minded friends and hold drafts for baseball, football,

Fantasy sports is the ultimate participatory vehicle for the arm-chair athlete. Without moving away from the computer or the telephone, it is possible for sports fans to "field" their own teams with players they have selected and compete against similarly stocked teams operated by friends, or even strangers. (AP Photo/Al Behrman)

basketball, hockey, and maybe even tiddlywinks. The general approach is the same, though any league may have its own quirks.

There are a large number of possible variations. While the early drafting process focused on individual stars, who usually produced impressive measurable stats such as touchdown passes or rushing yards in football, hits and home runs in baseball, or points and rebounds in basketball, eventually someone dreamed up the idea of paralleling real sports more closely. The draft in this approach is to have players choose entire teams to follow.

As interest kept growing, entrepreneurs thought of ways to make money off fantasy sports. Books appeared on fantasy sports. *Sports Illustrated* began running a weekly column. In August 2014 *SI* reported that there was a new FanNation fantasy sports app for phones that would allow players to load fresh contests onto their phones.

"In the Baseball Throwdown, pick a pitcher, an infielder, and an outfielder and see who beats their daily projections," the magazine noted.[1]

Software programs were developed for computers.

A Fantasy Sports Trade Association was formed in 1997 and calls itself "the voice of more than 41 million" fantasy sports players in the United States and Canada.[2] The association is headquartered in Chicago and performs surveys studying the demographics of the hobby. It estimated that 41 million people at least 12 years old in the United States and Canada played fantasy sports of some kind in 2014. This represented an estimated growth of about 7 million people, mostly attributable to a fresh wave of interest in hockey fantasy sports in Canada.

Following a winter conference in early 2015, the association predicted that by 2020 fantasy sports will be a $17 billion industry. "The fantasy sports industry is riding a wave of growth and industry experts at the Fantasy Sports Trade Association's 2015 Winter Conference on January 15 and 16 at the Bellagio in Las Vegas see a tsunami coming," a report from the conference said.[3]

While football and baseball were the engine drivers of fantasy sports leagues years ago, the modern-era fantasy player, depending on his or her home base, indulges in soccer and cricket as well.

From the original friends-meeting-at-a-bar concept of drafting players, far more sophisticated operations exist in which sports fans indulge with strangers via their home computers. The permutations are sometimes complex and offer wide varieties of ways to play.

Unsurprisingly, one thing some players have come to understand is that they are addicted to fantasy sports and no longer watch sports merely for fun and entertainment.

"I cannot watch football the way it was meant to be watched," a writer stated in the *New York Times*. "I watch for stats. I fret about fantasy points, not game outcomes. The game, in short, is meaningless. I don't watch playoff games. I don't care who wins the Super Bowl. I have loyalty to no one but myself and my pretend roster of random players from across the league. I can't recall the agony of emotional investment in a real team—the ability to feel that joy and pain has long left me, crowded out by fantasy obsession.

"There is no joy, only anxiety, only pain, only disappointment. When I win a fantasy game, I'm only happy not to lose. When I lose, I'm crushed."[4]

Even before the invention of a Fantasy Sports Trade Association the Center for Internet Addiction was created. It has a site people can visit to discuss fantasies that have gotten out of hand.

NOTES

1. "FanNation," *Sports Illustrated*, August 4, 2014.

2. Megan Van Petten, "Welcome to the Fantasy Sports Trade Association (FSTA)," Fantasy Sports Trade Association, http://www.fsta.org/?page=LetterDirector (accessed December 12, 2014).

3. Greg Smith, "2015 FSTA Winter Conference Recap," Fantasy Sports Trade Association, January 26, 2015, http://www.fsta.org/news/212864/2015-FSTA-Winter-Conference-Recap.htm.

4. C. D. Carter, "When Fantasy Becomes an Addiction," *New York Times*, November 27, 2012.

FURTHER READING

Berry, Matthew. *Fantasy Life: The Outrageous, Uplifting, and Heartbreaking World of Fantasy Sports from the Guy Who's Lived It*. New York: Riverhead Books, 2014.

Holleman, M. Christine. "Fantasy football: Illegal Gambling or Legal Game of Skill." *NCJL & Technology* 8 (2006): 59.

Nesbit, Todd M., and Kerry A. King. "The Impact of Fantasy Football Participation on NFL Attendance." *Atlantic Economic Journal* 38, no. 1 (2010): 95–108.

Schecter, Larry. *Winning Fantasy Baseball: Secret Strategies of a Nine-Time National Champion*. Austin, TX: Emerald Book Company, 2014.

#100 Soap Opera on Skates

The events leading up to the 1994 Winter Olympics were some of the most bizarre ever involving sports figures, astonishing the United States and the figure skating world as the truth gradually leaked out.

In early January, as the U.S. Figure Skating Championships were about to unfold in Detroit, top American skater Nancy Kerrigan, vying for a spot on her second Olympic team, was smashed in the right knee by an assailant with a police baton after a practice.

The seemingly incomprehensible action, aimed at hurting the 1993 national champion from Massachusetts and already a bronze medalist from the 1992 Games, threw the competition into a tizzy and made headlines around the world, even in places that had little interest in figure skating.

Kerrigan was the top American hope for the 1994 Games in Lillehammer, Norway, after her international performance in Albertville, France, in 1992 and her domestic triumphs. A contender for a spot on the U.S. team was Tonya Harding, who was the 1991 American champion and a silver medalist at the world championships in 1993.

One of the most distasteful and bizarre occurrences in sports history took place leading up to the 1994 Winter Olympics when top U.S. figure skater Nancy Kerrigan was attacked by crow-bar-wielding supporters of Tonya Harding, another contender. Kerrigan prevailed by winning a silver medal, and several assailants went to jail. (AP Photo/Merline Summers)

Harding, from Portland, Oregon, was known as a particularly athletic skater who was the first American woman to land a triple axel jump in competition.

At the time of the U.S trials, Harding had just been divorced from Jeff Gillooly. After the surprise attack on Kerrigan, police suspicion turned to Harding and her supporters, but when the story came out it appeared at first that Harding herself was in the clear. It seemed her friends had hatched the plot to disable Kerrigan, shove her aside, and help clear a path to the Games for Harding.

An astounded nation cringed as details came out of the behind-the-scenes doings. In the ultimate act of unsportsmanlike conduct, Gillooly and Harding's bodyguard, Shawn Eckhardt, hired Shane Stant to play the thug's role and bash Kerrigan's leg. The goal was at the least to break her leg. Stant had searched for Kerrigan in Massachusetts, but could not catch up with her before she departed for Michigan.

Stant found Kerrigan at Cobo Arena as she came off the ice from practice, and in a quiet corridor he slugged her, smacking her in the thigh. The blow did not break Kerrigan's leg as planned, but she did have to withdraw from the U.S. championships. Harding won the gold at that meet, cementing her place on the Olympic team. Officials voted to include Kerrigan on the Olympic squad anyway.

The unprecedented nature of the attack, coupled with sympathy for Kerrigan, made her an international news figure in an unflinching spotlight. She was on the cover of *Time* and *Newsweek* and was followed by hordes of reporters any time she stepped outdoors.

A couple of breaks quickly led investigators to the principals in the attack. On February 1, before the Games began, Gillooly cut a deal with a plea bargain in exchange for testimony against Harding. Progress on the case did not reach resolution before the competition in Norway was held, and U.S. officials talked of removing Harding. She threatened to sue, and that was enough to keep her in the Games. The sensational story's denouement played out on the ice. Harding skated poorly and finished eighth in ladies' singles figure skating. Kerrigan won the silver medal. Given the time difference between the United States and Norway, the figure skating was shown on tape delay, but garnered a huge audience.

At the Games, Kerrigan said her face was so familiar from the coverage that when she entered the athletes' cafeteria for meals, she was stared at.

"Do I have three heads?" she remembered thinking. "Why are you staring?"[1]

Later, once the investigation into the assault on Kerrigan was concluded, Gillooly, Eckhardt, Stant, and a getaway driver named Derrick Smith all served jail time for the incident. Harding escaped incarceration. She pled guilty to hindering prosecution of the attackers.

Her penalty was three years' probation, 500 hours of community service, and a $160,000 fine. Also, part of her official plea bargain was withdrawing from the 1994 World Figure Skating Championships and withdrawing her membership in the U.S. Figure Skating Association.

Kerrigan never imagined a fellow competitor would be behind the attack. But in a 2014 television interview, addressing the incident publicly for the first time in 20 years, she said, "I truly wanted to believe she had nothing to do with it at all. It's sad. I hated hearing it. It stinks."[2]

Kerrigan said she read FBI transcripts of interviews with the perpetrators in which they admitted that they had discussed killing her or options that would more seriously harm her than using the police baton to the knee.

After conducting its own investigation, the figure skating association piled more penalties on Harding. The organization stripped Harding of the U.S. title she had won in Detroit while Kerrigan was disabled and banned her for life from association events as either a skater or, looking ahead to the future, a coach.

The reasoning behind the association's additional harsh penalty for Harding was the conclusion that she was aware of the attack before it happened, which represented poor sportsmanship and unethical behavior.

Harding later claimed that she intended to go to the FBI to tell on Gillooly, but he threatened her and she backed off. Harding has always denied she had advance knowledge of the attack. The FBI, however, had some handwritten notes found in a trash dumpster that suggested otherwise.

In the years since her skates were retired, Harding has lived a life that has brought her to supermarket tabloids' attention more than once. One controversy revolved around a sex tape of her and Gillooly that was sold to *Playboy* magazine and still pictures from it that were printed in *Penthouse*. She appeared in a wrestling show; tried to make it as a singer, but was booed with her band; and competed in a celebrity boxing tournament.

On the plus side of the ledger, Harding was credited with saving an 81-year-old woman in a bar in Portland with mouth-to-mouth resuscitation.

After she won her silver medal in Norway, Kerrigan did not make a good impression on the media, and there was a backlash about her personality that appeared to diminish her image. She promptly left amateur skating and moved on to skating in professional ice shows. Over the years Kerrigan has served as a skating commentator on televised events and appeared on some television shows and in some movies.

To those looking back at the tumultuous times surrounding the U.S. figure skating trials of 1994 and the Winter Olympics the next month, the events seem to be as unbelievable now as they were two decades ago.

After watching a 2014 documentary made about the Harding-Kerrigan incident, Kerrigan used the word "surreal" to describe her feelings. Married with three children, long removed from competition, she said, "To some degree at this point it doesn't seem like it's me."[3]

NOTES

1. Willie Geist, interview with Nancy Kerrigan, *MSNBC*, February 24, 2014, http://www.msnbc.com/morning-joe/watch/nancy-kerrigan-opens-up-on-attack-16796576 3757.
2. Ibid.
3. Ibid.

FURTHER READING

Coffey, Wayne, and Filip Bondy. *Dreams of Gold: The Nancy Kerrigan Story*. New York: St. Martin's Press, 1994.

Kerrigan, Nancy, and Mary Spencer. *Artistry on Ice: Figure Skating Skills and Style*. Champaign, IL: Human Kinetics, 2003.

Kerrigan, Nancy, and Steve Woodward. *Nancy Kerrigan: In My Own Words*. New York: Hyperion, 1996.

Index

Aaron, Hank, xxiii, 76, 77, 78, 80, 143
Abrisomova, Svetlana, 213
Ackerman, Val, 161
Adelphi University, 325
Adidas, 226
Afghanistan, 6
Africa, 35
AIDS virus, 203, 204, 205, 206
A.J. Foyt Enterprises, 293
Akers, Michelle, 172, 173
Akron Indians, 81
Akron, Ohio, 307
Akron Pros, 81, 82
Alabama, 18, 38, 273
Alaska, 134, 343, 345
Alaskan Gold Rush, 343
Albertville, France, 302, 363
Alcindor, Lew (Kareem Abdul-Jabbar), 207, 208, 209, 210, 333, 335
Alexander Grover Cleveland, 180
Ali, Muhammad (Cassius Clay), xxii, xxiii, 15, 32, 33, 35, 36, 98
All-America Football Conference, 188, 346
Allegheny Athletic Association, xiii
Allen, Lucius, 333, 335
Allen, Mel, 25
Allison, Doug, 42
All-Star Game (baseball, Game of the Century), 187, 189, 190

Alou, Felipe, 46
Alston, Walt, 94
Alzheimer's disease, 223, 226
Amateur Athletic Union, 120, 254
Ameche, Alan, 60
Amer-I-Can, 280
American Association, xiii, 66
American Athletic Conference, 213
American Basketball Association (men), 43, 74
American Basketball League (first, men), 13
American Basketball League (second, men), 140
American Basketball League (women), 161, 162, 263
American Football Conference, 151, 251
American Football League (first), 53
American Football League (second), 43, 61, 96, 97, 136, 137, 138, 284, 347
American League, xvi, xxiv, 24, 43, 44, 45, 45, 47, 48, 66, 80, 84, 86, 103, 109, 144, 153, 181, 189, 190, 192, 234, 281, 294, 297, 298, 326, 338, 339, 340, 346
American Legion, 248
American Professional Football Association, xiv, 57, 81

American Tobacco Company, 247
Anaheim Angels, 297
Anchorage, Alaska, 343
Anderson, Chic, 102
Anderson, Dave, 98
Anderson, Dick, 151
Anderson, Frankie, 270
Andrie, George, 286
Angola, 122, 123
Antetokounpo, Giannis, 123
Argentina, 123
Arizin, Paul, 177, 178
Arizona Cardinals, 57, 81, 349
Arkansas, 181
Arlin, Harold, 24
Arlington National Cemetery, 18
Armed Forces Boxing Championships, 288
Armstrong, Lance, 128, 129, 130, 131
Artis, Orsten, 73, 75
Ashland, Massachusetts, 237
Associated Press, 256, 258
Association for Intercollegiate Athletics for Women, 21, 140, 223
Athens, 197, 236
Atlanta, 36, 80, 125, 161, 261, 311, 353
Atlanta Braves, 78, 79, 80
Atlanta Dream, 263
Atlanta Hawks, 114
Atlantic Coast Conference, 316
Attles, Al, 177, 178

Auerbach, Red, 88, 89, 90, 91
Augusta, Georgia, 118, 119, 243
Auriemma, Geno, 212, 213, 214, 215, 226
Austin, Texas, 1
Australia, 28, 123, 161, 228, 240, 275, 352
Australian Olympic Committee, 276
Australian Open tennis, 157, 199, 350, 354
Australian Rules Football, 29
Averill, Earl, 189
Azzi, Jennifer, 161, 262, 263

Babe Didrikson Cancer Clinics, 256
Bahamas, 30
Baker, Dusty, 340
Baker, Sam, 135
Baker Field, 26
Baltimore, xii, xvi, 47, 101, 218
Baltimore Colts, 58, 59, 60, 61, 96, 97, 98, 99, 149, 150, 151, 349
Baltimore Orioles, 63, 68, 92, 153, 155, 215, 217, 218, 234, 328, 347, 349
Baltimore Orioles (first Orioles), 346
Baltimore Ravens, 322, 349
Banks, Ernie, 143
Barber, Red, 25, 26
Barcelona, Spain, 121, 123, 161, 205, 258, 310
Barkley, Charles, 122, 123
Barrett, Angela Mortimer, 159
Barrow, Ed, 47
Barry, Dave, 185
BART Series, 340
Bascom, Kerry, 213
baseball cards, 246, 247, 248, 249
Baseball Hall of Fame, xx, 25, 42, 62, 65, 68, 71, 77, 87, 103, 105, 140, 144, 153, 155,

165, 166, 180, 189, 192, 233, 248, 283, 339, 356
Baseball Seminar, 360
Basketball Association of America, xiv, 13
Basketball Hall of Fame, 12, 42, 70, 73, 76, 80, 88, 114, 115, 133, 134, 177, 204, 207, 263, 338
basketball shot clock, 133, 139, 140, 142
The Battle of the Sexes, 355
Bayah, Birch, 19
Bay Bridge, 341
Baylor, Elgin, 91
Bazooka gum, 247
Beamon, Bob, 275, 323, 324, 325
Beatles, 121
Beaumont, Texas, 153
Beaver Dam, Kentucky, 336
Beijing (Peking), 146, 148, 195, 196
Bell, Bert, 59
Bell, Cool Papa, 2
Bellagio Hotel, 362
Bellamy, Walt, 121
Bellows, George, 184
Belmont Stakes, xii, xxii, 99, 102
Benton Harbor, Michigan, 23
Berger, Wally, 166
Bering Sea Coast, 343, 344
Berkus, Mike, 249
Berlin, 12, 37, 38, 39
Berlin Wall, xvii
Berman, Chris, 31
Berra, Yogi, 95, 192
Berry, Raymond, 58, 59
Bias, Len, 316, 317, 318, 319
Bias, Lonise, 319
Biasone, Danny, 13, 140
Big East Conference, 213
Big Six (Seven, Eight) Conference, 269
Big Ten Conference, xiii, 37, 51, 259

Billingham, Jack, 78
Bird, Larry, 122, 204, 257, 258, 259, 260
Bird, Sue, 213
Biyombo, Bismack, 123
Black Muslims, 34
Black Panther Party, 147
Black Sox Scandal, 47, 84, 85, 86, 87, 144, 145
Blanda, George, 322
Blazjowski, Carol, 161
Bleier, Rocky, 253
Bloomington, Indiana, 258
Bogdanovic, Bogan, 123
Boggan, Tim, 147, 148
Bogut, Andrew, 123
Bold Ruler, 101
Bolton, Ruthie, 161, 262, 263, 265
Bonds, Barry, 77
Borden, Amanda, 310
Boston, xvi, 42, 90, 108, 213, 236, 237, 288, 317
Boston, Ralph, 324, 325
Boston Beaneaters, 107
Boston Braves, 24, 76 166, 346, 347
Boston Bruins, 330
Boston Celtics, 69, 70, 88, 89, 90, 91, 140, 162, 176, 177, 204, 258, 316, 317, 318, 335
Boston Marathon, 236, 237
Boston Patriots, 137
Boston Red Sox (Boston Red Stockings), 2, 24, 25, 42, 44, 45, 47, 103, 106, 107, 109, 181, 221, 297, 298, 299, 328, 336, 337, 338, 346
Boston University, 7, 10, 263, 347
Boulder, Colorado, 238
Bowling Green University, 314
Bowman, Scotty, 331
Bowman baseball cards, 248
Boyd, Bob, 96
Boyer, Clete, 192
Boys and Girls Club, 198

Braddock, James J., 14, 15, 16
Bradshaw, Ahmad, 267
Bradshaw, Terry, 252, 253
Brady, Tom, 321
Brainard, Asa, 42
Branca, Ralph, 294, 295, 296
Brantford, Ontario, 219
Braves Field, 347
Brazil, 123, 161, 172, 173, 261
Brennan, Terry, 270
Brett, George, 109
Brickhouse, Jack, 282
Brigham Young University, 324
Bristol, Connecticut, 29
Bristol, Tennessee, 125
British Ladies Amateur (golf),
    256
British Open (golf), 117, 118,
    119, 245
Brockton, Massachusetts, 288,
    290
Brockton High School, 290
Bronx, New York, 183, 193
Brookline, Massachusetts, 237
Brooklyn Atlantics, xii
Brooklyn Dodgers, xx, 1, 2, 3,
    4, 5, 25, 26, 27, 93, 94, 95,
    153, 166, 191, 281, 294, 295,
    330, 346, 347, 348
Brooklyn Dodgers (football),
    27, 93
Brooklyn Excelsiors, 42
Brooks, Herb, 6, 7, 10
Brown, Jim, 277, 278, 279, 280,
    320
Brown, Paul, 278
Brown, Rita Mae, 200
Brown, Roosevelt, 59
Brown, Walter, 69
Brown, Warren, 51
Brown University, 81
Brumel, Valeri, 303, 304
Brundage, Avery, 276
Bryant, Emmette, 91
Buckner, Cleveland, 178
Bucyk, Johnny, 331
Budweiser (Anheiser-Busch), 31

Buffalo Bill Cody, xv
Buffalo Bills, 136, 137, 138, 151
Buoniconti, Nick, 151
Burgess, Smokey, 192
Burk, Adrian, 322
Burnett, A.J., 359
Burns, Tommy, 228
Burris, Buddy, 270
Burt High School (Tennessee),
    240
Busby Berkeley, 355
Bush, George W., 36, 80
Butch Cassidy and the Sundance
    Kid, 150
Butcher, Susan, 344
Butler, Al, 177
Buxton, Angela, 159

Caesars Palace, 18
Cager, Willie, 73
Cairo, Georgia, 1
Calgary, 300
Calgary Flames, 330
California, 1, 55, 82, 222, 330,
    340, 346s
California Golden Seals
    (California Seals), 330, 332
Camden Yards, 217
Campanella, Roy, 4, 94
Campbell, Bill, 177, 178
Canada, 35, 120, 219, 220, 221,
    222, 228, 300, 330, 362
Candlestick Park, 340
Canton, Ohio, 54, 57, 152, 251,
    284
Canton Bulldogs, 57
Cappaletti, Gino, 135
Caray, Harry, 28
Carew, Rod, 109
Carlisle Indian School, 56, 57
Carlos, John, 273, 275, 276
Carnegie, Pennsylvania, 248
Carnera, Primo, 15, 16
Carolina, Puerto Rico, 62
Carpenter, Chris, 359
Carpentier, Georges, 184
Carter, Jimmy, 6, 10, 146, 237

Carter, Joe, 194
Cash, Dave, 63
Cash, Swin, 213
Catchings, Tamika, 225
CBS Sports, 334
Center for Internet Addiction,
    362
Cepeda, Orlando, 63
Chadwick, Henry, xi, xii
Chairman Mao, 146, 148
Chalmers County, Alabama, 15
Chamberlain, Wilt, xxiii, 90, 91,
    175, 176, 177, 178, 179
Chambers, Jerry, 74
Champaign, Illinois, 51, 52
Chandler, A.B. "Happy," 3
Chandler, Don, 286
Chaney, Don, 91, 210, 333,
    335
Chapman, Aroldis, 339
Chapman, Ben, 4
Chapman, Katie, 338
Chapman, Ray, xxiv, 336, 337,
    338, 339
Charles, Deadra, 224
Charles, Ezzard, 290
Charles, Tina, 213, 214
Charleston (dance), xix
Charleston, Oscar, 2
Charlotte, North Carolina, 125
Charlotte Motor Speedway,
    111
Chastain, Brandi, 172
Chattanooga, Tennessee, 264
Cheers, 28
Chenery (Tweedy) Penny, 101,
    102
Chesbro, Jack, 180
Chicago, 5, 53, 70, 83, 85, 185,
    187, 189, 228, 282, 306, 313,
    362
Chicago Bears, 51, 52, 53, 54,
    81, 320
Chicago Black Hawks (football)
    83
Chicago Blackhawks (hockey),
    330

Chicago Bulls, 114, 115, 116, 221
Chicago Cardinals, 57, 81, 349
Chicago Criminal Court, 86
Chicago Cubs, 24, 49, 143, 188, 191, 288, 296, 308, 338, 340, 346
Chicago Marathon, 237
Chicago Stadium, 290
Chicago Tribune, 187, 188
Chicago White Sox, 24, 47, 56, 65, 84, 85, 104, 106, 145, 188, 189, 334, 346, 357
Chicago World's Fair (A Century of Progress International Exposition), 187
Childs, Frank, 228
China, 145, 146, 147, 148, 172, 196
China (plates), 249
Chinese Taipei, 173
Chou En-Lai, 148
Christian, Bill 10
Christian, Dave, 8, 10
Christian, Roger, 10
Chow, Amy, 310
Choynski, Joe, 227, 228
Churchill Downs, 101
Cicotte, Ed, 85, 86, 87
Cimoli, Gino, 194
Cincinnati (Queen City), xii, 40, 41, 42, 78, 153
Cincinnati Bengals, 285
Cincinnati Red Stockings, xi, xii, xiv, 40, 41, 42
Cincinnati Reds, xii, 25, 26, 42, 78, 84, 85, 142, 143, 153, 164, 165, 166, 338, 346
Cincinnati Royals, 349
Civil War, xi, xiii, xiv, xv, 42, 273
Clancy, Powell, 25
Clark, Ellery, 303
Clarke, Bobby, 332
Clarke, Fred, 44
Clarksville, Tennessee, 223, 241

Clemente, Roberto, xxiii, xxiv, 61, 62, 63, 64, 65, 192
Clemente, Vera, 65
Clemente Park, 65
Cleveland, 37, 338
Cleveland Barons, 332
Cleveland Browns, 97, 151, 277, 279, 349
Cleveland Indians (Spiders), 4, 103, 105, 106, 153, 154, 166, 181, 182, 281, 282, 283, 327, 336, 338, 346, 357
Clifton, Nate "Sweetwater," 69, 70, 71
Clines, Gene, 63
Clinton, Bill, 217, 312
Cobb, Ty, 48, 49, 107, 143, 144, 248
Cobo Arena, 364
Cockell, Don, 290
Cochrane, Mickey, 338
Cold War, xxi, 6
Cole Fieldhouse, 72
College Basketball Hall of Fame, 76, 132, 134, 316
College Football Hall of Fame, 83, 272
College Park, Maryland, 72
Collins, Jason, 202
Collins, Jimmy, 44
Colombo, Allie, 288
Colorado, xiv, 183
Colorado Springs, 183
Columbia, South Carolina, 125
Columbia University, 26, 28, 82
Colvard, Dean, 315
Comaneci, Nadia, 309, 310
Comiskey, Charles, 85, 86, 87
Comiskey Park, 188
Communism, 6, 146, 147
Conerly, Charlie, 59
Congo, 123
Congress, xviii, 19
Congressional Gold Medal, 5, 18, 39
Conigliaro, Tony, 338
Conley, Larry, 74

Connecticut Sun, 214
Connolly, James, 303
Cooper, Chuck, 69, 70, 71
Cooper, Cynthia, 162
Cooperstown, New York, xi, xii
Cope, Myron, 253
Corcoran, Larry, 165
Cornell University, 135, 136, 274
Cosell, Howard, 28, 276
Costas, Bob, 28
Cousy, Bob, 70, 91, 140
Cowan, Glen, 147
Cowens, Dave, 162
Craft, Harry, 166
Craig, Jimmy, 7, 8, 9
Cricket, xii
Croatia, 123
Cronin, Joe, 109, 189
Csonka, Larry, 150
Cuba, 161, 233
Cuellar, Mike, 233
Cuhna, Victorino, 123
Curtis, Mike, 96
Cuyler, Kiki, 166
Cypress, California, 243
Cy Young Award, 179, 192, 232
Czechoslovakia, 7, 199, 200
Czech Republic, 213

Dahlgren, Babe, 217
Dailey, Chris, 214
Dallas Cowboys, 152, 284, 285
Dallas Stars, 332
Daly, Chuck, 121, 122
Dampier, Louie, 74, 75
Dark, Alvin, 295
Darlington, 125
Dawes, Dominique, 310
Dawson, Red, 266, 267, 268
Davenport, Willie, 274
Davies, Lynn, 324, 325
Davis Cup, 28
Dayton, Ohio, xii
Daytona Beach, Florida, 126
Daytona 500, 112, 125, 291

Daytona International Speedway, 110
Dayton University, 74
D.C. Stadium, 137
Decatur Staleys, 81
DeFranz, Anita, 242
Delta Center, 116
Delvecchio, Alex, 331
Dempsey, Jack, xix, xxii, 23, 53, 183, 184, 185, 186
Denmark, 206
Denver Broncos, 320, 321, 322
DePaul University, 139, 259
Detroit, 15, 23, 73, 87, 363, 365
Detroit Lions, 271
Detroit Pistons, 71, 121, 162
Detroit Red Wings, 18, 330, 331
Detroit Tigers, 107, 144, 338, 346
DeZonie, Harold, 72
Dickey, Bill, 189
DiMaggio, Dom, 103, 106
DiMaggio, Joe, 103, 104, 105, 106, 109, 144, 218, 326
DiMaggio, Vince, 103, 166
Dineen, Bill, 44
The Dirty Dozen, 278, 279, 280
Disney World, 335
Ditmar, Art, 193
Doby, Larry, 4, 282, 283
Dodge City, Kansas, xiv
Dominican Republic, 63, 233
Donnelly, Terry, 259
Donovan, Anne, 162
Donovan, Art, 59
Donruss baseball cards, 249
Dorrance, Anson, 172
Doubleday, Abner, xi, xii
Dowler, Boyd, 286
Downing, Al, 79
Dream Team (U.S. National Basketball Team), 120, 121, 122, 161, 205, 258
Dressen, Chuck, 295
Drexler, Clyde, 122
Dreyfuss, Barney, 44
Driesell, Lefty, 318

Dube, Clayton, 146
Duffy, Hugh, 107
Duke University, 74, 122, 208, 314, 315
Dull, Dick, 318
Dumas, Charlie, 303
Dungy, Tony, 320
Duquesne University, 69
Durocher, Leo, 166, 167, 282, 348
Dykes, Jimmie, 189
Dynamo Gymnastics Club, 310

Eagan, Ed, 30
Earnhardt, Dale, Jr., 111, 112, 113
Earnhardt, Dale, Sr., xxiv, 110, 111, 112, 114, 126
Earnhardt, Ralph, 111
East Carolina University, 265, 266, 267
East St. Louis, 274
Ebbetts Field, 3, 93, 294
Eckersley, Dennis, 341
Eckhardt, Shawn, 364, 365
Edge, Bob, 28
Edmond, Oklahoma, 310
Edmonton Oilers, 220, 221, 222
Edwards, Harry, 274, 276
Edwards, Teresa, 161, 262, 263
Egan, Johnny, 313, 315
Einhorn, Eddie, 334, 335
Einstein, Albert, 284
Ellard, George, 40, 41
Ellis, Dock, 63
El Paso, Texas, 72, 76
Enberg, Dick, 28, 334
England, 35, 324
Eruzione, Mike, 7, 8, 10
ESPN, 29, 30, 31, 32, 134, 163, 263
ESPN Classic, 32
ESPN The Magazine, 32
ESPN2, 32
ESPNU, 32
Esposito, Phil, 331
Ethiopia, 15

European Tour (golf), 245
Evans, Lee, 274
Evanston, Illinois, 13
Evert, Chris, 199, 200, 201, 352
Ewbank, Weeb, 58, 98
Ewing, Patrick, 121, 122
Ewry, Ray, 303

Faber, Red, 87
Face, Roy, 192, 193, 194
Fairfield Stadium, 267
Falls, Joe, 87
FanNation, 361
Fantasy Sports, 360, 361, 362
Fantasy Sports Trade Association, 362
Faris, Kelly, 214
Farrell, Duke, 182
Farrell, Tom, 274
Favre, Brett, 320, 321
FBI, 78, 365
Federal League, 66
Federation Cup, 354
Federation Internationale de Football Association (FIFA), 172
Feller, Bob, 165
Felsch, "Happy" Oscar, 86
Fenway Park, 297
Ferrell, Rick, 189
Fessenden, Reginald, 23
Fight of the Century (boxing), 230
Finland, xxi, 10
Finley, Charlie, 68
Firpo, Luis, 184
Fisher, Jack, 328
Fitzsimmons, Bob, 228
Flatbush Avenue, 348
Fleer baseball cards, 249
Flood, Curt, 66, 67
Florida, 3, 110, 350
Florida A&M, 158
Flournoy, Henry, 73
Fly, Monica, Fly, 352
Flynn, Jim, 229
Forbes Field, 62, 193, 194

Ford (cars), 124
Ford, Gerald, 39
Ford, John, xxi
Ford, Whitey, 192, 193
Fordham University, 27
Foreman, George, 35, 36
Forksville, Pennsylvania, 51
Forrest Gump (1994), 264
Fort Dix, New Jersey, 251
Fort Lauderdale, Florida, 98
Fort Wayne, Indiana, 198
Fort Wayne Pistons, 13, 139, 140
The Forum, 91
Fosbury, Dick (Fosbury Flop), 275, 303, 304, 305, 306
Foudy, Julie, 172
42 (movie), 5
Fox Sports, 30
Foxx, Jimmie, 189, 326
Foyt, A.J., 291, 292, 293
Framingham, Massachusetts, 237
France, 123, 128, 230, 239
Franco's Italian Army, 251
Frazee, Harry, 47, 297
Frazier, Joe, xxii, 35, 36
Freeman, Ron, 274
French Open tennis, 157, 159, 199, 350, 354
Frick, Ford, 3, 327, 328
Friend, Bob, 192, 193
Frisch, Frank, 189
Frost, Sheila, 224
Fukuoka, Japan, 237
Fuller, Buckminster, 168
Fullerton, Hugh, 85
Fulton County Stadium, 79
Fuqua, John "Frenchy", 252
Furillo, Carl, 94
Futch, Eddie, 36

Gaedel, Eddie, 347
Galveston, Texas, 227, 256
Game of the Century (college basketball), 334
Game of the Week (baseball), 27, 77

Gamson, William, 360
Gandihl, "Chick" Arnold, 86, 87
Garnie, Joe, 344
Garvey, Steve, 216
Gary, Indiana, 73
Gashouse Gang, 3
Gehrig, Lou, 189, 215, 216, 217, 218
Gehringer, Charlie, 189
Georgetown University, 90, 133
Georgia, 80, 213
Georgia Tech, 214
Germany, 37, 123, 172, 173, 235, 351
Gettysburg Address, 31
Giamatti, Bart, 341
Gibson, Althea, xxiii, 157, 158, 159
Gibbs, Ron, 59
Gibson, Josh, 2
Gifford, Frank, 59
Gilbert, Rod, 331
Gillooly, Jeff, 364, 365, 366
Gilmore, Ohio, 180
Ginobili, Manu, 123
Gipp, George, 307, 308, 309
Glassboro State College, 360
Gleason, Kid, 85
Glory Road, 76
Gobert, Rudy, 123
Gogolak, Charlie, 137
Gogolak, Pete, 135, 136, 137, 138
Golden Ball, 173
Golden Shoe, 173
Goldman, Charlie, 288
Gomez, Lefy, 189, 190
Goodrich, Gail, 208
Goolagong, Evonne, 159
Gorbachev, Mikhail, 6
Gordon, Jeff, 125, 126
Gordon, Melvin, xxiv
Gore, Al, 217
Gould, Charlie, 42
Gowdy, Curt, 25
Graf, Steffi, 200, 350, 351
Graham, Mal, 91

Grande, George, 30
Grand Slam tennis, 157,158, 159, 199, 200, 201, 350, 354
Grange, Red, xix, 51, 52, 53, 54, 183
Graves, Abner, xi
Great Depression, xix, 49, 83, 157
The Greater Oakland Professional Pigskin Prognosticators League, 360
Great Migration, 38
Great White Hope, 229
Greece, xiii, 236, 264
Greek Idea, xiv
Green, Edith, 19
Green, Johnny, 177
Green, Sihugo, 90
Green Bay, 286
Green Bay Packers, 28, 81, 96, 284, 285, 286
Greenberg, Adam, 338
Greenberg, Hank, 326
Greene, Charlie, 274
Greene, Kalana, 214
Greene, "Mean Joe," 253
Greenville, North Carolina, 265
Gregg, David, 318
Gregg, Forrest, 286
Gretzky, Wayne, 219, 220, 221, 222
Griese, Bob, 98, 149, 150, 151
Groat, Dick, 192
Groza, Lou, 135
Guangdong, China, 172
Guerin, Richie, 177
Gullick, Dr. Luther, 11
Gwynn, Tony, 109

Haddix, Harvey, 192, 193
Hadl, John, 98
Hafey, Chick, 189
Halas, George, 51, 52
Hall, Erv, 274
Hall, Glenn, 330, 331, 332
Hall, Indiana, 207
Ham, Jack, 253

Hamburg, Germany, 350
Hamm, Mia, 172, 174
Hammond Pros, 81, 83
Hank Aaron Award, 80
Hanks, Tom, 264
HANS Safety Device, 112
Happ, J.A., 339
Hard, Darlene, 159
Harding, Tonya, 363, 364, 365, 366
Harkness, Jerry, 313, 315
Harlem Globetrotters, 70, 176
Harper, Ron, 114
Harrington, John, 9
Harris, Franco, 250, 251, 252, 253
Harris County Domed Stadium, 168
Hartford, Connecticut, 213
Hart, Marvin, 229
Hart Memorial Trophy, 220
Hartnett, Gabby, 189
Harvard University, xv, 56, 360
Haskell Institute, 55
Haskins, Don, 73, 75, 76
Hassett, Billy, 133
Havana, Cuba, 230
Havlicek, John, 91
Hawaii Braves, 1
Hayes, Elvin, 210, 333, 335
Hayes, Tiffany, 214
Hazzard, Walt, 208
Head, Dena, 224
Hearn, Jim, 294
Heathcote, Jud, 259
Heffelfinger, William "Pudge," xiii, xvii
Heilmann, Harry, 107
Heinrichs, April, 172, 174
Heinsohn, Tommy, 90, 91
Heinz 57, 106
Heisman Trophy, 270
Hernandez, Jackie, 63
Hershey, Pennsylvania, 175, 177
Hershey Sports Arena, 175
Hershiser, Orel, 359
Hill, Bobby Joe, 73, 75

Hillsboro, Virginia, 125
Hillsdale, Wyoming, 132
Hines, Jim, 274
Hitler, Adolf, xxii, 16, 37, 39
Hoak, Don, 192
Hockey Hall of Fame, 330
Hodges, Bill, 258
Hodges, Russ, 296
Hofheinz, Roy, 168
Holdsclaw, Chamique, 225
Hollywood, xxi, 266, 279
Homestead Grays, 2
Honolulu, 1
Hoover, Herbert, 48
Hope, Bob, 243
Hopkinton, Massachusetts, 237
Hornsby, Rogers, 107
House, Tom, 79
Houston, Texas, 73, 170, 291, 310, 313
Houston Astrodome, 168, 169, 170, 171, 210, 333, 335, 355
Houston Astros, 168, 169, 170, 233
Houston Colt .45s, 168
Houston Oilers, 151, 169
Houston Texans, 170
Howard, Elston, 192
Howard University, 214
Howe, Gordie, 219, 331
Howell, Bailey, 90
Hubbell, Carl, 189, 233
Hudson, Daniel, 359
Huff, Sam, 59
Hull, Bobby, 331
Hungary, 135
Hunter, Harold, 71
Hunter, Jim "Catfish," 67, 68
Hunter, Les, 313, 315
Huntington, West Virginia, 265, 266, 267, 268
Huntington Avenue Grounds, 44, 181
Huntsville, Alabama, 125
Hurricane Katrina, 170
Hurley, Dick, 42

Iba, Moe, 76
Ice Bowl, 284, 285
Ice Station Zebra, 280
Iditarod, Alaska, 343, 344, 345
Iditarod Trail Committee, 345
Iditarod Trail Sled Dog Race, xxiii, 343, 344, 345
Imhoff, Darrall, 177, 179
Immaculata Mighty Macs, 21
Immaculate Reception, 250, 253
Indiana, 12, 83, 207, 211, 257
Indiana Fever, 163
Indiana Pacers, 260
Indiana State Sycamores, 204, 207, 257, 258, 259, 260
Indiana University, 258
Indianapolis Colts, 320, 321, 322, 349
Indianapolis 500, xvi, 28, 45, 170, 291, 292, 293
Indianapolis Motor Speedway, 291, 292
Indianapolis Racers, 220
Indonesia, 35
IndyCar Racing, 291
Inside Sports, 360
Integration, 5, 69, 70, 71, 72
Internal Revenue Service, 17, 288
International Olympic Committee, 121, 242, 276
International Race of Champions, 292
International Table Tennis Federation, 148
Iowa State University, 270
Ireland, 35
Ireland, George, 313, 315
Irvin, Monte, 283
Italy, 15, 264
Ivy League, xiii, xv, 138

Jackie Robinson Little League, 5
Jackson, Keith, 28
Jackson, Lauren, 163
Jackson, Peter, 228
Jackson, Phil, 114, 116

Jackson, Reggie, 111
Jackson, "Shoeless" Joe, 85, 86, 87
Jacksonville, 77
Jamaica, New York, 323
James, Larry, 274
Jansen, Dan, 300, 301, 302
Jansen, Jane, 300, 301, 302
Jansen, Larry 295
Japan, 1, 35, 50, 146, 161, 172, 173, 245, 264
Jaracz, Thad, 74
Jeffries, James, 228, 229, 230
Jennings, Carin, 172, 173
Jeopardy, 28
Jesse Owens Track Classic, 39
Jim Brown, All-American, 280
Jimmy The Greek, 97
Jim Thorpe, Pennsylvania, 57
Jobe, Dr. Frank, 357, 358, 359
Joe Louis Arena, 18
John, Tommy, 356, 357, 358, 359
Jolson, Al, 53
Johnson, Earvin (Magic), 122, 203, 204, 205, 206, 257, 258, 259, 260
Johnson, Jack, xv, 15, 227, 228, 229, 230, 231
Johnson, Jim, 229
Johnson, Judy, 2
Johnson, Lady Bird, 169
Johnson, Lyndon, 169
Johnson, Mark, 7, 8, 10
Johnson, Marques, 210
Johnson, Walter, 180, 349
Jones, Bobby, 117, 183, 245
Jones, Buddy, 270
Jones, Jolanda, 171
Jones, K.C., 90, 91, 121
Jones, Sam, 90, 91
Jordan, Michael, 114, 115, 116, 117, 121, 122, 221

KDKA Radio, 24
Kansas, 55
Kansas City, 132, 208, 316

Kansas City Athletics, 327, 347
Kansas City Chiefs, 96, 151
Kansas City Monarchs, 1, 3
Kansas City Omaha-Kings, 349
Kansas City Royals, 45, 109
Kansas State University, 270
Kansas University, 12, 73, 74, 270
Kapp, Joe, 322
Karolyi, Bela, 310, 311, 312
Kaufman, Al, 229
Kearns, Jack, 18
Keeler, Wee Willie, 103, 105, 144
Kelly, Ed, 187
Kelser, Greg, 259
Keltner, Ken, 105
Kennedy, John F., xxii, 272, 273
Kennedy, Robert F., 273
Kentucky, 3, 102, 207, 210
Kentucky Derby, xii, xxii, 45, 99, 101
Kerlan, Dr. Robert, 359
Kerr, Steve, 114
Kerrigan, Nancy, 363, 364, 365, 366
Ketchel, Stanley, 229
Kiick, Jim, 150, 151
Kilillea, Harry, 44
King, Billie Jean, xxiii, 21, 201, 353, 354, 355, 356
King, Martin Luther, Jr., 5, 273, 313
King, Nellie, 62
Kingdome, 170
King Gustav V, 54
Kissinger, Henry, 146, 148
Kite, Tom, 119
Kitty Hawk, North Carolina, xii
Klein, Chuck, 189
Knight, Bob, 134
Knoxville, Tennessee, 225
Knute Rockne All-American, 308
Konerko, Paul, 65
Korean War, 107, 146
Koufax, Sandy, 165

Krakauskus, Joe, 106
Kron, Tommy, 74
Krutov, Vladimir, 8, 9
Kubek, Tony, 192, 194
Kuechenberg, Bob, 151
Kuhn, Bowie, 78
Kukoc, Toni, 114

Labine, Clem, 294
Lackey, John, 359
Lacy, Venus, 161, 261, 262, 264
Ladies Professional Golf Association, 160, 256,
Ladies Professional Golf Association Hall of Fame, 256
Lady Byng Trophy, 220
Laettner, Christian, 122
Laimbeer, Bill, 162
Lake Placid, N.Y., 6
Lake Placid Olympic Fieldhouse, 7, 8, 10
Lamar University, 259
Lambeau Field, 284, 285
Lambert, Jack, 253
Lamonica, Daryle, 98
Lance Armstrong Foundation, 129, 131
Landis, Floyd, 130
Landis, Kenesaw Mountain, 2, 85, 86, 87, 145, 187
Landry, Tom, 285
Lane Tech, 81
Langer, Jim, 151
Lansford, Carney, 340
Lansing, Michigan 204, 257
Lapchick, Joe, 133, 134
La Rotisserie Francaise, 360
Larsen, Don, xxiii, 92, 93, 94, 95
The Last Great Race on Earth, 343
La Starza, Roland, 288, 290
Las Vegas, xxiv, 18, 355, 362
Lattin, David, 73, 75
Laurin, Lucien, 99, 100, 102

Law, Vernon, 192, 193
Lazzari, Tony, 189
Lee, Spike, 280
Leftwich, Byron, 267
Lehigh University, 214
Lemigova, Julia, 202
Lengyel, Jack, 267, 268
Leonard, Andy, 42
Leonard, Buck, 2
Leonard, Lee, 30
Leslie, Lisa, 161, 164, 262, 263
Levinsky, Battling, 184
Lewis, Guy, 333
Lew, Harry "Bucky," 72
Ley, Bob, 31
Liberty, Kentucky, 336
Liddle, Don, 282
Lieberman, Nancy, 161, 162, 200
Life magazine, 133
Lillehammer, Norway, 302, 363
Lilly, Kristine, 172
Liston, Sonny, 33, 36
Lithuania, 123
Littell, Mark, 143
Little, Larry, 151, 152
Little League, 20
Lloyd, Earl, 69, 70, 71
Lloyd, John Henry, 2
Lobo, Rebecca, 161, 213, 262, 263
Lockman, Whitey, 295
Loma Prieta Earthquake, 341
Lombardi, Ernie, 166, 167
Lombardi, Vince, 285, 286
London, 197, 213
London, Jack, 343
Long, Terry, 316, 318
Long Island, 279, 325
Longley, Luc, 114
Lopez, Al, 283
Louis, Joe, xix, xxii, 5, 14, 15, 16, 17, 18, 38, 55, 288, 289
Louisiana, 170, 313
Louisiana Sports Hall of Fame, 264

Louisiana State University, 214, 259
Louisiana Tech, 224, 225, 226, 264
Louisville, xvi, 32, 101, 210
Los Angeles, 91, 148, 207, 208, 211, 221, 222, 233, 234, 240, 273, 330, 332
Los Angeles Angels, 234
Los Angeles Bulldogs, 1
Los Angeles Clippers, 115
Los Angeles Coliseum, 254
Los Angeles Dodgers, 68, 78, 79, 206, 231, 232, 357, 358
Los Angeles Kings, 221, 222, 330
Los Angeles Lakers, 91, 115, 204, 205, 206, 259
Los Angeles Raiders, 83
Los Angeles Rams, 284
Los Angeles Sparks, 164
Lovellette, Clyde, 90, 121
Lowe, Derek, 298
Lowell, Massachusetts, 72
Loyola University (of Chicago) Ramblers, 313, 314, 315
Lynch, Dick, 271
Lynn, Mike, 333

Mack, Connie, 189, 347
Mackey, John, 96, 279
MacPhail, Larry, 25
Madden, John, 28, 251
Madison Square Garden, 6, 13, 35, 133, 288
Magic Johnson All-Stars, 206
Magic Johnson Enterprises, 206
Maglie, Sal, 94, 281, 294
The Magnificent Seven (gymnastics), 310, 312
Magnolia Lane, 245
Major League Baseball, x, xvi, xvii, xx, xxv, 41, 55, 62, 65, 66, 69, 83, 92, 105, 107, 142, 144, 155, 163, 165, 168, 179, 187, 188, 294, 330, 336, 346, 349, 360

Major League Baseball Players Association, 66
Maleeeva, Magdalena, 350
Malone, Karl, 115, 122, 123
Managua, Nicaragua, 63
Manassa, Colorado, 183
Manfred, Rob, 145
Manhasset, New York, 279
Mann Act, 230
Manning, Archie, 320
Manning, Eli, 320
Manning, Peyton, xxiv, 319, 320, 321
Man O' War, 53
Mantle, Mickey, 94, 105, 192, 193, 248, 326, 327
Mara, Tim, 52
Marble, Alice, 158
Marchetti, Gino, 59
Marciano, Rocky (Rocco Francis Marchegiano), 287, 288, 289, 290
Marconi, Guglilimo, 23
Marina District, 341
Maris, Roger, 48, 105, 192, 326, 327, 328, 329
Markarov, Sergei, 8
Marquess of Queensbury, xiii
Marquette University, 214
Marshall, Bobby, 82
Marshall, George Preston, 13, 83
Marshall, Mike, 233, 358
Marshall University Fieldhouse, 266
Marshall University Thundering Herd, xxv, 265, 266, 267, 268
Martin, Seth, 331, 332
Martin, Sterling, 112, 113
Martinsville, Indiana, 207
Martinsville, Virginia, 125
Maryland, 74, 102, 217
Maryland Racing Commission, 101
M*A*S*H, 28
Massachusetts, 235, 363, 364
Massillon, Ohio, 307

Masters (golf tournament), 117, 118, 119, 243, 245

Mathews, Eddie, 77

Mathewson Christy 180, 233

Matlack, Jon, 63

Matson, Randy, 275

Mauch Chunk, Pennsylvania, 57

Maynard, Don, 96

Mayo Clinic, 217

Mays, Carl, 336, 337, 338

Mays, Charlie, 325

Mays, Willie, 2, 65, 281, 282, 283, 341

Mazeroski, Bill, xxiii, 191, 192, 194, 295

McCarthy, Brandon, 339

McCarver, Tim, 341

McClain, Katrina, 161, 262

McCongaughey, Matthew, 268

McCormick, Frank, 166

McCormick, Robert, 187

McCray, Nikki, 161, 262

McDonald, Tommy, 272

McGhee, Carla, 161, 262

McGraw, John, 45, 188, 189

McGraw, Muffet, 161

McGraw, Tug, 233

McGwire, Mark, 329

McKechnie, Bill, 167

McMullin, Fred, 86

McNally, Art, 252

McNally, Dave, 68

McNichol, William, 338

McVey, Carl, 42

The Meadow, 101

Mears, Rick, 291

Medlen, Kris, 359

Melbourne, Australia, 239, 240

Memorial Day, xvi

Mercein, Chuck, 286

Meschery, Tom, 177, 178

Messersmith, Andy, 68

Mexican League, 234

Mexican Student Movement, 273

Mexico, 63, 231, 233, 273

Mexico City, 273, 305, 323

Meyers, Ann, 161

Meyers, David, 210

Miami, 96, 98, 284, 286

Miami Dolphins, 98, 149, 150, 151, 152, 253

Miami Floridians, 338

Miami Heat, 114

Michael Phelps Foundation, 198

Michaels, Al, 28, 341

Michaels, Lou, 98, 135

Michigan, 87, 170, 208, 307, 315, 364

Michigan City, Indiana, 92

Michigan State, 204, 257, 259, 260

Middle Tennessee State University, 266

Middletown, New York, 235

Mildred "Babe" Dickinson Zaharias Award For Courage, 226

Mikan, George, 139

The Mike Douglas Show, 243

Mikita, Stan, 331

Miller, Marvin, 66, 67, 68, 249

Miller, Ray, 218

Miller, Ron, 313, 315

Miller, Shannon, 310

Milnar, Al, 106

Milwaukee, 80

Milwaukee Badgers, 82

Milwaukee Braves, 77, 347

Milwaukee Brewers, 80, 349

Minneapolis, 207

Minneapolis Lakers, 13, 139, 140, 330

Minnesota Fighting Saints, 330

Minnesota Lynx, 163, 214

Minnesota North Stars, 332

Minnesota Twins, 109, 297, 349

Minnesota Vikings, 151

Minnesota Wild, 332

Minute Maid Park, 170

Miracle at Coogan's Bluff, 295

Miske, Billy, 23, 184

Mississippi, 273

Mississippi State University, 314, 315

Missouri, 158

Mitchell, Dale, 94, 95

Mitchell, Jack, 270

Mitchell, Lydel, 253

Mizell, Vinegar Bend, 193

Mobile, Alabama, 77

Moceanu, Dominique, 310, 312

Modell, Art, 279

The Monicas, 352

Monroe, Earl, 134

Montella, Italy, 212

Montgomery, Alabama, 5

Montgomery, Rene, 213

Montreal, 230, 309

Montreal Canadiens, 27, 330, 331

Montreal Expos, 46, 142, 155, 349

Montreal Royals, 3

Moore, Archie, 287, 290

Moore, Jessica, 213

Moore, Lenny, 59

Moore, Maya, 213, 214

Moran, Frank, 229

Morehouse, Gene, 267

Morehouse, Kevin, 267

Morrall, Earl, 96, 97, 98, 149, 150

Morris, Mercury, 150

Morrow, Ken, 7, 10

Mosqueda-Lewis, Kaleena, 213

Moss, Randy, 267

The Mother's Day Massacre, 354

Mount Everest, 343

Mount Union, 269

Moyer, Jamie, 359

Mueller, Don, 295

Mullin, Chris, 121, 122

Munich, 120, 195, 235, 306, 353

Municipal Stadium (Philadelphia), 289

Murderers Row, 326

Murray, Jack, 229

Murtaugh, Danny, 63, 192, 193

Musial, Stan, 143, 144

Mutscheller, Jim, 61

Myhra, Steve, 59
Myshkin, Vladimir, 8, 9

NAACP, 70
Nagurski, Bronko, 53
NAIA, 70
Naismith, Dr. James, xiii, xiv, 11, 12, 14, 120, 131
Namath, Joe, xxiii, 95, 96, 97, 98, 99
Nantz, Jim, 119
NASA, 168
NASCAR, ix, 110, 111, 112, 124, 125, 126, 127, 291
NASCAR Hall of Fame, 127
Natick, Massachusetts, 237
National Association of Base Ball Players, 41, 42
National Basketball Association, x, xiv, xxiii, 11, 13, 14, 28, 31, 43, 69, 70, 71, 72, 88, 90, 114, 116, 117, 121, 123, 139, 140, 162, 175, 176, 177, 202, 204, 206, 207, 258, 317, 335, 346, 349
National Basketball Association All-Star Game, 205
National Basketball League, xiv, 13
National Center For Sports Safety And Security, 353
National Football League, x, xiv, xvi, xxiv, 28, 29, 31, 43, 51, 52, 57, 58, 61, 81, 82, 83, 89, 96, 136, 137, 138, 149, 250, 253, 277, 278, 279, 284, 319, 320, 322, 346, 349
National Historic Trail, 343
National Hockey League (National Hockey Association), x, xiv, 6, 7, 27, 43, 84, 219, 220, 329, 330, 331, 332
National Invitational Tournament, 13
National League, xvi, 3, 24, 41, 42, 44, 46, 48, 62, 63, 78, 94,

143, 153, 166, 181,189, 191, 192, 231, 233, 234, 281, 294, 297, 298, 336, 339, 346, 348, 349, 358
National Sports Collectors Convention, 249
Naulls, Willie, 90, 177
Navratilova, Martina, xxiii, 198, 199, 200, 201, 202, 352
Navy Seals, 122
Nazis, xx, 17, 37
NBC, 26, 79
NCAA, xxi, 1, 7, 13, 21, 28, 30, 72, 73, 88, 114, 132, 133, 141, 165, 204, 207, 208, 211, 212, 213, 214, 215, 223, 224, 225, 226, 235, 243, 257, 258, 259, 260, 261, 267, 269, 305, 313, 314, 315, 334, 335
Negro Leagues, 2, 3
Negro Leagues Museum, 155
Nenana, Alaska, 343
Nevada, 183
Newark, New Jersey, 160
Newcombe, Don, 4, 294
Newcomerstown, Ohio, 182
New England, 297, 321
New England Patriots, 151, 152
New Jersey, 160, 166, 169, 268, 360
New Mexico, xiv
New Orleans, 170, 320
New Orleans Saints, 320
Newsweek, 364
Newton, Massachusetts, 237
New York Celtics, 13
New York City, xii, xiv, xvi, xxi, 3, 25, 26, 35, 53, 73, 95, 96, 102, 105, 114, 157, 184, 186, 213, 225, 288, 338, 340, 348, 360
New York Daily News, 97, 280
New York Giants (baseball), xxiii, 24, 45, 56, 107, 188, 191, 281, 283, 294, 295, 296, 338, 346, 347

New York Giants (football), 52, 58, 59, 60, 61, 137, 151, 152, 169, 271
New York Highlanders, 45, 181, 346
New York Islanders, 10
New York Jets, xxii, 95, 96, 97, 98, 99, 151, 169
New York Knickerbockers (baseball), xii
New York Knickerbockers (basketball), 69, 70, 175, 177, 178
New York Marathon, 237
New York Mercury, xii
New York Mets, 348
New York Rangers, 27, 222, 330
New York Rens, 13, 70
New York (state), 6
New York Times, xv, 98, 335, 338, 362
New York Yankees, 24, 25, 27, 46, 47, 48, 49, 50, 68, 92, 94, 95, 103, 109, 169, 189, 191, 192, 193, 194, 215, 216, 218, 281, 296, 297, 298, 326, 336, 337, 338, 346, 348, 357
New York Yankees (football), 53
NFL Films, 82
Nicaragua, 61, 63, 233
Nick Bollettieri Tennis Academy, 350
Nicklaus, Jack, 117, 118, 119, 245, 360
Nicks, Carl, 259
Nigeria, 172
Nike (shoes), 243
Nixon, Richard, 19, 145, 146, 148, 267
Noll, Chuck, 253
Nome, Alaska, 343
Norman, Greg, 119
Norman, Jerry, 208
Norman, Oklahoma, 270
Norman, Peter, 275, 276
North America, 329
North Carolina, 110, 114, 124

North Korea, 146
Northwestern University, 13
North Wilkesboro, North
   Carolina, 125
Norway, 7, 172, 173, 308, 365,
   366
Notre Dame Fighting Irish, 210,
   214, 259, 270, 271, 306, 307,
   308
NRG Stadium, 170
Nunno, Steve, 310
Nurmi Paavo, 53

Oakland, California, 153
Oakland Alameda County
   Coliseum, 340
Oakland Athletics, 67, 339, 340,
   341, 347
Oakland Raiders, 96, 98, 250,
   251, 252, 253
Oakland Seals, 332
Oakville, Alabama, 37
Obama, Barrack, 152, 214, 316
Oberlin College, xiii
O'Brien, Jack, 229
O'Brien, Pat, 308
Oerter, Al, 275
Ohio State University, 37, 117,
   214
Oklahoma, 55, 57
Oklahoma City University, 73, 74
Oklahoma Memorial Stadium,
   270
Oklahoma State University, 266
Okrent, Daniel, 360
Olbermann, Keith, 31
Oldsmobile, 124
Old West, xxi
Oliver, Al, 63
Olympic Games, xiii, xvi, xxi,
   xxii, xxiii, 1, 6, 7, 8, 10, 12,
   14, 28, 30, 33, 37, 38, 39, 54,
   56, 57, 71, 88, 120, 121, 122,
   123, 160,163, 171, 174, 195,
   196, 197, 198, 206, 213, 223,
   235, 236, 237, 239, 240, 241,
   254, 258, 261, 263, 273, 274,

275, 276, 300, 301, 302, 303,
   305, 309, 310, 323, 324, 325,
   350, 353, 363, 364, 365, 366
Olympic Project For Human
   Rights, 274
O'Malley, Walter, 348
100 Rifles (1969) 280
O'Neil, Buck, 1
Orange Bowl, 270, 284
Oregon, 19, 304
Oregon State University, 304,
   305, 314
Original Celtics, 13
Original Six, 329, 330
Orlando, Florida, 205
Orlando, Johnny, 109
Orr, Bobby, 219
Ortiz, David, 298
Owens, Jesse, xix, xxii, 37, 38,
   39, 55

Pacific Coast League, 104
Pacific University, 214
Paige, Satchel, 169
Palmer, Arnold, 117, 360
Palmer, Jim, 341
Pan American Games, 235
Pan Pacific Games (swimming),
   195
Parche, Gunter, 350, 351
Parent, Bernie, 332
Parilli, Babe, 98
Paris, France, 129, 229, 303
Parker, Jarrod, 359
Parker, Jim, 59
Parks, Rosa, 5, 273
Pasadena Junior College, 1
Patrick, Dan, 31
Pat Summit Alzheimer's Clinic
   at the University of Tennessee
   Medical Clinic, 226
Pat Summit Foundation, 226
Patterson, Reggie, 144
Pavelich, Mark, 7
Pearl Harbor, 1
Pearson, David, 125
Pennington, Chad, 267

Penn State, 250, 253
Pennsylvania, 21, 56, 95, 98
Penthouse magazine, 366
Pepsi 400, 126
Perine, Samaje, xxiv
Persians, 236
Pettitte, Andy, 167
Petty, Kyle, 124
Petty, Lee, 124
Petty, Richard, xxiii, 111, 124,
   125, 126, 127
Petty Enterprises, 127
PGA Tournament, 118, 245
Pheidippides, 236
Phelps, Jaycie, 310
Phelps, Michael, 195, 196, 197,
   198
Pierini, Lou, 346
Philadelphia, 35, 176, 184, 185,
   289
Philadelphia Athletics, xii, 108,
   109, 181, 189, 340, 346, 347
Philadelphia City Paper, 308
Philadelphia Eagles, 27, 322
Philadelphia Flyers (Broad
   Street Bullies), 330, 332
Philadelphia Phillies, 4, 24, 45,
   48, 65, 142, 143, 144, 234,
   346
Philadelphia 76ers, 90, 91
Philadelphia Warriors, 175, 177,
   178, 179
Philippines, 36
Phillippe, Deacon, 44
Phoenix Mercury, 163
Pietrosante, Nick, 271
Pimlico Race Course, 101
Ping-Pong diplomacy, 145, 146,
   147, 148
Pipp, Wally, 337
Pippen, Scottie, 114, 116, 122
Pittsburgh, xiii, 24, 62, 65, 191,
   192, 193, 253
Pittsburgh Crawfords, 2
Pittsburgh International Bakery,
   253
Pittsburgh Penguins, 330, 332

Pittsburgh Pirates, 2, 24, 44, 61, 62, 63, 65, 170, 181, 192, 193, 194, 247, 296, 297, 346
Pittsburgh Steelers, 28, 151, 250, 251, 252, 253
Plains of Marathon, 236
Plano, Texas, 128
Playboy magazine, 366
Plymouth, 124
PNC Park, 65
Pocklington, Peter, 221
Podoloff, Maurice, 140
Polish Airlines, 266
Pollard, Fritz, 81, 82, 83, 89
Pollock, Harvey, 178
Polo Grounds, 52, 281, 282, 294, 295, 336
Pontiac Dome, 170
Port Arthur, Texas, 254
Portland, Oregon, 364, 366
Prague, Czechoslovakia, 266
Preakness Stakes, xii, xxii, 99, 101
Presidential Medal of Freedom, 4, 36, 39, 80, 127, 226, 354
President's Council on Physical Fitness, 272
Presley, Elvis, 121, 192
Princeton, xiii, 26, 28, 137, 269
Professional Golfers Association, 117, 243, 245
Pro Football Hall of Fame, 54, 57, 58, 82, 83, 250, 279, 280, 284
Progressive Field, 339
Powell, Mike, 325
Puerto Rico, 63, 65, 123
Pujols, Albert, 249
Purdue University Boilermakers, 207, 208
Pyle, C.C., 52, 53

Quebec Nordiques, 330
Queen Elizabeth II, 159

Radio (sports), 22, 23, 24, 25
Ralph, Shea, 213

Ramirez, Manny, 298
Randall, Semeka, 225
Rasmussen, Bill, 30
Rasmussen, Leo, 345
Rasmussen, Scott, 30
Ratelle, Jean, 331
RCA Dome, 170
Reagan, Ronald, 18, 144, 308, 309
Reddick, Cat, 174
Redington, Joe, Sr., 343
Reebok, 317
Reese, Pee Wee, 94
Reeves, Dan, 286
Reno, Nevada, 230
Rentzel, Lance, 286
Resurrection Bay, 343
Retton, Mary Lou, 310
Reynolds, Burt, 280
Reynolds, George, 333, 335
Rice, Grantland, 51
Rice, Jerry, 280
Richard Nixon Foundation, 148
Richardson, Bobby, 192
Richardson, Nolan, 73
Richie, Laurel, 163
Rickey, Branch, xx, 2, 3, 4, 69
Riddles, Libby, xxiii, 344, 345
Riggs, Bobby, 354, 355, 356
Riggs, Lew, 167
Riley, Pat, 74, 75
The Ring magazine, 185, 289
Rio Conchos, 279
Rio de Janeiro, 198
Ripken, Billy, 215
Ripken, Cal, 215
Ripken, Cal Jr., 215, 216, 217, 218
Risberg, "Swede" Charles, 86, 87
Riverfront Stadium, 285
Rizzotti, Jennifer, 213
Roaring Twenties, xviii, 47, 183
Robeson, Paul, 82
Robbie, Joe, 152
Roberto Clemente Award, 65
Roberto Clemente Fan Club, 63

Robertson, Oscar, 121
Robinson, David, 122
Robinson, Frank, 153, 154, 155, 156
Robinson, Jackie, xvii, xx, 1, 2, 3, 4, 17, 65, 66, 69, 70, 77, 83, 153, 155, 156, 157, 294
Robinson, Jerry, 1
Robinson, Mack, 1
Robinson, Mallie, 1
Robinson, Rachel (Isum), 1, 4
Robustelli, Andy, 59
Rochester Royals, 70, 349
Rockingham, North Carolina, 125
Rockne, Knute, 306, 307, 308, 309
Rocky (1976), 290
Rodgers, Bill, 237
Rodgers, Guy, 177, 178
Rodman, Dennis, 114
Rogan, Bullet Joe, 2
Rolapp, Brian, 29
Rollins, Jimmy, 65
Romania, 309
Rome, Italy, 239, 303, 324
Rooney, Art, 251
Roosevelt, Franklin D., 39, 347
Root, Charlie, 49
Root, Jack, 229
Rose, Pete, 103, 142, 143, 144, 341
Rose Bowl, 81
Rosen, Al, 282, 283
Ross, Tony, 229
Ross Trophy, 220
Rote, Kyle, 59
Rothstein, Arnold, 84
Rotisserie League Baseball, 360
Rounders, xii
Rouse, Vic, 313, 315
Rowe, Curtis, 210
Royal, Darrell, 270
Rudolph, Blanche, 240
Rudolph, Wilma, xxiii, 239, 240, 241, 264

Runyon, Damon, 53
Rupp, Adolph, 73, 74
Ruppert, Jacob, 48
Rush, Cathy, 21
Russell, Bill, 88, 89, 90, 91, 121, 153, 176
Rutgers, xiii, 82
Ruth, Babe, xix, xxiii, xxiv, 46, 47, 48, 49, 50, 53, 66, 76, 78, 87, 105, 107, 183, 189, 190, 191, 248, 254, 296, 297, 326, 327, 328, 347
Ryan, Nolan, 165
Ryun, Jim, 274

St. Louis, xvi
St. Louis Blues, 222, 330, 332
St. Louis Browns, 105, 106, 346, 347
St. Louis Cardinals (baseball), 3, 66, 143, 144, 234, 298, 346, 347
St. Louis Cardinals (football), 151, 272, 349
St. Simons, Georgia, 279
Sac and Fox Indians, 55
Sacramento Kings, 349
Sacred Heart, 214
Sailors, Bud, 132
Sailors, Kenny, 13, 131, 132, 133, 134
Sain, Johnny, 347
Saint Bethlehem, Tennessee, 239
Salazar, Alberto, 237
Sales, Nykesha, 213
Sally League, 77
Salt Lake City, 116, 259
Sam Houston College, 1
Sample, Johnny, 96, 99
Samuelson, Joan Benoit, 237
San Andreas Fault, 340, 341
Sanders, Tom "Satch," 90, 91
San Diego, 107
San Diego Chargers, 98, 151
San Diego Padres, 109, 144, 234
San Francisco, 103

San Francisco Bay, 339, 341
San Francisco Giants, 46, 155, 339, 340, 341
San Francisco Seals, 104
San Jose State, 273, 276
San Juan, Puerto Rico, 64
Sanguillen, Manny, 63
Santa Clara, California, 340
Sarajevo, 300
Sather, Glen, 220
Sauer, George, 96
Sauldsberry, Woody, 90
Schalk, Ray, 87
Schenkel, Chris, 28
Schilling, Curt, 298
Schmeling, Max, 16, 17
Schneider, Buzz, 8
Schrader, Kenny, 112
Scola, Luis, 123
Score baseball cards, 249
Scott, Everett, 216
Scott, Jake, 151
Scully, Vince, 28, 79, 80, 232
Seagren, Bob, 275
Seattle Mariners, 349
Seattle Pilots, 349
Seattle Storm, 163
Secretariat, xxii, 99, 100, 101, 102
Seles, Monica, xxiii, 350, 351, 352, 353
Selig, Bud, 296
Serbia, 350, 351
Seward, Alaska, 343
Sewell, Joe, 216, 339
Shackelford, Lynn, 333
Shaktoolik, Alaska, 344
Sham, 101
Shaofang, Qui, 148
Sharkey, Jack, 185
Sharman, Bill, 91
Shed, Nevil, 73
Shek, Chiang Kai, 147
Shell, Art, 83
Shero, Fred, 332
Shoebridge, Ted, 268
Shoebridge, Tom, 268

Shorter, Frank, xxii, 235, 236, 237
Shot clock, NBA, 139, 140, 141
Show, Eric, 144
Shriver, Pam, 199
Shula, Don, 96, 98, 149, 150, 151
Siegfried, Larry, 91
Silver, South Carolina, 157
Simmons, Al, 189
Sisler, George, 105
Skinner, Bob, 192
Skowron, Bill, 192
Slate, Bill, 28
Sloan, Jerry, 115
Smith, Bubba, 96
Smith, Dean, 13, 141
Smith, Derrick, 365
Smith, Eddie, 106
Smith, Gunboat, 184
Smith, Margaret Court, 354, 355
Smith, Red, 295
Smith, Tommie, 273, 274, 275, 276
Smoltz, John, 359
Snead, Sam, 245
Snell, Matt, 96, 98
Softball Hall of Fame, 70
Soldier Field, 185
Somethingroyal, 101
Sonora State, Mexico, 232
Sosa, Sammy, 329
South Carolina, 35, 157
Southeast Asia, 6
Southeastern Conference, 73, 74, 224, 226
Southern Methodist University, 73
South Florida, 214
South Korea, 161
Spahn, Warren, 77, 180, 233, 347
Spain, 123
Spain, Ken, 333
Spalding, Albert, xi
Stallard, Tracy, 328
Spartanburg, South Carolina, 125
Speaker, Tris, 338

Speer, Albert, 39
Spitz, Mark, 195
Splitter, Tiago, 123
The Sporting News, 280
SportsCenter, 30, 31
Sports Illustrated, 20, 32, 202, 243, 270, 312, 345, 354, 361
Springfield, Massachusetts, xiii, 11, 12, 120, 134, 207, 261
Stabler, Kenny, 252
Stagg, Amos Alonzo, x
Staley, Dawn, 161, 262, 263
Stallworth, John, 253
Stanford University, 20, 161, 212, 214, 243, 261
Stanley Cup, 10, 220, 221, 222, 330, 331, 332
Stant, Shane, 364, 365
Stanton, Bob, 28
Stargell, Willie, 63
Starr, Bart, 286
Star Spangled Banner, 275
Steding, Katy, 161, 262, 263
Stengel, Casey, 92, 93, 192
Stennett, Rennie, 63
Stern, Bill, 26
Stewart, Brianna, 213
Stewart, Dave, 340, 341
Stockholm, 54
Stockton, John, 115, 122
Strasburg, Stephen, 359
Strug, Kerri, xxiii, 309, 310, 311, 312
Sullivan, John L., xiii
Sullivan Award, 241
Summerall, Pat, 28
Summit, Pat (Pat Head), xxiii, 212, 223, 224, 225, 226
Summit, Tyler, 226
Sunday Night Football, 31
SuperBakery, 253
Super Bowl, xxii, 58, 96, 149, 151, 152, 250, 253, 284, 286, 320, 340, 362
Super Dome, 170
Swann, Lynn, 253
Swearingen, Fred, 252

Sweasy, Charlie, 42
Sweden, 7, 39, 54, 57, 173, 206
Swift, Doug, 151
Switzerland, 35
Swoopes, Sheryl, 161, 262
Sydney, Australia, 229, 350
Syracuse Nationals, 13, 71, 140
Syracuse University, 269, 279

Taiwan, 146, 147
Tallahassee, Florida, 158
Tatum, Jack, 252
Taurasi, Diana, 213
Taylor, Lawrence, 280
Taylor, Penny, 163
Tebbetts, Birdie, 167
Tejada, Miguel, 216
Television, 26, 27, 28, 29, 45, 62
Teller, Alaska, 344, 345
Temple, Ed, 239, 240, 241
Temple University, 13, 263
Tennessee State University, 71, 239, 240, 241
Tennessee Tech, 314
Tennis Magazine, 158
Ter-Ovanesyan, Igor, 323, 324, 325
Terre Haute, Indiana, 258, 357
Terry, Bill, 107, 189
Terry, Ralph, 194
Texas, 73, 170, 291
Texas A&M (Mechanical College of Texas), 23
Texas Rangers, 349
Texas Tech University, 263
Texas Western (University of Texas at El Paso Miners), 72, 73, 74, 75, 76, 315, 316, 324
Thailand, 243
Third Reich, 39
Thomas, Demmaryis, 322
Thomas, John, 303, 304
Thomas, Julius, 322
Thompson, John, 90
Thomson, Bobby, xxiii, 294, 295, 296

Thorpe, Charlie, 56
Thorpe, Jim, xxiii, 54, 56, 57, 82, 256
Thorpe, Patricia, 57
Three Rivers Stadium, 62, 253
Tigerbelles, 239
Tikhonov, Vladimir, 8
Tilden, Bill, 183
Time magazine, 5, 354
Title IX, x, xviii, xxii, xxiii, 19, 20, 21, 172, 223
Tittle, Y.A., 322
Toyko, 303, 324
Toledo, Ohio, 184
Toledo Blue Stockings, xiii
Toledo University, 269
Tolley, Rick, 267
Tombstone, Arizona, xiv
Tommy John Surgery, 180, 356, 357, 358, 359
Toomey, Bill, 275
Topps baseball cards, 248, 249
Toronto Blue Jays, 194, 340
Toronto Maple Leafs, 330
Tour de France, 128, 129, 130, 131
Towson, Maryland, 195
Track and Field News, 305
Traynor, Pie, 62, 189
Tretiak, Vladimir, 7, 8
Trgovich, Pete, 210
Tribble, Brian, 318
Tri-Cities Airport, 265
Tri-Cities Hawks, 72
Triple Crown (horse racing), xii, xxii, 100, 101, 102
Truman, Harry, 5
Trump, Donald, 293
Tubbs, Jerry, 272
Tucson, Arizona, 310
Tunnell, Emlen, 59
Tunney, Gene, 183, 184, 185
Turcotte, Ron, 99
Turkey, 213
Turley, Bob, 193
Turner, Frederick Jackson, xv
Turner, Jim, 98

TVS Television Network, 334
24 Hours of Daytona, 291
24 Hours of Le Mans, 291
Tyson, Mike, xxii

UCLA (Bruins), 1, 207, 208,
209, 210, 214, 333, 334, 335
Ukraine, 161
Ullman, Norm, 331
Unitas, Johnny, 58, 59, 60, 61,
96, 98, 149, 150, 320
United Black Students For
Action, 274
Union Cricket Club, 40
United Center, 116
United States, ix, x, xi, xiv, xv,
xvi, xviii, xx, xxi, 4, 6, 7, 8, 9,
10, 14, 15, 16, 19, 28, 29, 35,
38, 39, 45, 56, 62, 65, 72, 81,
120, 121, 122, 123, 128, 129,
130, 148, 160, 161, 163, 170,
173, 174, 195, 196, 199, 200,
205, 213, 219, 222, 230, 231,
236, 244, 254, 257, 261, 262,
263, 273, 294, 302, 310, 325,
330, 343, 350, 352, 363
United States Football League,
170
United States Olympic
Committee, 39
United States Postal Service, 78
United States Sports Academy,
226
United States Supreme Court,
67
United Steel Workers, 66
University of Alabama, 95
University of Arkansas, 259
University of Chicago, 12
University of Cincinnati, 73, 74,
314, 315
University of Colorado, 238,
270
University of Connecticut, 211,
212, 213, 214, 263
University of Evansville, 266
University of Florida, 235

University of Houston, 210,
333, 334, 335
University of Illinois, 51, 314,
315
University of Iowa, 12
University of Kentucky, 72, 73,
314, 315
University of Maryland Terrapins,
270, 316, 317, 318, 319
University of Miami, 269
University of Michigan, 37, 74,
360
University of Minnesota Golden
Gophers, 6, 207, 208, 269
University of Missouri, 270
University of North Carolina,
13, 114, 141, 172
University of Oklahoma
Sooners, xxiv, 259, 269, 270,
271, 272
University of Oregon, 13
University of Pennsylvania, 259
University of Pittsburgh, 27, 270
University of San Francisco, 88
University of South Carolina,
263
University of Southern
California, 146, 207, 269
University of Tennessee, 212,
213, 214, 223, 224, 225, 226,
320
University of Tennessee-Martin,
223
University of Texas, 23, 270
University of Utah, 74
University of Washington, 269
University of Wisconsin, xxiv,
8, 10
University of Wyoming, 13,
132, 133, 134
Unser, Al, 291
Upper Deck baseball cards, 249
USA Basketball, 160, 205, 261,
265
U.S. Amateur golf, 117, 244
U.S. Anti-Doping Agency, 130
U.S. Army, 235, 288

USA Swimming, 197
USA Table Tennis, 146, 147
U.S. Auto Club, 292
U.S. Boxing Team, 266
U.S. China Institute, 146
U.S. Figure Skating Association,
365
U.S. Figure Skating
Championships, 363, 364
U.S. Figure Skating team, 266
U.S. hockey team, 6, 7, 8, 9, 10
U.S. Junior Amateur golf, 243
U.S. Olympic Trials, 305
U.S. Open golf, 117, 118, 245
U.S. Open tennis, 157, 158, 199,
350, 354
U.S. Register of Historic Places,
170
U.S. Senate, 272
USSR, 6, 120, 146, 259, 310,
323
USSR hockey, xxi, 6, 7, 8, 9, 10
U.S. State Department, 158
U.S. Tennis Association, 158
U.S. Women's Amateur (golf),
256
U.S Women's Soccer (91ers),
172, 173, 174
Utah, 183
Utah Jazz, 114, 115, 116
Utah State University, 266

Valenzuela, Fernando, 231, 232,
233, 234
Vancouver, 330
Vancouver Canucks, 330
Vander Meer, Johnny, 164, 165,
166, 167
VanDerveer, Tara, 20, 161, 261
Veeck, Bill, 347
Vessels, Billy, 270
Veterans Stadium, 143
Vietnam War, xxii, 6, 34, 35,
273
Villanueva, Pat, 286
Vincent, Fay, 341
Virdon, Bill, 192, 194

Virginia, 70, 101
Virginia Tech, 259
Vitale, Dick, 134
Voss, Norway, 306, 309

Waddell, Rube, 181, 182
Wagner, Billy, 30
Wagner, Honus, 44, 246, 247,
    248
Walcott, Jersey Joe, 289, 290
Walker, Harry, 63
Walker, Moses Fleetwood, xiii,
    xv
Walker, Tillie, 48
Walker, Wade, 270
Walter Camp All-American
    Team, 308
Walton, Bill, 207, 210
Wambach, Abby, 174
Waner, Paul, 189
Ward, Arch, 187, 188, 189
Warfield, Paul, 151
Warner, Pop, 56
Warren, Mike, 333, 335
Washington, Richard, 210
Washington Capitals
    (basketball), 69, 71
Washington, D.C., xvi, 217
Washington Freedom, 174
Washington Nationals, 155
Washington Redskins, 13, 83,
    137, 151
Washington Senators (first),
    105, 108, 180, 346, 349
Washington Senators (second),
    349
Washington Wizards, 114
Waterman, Fred, 42
Watson, Jimmy, 332
Wayne, John, 107
WCAU Radio, 177
We Are Marshall (2006), 265,
    268
Weatherall, Jim, 270
Weaver, Buck, 86, 87
Webster, Alex, 59
Webster's Dictionary, 360

Weill, Al, 288
Weitz, Grete, 237
Welch, Raquel, 280
Wellesley, Massachusetts, 237
Wells, Mark,
Wennington, Bill, 114
Wertz, Vic, 282, 283
West, Jerry, 91, 121
West Allis, Wisconsin, 300
Westfield, Alabama, 281
West Germany, 35, 123
Westhead, Paul, 162
West Virginia, xxv
West Virginia State, 70
WFAN Radio, 25
Wharram, Kenny, 331
Wheaties, 312, 320
Wheaton, Illinois, 51
White House, 10, 39, 152, 214,
    226, 316
Wichita State University, 265
Wicks, Sidney, 210
Wightman Cup, 354
Wilkes, Jamal, 210
Wilkinson, Charles Burnham
    "Bud", 269, 270, 272
Wilkinson, Jay, 271
Willard, Jess, 184, 230
Williams, Billy, 216
Williams, Claude (Lefty), 86
Williams, Cy, 48
Williams, Lucinda, 241
Williams, Smokey Joe, 2
Williams, Ted, 87, 107, 108,
    109, 110, 221
Wills, Harry, 228
Wilmington, North Carolina,
    158
Wilson, Ben, 266
Wimbledon, 28, 157, 159, 199,
    350, 354
Winfrey, Oprah, 130
Winnipeg Jets, 330
Winthrop, Massachusetts, 7
Winston Cup, 111
Wisconsin, 77, 284, 286
WJZ Radio, 24

Wolters, Kara, 213
Women's American Basketball
    Association, 161
Women's Basketball Hall of
    Fame, 263
Women's Basketball League,
    161, 263
Women's National Basketball
    Association, xxiii, 141, 161,
    162, 163, 164, 174, 214, 263
Women's Sports Foundation, 20,
    241, 345
Women's United Soccer
    Association, 174
Wood, Kerry, 359
Wooden, John, 207, 208, 209,
    210, 211, 215, 333, 335
Wooden, Nell, 207
Woods, Earl, 243
Woods, George, 275
Woods, Kultida, 243
Woods, Tiger, 242, 243, 244,
    245, 246
World Baseball Classic, 234
World Championships (women's
    basketball), 213
World Championships
    (swimming), 195
World Colored Heavyweight
    Championship, 228
World Cup (soccer), 172, 173,
    174
World Figure Skating
    Championships, 365
World Football League, 170
World Golf Championship,
    245
World Hockey Association, 220,
    222, 330
World Series, xvi, xxi, xxiii, 4,
    24, 27, 28, 43, 44, 45, 47, 49,
    63, 65, 77, 84, 85, 87, 92, 94,
    95, 143, 145, 154, 166, 191,
    192, 193, 194, 216, 232, 281,
    283, 294, 296, 297, 298, 299,
    336, 339, 340, 341, 357
World War I, xvi, xix, 183, 184

World War II, xvi, xvii, xix, xiii, 6, 13, 17, 50, 70, 83, 107, 139, 192, 207, 269, 288, 347
Worsley, Willie, 73, 74, 75
Wrestlemania, 170
Wright, George, xii, 40, 41, 42
Wright, Harry, xii, 41, 42
Wright, Orville, xii, xvii
Wright, Wilbur, xii, xvii
Wrigley Field, 49, 188
WTAW Radio, 23

WWJ Radio, 23
Wyoming, XIV

Xavier of Cincinnati, 153, 267
Xavier of New Orleans, 70

Yale University, 20, 235, 269
Yankee Stadium, 15, 17, 48, 58, 94, 193, 287, 298, 328
YMCA, xiii, 11, 120
Young, Cy (Denton True), xxiv, 44, 45, 165, 179, 180, 181,

182, 248
Young, George, 274
Young, Sophie, 163
Yugoslavia, 350

Zaharias, George, 255
Zaharias, Mildred "Babe" Didrikson, xxiii, 254, 255, 256
Zaire, 35, 161
Zedong, Zhaung, 148
Zuppke, Bob, 52

About the Author

Lew Freedman is a veteran sports journalist who has worked on the staffs of the *Chicago Tribune*, *Philadelphia Inquirer*, and *Anchorage Daily News*. The author of dozens of books, Freedman has won more than 250 journalism awards in his career.

His works for ABC-CLIO include biographies of LeBron James, Peyton Manning, and Pele, as well as books on the history of NASCAR and stock-car racing, an encyclopedia of the African American pioneers of baseball, and the story of Latino baseball legends.

He graduated from Boston University with a BS in journalism and earned a master's degree emphasizing international communication from Alaska Pacific University.

Currently, Freedman is a reporter and columnist for the Cody Enterprise in Cody, Wyoming.